JUSTICE IN A NEW WORLD

Justice in a New World

Negotiating Legal Intelligibility
in British, Iberian, and
Indigenous America

Edited by
Brian P. Owensby and Richard J. Ross

NEW YORK UNIVERSITY PRESS
New York

NEW YORK UNIVERSITY PRESS
New York
www.nyupress.org

References to Internet websites (URLs) were accurate at the time of writing. Neither the author nor New York University Press is responsible for URLs that may have expired or changed since the manuscript was prepared.

Library of Congress Cataloging-in-Publication Data
Names: Owensby, Brian Philip, 1959–   editor. | Ross, Richard Jeffrey, editor.
Title: Justice in a new world : negotiating legal intelligibility in British, Iberian, and indigenous America / edited by Richard J. Ross and Brian P. Owensby.
Description: New York : New York University Press, 2018. |
Includes bibliographical references and index.
Identifiers: LCCN 2017054990 | ISBN 978-1-4798-5012-9 (cl : alk. paper) |
ISBN 978-1-4798-0724-6 (pb : alk. paper)
Subjects: LCSH: Indians—Legal status, laws, etc.—History. | American—History—To 1810. |
Colonies—America—Law and legislation.
Classification: LCC KDZ481 .J869 2018 | DDC 342.708/72—dc23
LC record available at https://lccn.loc.gov/2017054990

New York University Press books are printed on acid-free paper, and their binding materials are chosen for strength and durability. We strive to use environmentally responsible suppliers and materials to the greatest extent possible in publishing our books.

Manufactured in the United States of America

10 9 8 7 6 5 4 3 2 1

Also available as an ebook

To our children:

Amanda Jin Yu Owensby

and

Benjamin Samuel Ross and Miriam Aviva Ross

CONTENTS

1

Making Law Intelligible in Comparative Context

BRIAN P. OWENSBY AND RICHARD J. ROSS

"Legal" historians start from the premise that the messiness of the world can in some meaningful way be tamed by legal precepts and procedures. We do so knowing that law, like any other facet of social life, is ultimately embedded within larger structures of human experience and meaning. To isolate law as an object of inquiry, then, simplifies so that we may discern subtleties of "legality" that might be lost to a coarser analytical resolution. In any given social context, the messiness of the world, and law's capacity to bring some order to it, is difficult enough to tease out. Legal actors—claimants, defendants, prosecutors, advocates, judges, witnesses, treatise writers, legislators—come to legal encounters with varying motives and disparate levels of knowledge and expertise. Unraveling the tangle of intent, ability, language, and meaning must always be something of a quixotic pursuit. The challenge of making sense of law is magnified dramatically when questions of messiness and order are confronted in intercultural settings, i.e., when distinct cultures, each bearing its own legal precepts, meanings, and procedures, interact. This has been the lesson of recent studies examining how Europeans and indigenous people faced each other through law in the context of the New World encounter from the sixteenth to the eighteenth centuries. Such work has begun to stretch the boundaries of legal history by questioning law's capacity to "tame" the unordered circumstances of cultural difference.

To date, the scholarship has tended to limit itself to specific imperial legal understandings—English and Iberian—as each came into contact with distinct indigenous conceptions of law and justice. In this vein, historians begin by assuming a culturally and historically bound legal framework—the common law and treaties between sovereigns for Anglo-America and a neo-Thomist casuistry for Latin America—and conduct their research and analysis largely within the confines of that set of assumptions.[1] For all their insights, such works are missing a deeper interrogation of underlying premises regarding what law is and how it works in any given encounter. Thus, to what extent and how does it matter that indigenous people and settlers in Ibero-America were considered part of a single social order, while in British America they were virtually always considered distinct nations? What difference does it make that in British America sovereignty and treaty law structured legal encounters between settlers and Natives, while in Ibero-America a specific Law of the Indies took shape to mediate this relationship? Did one approach promote a greater or lesser degree of mutual comprehension between Natives and settlers than did the other? Or does asking the question this way foreclose lines of inquiry? The only way to get at this set of concerns is to open our analytical gaze to a wider, comparative landscape. Doing so leads us away from the secure footing of grounding-assumptions regarding legality onto the slippery topography of context and antiformalism as baselines for analysis, a move made more difficult when intercultural legal encounters are themselves the subject of comparison. *Justice in a New World: Negotiating Legal Intelligibility in British, Iberian, and Indigenous America* takes this next step.

As the essays in this volume demonstrate, colonialism in the English and Iberian Atlantic brought settlers, soldiers, imperial officials, and indigenous peoples into contact with different conceptions of law and justice. At a grand level, perhaps especially in Spanish America, those seeking to legitimate or restrain conquest, dispossession, and forced labor in the Americas made claims about justice. On the ground in daily life— and here will be our focus—various groups of Europeans and Natives appealed to imperfect understandings of their interlocutors' notions of justice and advanced their own conceptions during workaday negotiations, disputes, and assertions of right. This was no easy matter. Settlers' and indigenous peoples' legal presuppositions shaped and sometimes misdirected their resort to each other's law. Each misconstrued the other's legal commitments while learning about them; and each strained to use the other's law as a political, strategic, and moral resource. In so doing, each changed its own practice of law and dialogue about justice. At the heart of this process is the problem of "legal intelligibility": How and to what extent did settler law and its associated notions of justice become intelligible—tactically, technically, and morally—to Natives, and vice versa? To address this question, the volume extends the existing scholarship, which juxtaposes settlers' and Natives' understanding in empire-specific circumstances, by adding another axis of comparison, that *between* English and Iberian New World empires. Understanding the conflict and transformation of notions of justice and law through a dual comparative study of legal intelligibility is the objective of this volume.

I. Contrasting British and Iberian Legal Spaces

One of the most profound insights to haunt historical thinking about the "New World" over the last seventy years is Mexican historian Edmundo O'Gorman's contention that "America," rather than being "discovered," had to be "invented."[2] For historians, the distinction between the two terms is crucial. "Discovery," argues O'Gorman, implies the unveiling of a thing—always already present and fully realized as such but previously unseen. "Invention" implies the creation of something new that reconfigures reality. The intellectual operation attending discovery is to catalogue that which is revealed and refine the preexisting picture of the world to accommodate it. Invention, by contrast, first ruptures and then remakes established understandings of how the world looks and works. For O'Gorman, invention *produces* historical entities rather than merely *discovers* them. More concretely, O'Gorman's point is that "America" should not be understood as a "merely physical discovery," just one more accretion to the map of the world. Rather, "America" was "an invention of Western thought," a fundamental rethinking of the world as a whole and how people were to live in it.[3]

The novelty of "America"—its ontological originality—is the historiographical (and phenomenological) starting point for this volume. For just as "America" had to be invented, so law and justice had to be *reinvented* in relation to the radical newness of the encounter between indigenous people and Europeans. What is often forgotten, or at least obscured, in discussing law and justice in the New World is how enormous a challenge indigenous people and settlers represented for each other when they met in the legal crucible—and how disorienting it can be for scholars to think about law through the prism of difference.

The comparative approach advocated in this volume is premised on the idea that we must pay close attention to difference in two registers.

One focuses on the relationship between indigenous peoples and the settlers who intruded upon them. We know from the existing scholarship that legal encounters across this intercultural divide were fraught affairs. As discussed in section 2 of this chapter, we seek to capture the nuances and import of these interactions through the idea of *intelligibility*. The other register of difference—the subject of this section—demands attention to the distinct European legal regimes in the New World, Iberian and British, and the way they adapted to novel circumstances. While these regimes diverged in a variety of ways, we contend that two contrasts stand in sharp relief for their relevance to the essays in this volume. The first of these has to do with how indigenous people figured in colonial social orders. In Ibero-America, indigenous people were incorporated relatively early on into colonial society as vassals of the king. As a result, they acquired legal personality commensurate to their status. In Anglo-America, indigenous people remained on the outside of colonial society, to be treated with at arm's length as circumstances demanded. The second, related contrast involved the discourse of law. Whereas in Iberian realms, strong notions of substantive justice, backed by a duty of royal protection, remained the backbone of legal relations between settlers and indigenous people, in British realms sovereignty played the central role in structuring their legal encounters. In what follows, we unpack these two points.

As O'Gorman and others have noted, indigenous people had no obvious place in the European cosmological imagination of the early sixteenth century. Cartographically, theologically, and politically, their place had to be invented. Thus, during much of the sixteenth century, it was not even clear whether "Indios," as they came to be called, would be treated as fully human—able to receive the faith, govern themselves in their daily lives, be free of enslavement, and live as vassals of the king. This issue became a matter of deep debate within the Spanish empire. Dominican friar Antonio de Montesinos called attention to the plight of the native Taínos of Hispaniola in 1511, and by 1517 Dominican Bartolomé de Las Casas had taken up the cause of indigenous people, accepting appointment as protector of the Indians. In 1539, Francisco de Vitoria concluded that the Spanish crown lacked a legal basis for outright conquest of the Indians. Natural law granted indigenous people true *dominium* over their lands and persons. As such, neither the pope nor the king could dispossess them without their consent, a consent they had not granted. This conclusion did not entirely close the door on Spanish activity in the New World. Natural law, insisted Vitoria, held that Spaniards had a right of unhindered travel and commerce among the Indians, a right that might be enforced by war, though it could not warrant dispossessing the Natives.

By 1550 the issue of the status of the New World's indigenous people had become so sharp that Charles V suspended conquest activities until the matter could be hashed out in the Valladolid debate between Las Casas and court theologian Juan Ginés de Sepúlveda. Though the debate was officially unresolved, the decades following Valladolid gradually cemented the idea that the Indians were entitled to the rights and protections befitting vassals of the Spanish monarchy.[4] As Jesuit José de Acosta stated in 1588, "[T]he multitude of Indians and Spaniards form one and the same political community. . . . They all have the same king, are subject to the same laws, are judged by a sole judiciary."[5] From that time forward, the chief challenge of Spanish law in the New World was to balance the acknowledged need to exploit the Indios against the legal and moral imperative to protect them as the vassals they were.[6]

In Spanish America, inclusion of the Indians *within* the New World's social order led to the creation of a body of law—theological and philosophical statements, royal decrees and ordinances, indigenous customary law and practice, learned treatises and compendia—that historians have referred to as *derecho indiano*, or the Law of the Indies. Though the term is a historiographical artifact and almost surely connotes a greater degree of cohesion than was ever the case, this legal corpus and the jurisprudence that developed from it grounded ideas of justice and governed concrete legal relations in the Spanish New World from the sixteenth century to the early nineteenth century.[7]

The situation in Brazil was more equivocal from the point of view of Indians' legal status. In the mid-sixteenth century, when in Mexico caciques and nobles were learning to litigate, the Indians of Brazil faced a condition of "absolute juridical inferiority, which made it impractical for them to have recourse to magistrates to secure their freedom."[8] In practice, they could be denied their liberty in order to save their lives from other Natives who might kill or eat them. At this point, the early 1550s, the Valladolid debates had only just concluded, and natural Indian liberty as a widely agreed upon principle was at least a couple of decades off in Spanish America. In a letter of 1558, Jesuit Manuel da Nóbrega noted that in Brazil it was widely held that the Indians did not have full rights before the law because, lacking a soul, they were not fully human.[9] In 1562, Lisbon issued a ruling allowing indigenous people who violated a 1559 law against anthropophagy to be enslaved by just war. After that, as attitudes hardened against Natives, many Portuguese came to the view that perhaps the entire Native population needed to be partitioned along the lines of the Spanish *encomienda* (which awarded to the conquerors the labor of particular groups of Indians).[10] But this did not lead to the creation of a system of equal vassalage and separation into a Republic of Indians and a Republic of Spaniards, as in Spanish America. Rather, it implied a "mixed" social model premised on a measure of social integration, but rooted in a fundamental inequality of legal condition.[11] In alliance with the governor of Salvador, the Jesuits responded by pushing for the *aldeamentos,* a village system under their own administration. Though supported by the crown, even this arrangement could not fully insulate indigenous groups from colonists' incessant demands for labor. In the mid-1560s, the Conscience Board in Salvador ruled that parents could sell their children into slavery when in extremis and Indians older than twenty could exchange their liberty for money.[12] Opportunities for abuse were rife and means to restrain it lacking.

And yet, the underlying theory of Portuguese law did not diverge sharply from Spanish conceptions. Indeed, in the early seventeenth century, Philip III of Spain, holder of the Portuguese crown as a consequence of the Iberian union in 1580, tried to extend Spanish principles to Brazil. Indians were not to be enslaved, and their land rights were to be recognized.[13] A royal order of 1609 established a High Court in Salvador. Under its authority, enslaved Indians were to be freed and treated as vassals of the crown. In addition, a judicial system reaching to the village level was to be created, a structure quite similar to the one implanted in the Spanish New World. Two years later, the reforms had failed, and for most of the colonial period, law in Brazil remained distinctly "convoluted" and "particularistic, localist and multiform," both in terms of jurisdiction and in terms of process. In the eighteenth century, Portuguese-American law converged with Spanish-American law, at least on paper, when all Indians were declared vassals of the king (which technically had been true except for those taken in a "just war") and their enslavement prohibited. Despite this, though we need much more research, indigenous people in Brazil appear to have had a more limited access to legal process throughout the colonial period, as compared to Spanish realms. Even so, they did not deal with the Portuguese at arms' length, as did indigenous people in the northern New World and in remoter areas of the Spanish empire.[14]

No development parallel to the Spanish New World characterized British America. As Richard Ross has put it, legal historians have not conceptualized the English experience in terms of a "*derecho británico indiano*."[15] Whereas Spanish thinking about the New World was driven chiefly by the fact of direct encounter with its inhabitants, English thought aimed above all to assert sovereign claims to an area already presumptively under Spanish sway by the latter decades of the sixteenth century. Both Richard Hakluyts (cousins, one a geographer, the other a lawyer) and astrologer, mathematician, and geographer John Dee, none of whom ever visited America, argued strenuously that Spain had no claim to New World dominions. This position was bolstered in 1580 by Alberico Gentili, an Italian professor of Roman law at Oxford, who argued that the Indians' "abominable lewdness"—especially cannibalism, incest, and sodomy—justified war against them "as against brutes."[16] Vitoria had insisted that the Indians' sins, abominable though they might be, did not negate their "true dominion" in their territories before the arrival of Spaniards. War could be pursued against them only if they violated the duties and obligations of sovereigns vis-à-vis each other and not otherwise.[17]

The strong legal presence of indigenous people in Spanish America and their relative legal absence in British America set quite distinct baselines regarding struggles between settlers and Indians over land. As Tamar Herzog has pointed out, the idea that Europeans might be entitled to occupy territory belonging to Native people had its roots in Thomas More's *Utopia*, which proposed that overpopulated communities could legitimately enter upon the territory of others "when anye people holdethe a piece of grounde voyde and vacant to no good nor profitable vfe."[18] Gentili, as we have seen, held to the view that Indians lacked true sovereignty, a fact that essentially created a rebuttable presumption of legitimacy to any occupation of territory by English colonists acting with license from the king. From this it was a short step to the view that Indian territory was unoccupied precisely because, for Gentili, it was not under any prior sovereign control. For all intents and purposes, indigenous territories not covered by buildings or cultivated fields were by law constructively empty, *terra nullius*, available to any sovereign, or his agents, who might occupy them and *settle* or *improve* them (though, in practice, English colonists obtained most Indian land through purchase or cession, implicitly recognizing Native possessory rights). By contrast, Vitoria had insisted that indigenous princes were sovereign unless shown to be otherwise.[19] On this view, they were entitled to hold their territories against would-be occupiers pending proof that they had failed to meet the obligations of sovereignty or had violated natural law in ways that would forfeit their exclusivity, such as by denying commerce and communication.[20]

Though much more could be said about this issue, the bottom line for our purposes may be stated as follows. In Spanish America, the sixteenth century resulted in the (always contested and often violated) inclusion of indigenous people in the social and legal order. In Portuguese America—though we have little to go on—indigenous people appear to have had an uncertain legal status and remained marginal legal actors through most of the colonial period.[21] In British America, "legally, the indigenous would remain on the other side of a westward advancing frontier" rather than be incorporated into the colonial social order.[22] These distinctions are crucial to thinking about how law and justice mediated the relationship between indigenous people and settlers in different regions of America.

A second important contrast bears on our understanding of distinct legal regimes in the New World. Starting in the sixteenth century, the very idea of law underwent a deep transformation in Europe. German legal historian Matthew Stolleis has argued that the terrain on which European law had long been legitimated—God, history, tradition—began to shift during the late medieval period.[23] Rather than theologically rooted truth (*veritas*), law was now coming to be seen as an expression of a secularized notion of sovereign will (*voluntas*). Put another way, where once law had been valid because God had ordained it so, on this new understanding law was valid because the ruler had decreed it so. English and Spanish law reacted very differently to this broad transformation.

As Portuguese historian Antônio Hespanha notes, medieval European juridical culture was rooted in the idea of an order established by God *prior* to human will.[24] Spain's thirteenth-century legal code, *Las Siete Partidas*, held that God had appointed the king "over the people to maintain them in justice and in truth in temporal matters," ensuring thereby "rights to every individual."[25] The law of men answered to natural law and thus constrained the monarch to act justly. In Iberia, this understanding had produced a juridical theory in which law was subordinated to other spheres of normativity—love, morality, religion. Kings were under a legal duty to conserve a set of interwoven moral precepts that governed the world. Theologians, jurists, and others conversant with these precepts could in principle check potential excesses, both by the monarch and by his subjects.[26]

This broad conception came under considerable pressure beginning in the sixteenth century. As warfare and struggles over religious convictions fragmented Christianity, the religious and theological foundations of law weakened. At the same time, Machiavelli's attention to "the true nature of things," rather than to an idealized understanding of how things should be, began to decouple politics from morality and in the process undermine the very idea of substantive justice. By the mid-seventeenth century, many worried that justice might no longer be able to assure "peace, which is the principle social good," as Aquinas had put it.[27] Jesuit Antônio Vieira, in a sermon delivered from Brazil, framed the problem this way: "[W]hat leads government and also the consciences and souls of princes astray is the idea that they *may* do anything because they *can* do anything. . . . The king may only do what is just; for the unjust he has no power whatever."[28] Vieira's concern is clear: if the king was no longer bound to act justly, then law was rooted in nothing more than the will of men, with all the perils that implied.

This trend toward the primacy of *will* was staunchly resisted by Iberian jurists. Neo-Scholastics, many of them Jesuits, wrote anti-Machiavellian tracts in the sixteenth century and insisted on the continued relevance of substantive justice in grounding any legitimate legal regime.[29] These writers asserted that law was the chief instrument for "conserving" society and assuring its unity. As a political imperative, this *conservation* was predicated on the love that grounded the cosmos as ordained by God, a love that bound all things into an organic net of hierarchically related sympathies. Justice as conservation, thus, assured each thing a place in the constituted order. God had made human beings to live together, and so each and every person had a place in forming what Aquinas had called the "perfect society."[30] The just political order was one that achieved peace through dynamic conservation. And because society could be disrupted by changing circumstances, the just ruler responded to change through law to bring about the common good. This was the broad matrix of ideas regarding law and justice that ultimately authorized the inclusion of indigenous people within colonial society.

The problem was that the New World's novelty flew in the face of the imperative to conservation. Indeed, during the earliest decades after contact it was not clear what it meant for the king to conserve or act justly vis-à-vis indigenous people. For their part, settlers, in their encounters with Indians, evinced little concern for questions of justice or the king's law. Only after midcentury, as indigenous populations began to drop precipitously, did conservation of the Indians as a whole become one of the crown's central preoccupations. Partly this was a recognition of their unique vulnerability to abuse by settlers.

It was in this context that the doctrine of *personas miserables* (wretched people) came to be applied to the indigenous people from the late sixteenth century forward. Traditionally, *miserables* were orphans, widows, and all others lacking paternal protection from abuse by the powerful. The need to protect such people was obvious, for as Juan de Mariana put it in 1599, "The rich are corrupted by power [and] to a man seeking power every poor man is a very great opportunity."[31] In the New World, this doctrine of protection was extended to "Indios" as a legal category. By 1593, the king had ordered that the Indians "be more protected as people who are more miserable and of less defense" against the powerful.[32] From this point forward, "Indios" enjoyed a special claim at law to the king's pastoral and judicial attention. Yet even when they had been afforded special legal recognition, indigenous litigants were often exposed to those who Juan Solórzano y Pereira noted were "less affected to the love and service of our kings and their commands."[33]

In concrete terms, the doctrine of *miserables* recognized that Indios were entitled to speedier process, free legal counsel, interpreters, diminished responsibility for truth telling, choice of judges under certain circumstances, lesser punishments, and a right to the king's jurisdiction in the first instance.[34] These privileges might be unevenly available—the Andean highlands and the South American lowlands were not the Central Valley of Mexico—or unevenly honored in the breach. But they were, broadly speaking, part of the legal structure for indigenous people who appealed to the king and his judges for *justicia* in the face of mistreatment.[35] In this way, substantive justice remained a touchstone in Spanish America, perhaps more so for indigenous people than for Spanish colonists themselves—a critical part of the story about how law mediated their relationships.

In England, substantive justice had been less central to understandings of law. Jurists primarily conceived of law in terms of immemorial custom, what historians have called the "ancient constitution."[36] Through the Middle Ages, the truth of ordinances had been rooted less in precepts of nature than in the timelessness and antiquity of English common law, which jurists assumed was in accordance with the law of nature. And because common law had originated prior to any sovereign act, the monarch could make no special claim on it. From this vantage point, law was an artifact of custom (not inconsistent with the demands of nature) rather than a product of will. In the mid-seventeenth century, Hobbes and others challenged this idea, asserting instead that sovereignty alone authorized law as it pertained to men: "*auctoritas non veritas facit legem*"—authority, not truth, makes the laws. Law had not originated in antiquity, said Hobbes, but in an act of will transmitted through time as sovereign authority and subject to such authority thereafter. In the century after the English Civil War, sovereignty became a progressively more salient foundation for law. Or, as Pocock argued long ago, the "medieval concept of universal unmade law collapsed" and a new theory rooted in sovereignty came to legitimize law.[37]

This shift had important consequences for the legal encounter between English settlers and indigenous people in the New World. The English sovereign, as the "fountain" of law, could choose to make ordinances and grant them to indigenous people. But he was under no binding obligation to enact particular provisions of law determined by an objective standard of justice standing outside and above his will. The law that European invaders extended to Native inhabitants remained ungrounded in any particular principle of justice beyond that of the sovereignty Britain claimed over New World territory.

Indeed, where Spanish jurists of the sixteenth century treated *justice* in great depth and at great length, English documents from the period emphasized *freedom* and *rights*.[38] Because both imperial administrators and colonists disagreed among themselves over whether indigenous people were true sovereigns, freedoms and rights had little bearing on them as such. As some of the essays in this volume show, indigenous litigants learned to deploy the language of freedom and rights, much as in Spanish realms litigants referred to *libertad* (liberty) and *derecho* (law, right). But lacking any clearly defined place in the English legal imagination, the Indians neither posed an insuperable legal obstacle to settler designs nor presented a particular incentive for the crown to broaden the reach of law or justice, as royal letters patent authorizing conquest and discovery made clear by their silence on the matter.[39] This had deep repercussions: indigenous people, quite simply, were legally relevant only insofar as English advance might provoke an encounter requiring resolution. How law was to operate at these moments was left to be worked out in practice.

This does not imply the absence of an English legal corpus applicable to the New World. Parliament produced statutory law and the colonies themselves produced abundant police regulations.[40] London, as well as colonial governments, entered into "treaties" with Indian nations. But the absence of guiding principles of justice applicable to the Indians and the decentralized qualities of the common law made British colonial law highly variable. Thus, between settlers or traders and Indians, legal arrangements seem to have been a loose admixture of law and legal procedure, negotiation and contractual haggling, and diplomacy and saber rattling.[41] Law's role was not, even in principle, to check settler power so much as to sort out relationships and, ideally, keep the peace. The irony here is that while settlers, traders, and other colonists constantly sought to expand their ability to make and enforce law locally—often to enhance their power to draft local inhabitants into labor relations, to secure land, or press agreements—indigenous people found it harder and harder to reach the ear of the king even as the king found it more difficult to restrain his English subjects in America. This legal diversity and the growing attenuation of a link to the crown through law is a crucial background condition for all legal encounters between indigenous people and English settlers described in the essays that follow.

II. Legal Intelligibility: Trajectories

Europeans and Natives, who often found themselves on opposite sides of legal conflicts, needed to comprehend the words, concepts, and forms of evidence (writing, pictograms, knotted cords) used by each other. As Yanna Yannakakis has shown, translation was the foundation of intelligibility.[42] But more broadly, law became intelligible as historical actors began to appreciate the values and history behind a legal idea, the concepts to which it was tacitly linked, its range of uses in a given culture, its limitations, and the meanings attached to it by different groups. Only with this deeper understanding did conceptions of justice approach, if seldom fully reach, mutual intelligibility. Imagine a gradient stretching from a high degree of intelligibility to almost complete incomprehensibility. We might situate historical actors along this gradient by focusing on (1) the extent to which they appropriated and cultivated the values and history behind legal ideas (2) while responding to the specific circumstances of a given conflict by (3) adapting legal concepts to concrete strategies (4) across a range of uses and limitations determined by the meanings attached to it by different groups. The further that settlers and Natives moved along this gradient towards intelligibility, the better they could meaningfully learn from, outmaneuver, resist, or accommodate each other. At least some degree of intelligibility was a precondition for what historians call "jurisdictional politics," "legal resistance," "popular justice," and "strategic engagement with law."

At the outset, we must acknowledge the limits of our claims for the importance of legal intelligibility. There is little doubt that settlers and Indians alike learned to use the law in navigating their complex relationships. In many instances, they faced each other across a fog of legal misunderstanding, as several essays in this volume attest. But in other cases, misunderstanding may not have been a product of law at all, but of how interests and mistrust played out in intercultural legal settings. In Juan Pomar-Zurita's report from the mid-sixteenth century, a local Mexican cacique argued that Indians had become so litigious since conquest "because you do not understand us, nor do we understand you or know what you want."[43] Here, the cacique seemed to suggest that in the face of a broader failure of understanding, law might be the basis for some kind of mutual intelligibility. Two and a half centuries later, the reaction of two farm laborers reminds us that legal intelligibility is perfectly consistent with sharp tensions between parties. In 1799, the tithe collector showed up in the town of Tule, Oaxaca, to collect for the cathedral from the local indigenous community. On the outskirts of the village, he came across a couple of sharecroppers and told them that it was time to pay up. They refused. According to this official's report, one of the men responded "insolently," insisting that they were exempt from payment, and, much to the collector's surprise, quoted chapter and verse of the *Recopilación* of 1680 to back up his point. Doubtless, the legal knowledge and confidence expressed by these men was uneven across the vast Spanish empire, and probably no less so in English realms. Perhaps it was laced with bravado, a bluff betting on mutual ignorance of the law. But the blustery, even arrogant confidence they expressed suggests how much and how little things had changed since the sixteenth century for such people. Because they understood the law, they had put the tithe collector off this time. And yet, that understanding could not prevent him from coming back and trying again, better armed this time with his own legal arguments. In short, failures of legal intelligibility may have been at once a cause and a result of social tensions and clashing interests.

Adjusting one's angle of vision on the past in this way can produce either an account of settlers and Natives gradually improving their understanding of each other's legal commitments and concepts of justice, or an account stressing persisting incomprehension. Each of these accounts is stylized and necessarily partial. Developing them will be a useful first step toward framing the approach of this volume. We will emphasize the profound variability in how different groups of Natives and settlers understood elements of the other's notions of justice—a variability that was not merely an initial challenge that faded after contact but a perennial challenge, endlessly taking on new complexions.

First Perspective—Improving Understanding: Much scholarship tacitly assumes that, over time, settlers and indigenous peoples gradually came to a better, though never full, appreciation of each other's legal principles. For instance, in British America, Natives and settlers fairly quickly grasped their contrary approaches to handling murder—colonists expected a public trial of the guilty, while Indians demanded compensation to the victim's family to stave off retaliatory killing. Diplomats and treaty negotiators spent much time working out which of these approaches would prevail in which circumstances. Colonists and indigenous people did not misunderstand each other so much as they strove to mediate between conflicting, deeply held notions about what constituted justice when a life had been taken. By contrast, early sales of Indian land to colonists tended to produce confusion, for settlers believed they had purchased full, exclusive ownership, while Natives assumed they had merely given the English the privilege to use land alongside themselves. Within a few years, certainly within a few decades, each side grasped the other's position and bargained accordingly.[44] This appears to have been the general trend: settlers' understanding of Indian government improved over time, and vice versa. Many settler accounts written in the first generation after contact misrepresented indigenous societies as nearly without law and public authority or, alternatively, as monarchies ruled by will and custom. By the late seventeenth- and early eighteenth centuries, some colonists showed greater awareness of how Indian rulers relied on kinship ties and extensive consultation with leading families to enforce norms of justice through mobilized public opinion rather than through coercive authority.

The practicalities involved in trade, land sales, and preventing occasional murders from provoking war encouraged settlers and Natives to work at better comprehending the other's law. Colonists seeking to buy land, for example, benefited from learning who among the Natives could legitimately alienate tribal property and who could usefully feign such powers.[45] Indian norms helped structure trade not only in obvious but also in unexpected ways. Carolina settlers, for example, contended that Indian slaves bought from the Cherokee were prisoners taken in "legitimate" wars, a point established by Native—not English—law.[46]

Trials and treaty negotiations led to conversations between Natives and settlers about conflicting legal norms. Indians revealed that, when hungry and in haste on a military expedition, they did not regard as "theft" the removal of food from a colonist's house despite protests. Settlers explained how their legal culture distinguished between manslaughter (killing "through heat of blood") and premeditated murder, and between rape and fornication.[47] Treaties often granted Indians the right to attend colonial trials to ensure that justice was done to members of their nation and that settlers did not escape punishment for offenses against Natives.[48] In cases involving Indians as defendants, Natives on occasion served as jurors alongside settlers, either on regular panels or on specially convened "mixed juries."[49] Colonies varied in the extent to which they would accept Indian testimony—sometimes allowing it, sometimes restricting it to certain classes of cases or to proceedings involving other Natives.[50] Within these limitations, Natives gained experience in giving depositions and recounting events before tribunals.

Settlers and Natives in Spanish America also learned about each other's law over time. Spanish jurisprudence specifically recognized local custom as a source of authority in legal disputes, so long as it did not conflict with divine or natural law. This principle, forged in Iberia's highly fragmented medieval political and legal landscape, was critical to indigenous communities, because it meant that even in contests between Spaniards and Indians, *costumbre* (custom) carried an important weight. This was entirely consistent with the broader principle that the law's role—and the king's responsibility—was to *conserve* the social order, rather than innovate. Recognition of *costumbre*, thus, was a means of doing so, one that indigenous litigants leaned on heavily in their encounters with Spaniards. Of course, there was still ample room for disagreement and misunderstanding; Spanish and indigenous customs might conflict, or custom might be at odds with natural law or the law of God. Nevertheless, the fact that *costumbre* had a recognized place in Spanish jurisprudence as a legitimate source of law was critical to Natives' capacity to enter legal conversations on their own terms, which forced Spanish litigants to confront the legitimacy of Native custom in legal encounters. Thus, even as indigenous litigants gradually came to accept Spanish notions of land use and property, customary understandings of usufruct, community rights, productive use, and possession ensured the continued relevance of Native principles throughout the colonial period.[51]

Second Perspective—Persisting Incomprehension: We can, however, shift perspective and sketch a contrary picture—a colonial encounter where, for a variety of structural and ideological reasons, many colonists and Natives understood each other's notions of justice at little better than surface levels. The charters issued by the English crown to authorize the colonization of North America said little if anything about the status of indigenous law, leaving unexplained the terms of its interaction with crown and settler ordinances. Above all, the English did not acknowledge indigenous law as binding in any way, giving them little reason to look beneath the surface of what appeared to be strange and even senseless ideas. They did not treat the Indians' law as one of the various colonial, imperial, and transnational legalities whose complicated interaction governed affairs within English settlements. The reach of indigenous law became a question for diplomacy rather than a "choice of law" problem within the core areas of European colonization. The English erased the claims of Indian law over land acquired from Natives, subjecting it only to English principles and regulations.[52] Treaties that specified the circumstances under which Indian offenders would be tried under English law exempted settlers from Indian justice.[53] Indigenous law mattered politically in relations with Natives but exerted almost no claim over colonists *as law*.

This largely dismissive approach to Native law set the North American English colonies apart from other contemporaneous British imperial areas no less than from Spanish realms. East India Company (EIC) settlements in Madras and Calcutta, for example, operated not only under crown and parliamentary permissions but also under grants and contracts from South Asian sovereigns, which authorized jurisdiction over Native residents and shaped the concepts and techniques through which the English governed. In a region where South Asians allowed late-seventeenth-century Calcutta to exercise the jurisdictional privileges of a landholding *zamindar*, and where the EIC expanded effective control of territory in Bengal by assuming the office of a *diwan* (a Mughal revenue collector and administrator), the English needed to deploy South Asian legal concepts in order to rule. In certain classes of cases, EIC and English tribunals reached or ratified decisions based on what they imagined to be Hindu and Muslim law for adherents of those religions.[54] For all of their critiques of Hindu and Muslim law, Englishmen acknowledged these legal traditions as sophisticated and impressive. In the eighteenth century, some EIC administrators tried to reconstruct an "ancient Mughal constitution" and to establish "authentic" written accounts of Hindu and Muslim law in order to break free of reliance on Native interpreters.[55] The contrast of all of this to North America is striking. Amerindian grants and contracts did not provide permission for English settlement or suggest techniques of government. Settler tribunals did not pronounce or ratify decisions made under Seneca or Cherokee law. Colonists wondered to what extent "barbarous" Natives actually had law (as opposed to custom, will, and public opinion). They did not inquire into and respect Pequot or Powhatan law as longstanding traditions of high intellectual accomplishment.

Comparison to the Spanish empire further illuminates the reasons for and implications of the limited English interest in Native law. Sixteenth- and seventeenth-century Castilians established themselves, greatly outnumbered, among millions of Indians. The Spanish expected most Natives to be enveloped within their empire while settlers lived off indigenous labor and tribute, evangelized Indians, reordered their towns, invited or drove them into imperial tribunals, and tried to partially "Hispanicize" their customs and governance. By contrast, the English did not rely on Indian labor and tribute. The colonial legal system did not calibrate and enforce the extraction of work, money, and goods from indigenous peoples, nor did it coordinate large-scale economic enterprises (such as the mining and shipment of South American bullion) that drew on Indians from numerous local jurisdictions. Settlers made no systematic effort to anglicize the legal systems of Native American communities on the model of the (ambivalent) campaign of Christianization. Nor did the English follow the Spanish policy of treating Indians as subjects or "vassals" of the crown. Unless naturalized, the Indians remained foreigners. Colonial officials, therefore, typically knew less of indigenous legal principles than their counterparts in British India and in Spanish America. The practicalities of trade and land transfer created only limited incentives for colonists to learn Indian concepts of justice in any depth. The foundation of colonial government in crown rather than Native permission, the lack of respect for indigenous law as an intellectual system, and the lack of interest in "reforming" that law or in manipulating it to coordinate labor and tribute all combined to offer settlers very little reason to acquire a working knowledge of Native legality as anything other than an obstacle to be overcome.

By the same token, Natives often had limited reasons and means to understand English law in great detail. One very practical barrier was linguistic. Few Natives and settlers knew each other's languages, and interpreters were never plentiful enough. By 1700, New England tribunals no longer felt obliged to provide a translator to Indians living within their borders.[56] In Spanish realms by the seventeenth century, the law demanded the presence of an interpreter in all legal proceedings, and indigenous litigants often insisted on having them, even when they spoke perfectly adequate Spanish. But the divide between Indian and English settler legal cultures was deeper—not just linguistic (failure to understand words) but conceptual (as indicated by continual Native complaints that "they could not understand the way of our proceedings").[57] Core ideas of the English legal system, such as corroboration of evidence and adversary procedure, grated on Indians. Under the direction of Pennsylvania judge and councilor James Logan, English representatives investigating a 1722 murder by settlers took depositions from Indian witnesses. After one Native testified, others steadfastly refused to discuss the same matter and wondered why they were expected to repeat what had already been said. Their norms contradicted the English practice of cross-checking accounts and obtaining corroboration from multiple sources. Algonquian notions of reciprocity expected disputes to end, as Katherine Hermes observes, with exchanges by both sides so that each obtained "a material and psychological 'gift.'" English tribunals irritated Indians by declaring a "winner" at trial and demanding that the "loser" pay in a one-way transaction. In many instances, Natives asked for arbitration by a governor, councilor, or local magistrate rather than litigation under unfamiliar law and irritating adversary procedure.[58]

In British America, Natives may also have resisted engaging English law for reasons of cultural unpalatability. Within a few decades of contact, settlers came to appreciate that indigenous peoples in North America lacked a state in the European sense, where rulers could set policy and punish offenders according to a detailed set of established laws. In at least some nations, Indians might ignore sachems or headmen who tried to push beyond what public opinion would accept. Indian leaders relied on kinship networks, charisma, gift exchange, and, above all, on their power to persuade. Tribal public opinion served simultaneously as their greatest ally and their most profound constraint.[59] Thomas Pownall, when serving as lieutenant governor of New Jersey, observed that the indigenous peoples of the middle and northern colonies "know no such thing as an administrative or executive power, properly so called. They allow the authority of advice, a kind of legislative authority. But there is no civil coercion. They never had any one collective actuating power of the whole, nor any magistrate or magistrates to execute such."[60]

More acute European observers went further and contended that Indian political organization fostered a distaste for the well-articulated, precise, and technical ordinances that Europeans thought necessary to a "government of law, not of men." Such ordinances appeared to Natives not as limitations on potentially overreaching rulers—Indians restrained them through family and social pressure—nor as necessary foundations for property rights and trade. Instead, these convoluted "quibbles of art" seemed to set traps ensnaring ordinary people. Indian trader James Adair reported on the difficulty of impressing Natives

> with a favorable opinion of the wisdom and justice of our voluminous laws—They say, if our laws were honest, or wisely framed, they would be plain and few, that the poor people might understand and remember them, as well as the rich—That right and wrong, an honest man and a rogue, with as many other names as our large crabbed books could contain, are only two contraries; that simple nature enables every person to be a proper judge of promoting good, and preventing evil, either by determinations, rewards, or punishments; and that people cannot in justice be accused of violating any laws, when it is out of their power to have a proper knowledge of them.[61]

Even those Indians inclined to master European law faced difficulties since the colonists' law emerged in societies relying on skills and ideas absent or less evident in indigenous societies—a specialized legal profession devoted to analysis and application of law; the routine use of writing to record ordinances and precedents; the existence of judicial tribunals conceived of as separate from clans and tribal councils; and the maintenance of conceptual distinctions between criminal and civil, legislation and execution, and public and private.

In Ibero-America, situations varied, depending on Native structures. In central Mexico and in Incaic Peru, the idea of an authority that could order, dispose, and punish was well understood before European arrival. There, indigenous people, especially Native nobility, took to litigation quite readily. Even so, local communities often sought to reestablish a disrupted harmony by encouraging compromise, something to which Spanish law itself was open in many circumstances. Tribal peoples, such as those in the Amazon and South American lowlands, often operated much more like those of North America, resistant to "state"-like understandings of authority and inclined to settle disputes through kinship networks and gift exchanges (or warfare and anthropophagy in extreme cases).[62]

The differences in British America between European and Native orientations to law became important evidence for eighteenth-century Scottish Enlightenment thinkers articulating sweeping four-stage theories of evolutionary development. These theories were stories that Europeans told themselves rather than accurate depictions of Indian behavior. Lord Kames, Adam Smith, Adam Ferguson, William Robertson, and John Millar contended that much of humanity, at different times and rates, became more mature and civilized as it progressed through four developmental epochs—hunting, pastoral, agricultural, and commercial.[63] The common impulse among these writers was to look at a society's "mode of subsistence. Accordingly, as that varies, their laws and policy must be different."[64] Indians played an important role in these accounts. Relying on deeply misleading accounts of Indian society, evolutionary theorists saw Natives, inaccurately, as stuck in an early stage as hunters and fishermen with rudimentary agriculture, living with little sense of property rights and scarcely any government.[65] None of these writers believed that Natives' trade with each other and with settlers had advanced them into the civilized and polished commercial stage of Europeans and their overseas colonists. Commercial societies produced "a regular administration of justice," a predictable, specific set of "written and formal laws" of contract, debt, inheritance, and criminal procedure articulated and enforced by a state.[66] By contrast, Native hunters and simple agriculturalists had "occasion for very few regulations" as they lived with "imperfect conceptions of property," little of the social inequality that encouraged repression by the rich and envy by the poor, and a largely privatized response to violence through compensation and vengeance.[67] Reading the Scottish Enlightenment stadial theorists leaves the impression that Indians' awkwardness with formal, technical law was a normal consequence of the relatively early stage they occupied in a global, progressive evolutionary scheme, a stage that European and Middle Eastern civilizations had long ago surpassed and that had once produced similar political and legal practices—and limitations. We need not accept the four-stage model of evolutionary development as "true" nor countenance its dismissive and condescending account of Indian societies to extract a more limited point. Europeans told themselves that the economy and politics characteristic of Indian life gave Natives little experience in manipulating complex, technical law and created a distaste that discouraged the work of mastering it. From the fashionable thinkers of the Scottish Enlightenment came the most sweeping structuralist explanation of why Natives strained to find English law intelligible.[68]

For Natives and settlers alike, then, there were both encouragements and impediments to making the law intelligible. In the historiography, accounts tend to vary by the extent to which practical obstacles to engagement and cultural distinctions between Natives and Europeans are placed in the foreground or left in the background. This volume proposes to bring all of these considerations as much as possible front and center. That is, rather than accept the idea that law was either intelligible or unintelligible, we emphasize the extraordinary variability in how, why, and under what circumstances different groups of Indians and colonists came to understand or failed to understand specific features of each other's conceptions of justice. We see not so much a middle ground, implying a place upon which a solid stance was possible, as a terrain of tricky and always unreliable footing. It is a story, thus, not of ever-growing familiarity or persisting minimal comprehension, or even of an agreement to disagree, possibilities that presume some kind of endpoint, but of ebbs and flows, reversible gains, and a kind of permanent tenuousness.

Of course, historical actors did not intend such an outcome. People acting from their own understandings rarely strive to produce uncertainty. Our point is that historical analysis of New World legal encounters, written without a comparative perspective, has produced an overly sharp but simultaneously underconceptualized sense of legal (un)intelligibility. We see this volume as a corrective to this position and a spur for scholars to be more explicitly comparative in their outlook. Doing so, we contend, will open up new vistas on issues of jurisdiction, sovereignty, legal inclusion and exclusion, the quality and role of intermediation in structuring legal encounters and producing legal outcomes, and the intellectual foundations of justice as a guiding idea for legal engagement.

Our Perspective—Local Variability and Ebb and Flow: In Spanish America, jurisdictional and institutional changes had profound effects. In the central valley of Mexico, for instance, indigenous people very quickly began to litigate in reaction to threats to their lands and autonomy and in response to new political fissures within Native communities. Within a decade of the fall of Tenochtitlán to Cortés, caciques had begun to file lawsuits with the *Audiencia* (high court) in Mexico City. Legal process and dispute was hardly a novelty among the Aztecs. Bernardino de Sahagún had noted early on that the Aztecs had been known for the rigor and prudence of their system of justice. Few distinctions, informants told Sahagún, had been made between people "important or common, rich or poor." One crucial change resulting from the irruption of Spanish imperial law into indigenous lives, thus, is that legality initially became more oriented to status. Native caciques often could bring a case to the Audiencia where commoners—"*macehaules*" in Nahuatl—could not. And while local leaders might once have done so on behalf of their communities, now, as one commentator noted, litigious caciques were dispossessing ordinary Indians in order to afford litigation for self-interested ends. At the same time, Alonso de Zurita reported a complaint by an Indian noble that the conquerors had forced indigenous people into litigation just to defend themselves against unscrupulous Spaniards. And these lawsuits, stated Zurita's informant, were rarely successful, "because you [the Spanish] are the law and the judges and the parties, and you cut into us wherever you want, and whenever and however you like," making it difficult for Indians to get justice.[69]

The issue in these instances was not just a lack of understanding on the part of indigenous litigants; it was also a failure of law to be readily available to all those who sought justice in response to the disruptions of conquest. In other words, what the law could be understood to do, what role it could play in everyday life, was also a function of hierarchy and power relations—between Natives and colonists, but among Natives as well—that were themselves being transformed. By the late sixteenth century, complaints from New Spain that ordinary people could not reach the king's justice became a crisis that resulted in the creation of the General Court of the Indians in the 1590s. The Juzgado, as it was known, was charged to hear cases between indigenous litigants and cases in which indigenous litigants complained of misdeeds by Spanish officials.[70] In essence, the court lodged such cases within the viceroy's mixed administrative and judicial powers, an innovation that created a new kind of legality for all manner of intercultural judicial disputes.

The creation of the Juzgado opened the floodgates to indigenous litigation in Mexico, with deep implications for individual and corporate land disputes, individual claims for liberty, labor relations, rights of movement, and community rights to self-government. Any given individual might know little about the workings of law, but communities became repositories of legal knowledge and practice. Community archives contained the paper trails of earlier lawsuits, and local leaders were rarely without some legal experience to draw on. Moreover, royal decrees gave litigants a right to free legal counsel. In terms of incentives to "know" the law, this could cut both ways. On the one hand, the presence of a legal adviser could mean that even a completely uninformed complainant might retain counsel. On the other hand, advocates rarely prepared cases without closely consulting with their clients, whose input was crucial to establishing the facts and determining legal strategies. In Peru, concerns similar to those that prompted creation of the Juzgado led to a series of reforms by the viceroy in Lima. These reforms established indigenous rights to justice but did so in ways that made Indian access to the judicial system somewhat narrower and more tenuous than in Mexico, which speaks to the centrality of circumstance in thinking about legal intelligibility.

Natives in English America maintained a variety of relationships to the colonists' law depending on geography and on whether they belonged to an independent or tributary Indian nation or lived in an English settlement without tribal ties. To begin with, nations beyond the frontier of settlement that were independent or under merely nominal allegiance to the English ("foreign Indians") exercised nearly unqualified sovereignty. They might turn over offenders for trial or accept the conclusions of the colonists' law in particular cases, but only as a result of diplomatic negotiations. Second, nations that acknowledged English sovereignty but lived collectively in an Indian community near or within colonial borders maintained selective, ad hoc connection to the settlers' law. "Tributary" and reservation Indians in the Chesapeake seldom took their disputes to English courts. Crimes and breakdowns in trade would more readily be treated as communal problems to be handled politically than as individual offenses to be litigated. Indian sachems and colonial leaders accepted responsibility for the offenses of their people and made amends by punishing miscreants, offering compensation to victims, and restoring relationships through diplomacy accompanied by gift giving. Within New England, Indians who had submitted to colonial authority were expected to enforce selected Puritan morals regulations as well as their own laws. Over the course of the seventeenth century, an increasing percentage of Natives remaining within the core areas of settlement lived collectively as "praying" or "plantation" Indians in towns at first governed by mixed English/indigenous tribunals and, later, overseen by colonial guardians or commissioners. Finally, Natives who resided not in Indian towns but in English ones submitted to the settlers' legal system directly, without special jurisdictions or procedures.[71]

From the middle of the seventeenth century forward, Natives in the British New World suffered a relative decline in political and legal autonomy because of reductions in population and curtailment of military power. Fewer Natives within settled areas of colonies lived in independent nations. Among the shrinking overall indigenous population, more lived as plantation or tributary Indians or as unattached individuals. English law had scant impact on the lives of Natives in independent nations in the backcountry or beyond the frontier. They had little contact with English legal concepts outside of occasional diplomatic negotiations. The shift towards tributary, plantation, or unattached individual status encouraged relatively greater Indian use and understanding, if not approval, of English law—albeit among a declining population. This is especially true of residents in designated Indian towns and among Christianized Indians. Our claim is modest. Such Indians did not become legal adepts. But, over time, they found settlers' law somewhat more intelligible, at least in comparison to the experience of previous generations and of Natives in independent nations.

Sometimes Indians within colonial borders were the audience for programs of legal education; sometimes they observed settlers' tribunals or negotiated about what justice demanded in particular cases; and sometimes they used English legal forms in their own affairs. Several New England colonies published or yearly read aloud to Natives criminal laws and regulations against immorality.[72] A few Christianized Indians worked as lay attorneys.[73] By the eighteenth century, there is increasing evidence of Natives memorializing rights and obligations not only through oral tradition but in the written documents—the letters, deeds, and treaties—that settler authorities preferred, often demanded, as proof.[74] Slowly at first, and increasingly in the eighteenth century, Indians brought suits in English courts and became more skilled at petitioning.[75]

Above all, Natives gained experience with the law by being involved in actual proceedings. In the English colonies, Indians served alongside settlers in the governance of Indian towns and in mixed tribunals devoted to mediating disputes. North Carolina provided that trade disputes with an Indian village might be resolved by its "head man" sitting with commissioners appointed by the governor.[76] Massachusetts similarly established an elaborate system of mixed Native and settler governance for the Indian towns within their borders—from "praying towns" for Christianized Indians to treaties between Algonquian nations and the colony regarding Native rendition for murder of a colonist. King Philip's War (1675–1678) set in motion two contrary trends. Native officials lost some of their governing authority while Indians became more enmeshed in English law, with progressively less ability to escape it. Indeed, after the war, the colony confined all of the greatly reduced Indian population within its jurisdiction to a handful of plantations.[77] The pre-1676 praying towns, designed to "civilize" Indians, had prohibited "barbarous" practices while teaching colonial criminal law and morals regulation. By the eighteenth century, the colony spoke less of civilizing but expected plantation Indians to conform to almost all colonial legal precepts, civil as well as criminal. Massachusetts also became more willing to seize Indians for trial without, as in the seventeenth century, an interpreter and a sachem present as intermediary.[78] From the late seventeenth century forward, Natives kept their laws increasingly at English sufferance and were under closer supervision by settlers. Because Indians found it much harder to escape English law, learning about it became more important to the reduced number who remained within colonial borders after war and population loss. In effect, they were experiencing a kind of forced program of legal intelligibility.

Some of the strongest evidence that English law was becoming more intelligible to plantation Indians from the late seventeenth century forward was that, among themselves, they occasionally used settler legal ideas and techniques. Natives in Indian towns who traditionally assumed that communities controlled land came to understand the rights and duties of individuals who owned land in the English fashion. By doing so they became better able to deploy English legal forms—such as written deeds, a recording system, surveying, and descriptions of plots as rectangles rather than by natural boundaries—in order to extend their landholdings vis-à-vis other Indians, raise capital through sales, and define and defend their property from settlers.[79] By the late seventeenth century, Natives in New England, particularly women, were writing wills to ensure that property passed as they wished.[80]

The distinction among independent nations, plantation/tributary nations, and individuals living without tribal ties only begins to suggest the degree of variation in the way indigenous peoples used and understood English laws. Within each of these categories, Natives in certain colonies and towns invested more (or less) effort in familiarizing themselves with English concepts of justice. Consider, as a proxy, the rate of Indian participation in civil litigation in English-controlled tribunals. Tributary Indians in Virginia, who tended to live on the outskirts or frontier of the colony, brought or defended fewer lawsuits than their counterparts in New England. Within Massachusetts and Plymouth, most Indian litigants emerged from a particular social context: they came "from areas where there was a heavy concentration of Indians, most of them plantation Indians, who not only either owned land or had the right to utilize it but also were under the supervision of white guardians who could serve them—defendants as well as plaintiffs—as informal legal advisors and even attorneys."[81] Natives were particularly active in the English courts of Martha's Vineyard and Nantucket. In many years between 1677 and 1686, well over 50 percent of court actions and orders involved Indians. Here, too, a particular social setting encouraged participation—a sizable, concentrated Native population, early and extensive Christianization, and an outnumbered group of settlers who "may have worked harder here than elsewhere to integrate Indians into the English court system as a way of earning Native allegiance and forestalling violent resistance."[82]

In Spanish America, the quality of legal experience had less to do with independence or tributary status as such. In principle, all indigenous people were vassals of the Spanish king and therefore entitled to the king's justice. Instead, law tended to vary by geographical distance from viceregal capitals—initially Mexico City and Lima. In Mexico, the Audiencia's effective (rather than de jure) jurisdiction extended as far as indigenous litigants were willing to travel to have their cases heard. For the most part, this appears to have been within a five-hundred-kilometer radius of Mexico City (a trip that could take several weeks on foot), beyond which the number of cases being heard dropped off considerably.[83] In more distant reaches, such as northern New Spain where travel to the capital was all but impractical, law remained the same in principle, while in practice depending far more heavily on the local judiciary, from which appeal was much harder.[84] Something similar may have been the case in the viceroyalty of Peru, for reasons of geography rather than raw distance. In Lima and Quito, law appears to have been a central part of life among colonists and indigenous people.[85] Outside of urban centers, however, communities further up into the rugged highlands, separated from each other and from Spanish communities by mountain ranges and severe changes in altitude, may have been less likely to engage in legal proceedings beyond their local arena. In such places, Spanish law and procedure still applied, but, as in northern Mexico, many of the niceties may not have been observed quite so punctiliously as in more central locations. During the eighteenth century, in areas at the very edges of empire populated by unconquered indigenous groups—such as the Apaches, Utes, and Pawnee in northern New Spain, the peoples of the Chaco in the Bolivian lowlands, and the Araucanians in southern Chile—legal relations remained much more improvised and negotiated, a subject of trading, gifting, treatying, and warfare.[86] In these areas, there was little sense that an appeal to the Audiencia would resolve matters, and encounters tended to be improvised, much as they were in English realms in the northern New World.

Making our focus more precise as we look from one to another of these highly variable social settings sharpens our picture, but still not enough. Within each local context, intermediaries and brokers between indigenous and settler cultures developed vastly better understandings of contrasting notions of justice than the average settler or Indian.[87] At a general level in English America, intermarriage, longstanding trade relations, and Indian apprenticeship and enrollment in colonial colleges created partially or fully bilingual Natives and settlers who could explain cultural commitments, including legal ones. More particularly, certain intermediaries paid special attention to law. In Spanish America, intermarriage, commercial dealings, patronage, and local politics created a whole class of individuals who operated in a "mestizo" or interme-diary space between Spaniards and indigenous people. In both impe-rial realms, interpreters at trials and in negotiations sometimes served as lay attorneys and advisers. In New England and the middle colonies, Christianized Indians did much of this work, with the Delaware Indians being particularly active in Pennsylvania. Through the seventeenth cen-tury and fading slowly in the eighteenth century, sachems and headmen mediated Natives' experience of colonial justice—whether in a formal tribunal, arbitration, or negotiation. They advised Indians behind the scenes, conveyed or received payments of damages, represented specific litigants or defendants or spoke for their nation as a whole, and observed proceedings, reporting back on what the English thought justice meant. A handful of Natives served as judges, selectmen, and constables in Indian towns within colonial borders. They acquired a deeper under-standing of English justice that they variously enforced, melded with tra-ditional Indian norms, or quietly subverted. In New Spain, caciques and local leaders would meet in *cabildo* to discuss matters of legal moment, drawing on collective memory and practice. Earlier successes seem to have encouraged later attempts to have grievances heard or to seek pro-tection against prospective harms and also did much to sustain commu-nities through years and even decades of legal jousting.

Colonists too were deeply involved in legal processes. The Eng-lish judges and commissioners who worked with Natives to govern seventeenth-century Indian towns and the "guardians" that colonies ap-pointed over Indian communities in the eighteenth century came to bet-ter appreciate indigenous norms of justice even as they compromised with or ignored them.

Spanish *vecinos*, especially in more remote areas, were expected to serve as judges in local cases, and were presumed to know the rudi-ments of legal proceedings.[88] Some Indian nations hired English at-torneys as their long-term representatives to colonial governments. Likewise, Indian towns in the Spanish empire might develop long and intimate relationships with the local *procuradores de indios* who sat out-side the courts and whose job it was to represent Native claims before judges. These men, some of whom spoke Native languages, very often spared no effort to ensure indigenous litigants were heard and handled according to law. English colonies appointed ad hoc and standing groups of commissioners to manage trade and settle disputes with Natives. The British empire in the middle of the eighteenth century named superintendents of Indian affairs to oversee conflicting colonial approaches to trade regulation and the management of disputes. Brokers at the village, colonial, and imperial levels who mediated between conflicting notions of justice stand out from the majority of settlers and Natives with scant understanding. To ask to what extent a "community" found others' law intelligible is to pose an indiscriminate question.

Indeed, particularly in the British context, the term "community" implies a misleading stability. Up and down the Atlantic seaboard, war and disease decimated first one, then another Indian nation. Survivors integrated into more stable neighboring tribes or formed polyglot villages mixing families from several nations.[89] The refugees brought different levels of knowledge about English justice, dissimilar experiences with it, and various strategies for engaging with it. Among settlers, ongoing large-scale European immigration and transportation of Africans continually introduced colonists with little understanding of Indian norms of justice. Europeans moved among towns and colonies. One is tempted to find trends that bring order to the past. And there were some. The shrinking population of tributary/plantation Indians in the eighteenth century deepened their understanding of English justice as they lived among settlers more willing to override indigenous law, force Natives into court without translators and without sachems as intermediaries, and erode Indian towns' (partial) rights of self-government. But we must be cautious. The continual reconstitution of indigenous and European communities introduced new sources of confusion amid ever-altering configurations of settlers and Natives straining to understand each other's notions of justice. The pursuit of legal intelligibility was not a challenge for only the first generation after contact, a problem that faded. It was a persistent challenge, always present and never overcome, met to varying degrees by different people and groups in British America.

The situation appears to have been both similar and somewhat different in Iberian America, at least after the Native hecatomb of the sixteenth century finally bottomed out in the early seventeenth century. The first several decades of Spanish presence had deep and irreversible effects on Native social organization. In the central valley of Mexico, a series of epidemics wiped out communities, opening up lands and exposing survivors to a raw struggle for individual and collective survival, a challenge communities responded to in part through litigation. Villages emptied out and reconstituted, or constituted anew with a novel configuration of partialities. By the late sixteenth century, the viceregal government responded by creating "congregations" to concentrate dispersed people into single communities that could sustain themselves but also be available as a pool of labor. Native caciques, initially favored by Spaniards, found that rotation in office, as specified by Spanish law, eroded their authority and created opportunities for commoners to assume positions previously closed to them. Similar processes played out in the Andes. Legal relations that obtained closer to Lima or Quito were broadly similar to those in the Central Valley of Mexico. In more out-of-the-way places, whether highlands communities in Peru or remoter parts of New Spain, such as Yucatán and the far north, and perhaps as well in Brazil, communities were able to isolate themselves to a greater extent than was possible for more central communities. Of course, the other side of this coin was that such communities could also suffer more from legal isolation than they would have liked, making it harder for them to seek redress. This suggests that a critical variable was neither geography nor culture, but relative degree of remoteness from an administrative and judicial center, as defined by ease of access, for both potential indigenous litigants and local Spanish officials. By the seventeenth century, community life in most places had begun to settle down again somewhat. Many towns, even quite remote ones, were perhaps more permeable to outsiders than they had been before the arrival of Europeans, and movement in and out of them may have become more common. Many communities did manage to retain a strong sense of identity as a bulwark against the pressures that bore upon them. For them, the law, however clouded its meaning might at times be and however uncertain its outcomes, represented a resource against disorder, abuse, and bewilderment.

As historians, we strain to find broad patterns and trends that will make sense of the past. It is a cliché that we must be cautious in doing so. But the reminder is perhaps especially a propos in talking about legal (un)intelligibility, since law as a subject matter embodies a presumption in favor of order and regularity. In other words, there is no such thing as chaotic law.[90] Thus, we do not deny the possibility of meaningful configurations of evidence and interpretation extending beyond specific instances. We do insist that any patterns or trends be qualified by the variabilities in legal (un)intelligibility revealed by the comparative framework we have proposed here. That being said, if there is a large conclusion to be drawn from the cases that make up this volume, it is that the distinct legal cultures of Spain and England mattered profoundly to the shape ultimately taken by relationships between settlers and indigenous peoples in each realm. We cannot truly understand one except in explicit comparison to the other. As a corollary, the variability in legal (un) intelligibility counsels against easy generalities about the effects of "European" law on Native lives, whether for ill or good. The term "European" simply hides too much to be very useful in making sense of complex realities. Finally, we maintain that focusing on intelligibility as a relation between actors, individual and collective, rather than as a metric—i.e., how "much" intelligibility there was—makes clear that the burden of "misunderstanding," so long attributed to some Native deficiency, cultural or otherwise, was shared between settlers and Natives, even as the consequences of that misunderstanding tended to fall disproportionately on the latter.

III. Architecture of the Volume

A. Mis-dialogues, Code Switching, and Mixing Languages of Law

In the beginning—and not just in the beginning—was misunderstanding. Natives and settlers brought disparate concepts of law and justice to their negotiations and conflicts. Through translators, each side may have more or less grasped the words exchanged back and forth. But the concepts and presuppositions animating those words, the assumed implications and limitations, proved more elusive. From this deeper level of tacit meanings and associations rather than from the surface level of words came the most interesting and consequential challenges of legal intelligibility. Tamar Herzog provides a glimpse of one such misaligned conversation in "Dialoguing with Barbarians: What Natives Said and How Europeans Responded in Late-Seventeenth- and Eighteenth-Century Portuguese America" (chapter 2). Hers is a case study of what she terms "mis-dialogues" between Portuguese and "not-yet-domesticated" Natives in the Amazon basin. She aims to uncover the "legal structures that gave words and actions a particular meaning" and guided what each side expected would result from their agreements. Indigenous negotiators intended their accords with the Portuguese to bring trade and, sometimes, protection, while preserving independence. The Portuguese, interpreting the agreements with reference to their own legal traditions, expected conversion and pacification through vassalage. Europeans and Natives spoke across one another because of "disagreements regarding the precise consequences of pacts." The crucial point for Herzog, however, is that despite the one-sidedness of available accounts of these encounters—all were produced by Portuguese officials and missionaries—indigenous understandings of justice can be glimpsed and can even be seen to have changed in the heat of their "mis-dialogues" with Europeans, who were sluggish in investigating precisely what the Natives were saying and why.

After sustained contact, some Natives and settlers—typically brokers and intermediaries of various sorts—became better able to understand each other's legal commitments and interventions. To serve their community and to manipulate or to ingratiate themselves with interlocutors, they learned to code switch, moving back and forth between their culture's and their interlocutors' notions of law and justice. As Jenny Pulsipher recounts, the mid-seventeenth-century Nipmuc Indian John Wompas familiarized himself with both Native and settler concepts of land tenure, distribution, and sales, becoming adept at switching opportunistically between them in his career as a speculator and (untrustworthy) intermediary ("Defending and Defrauding the Indians: John Wompas, Legal Hybridity, and the Sale of Indian Land" [chapter 3]). Wompas emerged out of a world where Natives used English law to defend their land rights, while colonists deployed Indian law to deny those rights. He outstripped his contemporaries in his skill at drawing on his Native identity to obtain land, then manipulating English law to sell and record this land, and later switching to Indian norms to evade obstacles put in his way by colonial authorities. By "simultaneously or interchangeably drawing from Native and English land ways," Wompas aimed to make "land transactions . . . intelligible to both English and Indians, thus increasing the likelihood that land sales would be accepted by both peoples."

Code switching also proved useful to treaty negotiators, another type of intermediary. At first, English no less than Iberian America was the site for mis-dialogues. The 1621 treaty that the Wampanoag sachem Massasoit made with Plymouth Colony created, he thought, an alliance against the Narragansetts. By contrast, the Pilgrims viewed the agreement as a Native submission to King James I and English sovereignty.[91] Over time, Natives and settlers not only came to appreciate the political implications of treaties but learned to manipulate each other's legal concepts. Craig Yirush shows the Iroquois' skill at sequentially deploying indigenous and English concepts during negotiations with delegates from Pennsylvania, Virginia, and Maryland in 1744 ("'Since We Came out of This Ground': Iroquois Legal Arguments at the Treaty of Lancaster" [chapter 4]). The Iroquois defended their claims to land in Maryland and Virginia by invoking their conquest of it and their long possession (prescription). Arguments from conquest and prescription, familiar in European colonial discourses, constituted part of the settlers' case at the treaty negotiations. The Iroquois reworked these arguments to their own advantage, mixing them with appeals rooted in Native legal and rhetorical traditions. Code switching was at once a mechanism for gaining advantages in negotiations, defending interests, outmaneuvering rivals, and enriching intermediaries.

Some Natives and settlers became adept at more than code switching, at moving back and forth between two cultures' already established legal ideas; they engaged in something deeper, an innovative mixing of legal languages that fused elements of each to create new legal devices and strategies. The ingenuity of Andean indigenous communities at this work is the subject of Karen Graubart's "'*Ynuvaciones malas e rreprouadas*': Seeking Justice in Early Colonial *Pueblos de Indios*" (chapter 5). Natives near the city of Lima around the late sixteenth and early seventeenth centuries tried to preserve their notions of justice amid the pressures of colonization. Customary practices, which as noted above enjoyed legitimacy as a source of law, became "interdependent with decisions made by Spanish jurists." Indian leaders grew skilled at the "active management of heterogeneous norms" in the zone of discretion allowed them by the Spanish empire's tolerance for (constrained) indigenous self-government and legal pluralism. Indian wills, for example, "reveal multiple conceptualizations of labor, property and resource management, drawing upon a variety of Spanish and pre-conquest Andean practices." This "entanglement" could also be found in indigenous regulation of agricultural leases, private urban residences, and wage labor. Each was a site where Andeans who found Spanish law intelligible creatively mixed legal languages to preserve as best they could their notions of justice under colonial rule.

Scholars who have looked at how law became intelligible have commonly limited their analytic focus to one or the other of the Iberian or English realms. Peering simultaneously through the lenses of both gives a three-dimensionality to themes and insights flattened or ignored by viewing each empire in isolation. This section of the volume consequently mixes two essays on North America (Pulsipher and Yirush) and two on South America (Herzog and Graubart). Throughout the New World, mis-dialogues, code switching, and mixing legal languages were components of the larger challenge of legal intelligibility. But these shared components did not play out the same way under the dissimilar social and political conditions of English and Iberian America, as a comparative approach reveals.

Consider the difference between code switching and mixing legal languages. In English America, code switching aided Natives in the interactions they most commonly had with settlers: land sales, trade, treaty negotiations. Compared to code switching, mixing legal languages was an act implying far greater familiarity between parties and an orientation to ongoing relationship within a shared social order. It required a much deeper level of understanding of the two sides' legal commitments and the ability to fuse them in order to form new devices and strategies. Perhaps, as in Graubart's essay, the Spanish "empire of inclusion" provided the sustained, intertwined social relations necessary for mixing legal languages far more thoroughly than did the northern "empire of exclusion." The more distant, episodic Native-settler relations of English America favored code switching over mixing legal languages. But the encouragement to mixing legal languages that benefited the indigenous peoples of Spanish America came with a price. Once Natives were "included" as vassals within the empire, it became harder for them to stand apart, both practically and ideologically. The Spanish promised Indians a form of "justice" in their interactions with settlers but at the cost of surrendering the right to maintain arms-length distance on the grounds of "sovereignty." To the extent that mixing legal languages was more likely in Spanish America, was it more likely for all of the king's vassals? It would be worth exploring how settlers and Natives in Spanish America differed in the rate and way they mixed legal languages.

Broadly speaking, these four essays suggest that the deep cultural differences of the New World encounter had the capacity to destabilize established understandings of law and justice on both sides of any given encounter, and not just in some initial period, but persistently. This is what accounts for mis-dialogues, code switching, and mixed legal languages wherever settlers and indigenous peoples have faced each other through law. This is not to say there was no basis for mutual understanding—what we call "intelligibility"—across lines of cultural difference. Rather, the point is that analysis of such encounters may not begin from an *assumption* of intelligibility. Intelligibility must be shown in every given circumstance and in some cases simply may not obtain. *Un*intelligibility is as much part of the story, therefore, as intelligibility. This realization underlies one of the crucial findings of the recent legal history of the New World: the operations of law can in some circumstances not only fail to tame the world's messiness, because they are unintelligible to one or all parties to an encounter, but may even contribute to it, perhaps especially in intercultural situations. As uncomfortable as this insight may be for certain notions of legal history, it represents a crucial intervention, for it unsettles the background notion that ultimately law may be understood monotonically as an ordering phenomenon.

B. At the Boundaries of Differing Conceptions of Justice

One way to study comparatively settler and Native notions of justice and problems of legal intelligibility is to group together case studies on the English and Iberian Atlantic, as we did in the previous section. Another way is to conduct comparisons not between but within essays. Each of the chapters discussed in this section uses the practices of one empire to highlight distinctive features of another, features whose full significance might be misconstrued or simply missed if each empire is viewed in isolation.

Might the Spanish empire's simultaneously protective and limiting notion of corporate Indian rights help identify trends in early Virginia's policies toward tributary Natives? Such is the agenda of Bradly Dixon's

"'Darling Indians' and 'Natural Lords': Virginia's Tributary Regime and Florida's Republic of Indians in the Seventeenth Century" (chapter 6). Dixon contends that between the 1640s and Bacon's Rebellion (1676), only Massachusetts exceeded Virginia in realizing the "Spanish ideal of incorporating Natives into the colonial polity." Reminiscent of the Spanish empire's "republic of Indians," the tributary Natives lived in "semi-autonomous communities, subject to but separate from the English for their better exploitation and protection." Virginia law granted tributary "kings and queens" a "privileged standing" to enhance their rule over potentially dangerous Indians. The colony (in theory) viewed Indians, particularly poorer ones, as "miserable persons with a special claim upon English justice." Indeed, comparing Virginia's to Spanish America's (more elaborate and theoretically developed) notions of corporate Indian rights suggests a model for grouping together early Virginia initiatives whose collective significance might otherwise be overlooked. The Spanish experience also highlights how Virginia's tributary system, like the "republic of Indians," claimed to uphold a particular vision of justice—one that purported to safeguard Natives against the worst "abuses of grasping colonists" in return for loyalty to the king. Did Virginia's limited recognition of Native corporate rights represent a "might have been" in American history—offering not only a method for managing the practicalities of communal interaction but a particular (if one-sided) vision of justice?

To pose this question is to invite us not only to rethink early Virginia history but to reflect more deeply on the difference between English and Spanish notions of justice in respect to Natives. The English version of the "republic of the Indians" and the accompanying notion of "miserables" seem especially fragile. Virginia's framework rested on an insecure foundation, not least because it lacked the theological and legal infrastructure built up in Spanish America. The colony could proclaim that Indians deserved "English justice," but would settlers have known what that meant when applied to Natives? The reason for their confusion was not only the novelty of the colonial encounter. More deeply, settlers found it difficult to restrain themselves in the service of justice owed to Natives when they viewed law as a product of the king's will and conceived of themselves as extensions of the crown's sovereignty.

By contrast, the governing ideology of Spanish America insisted that justice was a substantive standard independent of the king and his will, a standard implanted in the universe by God's command and natural law. Under this conception, the crown and colonists acted legitimately only when they remained within the bounds of objective justice, however much their interests and greed tempted them to redefine it in their favor. Justice was not something they devised, enacted through their sovereign will, and then extended to Natives; rather, justice was an independent constraint to which they were supposed to submit. The Spanish vision of justice empowered indigenous people to take up the law because its stated purpose was to limit the actions of those who acted unjustly. In Spanish law, therefore, the doctrine of "miserables" created a kind of rebuttable presumption against those who had greatest power in local circumstances—settlers. This is why Virginia's tentative efforts to define a doctrine of "miserables" never quite took: Natives might oppose English pressure and overreaching, but not from a position of presumed injury, as Indians in Spanish realms could. By comparison to the Spanish, the thin, self-generated English conception of justice not only made Virginia promises of justice to Natives a weak instrument for restraining the "abuses of grasping colonists"; it also gave those promises little staying power. As Dixon observes, Indians' corporate rights and legal status declined along with their numbers and military power in the late seventeenth and eighteenth centuries, making them more vulnerable to predations by settlers. If the "miserables" principle had held, growing Native vulnerability should have resulted in greater legal protection, not less. In sum, Virginia's limited recognition of Native corporate rights appears from one perspective as a "might have been" in American history; from another, it reveals how distinct the two empires' notions of justice were from one another.

Native and settler notions of justice diverged especially sharply in the aftermath of murders, with Europeans expecting state-run trials and Indians preferring compensation to the victim's family to forestall retaliatory violence. Nancy Gallman and Alan Taylor show how in both Spanish and English America, conflicts over which system would dominate made more salient the norms of justice underlying each ("Covering Blood and Graves: Murder and Law on Imperial Margins" [chapter 7]). In the latter half of the eighteenth century, the British needed to preserve peace with the Iroquois; the Spanish in East Florida valued the Lower Creeks and Seminoles as potential allies against the Americans.

Despite pressure from imperial superiors to insist on public trials of killers, local officials understood that pressing the issue would alienate Natives, straining alliances or provoking war. Europeans' need to sustain alliances and Indians' determination to protect their autonomy created pressures for each side to investigate and make intelligible the other's deeper assumptions about justice as revealed in their different ways of responding to murder. To the Spanish, an investigation of homicide by the governor reinforced the structured, hierarchical vision of society that the empire favored, one in which an elaborate system of law for the New World (*derecho indiano*) paternalistically gave settlers and Natives their due and protected them as it kept them in their assigned place. By contrast, the Lower Creeks and Seminoles assumed that "covering the grave" through compensation to the victim's kin signaled their aversion to coercive authority and upheld their ideal of social harmony achieved through negotiation and consent (albeit with the threat of private retaliation in the background). Meanwhile, the Iroquois opposed English execution of settlers who killed Natives lest that set a precedent for the trial of Indians who killed settlers. The more that imperial officials pressed upon the Iroquois the European system of state-supervised punishment of offenders, the more they insisted that "covering the grave" should prevail even for cross-communal murders in settler jurisdictions.

The implications of Gallman and Taylor's work stand out more clearly when placed besides Dixon's study. Dixon's reconstruction of a partial and relatively short-lived "republic of the Indians" in early Virginia draws attention to the profound differences in the way the Spanish and English empires conceived of justice for Natives. One is likewise tempted, upon first reading Gallman and Taylor, to note points of dissimilarity between the empires. The Spanish colonial legal system in East Florida was part of the civil law family and employed inquisitorial procedure with final decisions about guilt made by the governor and imperial officials. This form of justice grew out of and reinforced what the crown idealized as a paternal, hierarchical society. By contrast, the English common law system of the colonies entrusted the jury with the power to convict offenders. The jury symbolized the importance of communal self-government and the liberties of Englishmen. And yet Gallman and Taylor's British and Spanish American case studies suggest that despite the ideological and juridical differences between the empires, and despite the dissimilarities between the political organization of the Iroquois in the North and of the Lower Creeks and Seminoles in the South, common themes predominate over divergences. First, disputes over murders became proxies for contests over imperial primacy and Native autonomy. And second, local officials acquiesced in Native practices of covering the grave, even against contrary imperial pressure, because of diplomatic and military exigencies.

Conflicts between Native and settler conceptions of justice—in particular about the status of Indian corporate rights—emerged from 1810 onwards in the late stages of the Spanish empire and in the wars of independence. As Marcela Echeverri shows in her study of the viceroyalty of New Granada, indigenous people resisted anticolonial creole programs to reduce Indian corporate privileges and burdens in the service of liberal ideals of equal citizenship ("'Sovereignty Has Lost Its Rights': Liberal Experiments and Indigenous Citizenship in New Granada, 1810–1819" [chapter 8]). Liberals in newly independent Colombia championed a notion of justice resting on a particular conception of equality and inclusion of all communities (under creole leadership). But it was a vision rooted in the idea that indigenous people had no rights other than those of individual citizens. In this they diverged from the solution proposed by the Cádiz Constitution of 1812, which had made room for Indians' defense of communal rights. Of course, at the time Spain was trying to gain the allegiance of indigenous people against independence-seeking creoles. But the fact remains that the imperial liberalism of the Cádiz Constitution was, at least in principle, willing to uphold a right that liberals struggling for national independence were not. This is one reason indigenous people so often sided with royalist forces, at least early in the wars of independence. Against the creoles' vision, some indigenous people advanced a contrary vision of justice—one accepting their obligation to pay tribute as a foundation of their inherited privileges of special protection, legal representation by the *protector de indios*, communal land ownership, and partially autonomous self-government. Liberals who wanted to turn the Indians into citizens were met by indigenous suspicion of a program to "subsume them into a polity that granted sovereignty effectively to the creoles," as Echeverri puts it.

Liberals' invocation of sovereignty marked a critical change. Under viceregal law, settlers and Indians alike were vassals of the Spanish king;

neither group could make a privileged claim to sovereign right. Creole pretensions to sovereignty disrupted this rough parity, with adverse consequences for effective Native access to law. In principle, citizenship cloaked all *individuals* in the same legal protections. In practice, indigenous people were rarely recognized as full citizens even as the liberal insistence on equality refused to acknowledge that some citizens might be more vulnerable to arbitrary exercises of power than others. Where once the king bore a positive duty to shelter his most vulnerable subjects from the arbitrariness of the powerful, under the liberal regime, powerful and powerless alike were citizens, equal before the law and not otherwise to be distinguished, regardless of their actual positions and chances in society. Moreover, indigenous people quickly came to understand that individual citizenship, enshrined in constitutions, had no place for corporate rights, including those to land. From this perspective, nineteenth-century debates over whether to preserve or reduce Indian corporate status therefore represented not only a sustained effort to change the letter of the law but also an assault on a legal culture centuries in the making. By adopting sovereignty as the baseline for their efforts to remake law along liberal lines, creoles sought to replace the principle of substantive justice, rooted in a notion of moral truth and protection of the vulnerable, in favor of a conception of law emerging from the will of the sovereign. As founders of new nations, the creoles claimed the role of this newly empowered sovereign. For their part, indigenous people who might once have sought the king's justice against the powerful now had to face the will of those who had enshrined themselves constitutionally as holders of a sovereign power from which there was no appeal. In Latin America, it has been common to point out that the grounding premises of liberal individualism were at odds with colonial recognition of corporate rights. Echeverri's argument suggests another point of difference as well, a subtler and more easily missed one: the creole assumption of sovereignty fundamentally redistributed power within the legal system in a way that made it far more difficult for indigenous people to defend communal lands and rights other than by rebellion.

Echeverri asks how the situation in the newly born United States was different. Heir to the British empire of exclusion, the new American republic viewed Indians beyond the frontier as "foreign nations" entitled to no more protections than other nations might be. Americans did not think that their revolution or liberalism "entailed the integration of indigenous peoples as citizens." In legal encounters, indigenous peoples in English America had always faced Europeans through the prism of sovereignty. To this extent, the early United States continued the policy of its colonial predecessor, while the basic premises underlying Native-creole relations in Spanish America were being fundamentally renegotiated through disputes over the place and meaning of sovereignty.

The contested place of Native corporate rights ties Echeverri's essay to Dixon's and Gallman/Taylor's. Where Echeverri charts creole initiatives to reduce Indian corporate status in the name of liberal equality at the end of a colonial era, Dixon reconstructs the beginning of a colonial era—where settlers devised Native corporate protections in the interest of averting war and achieving sustainable levels of exploitation. Gallman and Taylor reveal how Iroquois leaders in the middle eighteenth century favored Indian "covering the grave" with compensation rather than public trials for killings of Natives upon English land, even if a settler committed the murder. Against colonists' notions of personal and territorial jurisdiction (we should hold a trial because our subject committed murder within our boundaries), Indians involved corporate rights (the presence of a Native in a homicide as *either* killer or victim required covering the grave). All three essays show Natives deploying notions of corporate status to best preserve autonomy and communal life and identities, and doing so fully exposed the tensions and contradictions of the legal spaces they occupied.

IV. Future Lines of Research

While we are certain that the discerning reader will find her own path through and beyond these essays, we would like to conclude by identifying some areas for further inquiry that grow quite naturally from the ideas at the core of this volume. An important issue for future scholarship emerges from the two "concluding perspectives" essays by Lauren Benton ("In Defense of Ignorance: Frameworks for Legal Politics in the Atlantic World" [chapter 9]) and Daniel Richter ("Intelligibility or Incommensurability?" [chapter 10]). How shall we negotiate the tension between related but analytically distinct conceptualizations of law? In different ways, Richter and Benton present interest-driven accounts of law.

Richter treats intelligibility as a less pressing challenge than "incommensurability," the "fundamentally incompatible aims that indigenous and colonizing peoples often sought through their legal systems, [and] the profoundly different scales of value they assigned to otherwise mutually intelligible terms like 'justice' and 'rights.'" Benton counsels scholars to reconstruct "patterned strategic behavior" rather than inquire into Natives' and settlers' "understanding" of law—"what historical actors believed, thought, perceived, or knew." Their "ability to act strategically in a shifting legal field" is the better object of study than their "capacity to grasp legal concepts," which she contends was not a "precondition or accompaniment" to negotiation and manipulation of law.

Both make important points. Cunning and tactical maneuver figured importantly in disputes ignited by profoundly different definitions of justice and proper relationships among the wide array of New World Natives and settlers, a matter by now well settled. But legal cunning was not independent of the broader challenge of intelligibility. To what extent can a historian reconstruct how Natives and settlers pursued their at times incommensurate aims through strategic behavior without probing how they comprehended or misconstrued the rules, ideas, and practices assumed by their interlocutors? Determining which principles and customs were relevant to a given dispute and figuring out how far these could be pushed by oneself or an adversary were crucial to deciding how to litigate and when to negotiate. We do not suppose such efforts necessarily resulted in mutual understanding between parties. Sometimes they did. At other times, a party seemed to have a relatively clear sense of its own goals, but a limited sense of an adversary's legal arguments and assumptions. At other times still, parties' views were essentially opaque to one another. There was no generally linear movement from perplexity toward comprehension but rather ebbs and flows and reversible gains in a colonial encounter featuring new immigration, contacts of previously separated peoples, deaths and replacements of trusted brokers, and the continual reconstitution of communities. Parties were given to mistakes and overconfidence as surface acquaintance with an interlocutor's law masked deeper ignorance or uncertainty about the values and history behind a legal idea and its range of uses and assumed limits. Intelligibility was always in play. It was never complete or completely lacking, for law, especially under New World circumstances, was not a static set of ideas, norms, and procedures capable of straightforward application. Behind every judgment about intelligibility are the implied questions who, what, where, when, for what purposes, and pursuant to what understanding of a just and proper outcome? The wide range of such possibilities is precisely what we have referred to as the challenge of "intelligibility."

The essays by Richter and Benton remind us that the next step is to develop concepts capacious and flexible enough to synthesize the challenge of intelligibility with interest-driven accounts of law. Thus, we agree that recognizing "different scales of values" (Richter) and focusing on "strategic behavior" (Benton) and "creative . . . misunderstandings" (Benton, quoting Richard White) are critical parts of a larger framework.[92] So too are ever-shifting notions of what law means and what it can be made to say. Attending to the perennial challenge of intelligibility does not displace but rather enriches the study of negotiation and strategic manipulation of law. Finding a way to bring these views into a shared analytical frame is a critical task for legal historians.

Descending from the conceptual heights, the essays here point toward a number of important paths for future scholarship. The first of these involves stretching, spatially and temporally, the comparative framework and the concern for intelligibility. In spatial terms, our focus has been on English and Iberian America. But what of French realms, Canada and St. Domingue? What of the Danish and Dutch Caribbean, or Surinam? And what of the Caribbean more broadly, that cauldron of empires and peoples? Indeed, the Caribbean, in particular, seems a place almost ready-made for the comparative legal perspective we advocate here. St. Croix, for example, was successively controlled by Spain, the Netherlands, the Knights of Malta, Great Britain, and France up to 1733. At that point it was sold to the kingdom of Norway-Denmark, was later invaded by Great Britain in the early nineteenth century, and subsequently returned to Denmark in 1815, until finally being sold to the United States in 1917. At each step, new administrations and new legal norms had to be layered on top of existing principles and practices, creating a legal palimpsest of extraordinary complexity just in relation to European legalities. But as the essays in this volume suggest, we would also want to ask whether and to what extent Taíno notions of justice and West African legal sensibilities impinged upon legal intelligibility. It suffices to name

Trinidad and Tobago, Dominica and St. Domingue to know that opportunities for such research abound in the Caribbean.[93]

Scholars could also expand our approach temporally. We have concentrated on the "early-modern" period between the seventeenth and
nineteenth centuries, with only one essay crossing the "boundary" beyond 1800. That frontier is a historiographical artifact corresponding
to the period of independence movements between 1776 and roughly
1830 that reoriented the fates of almost the entire hemisphere. The
gauntlet thrown to future researchers is to think *through* this boundary
in order to connect the earlier period emphasized in these essays to issues of legal intelligibility in the nineteenth century, and perhaps later.
No less than in the earlier period, the comparative lens would be indispensable in order to make sense of the continuities and disjunctures
between what came before and what came after. Echeverri's essay points
the way. Thus, in Colombia, where indigenous people had achieved a
considerable understanding and broad acceptance of colonial law and
justice, the decision by liberal creoles to supplant colonial law in favor
a new legal order can only have been disorienting and threatening for
indigenous people. In other words, legal (un)intelligibility was as much
an issue after independence in Spanish America as it had been before,
though in a new register. The self-conscious project of independence-era
elites to dismantle colonial legal structures, so critical to an indigenous
"politics" up to 1810, dramatically restricted litigation as a recourse in a
political system oriented not to justice as a principle but to representation. As in many other places in Latin America, Indians continued to
seek the king's justice even after it was no longer in force. They did so because at that point it was the law they knew best. They continued to appeal to royal law, and to the principle of justice it embodied, because the
alternative offered by liberal constitutions seemed to limit rather than
expand their capacity for meaningful action regarding the conditions
of their lives. For their part, new elites saw only a senseless, baseless refusal to adopt modern legal mores, a conclusion that almost surely contributed to the growing sense among these elites that Indian resistance
was proof positive of their racial inferiority. In the United States, the
situation was quite different. There, the newly independent government,
intent on territorial expansion, took up the approach pioneered by the
British—treating the Indians as sovereign nations rather than as integral

parts of a new society. Indigenous people saw little change in their fundamental relationship to the government. In the nineteenth century, as in the eighteenth and earlier, legal encounters remained negotiated matters that eluded and even defied systematization. Some version of systematic law only came to pass as Indian sovereignty collapsed under the assault of the nineteenth century and as Indian nations became, in effect, wards of the United States government. Here, too, intelligibility remained an unfinished project, one best approached with explicit comparisons to other places, laws, and times. Much of this remains speculative, especially for Latin America, a matter ripe for scholarly energy and innovation.

The study of legal intelligibility is, in part, about the acquisition, transmission, and interpretation of a specific form of knowledge. As such, it can contribute to ongoing comparative research about the communication of legal knowledge in empires and in indigenous societies exposed to colonialism. Scholars have looked at the relationship between the way empires communicated law and the way they governed and at the ways in which settlers and imperial officials reshaped legal principles as they preserved and transmitted them.[94] Such work implicitly treats New World Europeans as the (active and innovative rather than passive and retentive) periphery of a metropolitan core. By extension, Natives come to figure in such narratives as a periphery of the settlers, that is, as a subperiphery, the last link of a chain originating elsewhere. Against this tendency, researchers working comparatively might ask how different groups of indigenous peoples in the New World preserved and understood legal ideas obtained through a variety of channels from settlers, military officers, merchants, and imperial administrators who were themselves in the process of reshaping and ignoring metropolitan legal concepts. Moving away from a European core/New World periphery model invites perspectives that emphasize Native ingenuity. We might ask how Indian creativity in law—strategies for code shifting and devices generated from mixing legal languages—traveled and were reworked as they passed among different communities of Natives. In what ways did the political, trade, and diplomatic structures of Native life and European empires together shape Indian communication circuits? Alternatively, reversing the core-periphery model, we might treat European settlers as the periphery. How, across British and Iberian America, did various groups of settlers learn of Indian ideas about justice and discover Natives' imaginative mixing of legal languages?

A third broad area for future research would involve a methodological and conceptual effort to bring the anthropology of law to bear more systematically on legal history. This is especially important in order to raise indigenous ideas regarding law and justice into sharper relief. The weight of "written" European law can be almost crushing at times when layered over the top of Native legalities. Such sources, so concretely available as printed materials and in archives, so voluminous and detailed, can make efforts to spell out the nuances of Native understandings seem thin and reaching by comparison. Here, anthropologists have shown the way by looking deeply into indigenous cultures for evidence of attitudes toward law and justice. This approach can reveal that even something so basic as a "fact" may hardly be a transparent concept, or indicate how an ideology of "harmony" can represent a theory of justice to redress a breach of social order.[95] Pursuing this line requires a leap for most historians, but as Tamar Herzog's essay in this volume forcefully argues, it is essential if we are to recover whatever we can of the legal understandings of indigenous people, even when the sources might seem to suggest the impossibility of doing so. If we fail in this, we will have less than half a story.

Attending to Native legalities in the service of a deeper sense of the possibilities and limits of legal intelligibility can contribute to the effort already discussed to rethink the default "instrumental" treatment of legal encounters. Much of the extant literature on jurisdictional politics, legal resistance, and strategic engagement tacitly presumes that people pursue legal remedies much as they might any other "interest"-oriented activity—for the advantage doing so will bring. That people have concrete interests when they enter into legal encounters is undeniable. But precisely because law is explicitly about how societies bind themselves together, establish relationships among members, secure social order, and repair or at least respond to harms, it has a deeper moral valence than does other interest-seeking conduct. This is why justice, as a concept, is never separable from law.

In this regard, close attention to indigenous slavery may yield rich dividends. There is a scholarship on law and African slavery, demonstrating the extent to which even the unfree could mobilize legal systems on their own behalf.[96] Much less has been done to explore the related story of indigenous slaves. Partly this is the case because indigenous slavery is presumed to have been short-lived, a phenomenon of the sixteenth century that supposedly faded with the introduction of African slavery and the acceptance of the broad general principle that Indians in Spanish America were free. But as Nancy Van Deusen has shown, enslaved Indians had to struggle for justice on their own behalf through legal process, in the New World, but also in Spain itself, a story both "locally and imperially relevant."[97] Nor did the broad prohibition against enslaving Indians stop *encomenderos* and others, from Mexico to Peru to Paraguay, from subjecting Indians to conditions that were at times all but indistinguishable from slavery—forced labor, restricted movement, abusive tribute arrangements, and various forms of enclosure. Indigenous litigants fought back against such impositions by insisting over and over again that they were not slaves, could not be treated as though they were slaves, and were entitled to their natural "liberty." Recent scholarship suggests that similar sorts of issues may have been far more common across the length and breadth of the New World than we have generally imagined.[98]

That we can see indigenous litigants take not only customary law but European law seriously in a wide variety of situations is a crucial reminder of this fact. Indeed, one way to think about the legal encounters in these essays is as early examples of a "cosmopolitan legality" rooted not in the presumption of a shared moral community but in the unavoidable fact of cultural difference.[99] It is in these sorts of contests and contexts that distinct legal sensibilities came face to face and had to struggle toward mutual intelligibility in concrete circumstances. Success was ambivalent, at best, and never permanent, as we have argued. Accordingly, these cases, and many more as yet to be discovered, have much to tell us about the possibilities and limits of an intercultural history of law and justice.

NOTES

1 See, e.g., Richard White, *The Middle Ground: Indians, Empires, and Republics in the Great Lakes Region, 1650–1815* (Cambridge: Cambridge University Press, 2010); Tamar Herzog, *Upholding Justice: Society, State, and the Penal System in Quito (1650–1750)* (Ann Arbor: University of Michigan Press, 2004); Brian Owensby, *Empire of Law and Indian Justice in Colonial Mexico* (Stanford, CA: Stanford

University Press, 2008); Jeffrey Glover, *Paper Sovereigns: Anglo-Native Treaties and the Law of Nations, 1604–1644* (Philadelphia: University of Pennsylvania Press, 2014); Saliha Belmessous, ed., *Native Claims: Indigenous Law against Empire, 1500–1920* (Oxford: Oxford University Press, 2014); Victor Tau Anzoátegui, *Casuismo y Sistema. Indagación sobre el espíritu del Derecho indiano* (Buenos Aires: Instituto de Investigaciones de Historia del Derecho, 1992).

2 Edmundo O'Gorman, *La invención de América: investigación acerca de la estructura del Nuevo Mundo y del sentido de su devenir* (México: FCE, 2006). In English: *The Invention of America: An Inquiry into the Historical Nature of the New World and the Meaning of Its History* (Bloomington: Indiana University Press, 1961).

3 O'Gorman, *La invención*, 9.

4 The critical background for this development is Lewis Hanke's work, especially *Spanish Struggle for Justice in the Conquest of America* (Philadelphia: University of Pennsylvania Press, 1949); *All Mankind Is One: A Study of the Disputation between Bartolomé de Las Casas and Juan Gines de Sepúlveda in 1550 on the Intellectual Capacity of the American Indians* (Dekalb: Northern Illinois University Press, 1974).

5 José de Acosta, *De procuranda indorum salute* (Madrid: Consejo Superior de Investigaciones Científicas, 1984–87), 516.

6 Owensby, *Empire of Law*. Because the Indios' status was so manifestly a product of legal argumentation, one historian famously argued that America had been born under "the inspiration of law." Javier Malagón Barceló, "Una colonización de gente de leyes," *Estudios de historia y derecho* (Xalapa: Universidad Veracruzana, 1966), 99.

7 One of the seminal studies of this process is Victor Tau Anzoategui's *Casuismo y Sistema*.

8 Giuseppe Marcocci, *A Consciência de um Império: Portugal e o Seu Mundo (Secs. XV–XVII)* (Coimbra: Universidade de Coimbra, 2012), 437.

9 Marcocci, *A Consciência*, 437.

10 Marcocci, *A Consciência*, 440–41.

11 Marcocci, *A Consciência*, 441–42.

12 Marcocci, *A Consciência*, 448.

13 On land, see Tamar Herzog, *Frontiers of Possession: Spain and Portugal in Europe and the Americas* (Cambridge, MA: Harvard University Press, 2015), 125.

14 Stuart Schwartz, *Sovereignty and Society in Colonial Brazil* (Berkeley: University of California Press, 1973), 254. "Convoluted" is from Herzog, *Frontiers*, 125. The "particularistic" quotation comes from Antonio Manuel Hespanha, "O direito de Índias no contexto de historiografia das colonizações ibéricas" (2017, unpublished paper, with permission). Herzog notes that while Spain recognized Native land rights de facto and Portugal and England did not, "it is possible" that actual differences "were not particularly great." Herzog, *Frontiers*, 125. We need more research to test this proposition.

15 Richard J. Ross, "Spanish American and British American Law as Mirrors to Each Other: Implications of the Missing *Derecho Británico Indiano*," in Thomas Duvé

and Heikki Pihlajamäki, eds., *New Horizons in Spanish Colonial Law: Contributions to Transnational Early Modern Legal History* (Frankfurt am Main: Max Planck Institute, 2015), 9–28.

16 Alberici Gentilis, *De Iure Belli Libri Tres*, J. B. Scott, ed. (Washington, DC, 1933), 1: 61, 2: 122.

17 Christopher Tomlins, "The Legalities of English Colonizing: Discourses of European Intrusion upon the Americas, c. 1490–1830," in Shaunnagh Dorsett and Ian Hunter, *Law and Politics in British Colonial Thought: Transpositions of Empire* (New York: Palgrave, 2010), 56–60.

18 Herzog, *Frontiers*, 117; Thomas More, *Utopia* (London, 1869), Edward Arber, ed. [original translation by Ralph Robinson, 1551, 2nd edition 1556], 90.

19 Tomlins, "Legalities," 56–60.

20 Herzog has shown that in certain circumstances—territorial disputes in interimperial zones, such as the one between Spain and Portugal in South America—bringing indigenous peoples under the protective framework of social inclusion accelerated their dispossession. Herzog, *Frontiers*, 245.

21 Lauren Benton, *Law and Colonial Cultures: Legal Regimes in World History, 1400–1900* (Cambridge: Cambridge University Press, 2002), 49.

22 Tomlins, "Legalities," 65.

23 Michael Stolleis, "The Legitimation of Law through God, Tradition, Will, Nature, and Constitution," in Michael Stolleis and Lorraine Daston, *Natural Law and Laws of Nature in Early Modern Europe: Jurisprudence, Theology, Moral and Natural Philosophy* (Burlington, VT: Ashgate, 2016), 45–55.

24 Antônio Hespanha, "Las categorías de lo político y de lo jurídico en la época moderna," *Ius Fugit. Revista Interdisciplinar de Estudios Histórico-Jurídicos* 3–4 (1994): 63–100. Actas del Congreso Internacional, "El estado moderno a uno y otro lado del Atlántico," *Zaragoza*, 24–26 octubre, 1994. See also Hespanha, *Vísperas del Leviathán: Instituciones y Poder Político: Portugal, Siglo XVII* (Madrid, 1989).

25 Robert Burns, ed., *Las Siete Partidas* (Philadelphia: University of Pennsylvania Press, 2001), 2:271–72 (2.1.5).

26 Hespanha, "Las categorías."

27 Aquinas, *The Political Ideas of St. Thomas Aquinas*, Dino Bigongiari, ed. (New York: Free Press, 1997), 187.

28 Quoted in Antônio Hespanha, *La gracia del derecho. Economia de la cultura en la edad moderna*, trans. Ana Cañellas Haurie (Madrid: Centro de Estudios Constitucionales, 1993), 171. My emphasis.

29 The people in question here are Pedro de Ribadeneyra, Juan de Mariana, Francisco Suárez, Luis de Molina, and Dominican Domingo de Soto. See Bernice Hamilton, *Political Thought in Sixteenth-Century Spain: A Study of the Political Ideas of Vitoria, De Soto, Suárez, and Molina* (Oxford: Oxford University Press, 1963); Diego Alonso-Lasheras, *Luis de Molina's De Iustitia et Iure: Justice as Virtue in an Economic Context* (Leiden: Brill, 2011); Frank Bartholomew Costello, S.J.,

The Political Philosophy of Luis de Molina (1535–1600) (Spokane, WA: Gonzaga University Press, 1974).

30 Stolleis, "The Legitimation of Law," 49.

31 Juan de Mariana, *The King and the Education of the King (De Rege et Regis Institutione).* G. A. Moore, trans. (Washington, DC: Country Dollar Press, 1948), 338.

32 R. Konestske, ed., *Colección de documentos para la historia de la formación social de Hispanoamérica, 1493–1810* (Madrid: CSIC, 1953), 2:528.

33 Juan Solórzano y Pereira, *Política Indiana* (Madrid: Fundación José Antonio de Castro, 1996), 1:223 (3.32.48).

34 Owensby, *Empire of Law*, 56.

35 As Charles Cutter's work shows, these principles were the common point of reference for legal interactions even in an area remote from the center, though distance and lack of personnel might lead to a relaxation of rigorous adherence to procedural and substantive requirements. *The Legal Culture of Northern New Spain, 1700–1810* (Abuquerque: University of New Mexico Press, 1995).

36 J. G. A. Pocock, *The Ancient Constitution and the Feudal Law: A Study of English Historical Thought in the Seventeenth Century*, revised ed. (Cambridge: Cambridge University Press, 1987 [1957]).

37 Pocock, *Ancient Constitution*, 234–35.

38 For example, "The Agreement of the People" (1647, 1649) did not mention justice once, portraying law as negative restraint. "The Instrument of Government" (1653) did refer to justice once in passing.

39 Tomlins, "The Legalities," 65.

40 Heikki Pihlajamäki, "The Westernization of Police Regulation: Spanish and British Colonial Laws Compared," in Thomas Duve and Heikki Pihlajamäki, *New Horizons in Spanish Colonial Law: Contributions to Transnational Early Modern Legal History* (Frankfurt am Main: Max Planck Insitute, 2015), 97–124. Such regulations became a bone of contention between colonists and the crown in the eighteenth century.

41 John Phillip Reid, *A Better Kind of Hatchet: Law, Trade, and Diplomacy in the Cherokee Nation during the Early Years of European Contact* (University Park: Pennsylvania State University Press, 1976).

42 Yanna Yannakakis, "Making Law Intelligible: Networks of Translation in Mid-Colonial Oaxaca," in *Indigenous Intellectuals: Knowledge, Power, and Colonial Culture in Mexico and the Andes*, ed. Gabriela Ramos and Yanna Yannakakis (Durham, NC: Duke University Press, 2014), 79–103.

43 William Taylor, *Landlord and Peasant in Colonial Oaxaca* (Stanford, CA: Stanford University Press, 1972), 82; Juan de Pomar-Zurita, *Relaciones de Texcoco y de la Nueva España, Pomar-Zurita* (México: Ed. S. Chávez Hayhoe, 1941), 101.

44 Stuart Banner, *How the Indians Lost Their Land: Law and Power on the Frontier* (Cambridge, MA: Harvard University Press, 2005), 58–62; Helen C. Rountree, *Pocahontas's People: The Powhatan Indians of Virginia through Four Centuries* (Norman: University of Oklahoma Press, 1990), 128.

45 For one of many discussions of such matters, see John Bulkley, "An Inquiry into the Right of the Aboriginal Natives to the Lands of America," in *Poetical Meditations*, ed. Peter Wolcott (New London, 1725), xlv–xlix.

46 Reid, *Hatchet*, 44–45.

47 Speech by the King of the Catawbas, Treaty Negotiations with North Carolina, August 29, 1754, in Alden T. Vaughan, ed., *Early American Indian Documents: Treaties and Laws, 1607–1789* (Washington, DC: University Publications of America, 1979–2004), 13:350–51; Governor Keith to the Chiefs of the Five Nations at a Council in Philadelphia, May 11, 1722, in *ibid.*, 1:239; Proceedings of the Maryland Council, September 15, 1687, in *ibid.*, 6:197–98.

48 See, e.g., Article 7, Treaty of Peace with the Delaware Indians, Entered into by William Johnson, May 8, 1765, in *The Letters and Papers of Cadwallader Colden* (New York: New York Historical Society, 1918–37), 7:31; Speech of Pennsylvania Gov. William Denny to the King of the Delaware Indians, July 27, 1757, in Vaughan, ed., *Indian Documents*, 3:264.

49 Yasuhide Kawashima, *Puritan Justice and the Indian: White Man's Law in Massachusetts, 1630–1763* (Middletown, CT: Wesleyan University Press, 1986), 129, 142; Ann Marie Plane, *Colonial Intimacies: Indian Marriage in Early New England* (Ithaca, NY: Cornell University Press, 2000), 84–85; Alden T. Vaughan, *The New England Frontier: Puritans and Indians, 1620–1675* (Boston: Little, Brown, 1965), 192. On mixed juries, see Concessions and Agreements of West New Jersey, March 3, 1677, in Vaughan, *Indian Documents*, 17:661. In some instances, sachems picked the Native members of mixed juries. Rhode Island, Law to Allow Indians to Testify against Other Indians, October 29, 1673, in Vaughan, *Indian Documents*, 17:435. William Penn famously proposed mixed juries to the Delaware Lanape Indians for criminal cases, but there is no evidence that one was ever called between 1683 and 1722. John Smolenski, "The Death of Sawantaeny and the Problem of Justice on the Frontier," in *Friends and Enemies in Penn's Woods: Indians, Colonists, and the Racial Construction of Pennsylvania*, ed. William A. Pencak and Daniel K. Richter (University Park: Pennsylvania State University Press, 2004), 116.

50 Laws governing Indian testimony varied by colony and over time. Plymouth Colony provides an example of a statute empowering courts to accept evidence from Indians. Laws to Govern Indians, 2 June 1685, in Vaughan, *Indian Documents*, 17:59–60. New England appears to have been more accepting than other regions. Kawashima, *Puritan Justice*, 130–33, 142; Vaughan, *New England Frontier*, 192–93. Some colonies only admitted testimony from Christianized Indians, and some restricted Native evidence to cases involving other Natives or blacks. See, e.g., Virginia, Law to Limit Indians Serving as Witnesses, September 1744, in Vaughan, *Indian Documents*, 15:167; Maryland, Law to Limit Testimony of Indians in Court and to Punish Indian Miscreants, 28 May–8 June 1717, in *ibid.*, 15:318–19; North Carolina, Law to Limit Indians' Roles in Court, 1746, in *ibid.*, 16:45. On Virginia's changes in policy, see Rountree, *Pocahontas's People*, 167.

51 Closer analysis than is possible here reveals a complex terrain regarding how Native law fared during the colonial period. See Tamar Herzog, "Colonial Law and 'Native Customs': Indigenous Land Rights in Colonial Spanish America," *Americas* 63:3 (2013): 303–21.

52 William Cronon, *Changes in the Land: Indians, Colonists, and the Ecology of New England* (New York: Hill & Wang, 1983), 69–70.

53 A few (among many) examples include Treaty Concluded by Virginia Lt. Gov. Alexander Spotswood and Representatives of the Nottoway Nation, February 27, 1713, in Vaughan, *Indian Documents*, 4:221; Articles of Friendship and Commerce between South Carolina and the Lower and Upper Creeks, June 14, 1732, in *ibid.*, 13:151.

54 To be sure, much of this went on in special institutions by different procedures, among community and caste representatives, in personal rather than public law, and through a version of Hindu and Muslim law that the English could recognize by reshaping it in their image. Still, Hindu and Muslim judges were invited onto the early-eighteenth-century court of judicature in Bombay and were asked to pay "due regard to caste customs" as well as EIC and English ordinances. The court solicited preliminary investigations from Muslim *qadi* magistrates and Hindu caste headmen.

55 Bernard S. Cohn, *Colonialism and Its Forms of Knowledge: The British in India* (Princeton, NJ: Princeton University Press, 1996), 57–75; Charles Fawcett, *The First Century of British Justice in India* (Oxford: Clarendon, 1934), 82, 171–77, 182, 184, 208–11; Philip J. Stern, *The Company State: Corporate Sovereignty and the Early Modern Foundations of the British Empire in India* (Oxford: Oxford University Press, 2011), 7, 13, 23–29, 41–44, 200–208; Robert Travers, *Ideology and Empire in Eighteenth-Century India: The British in Bengal* (Cambridge: Cambridge University Press, 2007), 8–9, 100–185.

56 Katherine Hermes, "'Justice Will Be Done Us': Algonquian Demands for Reciprocity in the Courts of European Settlers," in *The Many Legalities of Early America*, ed. Christopher L. Tomlins and Bruce H. Mann (Chapel Hill: University of North Carolina Press, 2001), 143; Daniel R. Mandell, *Behind the Frontier: Indians in Eighteenth-Century Eastern Massachusetts* (Lincoln: University of Nebraska Press, 1996), 73, 145–46; Plane, *Colonial Intimacies*, 74–75.

57 Vaughan, *New England Frontier*, 193. Indians in Teticut in Massachusetts complained to an early-eighteenth-century court that they lacked "a true Understanding of the English laws." Mandell, *Behind the Frontier*, 73.

58 James H. Merrell, *Into the American Woods: Negotiators on the Pennsylvania Frontier* (New York: Norton, 1999), 120; Hermes, "Justice," 127 ["gift"]; Katherine Hermes, "The Law of Native Americans, to 1815," in *Cambridge History of Law in America*, volume 1, *Early America (1580–1815)*, ed. Christopher L. Tomlins and Michael Grossberg (Cambridge: Cambridge University Press, 2008), 34–35, 39–40; Allen W. Trelease, *Indian Affairs in Colonial New York: The Seventeenth Century* (Ithaca, NY: Cornell University Press, 1960), 186; Edgar J. McManus, *Law and*

Liberty in Early New England: Criminal Justice and Due Process, 1620–1692
(Amherst: University of Massachusetts Press, 1993), 124–25.

59 Anonymous, *A new voyage to Georgia: By a young gentleman. Giving an account of his travels to South Carolina, and part of North Carolina. To which is added, a curious account of the Indians* (London, 1737), 58; W. A. Young, *The History of North and South America* (London, 1776), 159–60; Cronon, *Changes*, 59; John Philip Reid, *A Law of Blood: The Primitive Law of the Cherokee Nation* (New York: NYU Press, 1970), 54–55; Colin G. Calloway, *New Worlds for All: Indians, Europeans, and the Remaking of Early America* (Baltimore, MD: Johns Hopkins University Press, 1997), 192–93; Jenny Hale Pulsipher, *Subjects unto the Same King: Indians, English, and the Contest for Authority in Colonial New England* (Philadelphia: University of Pennsylvania Press, 2005), 11–12.

60 Thomas Pownall, *Considerations towards a General Plan of Measures for the English Provinces. Laid before the Board of Commissioners at Albany* (Edinburgh, 1756), 18. One after another European writer pointed to the lack of "coercive power" in Indian nations to explain their treatment of crimes—the absence of fines and imprisonment and the preference for restoration of harmony over punishment, expressed most famously in the instance that a killer's relatives or clan pay compensation to the relatives or clan of a victim lest the injured parties resort to private vengeance. James Adair, *The History of the American Indians* (New York: Johnson Reprint Corporation, 1968 [1775]), 429–30; Anonymous, *Voyage to Georgia*, 58 ["coercive power"]; Joseph-François Lafitau, *Customs of the American Indians Compared with the Customs of Primitive Times*, trans. William N. Fenton and Elizabeth L. Moore (Toronto: Champlain Society, 1974–77 [1724]), 1:300–305; Reid, *Law of Blood*, 75–76, 92; W. A. Young, *The History of North and South America* (London, 1776), 1:63–64.

61 Adair, *History*, 434. For more commentary along these lines, see Lafitau, *Customs*, 1:299–300; Louis Armand de Lom d'Arce, Baron de Lahontan, *New Voyages to North America: Reprinted from the English Edition of 1703*, ed. Reuben Gold Thwaites (Chicago: A. C. McClurg, 1905), 2:552–55.

62 Pierre Clastres has famously argued that among such groups, the very essence of the social order sought to preclude the emergence of a centralized "state"-like apparatus. Pierre Clastres, *Society against the State: Essays in Political Anthropology* (New York: Zone Books, 1987).

63 See, e.g., Henry Home, Lord Kames, *Sketches of the History of Man*, ed. James A. Harris (Indianapolis: Liberty Fund, 2007 [1774]), esp. 1:11; 1:373–74, 565–66; Henry Homes, Lord Kames, *Historical Law Tracts*, 2nd ed. (Edinburgh, 1761), esp. v; Adam Smith, *Lectures on Jurisprudence*, ed. R. L. Meek, D. D. Raphael, and P. G. Stein (Indianapolis: Liberty Fund, 1982 [1762–66]), esp. 14; Adam Ferguson, *An Essay on the History of Civil Society*, ed. Fania Oz-Salzberger (Cambridge: Cambridge University Press, 2007 [1767]); William Robertson, *The History of America* (Philadelphia: Johnson and Warner, 1812 [1777, 1796]); John Millar, *The Origin of the Distinctions of Ranks; or, An Inquiry into the Circumstances Which Give Rise*

to Influence and Authority in the Different Members of Society, ed. Aaron Garrett (Indianapolis: Liberty Fund, 2006 [1806]). The following paragraph will emphasize these theorists' similarities rather than their differences. On four-stage theory, see generally Robert F. Berkhofer, *The White Man's Indian: Images of the American Indian from Columbus to the Present* (New York: Vintage, 1979), 47–49; Ronald L. Meek, *Social Science and the Ignoble Savage* (Cambridge: Cambridge University Press, 1975); Robert A. Williams Jr., *Savage Anxieties: The Invention of Western Civilization* (New York: Palgrave Macmillan, 2012), 206–10.

64 Robertson, *History*, 1:301.

65 Kames, *Sketches*, 2:362, 561, 565; Ferguson, *Essay*, 75, 81–84; Robertson, *History*, 1:305; Smith, *Lectures*, 15, 459.

66 Adam Smith, *An Inquiry into the Nature and Causes of the Wealth of Nations*, ed. R. H. Campbell and A. S. Skinner (Indianapolis: Liberty Fund, 1981 [1776]), 910; Smith, *Lectures*, 203, 213; Ferguson, *Essay*, 247; Robertson, *History*, 1:4. "The more improved any society is and the greater length the several means of supporting the inhabitants are carried," wrote Adam Smith, "the greater will be the number of their laws and regulations necessary to maintain justice, and prevent infringements of property." Smith, *Lectures*, 16; see also Millar, *Origin*, 84–85.

67 Robertson, *History*, 1:315; Smith, *Lectures*, 202; Smith, *Wealth*, 709–10.

68 For a detailed discussion of how Spanish and Spanish-American authors responded to stadial theory and conjectural histories, see Jorge Cañizares Esguerra's *How to Write the History of the New World: Histories, Espistemologies, and Identities in the Eighteenth-Century Atlantic World* (Stanford, CA: Stanford University Press, 2001).

69 Owensby, *Empire of Law*, 42–43.

70 This arrangement took the pressures of such cases off the Audiencia, which continued to hear lawsuits between Indians and Spaniards as private citizens.

71 Kawashima, *Puritan Justice*, 21–40; Vaughan, *Puritan Frontier*, 186–90; Helen C. Rountree and Thomas E. Davidson, *Eastern Shore Indians of Virginia and Maryland* (Charlottesville: University Press of Virginia, 1997); W. Stitt Robinson Jr., "The Legal Status of the Indian in Colonial Virginia," *Virginia Magazine of History and Biography* 61 (1953): 247–49; Michelle LeMaster, "In the 'Scolding Houses': Indians and the Law in Eastern North Carolina, 1684–1760," *North Carolina Historical Review* 83 (2006): 204, 222.

72 See, e.g., Massachusetts, *Book of the General Laws and Liberties* (1660), in *The Laws and Liberties of Massachusetts, 1641–1691: A Facsimile Edition*, ed. John D. Cushing (Wilmington, DE: Scholarly Resources, 1976), 1:112; Plymouth Colony, Law to Regulate Indians, July 7, 1682, in Vaughan, ed., *American Indian Documents*, 17:54; Connecticut, Law to Encourage Christianity among Indians, October 10–November 1, 1717, in *ibid.*, 17:336. Cotton Mather, for the benefit of Christianized Indians, published in English and the Massachuset language a summary of selected colonial laws with a heavy emphasis on morals regulations. Cotton Mather, *The Hatchets, to Hew Down the Tree of Sin, Which Bears the Fruit*

of Death; or, The Laws, by Which the Magistrates Are to Punish Offences, among the Indians, as well as among the English (Boston, 1705).

73 Matthew Mayhew, *A Brief Narrative of the Success Which the Gospel Hath Had, among the Indians, of Martha's Vineyard* (Boston, 1694), 38; Merrell, *American Woods*, 90; James H. Merrell, "'The Customes of Our Country': Indians and Colonists in Early America," in *Strangers within the Realm: Cultural Margins of the First British Empire*, ed. Bernard Bailyn and Philip D. Morgan (Chapel Hill: University of North Carolina Press, 1991), 144; Kawashima, *Puritan Justice*, 147. More generally, Natives discovered what persuaded the English. Algonquian defendants in New England courts, who were initially defiant, learned by the 1650s to express remorse in phrases expected by English judges. The Meherrin in North Carolina protected their lands against encroachments by asking the English courts to uphold their "equitable right." Hermes, "Justice," 139; LeMaster, "Scolding," 220.

74 Kevin Kenny, *Peaceable Kingdom Lost: The Paxton Boys and the Destruction of William Penn's Holy Experiment* (New York: Oxford University Press, 2009), 136; LeMaster, "Scolding," 221. Christianized Indians in Natick learned to keep written records both in English and in transliterated Massachuset language. Jean M. O'Brien, *Dispossession by Degrees: Indian Land and Identity in Natick, Massachusetts, 1650–1790* (Cambridge: Cambridge University Press, 1997), 92, 97–98.

75 O'Brien, *Dispossession*, 168–69; Hermes, "Law of Native Americans," 45, 49; Kawashima, *Puritan Justice*, 66, 126, 128; LeMaster, "Scolding," 223, 226–28.

76 North Carolina, Law to Improve Relations between Indians and Colonists, Nov. 17, 1715–Jan. 19, 1716, in Vaughan, *Early Indian Documents*, 16:21.

77 Some Indians continued to live in English communities without tribal ties.

78 Although Native officials continued to undertake much routine governing, they enjoyed even less relative autonomy than in the days of the praying towns. The colony appointed English commissioners or "guardians" to exercise the powers of justice of the peace and to promote the welfare of the Indian village. Natick, one of the most prominent Indian villages, began electing white as well as Native officers by the middle third of the eighteenth century as settlers increasingly purchased land there. O'Brien, *Dispossession*, 48–51, 117, 124–25, 170; Neal Salisbury, "Red Puritans: The 'Praying Indians' of Massachusetts Bay and John Eliot," *William and Mary Quarterly* 31 (1974): 32–54; Kawashima, *Puritan Justice*, 28–33; Hermes, "Law of Native Americans," 45–46; Hermes, "Justice," 143; Merrell, "Customes," 145.

79 O'Brien, *Dispossession*, 75–78, 91–92, 97–106; Banner, *How the Indians*, 61–62; Paulette Crone-Morange and Lucianne Lavin, "The Schaghticoke Tribe and English Law: A Study of Community Survival," *Connecticut History* 43 (2004): 132–62; LeMaster, "Scolding," 221.

80 A will could direct property to women or distant relatives disfavored or excluded by English intestate succession. Indians served alongside settlers as estate

administrators and witnesses. Katherine Hermes, "'By Their Desire Recorded': Native American Wills and Estate Papers in Colonial Connecticut," *Connecticut History* 38 (1999): 151, 155; O'Brien, *Dispossession*, 114–15.

81 Kawashima, *Puritan Justice*, 181–82 [quotation]; Hermes, "Law of Native Americans," 47–48.

82 Plane, *Colonial Intimacies*, 85–93.

83 Owensby, *Empire of Law*, 57.

84 Cutter, *Legal Culture of Northern New Spain*.

85 See, e.g., Tamar Herzog, *La administración como un fenómeno social: la justicia penal de la ciudad de Quito (1650–1750)* (Madrid: CEC, 1995).

86 David Weber, *Bárbaros: Spaniards and Their Savages in the Age of Enlightenment* (New Haven, CT: Yale University Press, 2005).

87 The study of brokers and intermediaries has been at the heart of rich scholarship on the encounter of Natives and settlers. See, e.g., Merrell, *American Woods*; Daniel K. Richter, "Cultural Brokers and Intercultural Politics: New York–Iroquois Relations, 1664–1701," *Journal of American History* 75 (1988): 40–67; Daniel K. Richter, "Whose Indian History?" *William and Mary Quarterly* 50 (1993): 379–93; White, *Middle Ground*.

88 See Cutter, *Legal Culture of Northern New Spain*.

89 This was true even within established Massachusetts Indian settlements such as Mashpee, Stockbridge, and Martha's Vineyard, which mixed Natives from different tribes. Yasuhide Kawashima, "Legal Origins of the Indian Reservation in Colonial Massachusetts," *American Journal of Legal History* 13 (1969): 54.

90 An ordered legality can, of course, fall *into* chaos on its own terms under certain circumstances. At that point it would be a legal system in chaos. But that chaos could not be referred to as law per se, unless the terms of what constituted the law in the first place were changed to somehow reconceptualize what appeared to be chaos as some sort of ordered arrangement.

91 Colin G. Calloway, *Pen and Ink Witchcraft: Treaties and Treaty Making in American Indian History* (Oxford: Oxford University Press, 2013), 13–14.

92 White, *Middle Ground*, x.

93 While Eric Williams's *History of the People of Trinidad and Tobago* (London: A. Deutsch, 1963), *From Columbus to Castro: A History of the Caribbean* (New York: Vintage, 1984), and *Capitalism and Slavery* (Chapel Hill: University of North Carolina Press, 1994) do not make an analytical point of law, issues of legality and justice are woven into the fabric of his works.

94 See, e.g., Kenneth J. Banks, *Chasing Empire across the Sea: Communications and the State in the French Atlantic, 1713–1763* (Montreal: McGill-Queen's University Press, 2002); Herzog, *Upholding Justice*; Richard J. Ross, "Legal Communications and Imperial Governance: British North America and Spanish America Compared," in *The Cambridge History of Law in America*, volume 1, *Early America (1580–1815)*, ed. Michael Grossberg and Christopher Tomlins (Cambridge: Cambridge University Press, 2008), 104–43.

95 For a few such works, see Sally Falk Moore, *Social Facts and Fabrications: "Customary" Law on Kilimanjaro, 1880–1980* (Cambridge: Cambridge University Press, 1986); Laura Nader, *Harmony Ideology: Justice and Control in a Zapotec Mountain Village* (Stanford, CA: Stanford University Press, 1991); Laurelyn Whitt, *Science, Colonialism, and Indigenous People: The Cultural Politics of Law and Knowledge* (Cambridge: Cambridge University Press, 2014); Paul Bohannan, *Justice and Judgment among the Tiv* (London: Oxford University Press, 1957); Karl N. Llewellyn and E. Adamson Hoebel, *The Cheyenne Way: Conflict and Case Law in Primitive Jurisprudence* (Norman: University of Oklahoma Press, 1941); E. Adamson Hoebel, *The Law of Primitive Man: A Study in Comparative Legal Dynamics* (Cambridge, MA: Harvard University Press, 2006).

96 See, e.g., Michelle A. McKinley, *Fractional Freedoms: Slavery, Intimacy, and Legal Mobilization in Colonial Lima, 1600–1700* (Cambridge: Cambridge University Press, 2016); Thomas D. Morris, *Southern Slavery and the Law, 1619–1860* (Raleigh: University of North Carolina Press, 1996).

97 Nancy E. Van Deusen, *Global Indios: The Indigenous Struggle for Justice in Sixteenth-Century Spain* (Durham, NC: Duke University Press, 2015), 226. See also Tatiana Seijas, *Asian Slaves in Colonial Mexico: From Chinos to Indians* (Cambridge: Cambridge University Press, 2015).

98 Allan Gallay, ed., *Indian Slavery in Colonial America* (Lincoln: University of Nebraska Press, 2009).

99 Kant long ago argued for a "cosmopolitan law" premised on the notion that all rational beings shared a single moral community. More recently, Portuguese sociologist Boaventura de Sousa Santos has argued for a subaltern "cosmopolitan legality" to redress the imbalances of power in a globalized world. See Boaventura de Sousa Santos, *Toward a New Legal Common Sense* (Cambridge: Cambridge University Press, 2002); with César A. Rodriguez-Garavito, *Law and Globalization from Below: Toward a Cosmopolitan Legality* (Cambridge: Cambridge University Press, 2005). For our purposes, "cosmopolitan legality" may be understood as the recognition that in the encounter between very different legal worlds, no one system, however obvious and self-explanatory its premises may seem to those who hold them, may be taken as dispositive or foundational vis-à-vis another.

PART I

Mis-Dialogues, Code Switching, and
Mixing Languages of Law

2

Dialoguing with Barbarians

What Natives Said and How Europeans Responded in Late-Seventeenth- and Eighteenth-Century Portuguese America

TAMAR HERZOG

The expansion of European powers overseas brought their inhabitants into conflict with the aborigines who resided in these territories. Whether attempting to annihilate natives or to integrate them into an emerging colonial commonwealth, European agents knew that unless they neutralized the Indigenous, they would never become true masters of the land. These considerations were particularly important in areas where different European powers competed for hegemony. In these territories, monarchs, administrators, settlers, and missionaries urged one another to act quickly and decisively so as to guarantee not only that natives would not hinder their expansion but also that they would not facilitate that of their rivals. Such was the case in the Amazon basin in the seventeenth and eighteenth centuries as Spaniards and Portuguese fought one another with the aim of establishing their dominion.[1]

In their attempts to control the local population, the Portuguese held hundreds of conversations with "not-yet-domesticated" native groups.[2] Historians who had studied these interactions focused their attention on identifying agents and describing negotiations. Many pointed out that natives enjoyed at least some liberty to choose between several possible options.[3] They suggested that whereas in some areas Indigenous and European interlocutors established a middle ground where neither purely Indigenous nor entirely European standards prevailed, in others still under native control, native initiative, rituals, and vocabularies dominated. Indian prominence, however, waned over time. A gradual shift from native to European forms took place, mimicking the process that witnessed the power of Europeans grow and that of natives diminish.[4]

While many historians pointed out the complexities of these European-Indigenous dialogues, others insisted that exchanges between natives and Europeans were channeled through European dichotomies that divided people into barbarians and civilized.[5] According to this vision, if the Portuguese agreed to converse with natives, they did so because they failed to conquer and subject them in other ways. They thus manipulated Indians into believing that their intentions were good when they were not, and that natives would be treated as equals, when they never were. In this second story, Europeans rather than natives were the sole agents, and their standards were the ones carrying the day.

Exploring power relations between groups and exposing the importance of mediators and translators, historians have thus far neglected to ask questions about the law.[6] Yet, the way the parties interacted necessarily referenced their expectations of what produced certain results. If they did or said certain things, they did them because they imagined those things would bring about particular outcomes, which they desired to obtain. In what follows, rather than asking whether natives or Europeans controlled these dialogues or whether they employed a common vocabulary or imposed (when they could) their own concepts, I seek to undercover the codes that guided their behavior. I argue that beyond what was said and done, silently operating in the background were rules that linked speech and action to certain consequences. These rules, anchored in culture and experience, were legal in the sense that they were normative. They prescribed which actions could be taken, which words could be pronounced, and what their results might be. The dialogues between the Portuguese and the natives, therefore, might have involved different degrees of agency, might have depended on shared or privative vocabulary, might have featured strategic actions, but they also were determined by structures that gave words and actions particular meanings. If we understood these structures, we would recover what happened in the American interior by focusing not on who did what, but on what contemporaries expected would transpire as a result.

The aim of this exercise is both historical and methodological. Similar to what Ludwig Wittgenstein once did regarding the study of language, the task is to ask whether we can reconstruct rules by observing interactions. As spectators in a soccer match, if we watched it sufficiently long on a sufficient number of occasions, would we decipher what the norms of the game were? Neither intelligibility nor understanding are at stake here, and the norms that I seek to uncover were not written in law books, among other reasons because law books did not exist in the early modern period, at least not the way we know them today. During this period, laws (that is, legislation, including orders by the king, i.e., the Laws of the Indies) were but a secondary normative source of very limited importance, and they were indeed often unknown, ignored, or manipulated.[7] But royal mandates were *not* the law operating in the colonial world, or anywhere else, as a matter of fact. While reconstructing what the kings had ordered is of no interest to me, here the question would revolve around the employment of norms that required no juridical preparation but instead were widespread, among other reasons because they were not considered legal but part of the way things are and ought to be. Despite regional diversities, such norms were surprisingly common across large territories. Hundreds of conflicts (not law cases) from across a variety of regions suffice to attest how Europeans of extremely different legal traditions similarly advocated in their discussions with one another their right to land, or how they referenced their condition as members of communities.[8] To argue that actors interpreted these rules differently, leading to different results, or that different complementary or even contradictory norms existed, is to state the obvious. Strategic behavior may be the hero of the day, but it, too, sends us back to certain rules without which no strategy can ever be devised. Otherwise said, if "English and Spanish notions of justice" did not exist, that was the case because there were no such national divides, not because the English and the Spanish did not share basic guidelines that had to be followed in order to discuss (and eventually decide) what was just and what was not.[9] As Thomas Duve once suggested, without understanding those guidelines, we would only detect a senseless movement.[10]

Because documents describing native legal structures are mostly lacking, I propose to reconstruct these by closely reading Portuguese documentation. This documentation is flawed because it obscured what natives desired and it rarely addressed the question why they did certain things. Mainly originating in missionaries or military commanders, governors, and ministers, these records favor certain interpretations. Jesuit narratives highlight the importance of missionary activity for establishing relations with and domesticating Indians. Information produced by military commanders stresses the fierceness of natives because the more dangerous they were perceived to be, the more comprehensible a defeat and the more glorious a victory. Producing information that was meant to generate recognition or obtain specific rewards, the Portuguese who authored these reports carefully selected what they communicated, fabricating stories for the consumption of their immediate authorities and sometimes the wider public. Yet, despite the instrumentalized nature of these reports, they nevertheless contained plenty of details concerning native reaction and allow a window into the norms that may have guided natives in their interactions with the Portuguese.

My proposal, therefore, is to shy away from attesting that natives behaved irrationally (as contemporary Portuguese sources concluded), that they misunderstood what was proposed to them, or that, on the contrary, they were formidable agents who knew, recognized, and controlled, perhaps even engaged in, "cultivated ambiguity," "studied ignorance," "willful refusal to recognize," or "purposeful disregard" (all these versions exist in the literature).[11] Instead, I argue that, like all other peoples, natives were guided by what they considered just and what they perceived as possible. Their reactions to what happened when they contracted with the Portuguese can therefore be telling.

In what follows, I demonstrate that the dialogue between the Portuguese and the natives was compromised by the different conventions each of them held. The result was a true cacophony. This did not happen because the members of rival groups did not understand one another, because they lacked the ability to negotiate, or because they could not establish a basic working intelligibility. All of these factors were present and, indeed, treaties between the Portuguese and the Indians were extremely frequent, allowing them to arrive at agreements to which both sides consented. Yet—I would argue—each interpreted differently what those agreements included. Indigenous interlocutors argued that their accords with the Portuguese should lead to material exchanges and, on occasion, protection and that their behavior guaranteed both. The Portuguese, on the contrary, wanted to obtain pacification in the form of native vassalage and, hopefully, conversion. They too argued that, given the prevailing norms, what they were doing would lead them to that end. Thus, while natives suggested that accords should protect their independence and should guarantee that they would remain separate from other

Indigenous groups and the Portuguese, the Portuguese concluded that they would bring about native integration. Tracing these mis-dialogues, my argument is that at stake was not only the different position individuals and groups held within the colonial order or their ability to understand the meaning of terms or to enter into relationships. Instead, disjuncture was the consequence of the diverse expectations each party had as to the results of what it did, which in turn depended on what its members thought was legitimate and possible. In such a colonial setting, what was the meaning and extension of consent?

Alliance Making: The Common Ground

Late-seventeenth- and eighteenth-century Portuguese sources attested that both Portuguese and natives were willing to enter into mutual accords. The Portuguese imagined these pacts as a fairly simple transaction. They assumed that gift giving formed friendships and that friendships guaranteed native subjection. Gift giving often took place spontaneously and concerned very few people and a rather minimal material investment, and its importance was so evident to contemporaries that those involved in it often complained that poverty and the lack of resources hindered success and endangered the colonial enterprise altogether.[12]

The natives who received these gifts agreed that this behavior tied them to the Portuguese. The documents at our disposal include ample evidence that once gift giving began, natives usually returned to European posts requesting additional items and bringing with them some merchandise in return. Natives also indicated to the Portuguese which articles they desired and promised to bring what they thought the Portuguese might want. In order to perform these exchanges, the Indigenous either came disarmed or agreed to disarm themselves. They consented to speak with the Portuguese, usually through interpreters, or by using nonverbal communication such as gestures. The more frequent these exchanges, the more confident natives seemed to be that a relationship was established.

Contemporary chronicles support this understanding. As historians and anthropologists of Indigenous America have long suggested, these chronicles, for example, Jean de Léry's narrative of the Tupinamba

Indians of Brazil in the 1550s, contained evidence that the Tupi were interested in obtaining European products but that they also viewed gift giving as a distributive mechanism that established relationships.[13] The Tupinamba understood that trade required peaceful relations and that peaceful relations permitted trade. Under their optic, the acceptance of gifts could be read as a recognition of submission or an agreement to create an alliance, and its rejection could be understood as an assertion of independence or a refusal to contract. This behavior formed part of what scholars have identified as a "sociology of exchange" that targeted not only economic profit but also important political and religious consequences. The Tupi who received European gifts used exchanges as a method to incorporate these foreigners into their universe and, in the process, make them internal.[14] Contemporary authors also affirmed that natives desired European products and to gain them were willing to establish relations with the Portuguese. Those who were not interested in trade, on the contrary, preferred to avoid Europeans altogether by retiring to the interior, where they could not be reached.[15]

Alliance Making: The Portuguese Vision

Gift giving, therefore, was a shared European-Indigenous mechanism to establish relations between groups. But how were these relations established, and what was their purpose?

The reports Portuguese agents (military commanders, friars, and colonialists) sent to the authorities in order to corroborate their success at alliance making were extremely repetitive.[16] Although authored in different parts of the American continent by a variety of agents who were working under distinct circumstances, in different periods, and meeting different Indigenous groups, these reports were surprisingly similar. They usually began with the affirmation that Indians requested to meet with the Portuguese and offered to ally with them (part 1: native initiative). They continued by describing how in the following days, weeks, and months and over several encounters, the parties got acquainted (part 2: the conversations). Mediated by converted or domesticated Indians or by friars or experienced settlers, these dialogues involved Indian chiefs, on the one hand, and Portuguese missionaries, military commanders, or settlers on the other (part 3: the parties). During these conversations, gifts were exchanged and natives were informed of the need to establish peace, and were told that, if they agreed, they would become vassals and win royal protection (part 4: the conditions). On many occasions, natives immediately received either passports (*passaporte*) certifying that they were vassals or "certificates of services" (*certidão do serviço*), which would protect them from harm.[17] Native consent was given either verbally, or by signing papers, or by using gestures, for example, hugging and kissing, which Portuguese interlocutors interpreted as communicating acquiescence (part 5: native consent).[18]

In the absence of a formal protocol for peacemaking or general instructions that required compliance, Portuguese documentation does not clarify how very different local developments involving a diversity of actors, interests, situations, and periods produced such extremely repetitive narratives. If we take into account that the aim of writers was to demonstrate success at appeasing and subjecting Indians, it is plausible that the transformation of individual stories into a genre of account giving must have obeyed a certain ideological framework. This framework must have reproduced Portuguese expectations of what made for a valid agreement because only a valid agreement would convince readers that alliance with Indians was indeed achieved. Alliance included identifying the parties, describing the negotiation, enumerating the terms, exchanging gifts, and native consent. Because verifying that all these elements existed guaranteed legal validity, Portuguese agents spent time, effort, and paper to demonstrate that such was the case. As a result, rather than a reflection of reality, Portuguese narratives of alliance making, which were astonishly persistent over time, should be read as reproducing Portuguese understanding of how agreements were reached and what they could or must contain.

This understanding began by stressing native initiative (part 1). To do so, Portuguese informants continuously asserted that natives came to seek the Portuguese rather than the inverse. They explained this native predilection by referencing Portuguese superiority, which they took for granted, or by pointing out native interest in the (superior) goods that the Portuguese could supply. The negotiations that followed the arrival of natives (part 2) were distinguished in Portuguese sources with a particular term, "*praticas.*" They were described as verbal exchanges, usually through the mediation of acculturated Indians or experienced missionaries or settlers.

While fulfilling these first two conditions for a valid contract was fairly easy, understanding whom you spoke with (part 3: identifying the parties) was not. Aware of the need to identify their interlocutors, Portuguese governors, missionaries, settlers, and military commanders often hesitated or openly disagreed with one another as to whom they were dealing with.[19] They were unsure whether one or several native groups answering to a single denomination existed, what was the relation among them, and who headed them.[20] Appealing to their own experience in the interior, the Portuguese also depended on informants. In the Amazon, they heavily relied on data supplied by the Tupinambá, a complex and multivalent assemblage of Indigenous groups with whom they came into contact in the seventeenth century.[21] Involving a double translation (from local to Tupi and from Tupi to Portuguese), Tupi mediation was also compromised by the Tupis' particular position as members of an Indigenous group that immigrated from the coast to the interior, mainly following the Portuguese, and whose presence brought them into conflict with many local groups, which they sought to replace. The desire to classify Indians as either friends or enemies and transform the native world into a fully legible one led to Portuguese frustration (and impatience) with the continuing presence of Indians belonging to nations "totally unknown" whose language was "strange and unused" (*estranha e desusada língua*).[22]

If arranging groups and distinguishing between them was complex, no less so was the need to understand who could speak for which group. Because, following Portuguese legal traditions, leaders of groups could make pacts that could oblige all members, the Portuguese proceeded to identify such leaders, recognizing certain individuals as Indigenous *principais*. Historical research has nonetheless demonstrated that, on most occasions, the persons identified by the Portuguese as *principais* were individuals who had previous contacts with Europeans and were somewhat acculturated. Proclaiming themselves leaders, or selected by the Portuguese as such, these individuals rarely were designated according to native traditions. Because their power depended on their position as mediators, to consolidate it, the Portuguese, who recognized these *principais* as valid interlocutors, proceeded to designate them as such. They declared them hereditary leaders, often giving them also formal letters of nomination, as well as military distinctions.[23] On occasion, they even decorated them with "certificates of services" (*certidão do serviço*) that attested to their alliance with the Portuguese. Because the gifts given to these men were superior to those offered to their "vassals," individuals recognized as leaders were also distinguished from other natives by the dress and objects they possessed. By the end of this process, rather than the authorities of a group reaching an agreement, as it was often portrayed, what frequently happened in the interior of the Amazon region was that accords with natives instituted both the group and its authorities. In their aftermath, pacts that recognized the contracting parties as valid in fact made them thus, or so at least did the Portuguese believe.[24]

After the contracting parties were identified (or created), material exchanges followed. These were important as a means to "win over" natives, yet, for the Portuguese, they also had a legal significance. According to Portuguese understanding, some measure of "consideration," that is, material exchange, was needed to seal an alliance ceremoniously. As the Portuguese governor of São Paulo suggested in 1771, no true diplomatic undertaking could be achieved without it.[25] Because the Portuguese juridical system also determined that if you behaved as a friend (by giving gifts) and one acknowledged you as such (by receiving them), you became one, gift giving could also be perfomative, constituting rather than acknowledging relations.

While the processes of identifying the parties, establishing conversations with them, and exchanging gifts were profusely spelled out in Portuguese reports on alliance making, the precise conditions that the pacts included were not (part 4). Either natives were not clearly told what these accords meant or they were mainly informed that peace carried with it the duty to obey the monarch, to be a "friend of his friend and enemy of his enemies." For their part, the only promise the Portuguese explicitly made was not to harm natives. It was nevertheless clear that, in the Portuguese mind, agreements with natives also included additional conditions that were implied in their understanding of what vassalage meant and what their role in the American interior was. These implicit conditions included—as natives often discovered after they were agreed upon—conversion, resettlement, commercial exchanges, military service, and, most importantly, subjection to the Portuguese and loss of independence.

To all these conditions, Portuguese sources stated, natives consented of their free and spontaneous will (part 5). To prove this point, Portuguese informants stressed native initiative, which, according to them, was telling. They also insisted that natives knew what they were doing and agreed to the pacts of their own volition. So pressing was this need to confirm Indigenous choice that, in 1791, a Portuguese military commander recounted how the Guaicuru, who wanted to give proof of their recognition and gratitude to the Portuguese who had given them many presents (*uma evidente prova do seu reconhecimento, gratidão e sensibilidade pelo bom tratamento e repetida beneficia que ultimamente tem recebido dos portugueses*) and wishing to exhibit the "great respect and fidelity" (*grande respeito, e fidelidade*) they had for the Portuguese king, "spontaneously and anxiously" (*espontânea e ansiosamente*) arrived to the regional capital (Vila Bela, in Mato Grosso).[26] There, received with great demonstrations of friendship and given additional gifts, they promised that from that day onwards they would always obey royal commands. Asked if this promise was "born out of free will" (*era nascida de sua livre vontade*) and if it included subjection to Portuguese laws, "being friends of the king's friends and enemies of his enemies," they answered positively.

Native consent was often asserted verbally, but it could also be read into native behavior. "It was only by their actions that we perceived their willingness" to leave their original habitat and come to live next to the Portuguese, one Portuguese administrator reported in 1786.[27] Others pointed out that natives consented to the agreement by expressing happiness (*contentos*) and by undertaking "festivities," "dancing in their gentile ways" (*com muita festa e fizeram suas danças e bailes a seu modo gentílico*).[28] So strong was the belief in the ability to interpret behavior that accidently (*casualmente*) meeting with "wild Indians of unknown nation" (*índios silvestres de nação desconhecida*), the Portuguese nevertheless reported to their king that the members of this group had "manifested willingness and inclination to become civilized" (*com uma manifesta vontade e inclinação de admitir civilidade*).[29]

The quest to communicate good intentions and the wish to confirm native consent were also supported by the use of religious symbols. In the 1650s, an Indian chief whom the Portuguese sent to discuss peace with his relatives (*parentes*) requested that they give him proof that the

Portuguese could be trusted (*para ser melhor crido dos que já tão pouco se fiavam dos brancos, pediu lhe dessem um sinal que mostrasse aos contrários*).[30] The chief rejected the suggestion of the military commander that he would carry a paper in which the governor would offer these Indians his perpetual friendship. His relatives, he argued, did not trust papers.[31] He needed a more efficient sign (*dizendo que já não se fiavam de papéis, que lhe dessem outro sinal mais eficaz*). According to Jesuit narratives, the Portuguese present were confused by this answer, but Friar João de Souto Maior knew exactly what needed doing. He offered an image of Christ to the Indian, who was satisfied by it. The friar's decision indeed accomplished the desired miracle: the Indians ceased their hostilities, and by the end of that year, they made peace with the Portuguese.

Jesuit reports including such narratives might have been colored by the wish to stress both Jesuit contributions to peacemaking and the power of the cross to transform foes into friends, but contemporary sources confirm that the use of the cross was general and that it was also adopted even by the so-called not-yet-domesticated Indians for precisely the same end. In 1659, for example, the Jesuit António Vieira met with a group of "savage" Indians in the interior of the Amazon basin.[32] The conversations began when native leaders joined Vieira in his canoe and handed him a cross, which they had received four years earlier from another missionary. Even as late as 1771, native groups might have used the cross in similar ways. According to military correspondence, that year some thirty Indians who wanted to "talk" to the Portuguese came to the fort of Iguatemi in the Amazon region with crosses in hand, which they offered to the commander as a sign of their peaceful intentions.[33] The commander accepted the crosses, placed them on the ground, and ensured his interlocutors that they needed no other instrument to win over him and his soldiers.

Whether they understood the metaphysical meaning of the cross or not, natives learned that it could communicate peaceful intentions or even consent.[34] Returning to the encounter between Vieira and the Indians in 1659, to native offering of the cross Vieira responded by celebrating a mass with the participation, on the right, of Indigenous leaders of groups that had already converted to Christianity and were wearing European dress and bearing arms and, on the left, of the members of the new and not-yet-converted group in their "barbarian cloths and bows and arrows." In their role as intermediaries between these two Indigenous worlds, the middle ground was left for the Portuguese. Vieira preached to the not-yet-converted Indians, notifying them of the need to answer his questions with "clean hearts" and without "deceit" and informing them that after they did so, they would be bound by what they had promised. He then asked each cacique whether he was willing to convert and become a subject of the Portuguese crown. The Portuguese and the already-converted Indians explained in "one voice" that the main obligations of subjects included the duty to obey the king and his laws, and be friends with his friends, enemies with his foes. Because the unconverted-undomesticated Indian caciques responded positively, they each came to the altar, laid their bows and arrows on the ground, and, putting their hands in Vieira's, swore to be vassals and live in perpetual peace with the Portuguese. Kissing the hands of Vieira, the principals proceeded to embrace the friars, the Portuguese, and the domesticated Indians. They all sang together a Te Deum, accompanied by the sounds of trumpets, horns, and drums and the "continuous cries of infinite number of voices" in "multiple languages." Gift giving followed, as did music and dances. To commemorate what had transpired, a huge cross was erected and immediately venerated by both "Christians and pagans." The ritual took three days to conclude and might have included the participation of as many as fifty Indian principals and some forty thousand of their followers.

Free will (even if not free choice) was of course required by Portuguese law for agreement making. Because free will was not necessarily viewed in Europe (where theoretically, feudal vassals freely submitted themselves to the lord and where faith depended on free choice) as missing because of the presence of power relations or even extreme duress, in the American interior, Indians were said to have freely subjected themselves to the Portuguese. Not only did they exercise a choice, but they were happy and thus grateful to have been given the chance to do so.

Was Alliance Making That Simple?

While Portuguese narratives followed a storyline that was meant to validate the agreements reached with natives by systematizing and subjecting all information to that end, the complexity of what actually transpired (and how natives reacted to it) can be demonstrated by the following two examples. In 1771, the military commander of the fort of Iguatemi in the Amazon basin began conversations with a group of "undomesticated" Indians who had come to see him.[35] After the Indians disarmed themselves, and hugs and gifts were exchanged, he offered them peace, and they promised not to offend the Portuguese, receiving assurances that the Portuguese would do the same with them. Although according to the commander success was guaranteed because the Indians left the fort "very happy," the documentation nevertheless included indications that such might have not been the case. The Indians, the commander reported, asked several "impertinent" questions (*algumas impertinentes perguntas*). The first was why the Portuguese had come to take the lands that god had given them for their livelihood (*qual era razão por que lhes vinham tomar as suas terras que deus lhes tinha repartidas para suas vivendas*). The commander responded that the Portuguese did not want their lands because they had sufficient territory. Their sole aim, he said, was to acquire their friendship (*respondi-lhe que eu lhe não vinha tomar as terras e que delas não carecia antes vinha buscar a sua amizade que hera só o que queria*). To this, natives responded that "this was good and that they wanted the same, that is, to avoid deaths that god did not want" (*respondeu-me que estava bem e que isso mesmo queriam eles, para que entre nós não houvesse mortandades que deus não queria*). The commander then asked if they knew god, to which they responded that he had bled on the cross for men and kissed an image of Christ with "great reverence" (*o cacique com grande reverencia beijou a senhor*). The second and third questions natives asked, which the commander found equally offensive, were whether the governor of São Paulo and the king were married and had fathered children.

Why these queries were "impertinent" is hard to establish. Perhaps the commander had expected to take the leading role in the conversation and was annoyed that the Indians had taken the initiative or questioned his intentions. Perhaps he was surprised at their awareness that the Portuguese were after their land. Perhaps he was insulted by the implication that the land was Indigenous rather than Portuguese. But whatever the case might have been, as the Indians left the fort, the Portuguese commander had plenty of reasons to suspect that what he perceived as an easy, indeed a done, deal, was not to be thus. Not only did the Indians ask difficult questions, but when he inquired whether they and their families would come and live under the protection of the king and among the Portuguese, they answered that for the moment they would not. Furthermore, soon after the members of the group left, the house of a Portuguese settler was assailed. The commander was unsure whether the attack was carried out by the same group that had visited the fort or by other Indians. One could not tell, he reported, which was the case because these natives were barbarians, who could not be trusted. His disillusionment only grew after a second group visited the fort and he contracted, so he said, the same peace with them. Despite his efforts, the members of this second group left the Portuguese camp discontented, according to him, because they absurdly "wanted to receive everything they saw." Why he nevertheless thought they agreed to peace was unclear.

The exchanges reported by the commander might have responded to Portuguese legal requirements for alliance making, but they also revealed important tensions. While the Portuguese assumed that peace would imply settlement and conversion, the Indians—who were told about these conditions only a posteriori—responded that peace would be possible, but that they wanted to remain where their forefathers had lived. While the Portuguese suggested that after peace was achieved natives must become dependent on them, the Indians refused to comply. Clearly, by the 1770s, natives were afraid of Portuguese encroachment on their lands and might have sought out the Portuguese in order to halt, not to advance, their penetration. They might have wanted to check what the Portuguese were doing, and might have desired gifts. Evidently, they were not looking to convert or become vassals. Yet, despite clear evidence that they disagreed with the Portuguese, as long as they were not overtly hostile, the Portuguese commander concluded that they had "good faith" (*boa fé*) and that peace had been made.

This phantasmagoric conclusion was possible because, for the Portuguese, native consent operated not as the reflection of reality but as a legal construct. This legal construct was based not on what actually transpired in the American interior but on the understanding of how territories and their people were to be possessed. According to this understanding, the conversion of the Americas into a Portuguese dominion required taking hold of the land without suffering opposition.[36] Because, according to this theory, the absence of a violent response or

silence could be considered consent, the Portuguese could easily interpret the native response as signaling agreement. Otherwise said, as long
as Indians were not explicitly hostile, the Portuguese asserted that they
acquiesced to their presence.[37] Presupposing that the lack of explicit opposition meant acceptance, in their conversations with natives, therefore, what the Portuguese sought to establish was not a true exchange or
a manifest accord, but instead a confirmation that they were indeed (as
they thought they already were) supreme masters of the land.

If the encounter near Iguatemi was perplexing, even more so were
the "dialogues" held in the 1780s between the Portuguese and various
Indigenous groups that the Portuguese identified as belonging to the
"Mura" nation (my second example).[38] These dialogues began when
a small group of natives arrived "with no ill intention" (*em termos de
paz*) at Maripi in the Amazon basin. While its members requested to
receive tools and promised to return with tortoises, which they knew
the Portuguese desired, the Portuguese wished to find out whether the
Muras, whom they considered their enemies, were in reality spying on
them, their interest in peaceful exchanges expressing "more treason
than any other thing" (*mais traição que outra qualquer coisa*). Guided
by these suspicions, the Portuguese instructed the Indians that the first
step for exchanges would be to contract peace.

Before their next visit, the Muras sent a messenger. He explained to
the Portuguese that all the Muras wanted "was to come to talk," and he
promised that they would bring with them to the fort presents in the
form of five tortoises and some roots. The Portuguese, who classified
these gifts as "not much" (*cousa pouca*), nevertheless agreed to converse.
They insisted, however, that the Muras bring their wives along, and they
asked if and when they would be willing to settle near the Portuguese.
The answer the Mura chief gave on both accounts was, Not quite yet: he
first needed to consult with his relatives. He refused a Portuguese escort
back to Mura habitation because, according to him, he was sick and thus
ill disposed for "walking with whites."

In yet another meeting, the Mura chief agreed to contract peace with
the Portuguese—or so, at least, the Portuguese concluded. In order to
consecrate this understanding, the Portuguese instructed him that when
natives spotted a Portuguese canoe they would present themselves
unarmed, crying out "camarada Mathias," a password (*senha*) that would

demonstrate their "good intentions." This method, however, would not be reciprocal. Although the Portuguese agreed to the use of a password, contrary to natives, they would not use it themselves, nor would they have to disarm before they approached natives. The explanation for this divergence was that while they, the Portuguese, could be trusted not to attack the natives for no good cause, such was not the case with their opponents. After all, the Muras were barbarians who were used to treachery (*não obstante que desse logo não devamos dar inteiro credito ás promessas d'aqueles bárbaros, e que por ora sobre eles e sobre alguns seus pretendidos enganos, nos devamos com prudência e cautela regular*).

Asserting that he would not be surprised if the Muras broke this understanding, the Portuguese governor who received the news immediately moved to threaten rather than appease the Muras. He instructed the commander to tell the Muras that their "grave crimes" would be forgotten only if they converted to Christianity and became vassals of the king. If, on the contrary, they continued in their "insults and excesses," they would be brought to their complete destruction (*última ruína*). The governor also instructed his men to spy on the Indians in order to find out how many they were and where they lived. He ordered that even if they would be willing to settle near the Portuguese, they should be divided in groups and separated from one another, perhaps even mixed with other natives, so as to limit the possibility of rebellion.

During these conversations, the Portuguese were obsessed with knowing who the Muras "truly" were. They concluded that they belonged to a "very powerful nation," divided into many groups, extending over large territories, and enjoying great natural resources. The Muras, they suggested, disseminated havoc wherever they went, capturing and killing other Indians as well as many Portuguese. Because they were internally divided into many groups, for peace to persist it was vital to integrate into the conversation additional Indians. The Portuguese also attempted to force the Muras to abandon what the Portuguese argued was their nomadic way of life in favor of a permanent settlement.

The Muras sometimes agreed to these demands, yet after they established their domicile near the Portuguese, they often left the settlement for prolonged periods, visiting relatives or searching for food. And, while the Portuguese believed that resettlement would subject the Muras to the Portuguese, there is no suggestion in the documentation that the Muras imagined it would. On the contrary, the Muras apparently felt free to roam the countryside. They traded with the Portuguese, but when vicinity to the Portuguese was no longer convenient for them, many among them "resettled" in their original lands, which they either never completely abandoned or now wished to recuperate. Asked by the Portuguese who considered them vassals to perform certain tasks (regretfully, we do not know which), the Muras refused because they found them "repugnant to their customs." The Muras also maintained close contacts with their "relatives" (*parentes*) living both inside and on the fringes of the colonial world, in both Spanish and Portuguese territories, and they continued to have both friendship ties and animosity with other native groups, regardless of the question of whether members of these groups were friendly with the Portuguese or not.[39] Only a few of them ever converted.

Reading Law into These Exchanges

While what had transpired between the natives and the Portuguese could be explained by the different interests and agendas each side had, it also depended on expectations that were not spelled out, or verbalized. Most important among them was the way contemporaries inserted these accords into their understanding of how things operated. As established above, for the Portuguese, accords with Indians had to contain certain elements if they were to be valid. Once their existence was verified—as happened in Portuguese narratives of alliance making—the Portuguese concluded that they had contracted a binding agreement with natives. This agreement was to confirm that they were indeed masters of the Americas, which they thought they already were, or should soon become. It was to produce submission and subjection in the form of vassalage. Concluded with a native chief, in line with the Portuguese understanding of authority, the agreement could be enforced on all group members and was to apply in their relationships with any Portuguese. It was also to modify the relations that members of this native group could have with other natives as well as with other European powers because by becoming vassals, Indians were also transformed into friends of friends and enemies of enemies.

The Portuguese also assumed that these agreements were to lead to conversion and resettlement. That conversion would follow was almost an axiom. Sooner or later, all those under allegiance to the monarch would have to convert. As for resettlement, it was clearly in the background, as after agreements were concluded, the Portuguese usually asked natives if they would come to settle near them. From the Portuguese point of view, allowing natives to remain in their original habitat would be a tactical mistake because, strategically, vicinity ensured political and military control, it facilitated conversion, and it guaranteed the availability of a labor force.[40] Beyond these tactical considerations, insistence on settlement was also tied to Portuguese belief that their mission in the Americas was to transform the land. It was to ensure the "civilization" of all of the Indigenous, among other things, by converting nomads into "useful" members of civic communities, and by forcing them to incorporate into the emerging colonial order.

While this was what the Portuguese expected, native expectations might have been radically different. If we assumed that, rather than sporadic and senseless (as the Portuguese argued), native behavior was directed at obtaining certain goals, what were these goals and how did they go about obtaining them? Judging from the disagreements and disobedience that Portuguese sources registered, what did natives attempt to achieve by conversing and exchanging with the Portuguese?

The Portuguese, we already know, assumed that alliance making was a single act that, once concluded, would produce a permanent subjection, and they complained of native treachery when this did not occur. Yet, their own records indicated that natives might have considered alliance making a temporary arrangement. On occasions, natives suggested that the understandings with the Portuguese were seasonal. This was what an Indigenous principal argued in 1781, when he explained to the Portuguese that beforehand he was willing to come and settle next to the fort but that at the present time this was no longer true because he now needed to cultivate the land so as to sustain his family, vassals, and allies who were dispersed in the territory.[41] Native behavior also indicated that because alliances depended on exchanges and exchanges depended on reciprocity, these could cease if interests mutated or if natives received insufficient benefits. Because relations depended on exchanges, the delivery of bad-quality goods could lead to the renewal of violence. This happened in the late seventeenth century when a recently allied Indigenous group received "mixed *aguardiente*" that made natives vomit. This episode led to native "*desconfiança*" that, in turn, reconverted them into enemies as they had been before (*ficando inimigos como dantes*).[42] Understanding and exchanges could also be abandoned if, after natives had contracted peace, they reached the conclusion that they had made a mistake and changed their minds.[43] From a native point of view, therefore, there was a perfect logic and a full legal justification to the alternation between alliance with one European power or the other according to which treated them better or gave them larger rewards.[44] Said differently, if for Europeans this alternation involved treason, for natives it involved what was agreed upon.

Other disagreements regarding the meaning and extension of accords were also present. While the Portuguese assumed that contracting with natives was sufficient to appease them all with regards to all the Portuguese, natives often considered themselves only allies of certain individuals.[45] Rather than based on "national" designations, the mutual exchanges and understandings natives established linked them to concrete people. It is therefore not surprising that the Indigenous who met the Portuguese in Iguatemi in 1771 wanted to know who they were dealing with. Rather than accepting relations with "the Portuguese," they asked who was the king and who the governor.[46] For the same reason, the understanding reached in the 1780s with the Muras was based on the mutual recognition between the Muras and the person who had brokered the deal, Mathias, the administrator of Maripi. So omnipresent was the Muras' relationship with Mathias that they were to invoke his name as a password showing their good intentions.[47] These factors perhaps explained why many natives failed to understand why an alliance with the Portuguese eliminated the possibility of a relationship also with other European powers or with their nondomesticated native relatives, or why allowing some Portuguese to be present on their land implied that others could be as well.

If relations were concrete and personal, so were disappointments. In 1780, the Cupitá Indians ceased their conversations with the Portuguese because one of them was told by the local priest to abandon his concubine.[48] Enraged by this order, thereafter the Indians refused to listen to the Portuguese, "demonstrating in this way the independence they still had of them." When the Portuguese insisted that talks would continue, the native leader answered that he refused to return to the fort: he had nothing to do there, where he received nothing. He would only go, he explained, where it would be beneficial for him to go. When the Portuguese attempted to apprehend him so as "to teach him a lesson," the Indians reacted with violence. For the Portuguese, this mishap took place because the members of this Indigenous group were "newly" introduced to Portuguese ways and lacked civility (*novos e sem a civilidade*). But, for the Indians, it was probably tied to the personal relations that they had failed to establish and to the conclusion that the exchanges offered were insufficient.

Disagreement regarding the identity of the contracting parties also worked in other ways. According to the Portuguese, the understanding they reached with a single native (whom they identified as a leader) obliged all. Natives, on the contrary, might have considered each group independent, and it was unclear whether accords with the individuals whom the Portuguese identified as valid interlocutors were sufficient to coerce all members of the group. Those identified by the Portuguese as *principais*, at least, often doubted such was the case. They told the Portuguese (who refused to give it full credence) that they needed to speak to their relatives (*parentes*). Although, responding to Portuguese pressure, one principal brought another, it was also clear that all arrived accompanied by yet other individuals, and they continuously invoked the existence of additional members who should be consulted. Even in cases in which the alleged leader rejected the pact, some of "his" subjects could act independently and remain among the Portuguese. There was no indication in the documentation, therefore, that decisions by the so-called *principais* could bind all members.

It is also possible that, rather than implying vassalage, as Europeans assumed, for most Indians the understandings they reached with the Portuguese were about trade and protection. Trade and protection required peace, but they did not necessarily entail political subjection. As the Muras plainly asserted in the 1780s, if they came with "peaceful intentions" to the fort of Maripi, they did so because they wanted to exchange tortoises for Portuguese goods.[49] Judging by their behavior, they had no intention to convert, resettle, or submit to the Portuguese.

Perhaps clearest in the sources was the disagreement regarding removal. Natives expected that their accords with the Portuguese would lead to peace that would allow them to remain on the land of their ancestors.[50] These expectations were based on their friendship with the Portuguese and the assistance they gave them. Need was also invoked: natives expected to have sufficient territory to sustain themselves.[51] Indeed, even if they were chased away by missionaries who accused them of disobedience, since this was the original habitat where their ancestors had lived, and since they were now loyal vassals and were willing to live in peace and friendship with the Portuguese, they should be allowed back.[52] Their rights, natives suggested, were based on having resided in the territory, but entitlement was also anchored on the idea of a reciprocal pact that originated not in conquest but in a pacific (and voluntary) communion with both god and king.

Yet, while natives suggested that remaining on their ancestral lands was natural now that they were vassals and obedient, the Portuguese thought that by contracting with them, natives who submitted themselves to the Portuguese would resettle elsewhere. At stake was sometimes the wish to vacate Indigenous land so that it could be repossessed by the Portuguese. At others, the main goal was to settle Indians whom the Portuguese suggested were nomads or to ensure that they would reside near the Portuguese and would be more easily integrated, converted, and disciplined. Removal also ensured that Indians would no longer live on their ancestral land, where their past traditions were strong, as were social and political structures. But whatever the reasons for removal were, if for natives peacemaking was about nonintervention, for the Portuguese it implied change.

A Learning Curve?

Given these distinct understandings, it is easy to comprehend why both the Portuguese and the Indians (often) concluded that the *other* party contravened the accords. Portuguese sources were particularly adamant on this point, routinely arguing that native allies who had lived in "good peace and friendship" (*boa paz e amizade*) with the Portuguese, being "their confederates and friends," frequently turned hostile and committed "much tyranny and falsity."[53] This happened, the Portuguese explained, because the Indigenous were barbarians who could not be trusted and whose "natural brutality and inconsistency" led them to respect no agreement.[54]

Yet, natives were no less prone to accuse the Portuguese of infidelity. In 1659, for example, an Indigenous chief who was requested to swear allegiance to the king responded that there was no reason why he would. After all, he and his people had always been "faithful to the king and recognized him as their lord, and were always friends and servants of the Portuguese." If this friendship and obedience were broken, the break occurred because of what the Portuguese, not he and his people, did. As a result, the Portuguese and not they must now "re-do their promise."[55] Similarly, in 1671 and 1672, several Indian chiefs requested royal protection against the occupation of their lands by the inhabitants of São Paulo who pretended to enslave them. Alleging that they were already vassals of the crown and friends of the Portuguese, they lamented the fact that these factors were insufficient to shield them.[56]

While agreeing that violations were common and searching to identify the responsible party, contemporaries placed almost no effort on understanding *why* they happened. For the Portuguese, Indians were barbarians; for the Indians, the Portuguese promised protection they could not or had no intention to give. Thus, while these cross-accusations revealed a common adherence to the idea of alliance and a common expectation that it would produce certain results, what they disguised was the profound disagreement about what these results would be. Whether strategically used or fomented (as some have suggested) or instead genuine (as others have sustained), this disagreement was not necessarily due to the incapacity to dialogue or to simple communicative errors. Neither should miscommunication be attributed to one side lacking agency and the other having it all, or to the absence of mutual understanding or intelligibility. Instead, what was clearly at play was disagreement regarding the precise consequences of pacts. This diverse understanding did not necessarily hinge on what was said and what was done. It was anchored in deep-rooted conventions regarding the effects of certain things. Unless we understand how these normative structures operated, we will fail to grasp what transpired in the American interior. We will only see senseless movement.

NOTES

1 On the Spanish-Portuguese rivalry in the Americas and relations with Indians, see Tamar Herzog, *Frontiers of Possession: Spain and Portugal in Europe and the Americas* (Cambridge, MA: Harvard University Press, 2015).

2 This was the term contemporary documents used. However, by the mid-seventeenth century, almost all native groups had experienced at least some exposure to things European. Not completely "untouched," nor integrated in a colonial world, the so-called not-yet-domesticated Indians hovered between Spain and Portugal, colonialism and independence: Chiara Vengelista, "Los Guaikurú, españoles y portugueses en una región de frontera: Mato Grosso, 1770–1830," *Boletín del Instituto de Historia Argentina y Americana "Dr. Emilio Ravignani,"* 3rd serie, 8 (1993): 55–76; and Elisa Frühauf Garcia, *As diversas formas de ser índio. Políticas indígenas e políticas indigenistas no extremo sul da América portuguesa* (Rio de Janeiro: Arquivo Nacional, 2009).

3 Garcia, *As diversas formas,* 227–28 and 235–36.

4 Richard White, *The Middle Ground: Indians, Empires, and Republics in the Great Lakes Region, 1650–1815* (Cambridge: Cambridge University Press, 1991); James H. Merrel, "'The Customs of Our Country': Indians and Colonists in Early America," in Bernard Bailyn and Philip D. Morgan, eds., *Strangers within the Realm: Cultural Margins of the First British Empire* (Chapel Hill: University of North Carolina Press, 1991), 117–56; Juliana Barr, *Peace Came in the Form of a Woman: Indians and Spaniards in the Texas Borderlands* (Chapel Hill: University of North Carolina Press, 2007), 2–6, and 27–68; Carlos Lázaro Ávila, "Conquista, control y convicción: El papel de los parlamentos indígenas en México, el Chaco y Norteamérica," *Revista de Indias* 59 (217) (1999): 645–73; and Ned Blackhawk, *Violence over the Land: Indians and Empires in the Early American West* (Cambridge, MA: Harvard University Press, 2006).

5 Chantal Cramaussel, "Consideraciones sobre el papel de los gentiles en la Nueva Vizcaya del siglo XVII," in Christophe Giudicelli, ed., *Fronteras movedizas. Clasificaciones coloniales y dinámicas socioculturales en las fronteras americanas* (Mexico: CEMCA, 2010), 173–83, 175–79; and Christophe Giudicelli, "'¿Naciones de enemigos?' La identificación de los indios rebeldes en la Nueva Vizcaya (siglo XVII)," in Salvador Bernabéu Albert, coord., *El gran norte mexicano. Indios, misioneros y pobladores entre el mito y la historia* (Seville: SCIC, 2009), 27–57.

6 Alida C. Metcalf, "The Entradas of Bahia of the Sixteenth Century," *Americas* 16 (3) (2005): 373–400, 388–92; and Francismar Alex Lopes de Carvalho, "Lealdades negociadas: povos indígenas e a expansão dos impérios ibéricos nas regiões centrais da América do sul (segunda metade do século XVIII)." PhD dissertation, Universidade de São Paulo, 2012. Also see Jenny Hale Pulsipher, *Subjects unto the Same King: Indians, English, and the Contest for Authority in Colonial New England* (Philadelphia: University of Pennsylvania Press, 2005); and Cécile Carayon, "Beyond Words: Nonverbal Communication, Performance, and Acculturation in the Early French-Indian Atlantic (1500–1701)." PhD dissertation, College of William and Mary, 2010.

7 Tamar Herzog, "Colonial Law: Early Modern Normativity in Spanish America," in Jörg Alejandro Tellkamp, ed., *A Companion to Early Modern Iberian Imperial Political and Social Thought* (Leiden: Brill, forthcoming).

8 Herzog, *Frontiers of Possession*; and Tamar Herzog, *Defining Nations: Immigrants and Citizens in Early Modern Spain and Spanish America* (New Haven, CT: Yale University Press, 2003).

9 Lauren Benton, "In Defense of Ignorance: Frameworks for Legal Politics in the Atlantic World," in this volume.

10 Thomas Duve, "Grenzenlose Räume," *Rechtsgeschichte–Legal History* 23 (2015): 307–8.

11 For "cultivated ambiguity," see Lauren Benton chapter, this volume.

12 Letter of João Pereira Caldas, Barcellos 12.8.1787, Arquivo Histórico Ultramarino, Lisbon (henceforth ahu) acl_cu_ 020, cx. 13, d. 499.

13 Jean de Léry, *History of a Voyage to the Land of Brazil*, Janet Whatley trans. and introduction (Berkeley: University of California Press, 1990), 164, 168–69, 171, and 178–87. Among the historians and anthropologists who study such practices are Katherine A. Hermes, "The Law of Native Americans, to 1815," in Michael Grossberg and Christopher Tomlins, eds., *The Cambridge History of Law in America*. Vol. 1, *Early America (1580–1815)* (Cambridge: Cambridge University Press, 2008), 32–62, 39–40, 44, and 47; Barr, *Peace Came in the Form of a Woman*, 31–34; and Pulsipher, *Subjects unto the Same King*, 10.

14 Eduardo Viveiros de Castro, *The Inconsistency of the Indian Soul: The Encounter of Catholics and Cannibals in 16th-century Brazil*, Gregory Duff Morton, trans. (Chicago: Prickly Paradigm Press, 2011).

15 Mauricio de Heriarte, *Descripção do estado do Maranhão, Pará, Corupá e Rio das Amazonas* (Vienna: Gerold, 1874 [1662]), 20 and 35.

16 Diogo de Mendonça Corte Real to Francisco Xavier de Mendonça Furtado, Lisbon, 1.6.1756, ahu_acl_cu_020, cx.1, d. 44; information sent by Felipe Sturm, Boca Rio Tacucu 19.11.1775, ahu_acl_cu_013, cx.75, d.6279; João Pereira Caldas to Martinho de Melo e Castro, Barcelos, 21.6.1785, ahu_acl_cu_020, cx.9, d. 380; and Barcelos, 27.9.1787, ahu_acl_cu_020, cx. 13, d. 499. The analysis included in Pulsipher, *Subjects unto the Same King* (for example, p. 10) and Blackhawk, *Violence over the Land*, p. 62, suggests that such repetitive narratives were common also in Spanish and Anglo-America.

17 "Pasaporte del capitán general de Matogroso Joan de Albuquerque de Mello Pereira e Cáceres," 29.7.1791, Archivo Histórico Nacional, Madrid (hereafter AHN), Estado 4548.

18 On how gestures evolved into a "corpus of more or less standardized and mutually intelligible signs" see Carayon, "Beyond Words."

19 On European efforts to classify, see Lidia R. Nacuzzi, "Los cacicazgos del siglo XVIII en ámbitos de frontera de Pampa-Patagonia y el Chaco," in Mónica Quijada, ed., *De los Cacicazgos a la ciudadanía. Sistemas políticos en la frontera, Río de la Plata, Siglos XVIII–XX* (Berlin: Gebr. Mann Verlag, 2001), 23–77, 24, and 33; and Guillermo Wilde, "Orden y ambigüedad en la formación territorial del Río de la Plata a fines del siglo XVIII," *Horizontes antropológicos* 9 (19) (2003): 105–35, 113–15.

20 This confusion was also clear in chronicles such as Heriarte, *Descripção do estado do Maranhão*, which pointed out the numerous nations living in the various parts of the Amazon and the difficulty in identifying them. Heriarte also vacillated as to who led such groups. On the one hand, he argued that natives were divided by families and headed by a pater familias, but he also referred to *principais* who headed families but were also kings, or territorial rulers. Somewhat similar was the impression of Hans Staden, who, writing on the Tupi in the 1550s, argued that each hut had its own chief or king yet all chiefs belonged to one family with one common authority: Hans Staden, *The True History of His Captivity, 1557*, Malcolm Letts ed. and trans. (London: Routledge, 1928), 140 (part 2, chapter 12).

21 Almir Diniz de Carvalho Júnior, "Índios cristãos. A conversão dos gentios na Amazônia portuguesa (1653–1769)." PhD dissertation, História, Universidade Estadual de Campinas, 2005, 123–50 and 215–36. On the similar experience of the English: April Lee Hatfueld, "Spanish Colonization: Literature, Powhatan Geographies, and English Perceptions of Tsenacommacah/Virginia," *Journal of Southern History* 69 (2) (2003): 245–82, 248–49, and 260–62.

22 Ofício do governador e capitão geral de Goiás Tristão da Cunha Meneses ao secretário de estado da marinha e ultramar Martinho de Melo e Castro, Vila boa, 28.8.1787, ahu_acl_cu_008, cx. 36, d. 2242.

23 Francisco Coelho de Carvalho to the king, 28.2.1624, ahu_acl_cu_009, cx.1, d. 79 and "Carta Patente de principal," given by Francisco Xavier de Mendonça Furtado on 6.10.1752, petitions of Ignacio Coelho, Francisco de Souza de Menezes and Luís de Miranda to the king, all three dated 15.3.1755, and Sebastião José de Carvalho e Mello to the Conselho Ultramarino, 15.3.1755, all cited in Mauro Cezar Coelho, "De guerreiro a principal: integração das chefias indígenas à estrutura de poder colonial, sob o Diretório dos índios (1758–1798)," in *Actas do congresso internacional "Espaço Atlântico de Antigo Regime: Poderes e Sociedades—Lisboa 2 a 5 Novembro de 2005*, 6. Available at www.cvc.instituto-camoes.pt/eaar/coloquio /communicades/mauro_cezar_coelho.pdf. Also see Nádia Farage, *As muralhas dos sertões. Os povos indígenas no rio Branco e a colonização* (São Paulo: Paz e Terra, 1991), 160–63 and 170; and Garcia, *As diversas formas*, 48–49, 78–80, and 248–251.

24 These issues were also explored in Neil L. Whitehead, "Tribes Make States and States Make Tribes: Warfare and the Creation of Colonial Tribes and States in Northeastern South America," in R. Brian Ferguson and Neil L. Whitehead, eds., *War in the Tribal Zone: Expanding States and Indigenous Warfare* (Santa Fe, NM: School of American Research Press, 1992), 127–50; Guillaume Boccara, "Antropología política en los márgenes del Nuevo Mundo. Categorías coloniales, tipologías antropológicas y producción de la diferencia," in Christophe Giudicelli, ed., *Fronteras movedizas. Clasificaciones coloniales y dinámicas socioculturales en las fronteras americanas* (México: CEMCA, 2010), 103–35, on 119–20; Giudicelli, "'¿Naciones de enemigos?'"; Alexandra V. Roth, "The Xebero 'indios amigos'? Their Part in the Ancient Province of Mainas," in María Susana Cipolletti, ed., *Resistencia y adaptación nativas en las tierras bajas latinoamericanas*

(Quito: Abya-Yala, 1997), 107–22; Garcia, *As diversas formas*, 138–39 and 227–65; and Pedro Puntoni, *A guerra dos bárbaros. Povos indígenas e a colonização do sertão nordeste do Brasil, 1760–1720* (São Paulo: Universidade de São Paulo, 2000), 60–61, 68–69, and 77.

25 Luís Antônio de Sousa to Martinho de Melo e Castro, São Paulo, 21.4.1771, ahu_acl_cu_023–01, Cx. 27, D. 2553.

26 Ofício do governador e capitão geral da capitania de Mato Grosso Luís de Albuquerque de Melo Pereira e Cáceres ao secretário de estado da marinha e ultramar Martinho de Melo e Castro, Vila Bela, 9.9.1791, ahu_acl_cu_010, cx. 28, d. 1617.

27 *Só por ações se percebe pretenderem descer*: The director of Vila de Serpa in a letter dated 24.9.1786 in "Notícias da voluntária redução de paz da feroz nação do gentio Mura nos anos de 1784, 1785 e 1786," *Boletim de Pesquisa da CEDEAM* 3 (5) (1984): 17–87, 84–85.

28 João Felipe Bettendorff, *Crônica da missão dos padres da Companhia de Jesus no Estado do Maranhão* (Imperatriz, MA: Ética, 2008), 287. Historians have also suggested that singing and dancing served to communicate with natives: Metcalf, "The Entradas of Bahia," 388.

29 Ofício do governador e capitão geral da capitania de Mato Grosso Luís de Albuquerque de Melo Pereira e Cáceres ao secretário de estado da marinha e ultramar Martinho de Melo e Castro, Fortaleza da Conceição, 25.1.1774, ahu_acl_cu_10, cx. 17, d. 1060.

30 Bettendorff, *Crônica da missão*, 95. On the use of the cross in similar situations see Barr, *Peace Came in the Form of a Woman*, 38–42; and Blackhawk, *Violence over the Land*, 62.

31 According to Jean de Léry, who interacted with the Tupinamba Indians of Brazil in the 1550s, they were suspicious of European writing and considered it witchcraft: Léry, *History of a Voyage*, 134–35.

32 Bettendorff, *Crônica da missão*, 123–27. Presented as "undomesticated" and "savage," these natives nevertheless obviously had some (even if limited) contact with Europeans.

33 João Martins Barroso to Luís Antônio de Sousa, Iguatemi, 30.1.1771, ahu_acl_cu_023–01, cx. 27, d. 2553.

34 On the dialogue between natives and Spaniards regarding the meaning of the cross, see William B. Taylor, "Placing the Cross in Colonial Mexico," *Americas* 69 (2) (2012): 145–78, mainly 150–57.

35 João Martins Barroso to Luís Antônio de Sousa, Iguatemi, 30.1.1771, ahu_acl_cu_023–01, cx. 27, d. 2553.

36 On these questions Herzog, *Frontiers of Possession*.

37 According to Grotius, "[I]f a person knows his property to be in the possession of another, and allows it to remain so for a length of time, without asserting his claim, unless there appear sufficient reasons for his silence, he is construed to have entirely abandoned all pretentious to the same": Hugo Grotius, *On the Law of War and Peace*, trans. A. C. Campbell (London: Boothroyd, 1814 [1625]),

book 2, chapter 4, numbers 3 and 5. The Portuguese followed such understandings that equated the lack of protest with agreement: Arquivo Provincial Estado do Pará, Belém do Pará, Brazil (APEP), Cod. 122, Doc.1, 1r; and "Instrução que ao General Luiz Albuquerque de Mello Pereira e Cáceres deixou seu Antecessor Luiz Pinto de Souza Coutinho," Vila Bela, 24.12.1772, Arquivo Público do Estado de Mato Grosso, Cuiabá, Brazil (APMG), Livro C–03, Doc. 03, fols. 34v–53, on fol. 48v.

38 "Notícias da voluntária redução," for example, Manoel José Valladão comandante do destacamento do lugar de Santo António do Maripi, no rio Jupurá to João Pereira Caldas, 12.7.1781 and 15.1.1785, 17–18 and 20–22; João Baptista Mandel to João Pereira Caldas, Ega, 22.1.1785, 22–23; João Pereira Caldas to João Baptista Mardel, Barcellos, 4.2.1785, 23–25; João Baptista Mardel to João Pereira Caldas, Ega, 15.3.1775 25–29; and João Baptista Mardel to João Pereira Caldas, Nogueira, 1.6.1785, 32–41. On the contacts with the Muras in 1785–1789, see, for example, ahu_acl_cu_ 020, cx.9, d. 380, cx. 12, d. 468, cx. 13, d. 499, cx. 15, d. 558.

39 Other Indigenous groups might have reacted similarly: Lía Quarleri, *Rebelión y guerra en las fronteras del Plata. Guaraníes, jesuitas e imperios coloniales* (México: Fondo de Cultura Económica, 2009), 116–19; David J. Weber, *Bárbaros: Spaniards and Their Savages in the Age of Enlightenment* (New Haven, CT: Yale University Press, 2005), 17 and 247; and Wilde, "Orden y ambigüedad," 120–22.

40 Letter of João Pereira Caldas to Martinho de Melo e Castro, Barcelos, 19.1.1782, ahu_acl_cu_ 020, cx.4, d. 238.

41 Henrique João Wilckens, "Diário da viagem ao Jupurá, 23.2.1781," in Marta Rosa Amoroso and Nádia Farage, eds., *Relatos da fronteira amazônica no século XVIII. Documentos de Henrique João Wilckens e Alesandre Rodrigues Ferreira* (São Paulo: USP, 1994), 19–46, 28–29.

42 Bettendorff, *Crônica da missão*, 287.

43 Letter of Gomes Freire de Andrade to Sebastião Jose de Carvalho e Melo, Rio Grande de São Pedro, 14.12.1755, ahu_acl_cu_ 059, cx.1, d.90.

44 Letter of João Manuel de Melo to Francisco Xavier de Mendonça Furtado, Vila Boa, 7.6.1764, ahu_acl_cu_ 008, cx. 20, d. 1220. Also see Wilde, "Orden y ambigüedad," 122–23.

45 Rafael Chabouleyron and Vanice Siqueira de Melo, "Indios, engenhos e currais na fronteira oriental do estado do Maranhão e Pará (século XVII)," in Márcia Motta, José Vicente Serrão, and Marina Machado, eds., *Em terras lusas: Conflitos e fronteiras no Império Português* (Rio de Janeiro: Universidade Federal Fluminense, 2013), 231–59, 245–46.

46 João Martins Barroso to Luís Antônio de Sousa, Iguatemi, 30.1.1771, ahu_acl_cu_023–01, cx. 27, d. 2553.

47 "Notícias da voluntária redução."

48 Alexandre Rodrigues Ferreira, "Tratado histórico do Rio Branco, 1786," in Marta Rosa Amoroso and Nádia Farage, eds., *Relatos da fronteira amazônica no século*

XVIII. Documentos de Henrique João Wilckens e Alexandre Rodrigues Ferreira (São Paulo: USP, 1994), 97–134, 115–17.

49 Jesuits, for example, complained in the 1730s that natives only obeyed "the language of gifts": Peter Downes, "Jesuitas en la Amazonía: experiencias de Brasil y Quito," in José Jesús Hernández Palomo and Rodrigo Moreno Jeria, coord., *La Misión y los jesuitas en la América española, 1566–1767: cambios y permanencias* (Seville: Escuela de Estudios Hispanoamericanos, 2005), 151–86, on 153–55.

50 Consulta of the Conselho Ultramarino, Lisbon, 12.2.1716, ahu_acl_cu_ 013, cx.6, d.515; and sentencia cível movida pelo procurador geral dos índios. . . . Belém, 28.4.1737, ahu_acl_cu_ 013, cx.20, d.1842. Also see certidão de justificação do tabelião do público judicial, Francisco António de Lira Barros, Belém, 26.10.1742, ahu_acl_cu_ 013, cx.25, d.2330.

51 Letter of the governor of Maranhão e Pará João de Abreu Castelo Branco, Pará, 16.1.1746, ahu_acl_cu_ 013, cx.28, d. 2676.

52 Requerimento do índio principal da aldeia de Mortigura, before 9.3.1757, ahu_acl_cu_ 013, cx.42, d. 3841. A particularly energetic strand of such demands was made by Indigenous groups in the aftermaths of the Treaty of Madrid (1750), which required evacuating seven missions from the land that Spain was to hand over to Portugal: Quarleri, *Rebelión y guerra*, 153–92.

53 Letter of the governor of Maranhão Inácio Coelho da Silva para to the prince regent, Pará 20.4.1679, ahu_acl_cu_013, cx.2, d.178.

54 Letter of João Pereira Caldas to Martinho de Melo e Castro, Barcelos, 19.1.1782, ahu_acl_cu_ 020, cx.4, d. 238. On how and why these perceptions developed, see de Castro, *The Inconsistency of the Indian Soul*.

55 Bettendorff, *Crônica da missão*, 125. The original version reads,

[Q]ue as perguntas e as práticas que o padre lhes fazia que as fizesse aos portugueses e não a eles, porque eles sempre foram fiéis a El-Rei e o reconheceram por seu senhor desde o principio dessa conquista, que sempre foram amigos e servidores dos portugueses e que se essa amizade e obediência se quebrou e interrompeu fora por parte dos portugueses e não pela sua, e assim os portugueses eram os que agora haviam de fazer ou refazer as suas promessas, pois as tinham quebrando tantas vezes, e não ele e os seus, que sempre as guardaram.

56 Letter of the governor of Maranhão, Grão Pará e Rio Negro Pedro César de Meneses to the prince regent, Belém 20.7.1673, ahu_acl_cu_013, cx.2, d.150.

3

Defending and Defrauding the Indians

John Wompas, Legal Hybridity, and the Sale of Indian Land

JENNY HALE PULSIPHER

When the new Indian history emerged a generation ago, Francis Jennings and other writers portrayed Indians as victims of European ideologies that justified seizing land by conquest, royal grant, the doctrine of *vacuum domicilium*, or the use of legal trickery, taking advantage of Native ignorance of the subtleties of English law.[1] While that is still the dominant story line in popular history and contemporary politics, the scholarly literature has long since acknowledged that Native and English land laws and practices became mutually intelligible fairly soon after contact and that the English usually paid Indians for their land, albeit very little.[2] While scholars recognize that Indians and English did not long remain in ignorance of each other's land ways, a great deal more work remains to be done to elaborate how mutual intelligibility emerged over time and what its consequences were for both English and Indians. In this essay I trace the development of legal intelligibility from an initial phase of "creative misunderstanding" to a time when both Natives and English effectively used legal hybridity, drawing on each other's land ways to legitimize purchases of Native land and defend their possession. While the use of legal hybridity was effective for a time, its benefit to Indians was limited by the growing English population and political power, which ensured that the English legal system was dominant almost from the start of colonization. Wielding the tool of legal hybridity within that system was a two-edged sword that could be used by Natives and English not only to defend land but also to defraud each other. This essay examines the legal hybridity of seventeenth-century New England land sales through a number of cases, but chiefly through the experience of one particular actor, John Wompas, a Nipmuc Indian, sometime Harvard student, transatlantic sailor, and land speculator who used the tools of both cultures to sell Indian land.

John Wompas was born around 1640 to Christian Indian parents who placed him in an English home in his early adolescence, hoping that thereby he would "come to know God."[3] After gaining proficiency in English, Wompas attended Roxbury Grammar School, then Cambridge Grammar School, and finally became one of a handful of Native scholars to attend Harvard College. John entered the college in 1665 but left by 1668, abandoning his study of Latin and Greek in favor of a career as a sailor and land speculator. Wompas's first foray into Indian land sales occurred in the late 1650s, a full generation after English settlement of New England. Much had changed in the land market by that time; a review of initial Native and English understandings of land tenure helps set the groundwork for those later changes.

English and Indian Patterns of Land Tenure

Before the English arrived on the coast of Massachusetts, the Algonquian-speaking Indians of the region, including the Wampanoag, Narragansett, Massachusett, Nipmuc, Mohegan, Pequot, and Pennacook, claimed specific tracts of land, with distinct, recognized boundaries. Within these boundaries, Indian groups used different parcels of land at different times of the year, shifting locations at times of planting, fishing, hunting, and harvest.[4] The sachems, or Native leaders, had the right to distribute land within their bounds, but this right was constrained by the traditional use a particular family made of a parcel of land. While particular Indians had the right to use the land, some uses, such as access to hunting grounds, were shared with other Natives. Having the traditional right to use a particular piece of land did not confer the right to alienate that land, something that required the sachem's consent. Likewise, sachems could not give away land traditionally used by specific tribe members without their support for that action, as well as the consent of the elders of the tribe. Ignoring the wishes of either of these groups would alienate them, undermining the sachem's authority.[5]

The English came to the New World with different conceptions of land tenure and different expectations about what justified its possession. Among the English, land was commonly held in fee simple absolute, meaning that the owner of the land had the right to all of its uses as well as the right to alienate it by sale, bequest, or donation. It was also common among the English for a single person to hold title to land, rather than the multiple claimants in Native society. When land owners sold a piece of land, they lost all rights to plant, build, hunt, or use any resources on that land.[6] Colonists newly arrived on the shores of Massachusetts could draw on a number of justifications for claiming Indian land, including royal grant, natural law as embodied in legal principles such as *terra nullius* or *vacuum domicilium*, and God's commandment to Adam to "replenish the earth." By this understanding of natural law, no one had the right to unused land; the earth belonged to those who would subdue and improve it by planting crops, grazing livestock, and building houses and barns. In the English view, which was blind to the land uses of the Indians, most Indian land was unimproved and therefore free for the taking.[7] While many English would argue that natural law or royal grants were sufficient justification to claim land, in actual practice the colonists drew on as many justifications as they could to defend their right to land. These included right by conquest, which the English used in the aftermath of the Pequot War of 1637–38, and "the invitation of the Indians," which meant voluntary transfer of land by gift or sale.[8]

Contact, Preconceptions, and "Creative Misunderstanding"

When the English arrived to settle Plymouth and Massachusetts Bay, the Wampanoag and Massachusett Indians gave them land to build on. In return, the English gave the Indians some small items such as English peas, coats, and other trade goods.[9] Both societies had long traditions of gift giving as a means of establishing reciprocal relationships and conferring obligations, but those traditions depended on accurate understanding of the relative status, needs, and desires of the parties to the exchange. Such understanding was rare in initial interactions between Indians and English.[10] As a result, both parties saw their initial exchanges differently. The English believed that Providence had cleared the Indians from the land through disease, making way for their settlement. They also believed that the items they gave to the Indians constituted payment for the land the Indians had given them.[11] For their part, the Indians probably perceived their gift of land as a way of bringing the English into their sphere of authority. By accepting the land, the English implicitly accepted a relationship of submission to their neighbor Indians. Sachems, who held the power to distribute land, expected those who received land to pay regular tribute in acknowledgment of the sachems' authority. Indeed, some Indian sellers later built requirements into English payments that seemed designed to maintain such a tribute pattern. For instance, in 1640 the English, who had paid twenty-three pounds for the land on which Watertown and Cambridge were built, accepted the Indian stipulation that "Cambridge is to give Squa Sachem a coate every winter while shee liveth."[12] On the peripheries of New England, where Native power remained substantial much longer than it did in Massachusetts Bay, Indians continued to expect—and receive—tribute from the English who settled their land well into the 1680s.[13]

In the earliest years of English settlement, the relative equality of the Indian and English populations, and the benefit each saw in maintaining a relationship with the other, pushed them toward a mutual tolerance of differences that Richard White and other scholars have characterized as "creative misunderstanding."[14] The Indians could assume that English gifts were tribute, while the English could consider them payment for land. The Indians could assume that they had granted usufruct use of their lands to the English, and the English could assume that the land was theirs and that the Indians would move on once it got too crowded for comfort. Benefits for the English in tolerating Native land ways included safety and the possibility of military and trade relationships with their Indian neighbors. The Indians in the areas where the English settled hoped for similar benefits. Just four years before the Plymouth English arrived, the coastal Indians were devastated by an epidemic that killed up to 90 percent of their people. The Narragansett Indians to the southwest escaped the disease and were powerfully threatening to the coastal Wompanoag and Massachusett. For them, having the English nearby and obligated to them was a boon at a time of real crisis.[15]

Initially, making gifts of land was more beneficial than burdensome to the Indians. Much of the land that had formerly been the traditional property of particular Native persons or families was vacated by death from European diseases, so securing other Natives' consent to give land to the English was probably not difficult, especially considering the benefits the Indians expected from English proximity. Of course, because the Indians gave the land according to their own land ways, they were only giving the English the right to use the land—to plant and build on it.[16] They kept their own rights to plant and build on part of the land, and to use all of the land for other traditional uses. Shared use of the land was what made the gift useful to the Indians: the English would be nearby for trade and military assistance.

Wittingly or not, the English signaled conformity with Native land ways by accepting the gift of land but allowing the Indians to continue living, planting, fishing, and hunting on it.[17] The English also conformed to Native land ways by giving the Indian sachems gifts that the Natives probably viewed as tribute. During the years that Indians retained power relative to the English, it made sense for the English to tolerate shared use of land and to acknowledge Native land ways. It smoothed relations between groups and, particularly where the English were a minority, lent legitimacy to their land transactions. The same held true for the Indians, who also wanted their land exchanges to be recognized by both the English and their own people. Walter Woodward noted that John Winthrop Jr. honored Native land ways by acknowledging multiple claimants to Native land, obtaining the signed consent of all claimants and paying them for it, and repeating the process if additional claimants showed up days or even years later. Such efforts acknowledged Native expectations that both sachems' and followers' consent was needed to sell land, and attention to Native as well as English land ways established "cross-cultural authority" for land sales.[18]

By observing both Native and English land transfer ceremonies, colonists and Natives engaged in a form of legal hybridity, layering two traditions of legal land transfer.[19] An example of a public display of this legal hybridity appears in a 1643 transaction in which the sachem Tacomus gave possession of a parcel of land "by earth and grass delivered [to] sd Stephen Day," who was acting for Governor John Winthrop of Massachusetts Bay Colony. This physical transfer of a bit of earth and grass followed the archaic pattern of an English "turf and twig" or livery of seisin ceremony, which the colonists may have suggested because of its effectiveness in visually conveying the idea of land transfer. Second, Tacomus carried out what appeared to be a Native land transfer ceremony. He "cause[d] his eldest Son to lye or kneele down upon the ground and himselfe made his marke or signe on the Deed upon his Sons back and then he put himselfe in the same posture and caused his sd. Son to signe the same Deed upon his back and also caused his other Sons successively to do the like upon one anothers backs, the meaning whereof the deponent understood was that none of them might have any pretence of right by succession to disturb or molest sd mr Winthrop or his Children."[20] At least, that is what the English hoped the ceremony meant.

In his first recorded transaction involving Indian land, the Nipmuc Indian John Wompas similarly went to great lengths to observe both Indian and English land exchange practices, thereby ensuring that the sale would be recognized by both cultures. In 1656, Wompas went looking for a Connecticut Indian sachem named Romanock, the father of his long-time Roxbury neighbor Ann Prask, who had been enslaved to an English family since her capture in the Pequot War. As a sachem, Romanock had authority within Native culture to distribute land, a right that both Indians and English acknowledged. To lend added legitimacy to this conveyance of land, Wompas arranged for an Englishman, Thomas Minor, to travel seventy miles to witness the deed. Minor, a leading citizen of Connecticut Colony and a frequent deputy to the General Court, could testify that Romanock had tranferred title to his land in a manner binding under English law. Minor later testified that he saw Prask "take possession" of Romanock's land and witnessed Romanock carry out a traditional English "turf and twig" ceremony demonstrating his ownership of the land and transferring that possession to another: he "cut a stake, drove it into a hole, said, 'Mee narrowe,' &c . . . [and] he cut up a turf, and said, 'Mee narrowe,' &c."[21] Even as early as 1660, the turf and twig ceremony was considered archaic, demonstrating Romanock's—or Wompas's—determination to use every English tool available to underline the validity of the title.[22] Six months after Romanock transferred his land to his daughter Prask, John Wompas married her before an English magistrate, thus securing title of the land to himself under the English practice of coverture. Wompas would follow a similar pattern of using his Native identity and connections to obtain Indian land, then relying on English law and traditional practice to secure it in his later land sales, shifting from one to the other, or combining aspects of each as they suited his purposes. Although he was perfectly capable of signing his full name (in English or Latin), he adopted a symbol for his mark, perhaps as a way of identifying himself with Natives who used pictographs on English land deeds rather than alphabetic signatures. He obtained and registered deeds with English officials, and marked the bounds of his land in the English manner by carving a "J W" into trees, much as Thomas Minor did on his own land.[23]

The practice of legal hybridity—simultaneously or interchangeably drawing from Native and English land ways—was beneficial to both Indians and English. It smoothed relations between the two peoples by demonstrating a willingness to tolerate differences. But the use of legal hybridity is not evidence that Indians and English considered each other's land ways equally valid. The dramatic depopulation that preceded English settlement and the continued decline in Native power afterwards ensured that the English legal system would be dominant almost immediately, which forced Indians to adapt to it. Instead, legal hybridity was a practical strategy: it ensured that land transactions would be intelligible to both English and Indians, thus increasing the likelihood that land sales would be accepted by both peoples.

The Impact of English Dominance on Land Practices

Had English and Indian power remained relatively equal, they might have continued to tolerate each other's practices, ignoring conflicting interpretations because of the benefits each gained from the other. But power did not remain equal. The balance tipped toward the English almost immediately because of the dual factors of explosive population growth among the English and continued decline from European diseases among the Indians. The expanding English population created pressure on lands shared by Indians and English, making it increasingly difficult to avoid conflict over their differing uses of the land.

English grants of land proved to be an enormous wedge opening the door to Indian land sales. Colonial New England governments extended their authority over Indians as well as English. The conquest of Indians in the Pequot and King Philip's Wars and the submission of tribes such as the Massachusett, Wampanoag, and Nipmuc to English governments solidified that authority, as did colony charters, which gave English governments authority to grant land to English colonists. The New England colonies were jealous of their authority, and when they heard of people—Indian or English—selling Indian land without their permission, they usually voided such sales.[24] But they were not at all reluctant to give grants—usually of about nine miles square of land—to any group of people who intended to settle a plantation. The grants did not confer title. Colonists were still expected to treat with the Indians about payment for the lands. But grants often preceded purchase, and English efforts to lay out lots and even begin to build houses and barns effectually forced Indians to agree to sell their lands. Once the English had possession, it was very hard for the Indians to refuse to sell.

The establishment of an English plantation at Quinsigamog (Worcester) illustrates that process. The General Court granted land to establish an English plantation near Quinsigamog Pond in 1667. The settlement was slowed by the existence of conflicting claims on the land, but by the spring of 1674, these conflicts were resolved to the point that the plantation committee began laying out lots, planting crops, and even constructing some buildings. Not until July 1674 did the committee treat with Indians to purchase the land, and although their agreement specified that payment would be completed within three months, it was not actually delivered until August 1676. This was not "unimproved" Indian land. Early records of the English settlement at Quinsigamog frequently mention the "Indian broken up lands," or planting fields, and the plantation committee itself wrote of the need to obtain title from the Indians, "then numerous in the vicinity, that neighbors so dangerous and powerful might be propitiated."[25] English surveyors, traders, planters, and builders had been present at Quinsigamog to some degree for over a decade, and, by the time payment was finally made, King Philip's War had cut like a scythe through the Native population. By 1677 there was no question of resisting sale, merely of how much the Indians would be paid.[26]

Much has been made of the fact that early English settlers claimed the right to take Indian land without paying for it, using such justifications as the king's royal grant, the right to land by conquest, and the right to land under the legal doctrine of *vacuum domicilium*. While these arguments did provide justification for seizing Indian land, in actual practice the English almost always paid for the land, even the lands they obtained by conquest.[27] But while the English almost always paid the Indians, they paid very little, often expecting to secure absolute title for the price one might pay for a year's tribute.[28]

The most destructive element in the long history of Indian land sales was the English ability to set land prices that were far too low to sustain a Native population increasingly dependent on English goods and unable to continue their traditional land uses in the face of English expansion.[29] The settlers of early New England may have had statutes informed by Christian ethics and democratically expansive concepts of natural law, but they were also hard-headed businessmen, willing to pay as little as the market would bear. Colonist Nathaniel Saltonstall illustrated this approach in his narrative of King Philip's War. Defending Plymouth Colony against the implication that they had provoked the war by taking Native lands, he declared, "The English took not a Foot of Land from the Indians, but Bought all, and although they bought for an inconsiderable Value; yet they did Buy it."[30] Payments for Native land could be ridiculously low. In the first settlement period, payments typically consisted of a collection of trade goods. Later, payments were made in English pounds, or their equivalent in goods. As late as 1670, Joan, the daughter of Skatery Gusset of Casco Bay, sold four hundred acres of land to the Englishman Anthony Brackett for twenty shillings, or one pound. The price for an acre of unimproved land between two Englishmen was closer to a pound for four acres—one hundred times what Anthony Brackett paid Joan for her land.[31]

While the initial reason for such "inconsiderable" payments may have been the creative misunderstanding that allowed Indians to construe English coats and cloth as tribute and the English to consider it payment, the pattern of token payments remained throughout the seventeenth century, with few exceptions. Some scholars have argued that the low payments reflected the fact that Indian land was "unimproved," so lower in value than land sold between English buyers.[32] However, evidence suggests that even unimproved land sold for much higher prices between Englishmen than equivalent land sold to the English by Indians. English attitudes toward Indians—the tendency to consider them "barbarous" and "uncivilized"—is a more compelling explanation for the low prices Englishmen offered for Native land. Colonists persisted in believing that the Indians had no need for the sums that land sales between two English buyers typically commanded. English buyers needed payments that would sustain a "civilized" lifestyle, one replete with houses, barns, plows, domestic animals, pillows, bolsters, bedsteads, linens, plates, knives, spoons, undergarments, clothing, stockings, shoes, books, and candles to read them by. Indians, in the eyes of most English, were uncivilized. They did not need or want most of these things, so it followed that they did not need large sums of money. This attitude—an inability to consider Native needs as equivalent to English needs—suggests that most English were unable to conceive of the Indians as being like themselves.[33] Englishmen would not pay Indians more than what they considered a "fair" price, and that price was much, much lower for the lands of "barbarous" Natives than for lands sold between Englishmen.

By the time the English had enough power to impose their ideas of absolute sale on the Indians, the Indians lacked the power to insist on being paid the full value of their land. An example of this appears in a 1646 exchange between the Wampanoag sachem Massasoit and a group of Englishmen from Rhode Island. The Englishmen had been enjoying grazing privileges on the sachem's land for a number of years before they decided to secure the land by purchase. They offered Massasoit a payment of fifteen fathom of wampum for the land, but he requested more in English goods. The English went to fetch the wampum and goods and presented them to the sachem, but he requested still more. When the English refused, Massasoit attempted to return all the items the English had given him, rejecting the bargain. The Rhode Islanders refused to either accept the return or pay more for the land, declaring that they "were not willing to wrong our country in granting his desire of foure coats, and so unreasonably to raise ye price of such parcells of land in this barbarous wilderness." Despite the sachem's resistance, they proclaimed the land sold to the town of Providence "according to a faire and righteous bargaine," as determined by themselves.[34] This exchange illustrates the fact that, while the English were willing to pay for Indian land—even made a point of doing so—they were not willing to pay prices that would be considered fair between two English buyers.

John Wompas's long dwelling with and education among the English gave him a first-hand view of how land was exchanged among the English and what it was worth. It is very clear from his transactions that he believed that the Indians were paid far too little for their land, and he demanded much more. By his own report, Wompas sold a portion of the land his wife inherited from Romanock for 530 pounds, by far the largest sum paid to an Indian for land in seventeenth-century New England.[35]

If Wompas was truly able to command such a sum—the equivalent of two or three English householders' entire estates—it was a rare occurrence. Over time, as Native power continued to wane, even the culturally savvy Wompas would receive less and less for his land sales.

Indian Legal Strategies to Preserve and Profit from Their Land

In response to the growing pressure of English expansion and the diminishing ability of the Indians to maintain their traditional way of life on a shrinking land base, Indians adopted strategies of legal hybridity, using both Indian and English practices to preserve or profit from their land. One such strategy was to make Native assumptions about land tenure explicit in land deeds. There are few deeds from the earliest period of English settlement; most land seems to have been exchanged informally, accompanied by token gifts from the English, allowing for the kind of creative misunderstanding that maintained peace amidst differing customs.[36] By the 1650s, formal deeds became more common, and in many of these, Indians selling land to the English reserved rights to plant, set up weirs, hunt, sometimes even to continue living on land they conveyed to the English.[37] These reservations are a clear indication that Indians understood that the English concept of land sale meant complete alienation of land and were taking steps to preserve their own land ways. Reserving rights on deeds allowed Indians to protect the Native practice of usufruct within the dominant English legal system. Such reservations became less and less effective as the English population grew and succeeding generations felt little pressure to respect Indian land ways. Indeed, in the last quarter of the seventeenth century, English buyers began to limit the kinds of reservations Indians could make, allowing hunting but not trapping, or insisting that Indians fence in any lands they reserved for planting. For instance, in 1655 the United Colonies Commissioners declared their intention to respect the Mohegan sachem Uncas's "Just Rightes," but also insisted on limiting them: "Hee may nott without theire leave sett downe Wigwames or dwell within any p[ar]te of the land they [the English] justly possess."[38] In some deeds the English required that Indian sellers acknowledge that they were not reserving any rights at all.[39]

Another strategy the Indians used was to obtain the assistance of English allies or protectors in defending Indian land within the English court system. One example appears in an Indian petition to the English court at Plymouth in the early 1670s. Manaquo Woaoksunt, the sachem of Cowesit, explained that twenty-six years earlier, in the 1640s, his own father and the English colonist Mr. Browne made an agreement on shared use of the sachem's land. Woaoksunt explained that his "father And the said Mr Browne being soe loveing each to other, that Mr Browne promised my father if acasion should be he would Really and effectually Joyne with him for his preservation; And Assist him for the preserving of a Happie and well grounded pea[ce]: for the good of him and his posterity." Taking out a deed to the sachem's land in Browne's name seems to have been an effort to "joyne with [the sachem] for his preservation." Browne would hold the land and defend the title for the sachem. In return, the sachem gave Browne the right to harvest hay on the land. Similarly, the Mohegans of Connecticut deeded all of their land to the Mason family on the understanding that the well-connected Masons would defend Native title to the lands.[40] Patrons of the Christian Indians, such as John Eliot and Daniel Gookin, often intervened on the Indians' behalf in cases of trespass or other land violations.[41] Eliot's position as a minister and Gookin's as a magistrate meant that the Indians' cases at least got a hearing before the highest governing bodies in the colony.

The Indians also used agents—knowledgeable English and Indians—to help them navigate the English legal process for selling or securing land. Beginning in the 1660s, a number of Indians within the boundaries of Plymouth Colony began using the Plymouth courts to deed lands to other Indians, or to confirm their own lands to themselves. Richard Bourne, a missionary to the Indians in Plymouth Colony, encouraged the Indians to use this English legal mechanism to make the title to their lands more secure, and he appears as a witness on most of these deeds.[42] Similarly, the Nipmuc Indians employed John Wompas "[t]o inquire after & in our name & for our use to declare & endevor to get setled & Recorded, the indians title & Right to those lands." They asked Wompas, rather than an Englishman, not only because he was kin to many of them but "because he spake English well & was aqu[ainted] wth the English."[43]

Not only did Natives obtain English deeds to their own traditionally held land, but they also secured English grants to that land. The Massachusetts General Court declared its willingness to grant land to any groups of people, Indian or English, who professed the intent to settle and improve it as a plantation. Several groups of Christian Indians took advantage of this provision to secure grants of land for setting up praying towns, such as Natick and Okonnokamesitt.[44] Josias Chikataubut, sachem of the Massachusett Indians, asked for and received a deed for six thousand acres of land at Punkapoag, and the court granted it, despite the fact that it lay within the previously granted bounds of the English town of Dorchester.[45] The modern reader cannot help but notice the irony of Indians seeking English grants for their own traditional lands, but the grants offered another layer of protection, needed as more and more enterprising English—and Indians—sought ways to profit from Indian land sales. As Indian superintendant Daniel Gookin put it, the General Court "hath granted those Indians lands and townships, and thereby confirmed and settled them therein as the English; so that, besides their own natural right, they have this legal title, and stand possessed of them as the English are."[46]

Indians also used a combination of Indian land ways and English courts to fight dispossession. They did this by using English courts to challenge land sales that had been made contrary to Native practice, which required the consent of all the people concerned in a sale—the sachem, his counselors, and the traditional holders of the land.[47] The Indians were aided in this by the Massachusetts General Court's 1634 enactment of a set of laws regarding the sale of Indian lands. These laws prohibited the sale of Indian land without permission from the General Court and acknowledged the "just right" of the Indians to any lands that they "have possessed and improved, by subduing the same." In practice, English courts determined just right by both improvement and Indian testimony of their traditional possession. Thus, while English law recognized Native right to the land, it qualified that right with the English legal principle of *vacuum domicilium* that protected only improved land.[48] Similar laws requiring General Court permission for the sale of Indian land were enacted in other New England colonies as well.[49]

It is important to note that these laws were not put in place solely for the protection of the Indians. By publishing the laws, colony officials asserted their authority over the Indian as well as English residents of the region. Requiring colonial permission for Indian land sales was a public assertion that even the chief sachems of the Indians were inferior in authority to the officials of the English colonies.[50] While the prohibition of unauthorized sales served English purposes, it also gave Indians a consistent basis for lawsuits against English or Indians who sold Native land without proper approval. When illegal sales, trespass, or abuse of shared use agreements occurred, aggrieved Indians sought recourse in court, as Manaquo Woaoksunt did when James Browne pushed his usufruct rights too far. The English encouraged such appeals and took steps to train Indians to take their suits to lower, county courts rather than directly to the General Court, reinforcing their status as subjects under colonial authority.[51]

Many Indians took advantage of English courts to defend their land, and their appeals contained both Native and English legal justifications for Native possession. English courts frequently relied on Native testimony to determine whether or not a sale was legitimate, accepting Native definitions of what constituted legitimate land tenure. For instance, one frequent complaint was that Indian land had been sold without proper consent. That included the consent of the sachem who held the land, his counselors, and any followers who used the land. In a 1683 petition to the Massachusetts General Court, a group of Indians protested a sachem's land sale "which said Council & wise men in this case never consented unto." They carefully laid out their justification for this protest, declaring, "[W]e do testifie that according to the Custom of Indian Sachims, they never sell any Land without ye Consent of their Counsil or wise men."[52] After the Nipmuc sachem Oonamog complained that Englishman Job Tyler cut hay on his land, the English court ordered Tyler to pay damages, demonstrating that they would not allow even shared use without Native consent.[53] And, when two Natick Indians sold land to an Englishman without the consent of the other Native residents of the town, those residents appealed to the court and the sale was made void.[54]

John Wompas was clearly aware of the potential for protests of any Indian land sales that did not demonstrate proper consent. His 1671 sale of one hundred acres of land to fellow mariner Thomas Steadman demonstrates that awareness. In the deed, Wompas declared himself the owner of a fourteen-mile-square tract of land "appertaineing unto me . . . as my proper right & inheritance."[55] While Wompas was the only owner listed on the deed, it contains additional wording that suggests that Wompas knew his exclusive right could be questioned. Following the words "my proper right & inheritance" is a phrase inserted above the line: "or one third part thereof." Wompas's father, Old Wompooas, had died in 1651, but his father's brothers, Thomas Tray and Anthony, were still living in 1671.[56] Wompas's acknowledgment that his inheritance only extended to "one third part" of the tract shows that he knew the land was not his sole property. There is no evidence that Wompas asked his uncles to consent to his land sale or that they shared in the purchase price. He may have asked and been refused. Or he may have decided that, given the vast expanse of land the three men claimed, he could sell a tiny fraction without consulting his kin. Certainly, one hundred acres was far less than a third of the total. While according to Native practice, no part of a tract of land could be sold without the consent of all owners, Wompas seems to have imposed an English pattern on the land, dividing it among the heirs, and claiming exclusive right to one portion, thus giving lip service to Native ways while using English patterns of absolute alienation to obtain the profit for himself. In other words, he used legal hybridity to defraud rather than defend his fellow Nipmucs. Such actions eventually led Wompas's Nipmuc kin to revoke their permission for Wompas to act as their agent and to disavow his land dealings, and for the Massachusetts government to prohibit Wompas from selling any Indian lands.[57]

When the highest colonial authorities failed to satisfy Native grievances, there was another avenue of appeal within the English legal system—petitioning the king. The most famous example of such an appeal occurred in 1644, when the Narragansett sachem Miantonomi subjected himself, his people, and his lands to King Charles I of England, begging protection from the incursions of the Massachusetts English, who had forcibly restored a minor Narragansett sachem to the lands that the paramount Narragansett sachem Miantonomi sold out from under him.[58] Evidence suggests that this appeal to the crown was orchestrated by Samuel Gorton, Miantonomi's English buyer, but it is also clear that the Narragansetts embraced the tactic of royal appeal wholeheartedly, showing an astute understanding of the hierarchical English authority structure and skill in employing it over the course of several decades.[59] There are lesser-known examples of this strategy as well. In 1666, the Massachusett sachem Josias Wampatuck submitted his land to the English crown and offered to pay the king tribute of five pounds a year in return for his protection.[60] John Wompas also used this avenue of appeal, sending a petition to King Charles II and later appearing personally before him to protest the Massachusetts government's restriction on his land sales and ask to "be restored to his said lands or else that he may [have] free liberty to make Sale thereof." The king did write a letter to Massachusetts governor John Leverett "recommend[ing]" that Wompas "may have justice done him and what favour the matter will fairly beare," but the letter's qualification—"what . . . the matter will *fairly* beare"—gave Leverett room to reject Wompas's demand when he presented the letter to him.[61]

Abusing English and Indian Land Practices

As John Wompas's story illustrates, Native and English means of defending Indians could just as easily be used to defraud them. A generation after English settlement in New England, Indian and English land practices had become mutually intelligible, at least to those Indians and English who associated with each other frequently. The English, for instance, knew that sachems had the right to distribute land. Some buyers manipulated this pattern by persuading a paramount sachem to sell the land that an inferior sachem had refused to part with, as in the case of Samuel Gorton, Miantonomi, and Pomham.[62] Others bought land from sachems who were willing to sell without the consent of their followers, as in the case of Josias Wampatuck and the Englishman Richard Thayer. Some Natives, on their own or by the instigation of others, claimed to be sachems in order to lend legitimacy to their sale of land.[63] For instance, twenty years after Romanock signed a deed conveying land to his daughter, English settlers who disputed the sale obtained testimony from several local Indians who denied Romanock was a sachem, raising the possibility that John Wompas had lied about Romanock's status. Even if he were a sachem, the Indians protested, Prask could not have inherited from Romanock because the "right of lands is in the male line by their custom."[64] Ironically, in this case English settlers used Native land tenure practice to resist the claims of an Indian who used English law to establish possession.

Legal arrangements originally intended to provide protection to Indians could be turned to the opposite purpose in subsequent generations.

Uncas and the Mohegans found that, while the protection of the Mason family was quite effective for half a century or so, it broke down as succeeding generations reinterpreted agreements in favor of the English.[65] An example of such reinterpretation also appears in the case of the sachem Manaquo Woaoksunt and old Mr. Browne, mentioned earlier. The sachem had given Browne the right to mow grass on his lands in exchange for protection of those lands. Mr. Browne seemed to recognize that this was a grant of usufruct, or profitable use, not an absolute conveyance of the land, and he only used it for the granted purpose. After old Mr. Browne's death in 1662, the sachem gave the same right to Mr. Browne's son, James Browne, but the son used the land as if he owned it in the English fashion. Even though the deed contained language reserving rights to the Indians to live and plant on the land, James Browne's possession of the deed enabled him to alienate that land to others, and he seems to have felt entitled to do so. James Browne not only cut hay on Manaquo Woaoksunt's land, but conveyed pieces of it to other Englishmen who built homes on it and brought their livestock to graze on it, leading the sachem to lament, "[Their] cattle and hogs eats up our corn, besids the takeing away of our Lands."[66]

Indians as well as English used legal hybridity to benefit themselves at the expense of others. After the initial period of English settlement, the Indians knew that the English perceived their "gifts" as payments. Nevertheless, Indians continued to use their traditional interpretation of gifts as tribute in order to demand multiple payments for the same piece of land. The Wampanoag sachem Massasoit "sold" land to different Englishmen "indiscriminately and as often as possible," employing an "attitude towards land sale to the English [that], while not ignorant, seems to have been profitably elastic."[67] Indians also capitalized on the eagerness of English settlers to buy land by accepting payment for it and then demanding more payment later in the form of "confirmations" of the sale, or bringing forward additional Native claimants to the land who also demanded payment.[68] English exasperation over this practice is evident in a 1651 petition from the inhabitants of Rumneymarsh to the Massachusetts General Court, requesting an order that would "vest them and other inhabitants of the colony in the possession of their holdings in such manner as would serve to protect them from illegal and unjust claims to proprietorship put forward by Indians and others."[69] An attempt to limit such tactics appears in a 1674 Plymouth General Court ruling that any Indians claiming inheritance rights in lands possessed by the English had to sue for it within a year of reaching the age of majority or lose all right to sue for it.[70]

While the English grumbled at having to shell out payments two, three, or more times, the confirmations served English purposes as well as Indian. Even three or four payments for the same piece of land usually amounted to far less in total than the price an Englishman would later ask of another Englishman for a small portion of that land. And getting the signed consent of every Indian who could claim ownership in the land on a legally binding deed made English possession more secure in the end. Both the repeated demands and the token payments conformed to the traditional Native practice of tribute, a small, regular payment to the sachem in authority over one's land. Whether the Indians were consciously using the English courts' recognition of Native land tenure practices to perpetuate a form of tribute or were using cumulative payments to make up for what the orginal payments lacked is not clear.

Blatant fraud and abuse also occurred, although it was rare and came from both sides of the cultural divide, as John Wompas's career in land sales demonstrates.[71] We know about cases of fraud because they were challenged—usually successfully—in court, demonstrating that they were considered aberrant and worthy of prosecution.[72] For instance, in 1669 Josias Wampatuck and his wife Weetamoo complained to the Plymouth Court that the Englishman Captain John Sanford had illegally seized their land based on a deed of gift from their mother, Namumpum. Sanford had obtained the deed by assuring Namumpum that it would be "a means of protecting her land forever." Instead of preserving her title, however, Sanford claimed the title himself.[73] In another case, a Connecticut court turned over an Indian to an Englishman whose property he had damaged. The Englishman, John Griffin, held the Indian ransom and demanded five hundred fathoms of wampum for his release. Because the man's kinsmen could not pay it, they instead signed over all the rights of their land to Griffin. These apparently included the sachem's rights to distribute land, as several Indians later testified that "John Griffin was now the sachem of Mapachoe" and began going to him for permission to hunt and plant on the land. Given the fact that Griffin was able to set his own price for the ransom and then demand Native land when it could not be paid, this seems to be a clear case of misuse of English power.[74]

It is worth repeating that English court officials usually ruled against clear cases of abuse. But many cases never came to court. And, while English officials tried to uphold Native rights as articulated in English law, they were reluctant to order the English to remove themselves from land they had already improved. Thus, in some cases of fraud as well as in cases in which the English did not pay for land until after they had begun building on it, the Court's solution was not to order the English to leave Indian land but to grant Indians a small amount of acreage in place of the entire tract.[75] But being given a small amount of acreage—two to ten acres, typically—in the midst of English settlement simply delayed the process of dispossession. Just as James Browne's shared use of the sachem Manaquo Woaoksunt's land led to his cattle and hogs eating up all the Indians' corn, Native land surrounded by English settlement suffered from the encroachment of English animals, restricted access to hunting and fishing sites, and inadequate space for planting. Natives boxed in by English settlement often retreated to more distant lands, giving up possession but hoping to at least obtain payment for the lands they could no longer use.[76] Because the English persisted in paying minuscule sums for Native land, that approach did little to slow the process of dispossession and impoverishment.

Fighting over Land

By 1675, the Native population of New England had shrunk to around 18,000, while the English population approached 150,000, with new plantations as far west as the Hudson River.[77] There was little land remaining where Indians were free from the pressures of English settlement. Wampanoag sachem Philip Metacom complained that "English Catell and horses still incresed that when thay removed 30 mill from wher English had anithing to do, thay Could not kepe ther coren from being spoyled."[78] The Native pattern of shared use became increasingly difficult for Indians to maintain as English settlers used law and their numerical dominance to push back against Native assertions of rights. By the 1670s, the unrelenting pressure of English population growth became a primary cause of King Philip's War.[79] Philip himself listed land as a major grievance in his complaints to Rhode Island official John Easton in the days preceding the outbreak of violence, declaring, "[T]hay had . . . let them have a 100 times more land, then now the king [Philip] had for his own peopell."[80] Edward Randolph echoed the sachem's complaints in a 1688 letter to William Penn, writing that "[t]his Barbarous people [the Indians] were never civilly treated by the late Government, who made it their Business to encroach upon their Lands, and by Degrees to drive them out of all. That was the ground & the Beginning of the last War."[81]

In the aftermath of the war, Indian deaths from battle and disease and the flight of surviving Natives from the region reduced the already small population sharply, and English wariness of future attacks led them to create what was essentially a reservation system confining the remaining Indians in the region to a defined set of lands.[82] This, and the fact that the English could once again claim right of conquest, led to a huge increase in Indian land sales in the last decades of the seventeenth century.[83] By this point, the Indians had lost all power to regain their land, but they continued to petition for payment for the lands they had lost.

In seeking payment for their lands, the Indians once again drew from Native and English understandings of land tenure. Knowing that many of the English believed that their success in King Philip's War justified their right to Indian lands by conquest, the petitioning Indians underlined their unbroken status as friends to the English, "having approved our selves faithfull to ye English Interest, In ye Late Warr, and Served them Most of us As Souldiers." As faithful subjects of "his Majesty and his Government in this Jurisdiction," they had not forfeited their lands by conquest. In addition, the Indian petitioners called on both natural right—a concept present in both legal traditions—and religion to justify their claim, declaring that "wee and or predecessors had & have a naturall Right to [most] of the Lands Lying in the Nipmuck Country" and requesting the General Court to "[g]ive us a compensation, and sattisfaction for or Natural Rights to those Lands, that so Before God & Man things may be Clear."[84]

In response to such petitions, the English continued to pay for Indian land, but they continued to pay very little. As late as the 1680s, Joseph Dudley and other English speculators paid the Nipmuc Indians ten pounds for five miles square of land. Within the year, Dudley sold a two-thousand-acre parcel of that same land to Thomas Freake of London for 250 pounds.[85] Forced into an English lifestyle of sedentary agriculture, Indians required the same amount of profit from their lands as any Englishman would, but they never received it. Payments for land continued to be entirely inadequate to the needs of a Native population unable to continue its former patterns of seasonal mobility. For whatever reason, be it greed or an inability to consider Indian needs equally as valid as their own, English settlers did not pay Indians what would have been considered fair between themselves.

The long history of Indian dispossession of land has been blamed on English fraud, Native ignorance, and the dominant English systems of law and ideology. This claim, still perpetuated in popular history and contemporary politics, is an oversimplification that fails to recognize how quickly Natives and English gained a working knowledge of each other's land ways and used that knowledge to smooth relations between each other and to safeguard and purchase land. But while mutual legal intelligibility had significant benefits, it also allowed for fraud and abuse. And the dominance of the English increasingly meant that the benefits of legal hybridity accrued to the English, not the Indians. Thus, by the end of the seventeenth century, one of the main uses of legal hybridity was English colonists asserting the validity of their own land purchases on the basis of the proper consent of sachems, elders, and traditional Native holders of the land.[86] Philip Metacom's 1675 claim that "now ther kings wear forewarned not for to part with land for nothing in Cumpareson to the valew thereof" was a correct diagnosis of the problem, but one that came far too late.[87]

NOTES

1 Francis Jennings, *The Invasion of America: Indians, Colonialism, and the Cant of Conquest* (New York: Norton, 1976 [1975]), chapters 5, 8, 11; Neal Salisbury, *Manitou and Providence: Indians, Europeans, and the Making of New England, 1500–1643* (New York: Oxford University Press, 1982), chapter 6; William Cronon, *Changes in the Land* (New York: Hill and Wang, 1983), chapter 4. A number of historians have challenged Jennings's charges of English chicanery. See Peter S. Leavenworth, "'The Best Title That Indians Can Claim': Native Agency and Consent in the Transferral of Pawtucket Land in the Seventeenth Century," *New England Quarterly (NEQ)* 72, 2 (June 1999): 289, 298; Richard Cogley, *John Eliot's Mission to the Indians before King Philip's War* (Cambridge, MA: Harvard University Press, 1999); and Yasuhide Kawashima, *Puritan Justice*

and the Indian: White Man's Law in Massachusetts, 1630–1763 (Middletown, CT: Wesleyan University Press, 1986).

2 On contemporary political discussions of seizing Native land, see Suzanne Benally, "Sanctioned Theft: Tribal Land Loss in Massachusetts," in "We are still here: Tribes in New England Stand Their Ground," Cultural Survival Quarterly 38, 2 (June 2014), www.culturalsurvival.org. On mutual legal intelligibility, see Emerson W. Baker, "'A Scratch with a Bear's Paw': Anglo-Indian Land Deeds in Early Maine," Ethnohistory 36, 3 (1989): 240; and Leavenworth, "'The Best Title,'" 282–86. On the English paying Indians for their land, see James Warren Springer, "American Indians and the Law of Real Property in Colonial New England," American Journal of Legal History 30, 1 (1986): 25–58; Kawashima, Puritan Justice, 48–59; Stuart Banner, How the Indians Lost Their Land: Law and Power on the Frontier (Cambridge, MA: Harvard University Press, 2005), 1–8. While Francis Jennings emphasized English seizure of Native land, he acknowledged that they usually paid for it (Invasion, chapter 8). Jean M. O'Brien gives a nuanced description of Indian land loss at Natick "through the excruciating workings of business as usual" in Dispossession by Degrees: Indian Land and Identity in Natick, Massachusetts, 1650–1790 (Cambridge: Cambridge University Press, 1997), 8–9.

3 Michael P. Clark, ed., The Eliot Tracts: With Letters from John Eliot to Thomas Thorowgood and Richard Baxter (Santa Barbara, CA: Praeger, 2003), 95.

4 Roger Williams, A Key into the Language of America (Bedford, MA: Applewood Books, n.d. [London, 1643]), 94–96. Kathleen Bragdon describes three land-use patterns within Algonquian New England: the "conditional sedentism" of coastal dwellers, characterized by "very circumscribed movements within the same rather restricted zones year after year"; the more sedentary agricultural pattern of the riverine dwellers; and the "uplands" pattern, which combined some of the features of coastal and riverine dwellers (Native People of Southern New England, 1500–1650 [Norman: University of Oklahoma Press, 1996], 59–75).

5 Kathleen Joan Bragdon, "Another Tongue Brought In: An Ethnohistorical Study of Native Writings in Massachusett" (PhD dissertation, Brown University, 1981), 93–94, 106–8; Baker, "'A Scratch with a Bear's Paw,'" 240; Bragdon, Native People, chapter 5. Scholars debate whether land and political office passed matrilineally or patrilineally among the Natives of southern New England. See Bragdon, Native People, 145, 160–61; Frank G. Speck, "A Note on the Hassanamisco Band of Nipmuc," Bulletin of the Massachusetts Archaeological Society 4 (1944): 49–56; and Amy E. Den Ouden, Beyond Conquest: Native Peoples and the Struggle for History in New England (Lincoln: University of Nebraska Press, 2005), 83, 246–47, fn. 18.

6 This was true if owners sold in fee simple. But it was possible to qualify a sale or transfer, or to make it conditional.

7 The colony's first governor, John Winthrop, explained this thinking in his journal: "The Indians having only a natural right to so much land as they had

or could improve, so as the rest of the country lay open to any that could and would improve it" (*Winthrop's Journal "History of New England,"* 1630–1649, James Kendall Hosmer, ed., 2 vols. [New York: Scribner's, 1908], 1:294). Evidence that this view existed in old as well as New England appears in Thomas More's *Utopia,* which justified war "when any people holdeth a piece of ground void and vacant to no good or profitable use: keeping others from the use and possession of it, which, notwithstanding, by the law of nature, ought thereof to be nourished and relieved," cited in Wilcomb E. Washburn, *Red Man's Land, White Man's Law: The Past and Present Status of the American Indian,* 2nd ed. (Norman: University of Oklahoma Press, 1995), 40. See also Jeffrey Glover, *Paper Sovereigns: Anglo-Native Treaties and the Law of Nations, 1604–1664* (Philadelphia: University of Pennsylvania Press, 2014), 131.

8   *Public Records of the Colony of Connecticut (CCR),* J. Hammond Trumbull, ed. (Hartford, CT: F.A. Brown, 1852), 2:473–74; *Records of the Governor and Company of the Massachusetts Bay in New England (MBR),* Nathaniel B. Shurtleff, ed. (Boston: William White, 1854), 3:280.

9   *Winthrop Journal,* 59 (23 March 1631), 65 (13 July 1632); Jeremy Dupertuis Bangs, *Indian Deeds: Land Transactions in Plymouth Colony, 1620–1691* (Boston: New England Historical and Genealogical Society, 2002), 15.

10 For an excellent discussion of European and Indian traditions of gift giving and their meanings, see David Murray, *Indian Giving: Economies of Power in Indian-White Exchanges* (Amherst: University of Massachusetts Press, 2000), chapter 1. On gifts among New England Indians, see Salisbury, *Manitou and Providence,* 116.

11 On the providential view, see Roy Harvey Pearce, *Savagism and Civilization: A Study of the Indian and the American Mind* (Baltimore, MD: Johns Hopkins University Press, 1953 [1965]), 19.

12 *MBR* 1:292, 13 May 1640.

13 Emerson W. Baker and John G. Reid, "Amerindian Power in the Early Modern Northeast: A Reappraisal," *William and Mary Quarterly (WMQ)* 61 (Jan. 2004): 77–106. On tribute among Indians, see Bangs, *Indian Deeds,* 29. For examples of English paying tribute to Indians, see Bangs, *Indian Deeds,* 72, 257, 258; and Jenny Hale Pulsipher, "'Dark Cloud Rising in the East': Indian Sovereignty and the Coming of King William's War in New England," *New England Quarterly* 80, 4 (Dec. 2007): 593–95.

14 Alan Taylor, *American Colonies: The Settling of North America* (New York: Penguin, 2001), 380; Richard White, "Creative Misunderstandings and New Understandings," *WMQ* 63, 1 (Jan. 2006): 9–14.

15 Only in the last generation have scholars fully grasped the impact unfamiliar diseases had on the "virgin population" of America. Important contributions to the longstanding debate over Native population numbers before European settlement include Sherburne F. Cook, "Interracial Warfare and Population Decline among the New England Indians," *Ethnohistory* 20, 1 (1973): 1–24; and "The Significance of Disease in the Extinction of the New England Indians," *Human Biology* 45

(Sept. 1973); Dean Snow and Kim M. Lanphear, "European Contact and Indian Depopulation in the Northeast: The Timing of the First Epidemics," *Ethnohistory* 35 (1988): 351–83; Henry F. Dobyns, with the assistance of William R. Swagerty, *Their Number Become Thinned: Native Population Dynamics in Eastern North America* (Knoxville: University of Tennessee Press, 1983); Alfred Crosby, "Virgin Soil Epidemics as a Factor in the Aboriginal Depopulation in America," *WMQ* 3rd series, 33 (1976) and *The Columbian Exchange: Biological and Cultural Consequences of 1492* (Santa Barbara, CA: Praeger, 2003); David S. Jones, "Virgin Soils Revisited," *WMQ* 3rd ser., 60 (Oct. 2003): 703–42. There is wide but not universal consensus that Native American depopulation in the wake of European contact approached 90 percent. For a contrary view, see David P. Henige, *Numbers from Nowhere: The American Indian Contact Population Debate* (Norman: University of Oklahoma Press, 1998).

16 David J. Silverman, *Faith and Boundaries: Colonists, Christianity, and Community among the Wampanoag Indians of Martha's Vineyard, 1600–1871* (Cambridge: Cambridge University Press, 2005), 95, 125; Baker, "'A Scratch with a Bear's Paw,'" 235–56.

17 *Winthrop Journal,* 59 (23 March 1631), 65 (13 July 1632). Virginia DeJohn Anderson notes that the English persistently allowed joint use of land by both Indians and English in "King Philip's Herds: Indians, Colonists, and the Problem of Livestock in Early New England," *WMQ* 51, 4 (Oct. 1994): 610. See also her *Creatures of Empire: How Domestic Animals Transformed Early America* (New York: Oxford University Press, 2004).

18 Walter W. Woodward, *Prospero's America: John Winthrop, Jr.; Alchemy and the Creation of New England Culture, 1606–1676* (Chapel Hill: University of North Carolina Press, 2010), 109.

19 Seán Patrick Donlan, "Remembering: Legal Hybridity and Legal History," *Comparative Law Review* 2, 1 (2011): 1–35. On legal pluralism, see Richard J. Ross and Philip J. Stern, "Reconstructing Early Modern Notions of Legal Pluralism," in Richard J. Ross and Lauren Benton, eds., *Legal Pluralism and Empires, 1500–1850* (New York: NYU Press, 2013); and Lauren A. Benton, *Law and Colonial Cultures: Legal Regimes in World History, 1400–1900* (New York: Cambridge University Press, 2002).

20 *Suffolk Deeds* (SD) 13:344–45, Massachusetts State Archives, Columbia Point, MA. John Winthrop Jr's agent, Amos Richardson, was present to observe what appeared to be a similar Native land transfer ceremony in 1645, in which the Indian Webucksham declared that he "lay this Wishkeeg or Writing on Washcomos my Son and Heirs Breast and sett my mark and Seal and Wascomos my said Son according to Indian Custom freely makes his Mark and Seal hereunto on my Breast. This don with Consent of all the Indians of Tantiusques" (cited in Woodward, *Prospero's America*, 109).

21 *Collections of the Massachusetts Historical Society (MHSC)*, 5th ser., 9:132–34.

22 Peter Leavenworth argues that use of the turf and twig ceremony may have been
    more common than these few instances suggest because "the written record
    became a competing and corrective method of transfer only by the late 1650s"
    ("The Best Title," 290–91).

23 For John Wompas's mark, see SD 10:112–13. On Thomas Minor, see James Sav-
    age, *A Genealogical Dictionary of the First Settlers of New England, before 1692*
    (Baltimore, MD: Genealogical Publishing, 1994). On John Wompas and Thomas
    Minor carving their initials into tree trunks, see Massachusetts Archives Collec-
    tion (MAC), vol. 30:259a, Massachusetts State Archives; and *The Diary of Thomas
    Minor, Stonington, Connecticut, 1653 to 1684* (New London, CT: Day Publishing,
    1899), 205. See also Leavenworth, "The Best Title," 284, note 18.

24 Kawashima, *Puritan Justice*, 70. *MBR* 1:266, 4 June 1639: "John Bayly was fined 5
    L for buying land of the Indians wthout leave, wth condition, if hee yeld up the
    land, to be remitted."

25 William Lincoln, *History of Worcester, Massachusetts* (Worcester, MA: Charles
    Hersey, 1862), 13, 19. Other examples of purchase following grant appear in *MBR*
    1:254, 327, 346.

26 The eventual payment amounted to ninety-four pounds—just more than ten
    pounds per mile square (Lincoln, *History of Worcester*, 9–17).

27 In *John Eliot's Mission*, Richard Cogley wrote, "That Eliot's program stripped the
    praying Indians of their land is an article of orthodoxy in the literature" (233).
    In 1683, Rev. Higginson of Guilford, Connecticut, testified that as early as 1638,
    Indians "gave all land to Norwalk to English as conquered land and were paid in
    coats, hoes, etc." (William Samuel Johnson Papers, 3665, Connecticut Histori-
    cal Society; transcription by Laurie Pasteryak, Mashantucket Pequot Museum
    Research Center).

28 *Winthrop Journal*, 1:116. Samuel Gorton, another critic of Massachusetts policy,
    reminded John Winthrop Jr. that the king, too, expected his colonists to take no
    lands from the Indians "without giving satisfaction for them" (*MHSC* 4th ser.,
    7:627).

29 Bangs, *Indian Deeds*, 222–23.

30 Nathaniel Saltonstall, "The Present State of New-England with Respect to the
    Indian War, by N.S., 1675," in Charles H. Lincoln, ed., *Narratives of the Indian
    Wars, 1675–1699* (New York: Barnes & Noble, 1952 [1913]), 26.

31 Examples of very low prices for substantial tracts of land include the follow-
    ing: In 1668, the Wabanaki sagamore Wesumbe sold twenty square miles of
    land to an English trader for two large Indian blankets, two gallons of rum, two
    pounds of powder, four pounds of musket balls, and twenty strings of wampum
    (Coll. S-1262, Misc box 59/27, 2965, Maine Historical Society, Portland, Maine).
    In 1648, the inhabitants of Sudbury paid Cato five pounds for five miles square
    (SD 1:93). On prices for unimproved land between English buyers, see SD 1:37
    (sixty pounds for forty-eight acres); SD 8:10 (ninety pounds for three hundred

acres); SD 8:186–88 (twenty-five pounds for five hundred acres); SD 12:289 (approximately two hundred pounds for six hundred acres); SD 13:202 (one hundred pounds for one thousand acres); SD 14:120 (fifty pounds for five hundred acres); SD 38:72 (ninety pounds for two hundred fifty acres); SD 4:268 (fourteen pounds for five hundred acres).

32 A number of scholars, including Yasuhide Kawashima, Peter Leavenworth, and David Konig, acknowledge that the English assigned very low monetary value to "waste" or wilderness land. Kawashima offers the explanation that English colonists had to pay for their transport from England, and that in some places newly arrived English could claim fifty or more acres of land for free (Kawashima, *Puritan Law*, 59; Leavenworth, "The Best Title," 290). But the same English who assigned low values to unimproved lands sold those lands to fellow English for much higher prices than they ever offered to Native sellers.

33 I thank Tamar Herzog for pointing out Giovanni Levi's discussion of need as a factor in the fair price of land among early modern Europeans (*Inheriting Power: The Story of an Exorcist*, tr. Lydia G. Cochrane [Chicago: University of Chicago Press, 1988], 80–94).

34 *Records of the Colony of Rhode Island and Providence Plantations* (*RIR*) (Providence, RI: A. Crawford Greene and Brother, 1856), 1:33. Similarly, the Mohegan sachem Uncas complained to Connecticut officials of the attempt of some men from New London to buy more land: "He said that he could not spare all the land they desired, nor accept the price" (*MHSC* 4th ser., 7:556).

35 Petition of John Wompas to King Charles II, 14 March 1678/79, CO 1/43, no. 33, National Archives, London, United Kingdom.

36 Salisbury, *Manitou and Providence*, 184–85.

37 See, for example, the 1658 deed to Hadley, which included this phrase: "The Indians desired they might set their Wiggwoms at sometimes wth in ye tract of ground they sold withoute offence & that the English would be kinde & neighborlie to ym in not Prohibiting ym firewood out of ye Woods &c which was promised ym" (Harry Andrew Wright, ed., *Indian Deeds of Hampden County* [Springfield, MA: 1905], 33).

38 David Pulsifer, ed., *Records of the Colony of New Plymouth in New England*. Vols. 9–10, *Acts of the Commissioners of the United Colonies of New England* (*PCR*) (Boston: William White, 1859), 9:144.

39 Fairfield Land Records, 671, 673, Connecticut State Library, Hartford, CT. The purchase agreement for Quinsigamog specified that the purchase "included all and every part of the natural or civil right of the native chiefs, in all and singular the broken up land and wood land, woods, trees, rivers, . . . minerals, or things whatsoever, lying and being within the eight miles square" and that the land "should be held without any let, molestation, or disturbance by the grantors or their kindred, or people, or any claiming under them" (Lincoln, *History of Worcester*, 17).

40 Michael Leroy Oberg, *Uncas: First of the Mohegans* (Ithaca, NY: Cornell University Press, 2003), 155–56, 205. Oberg explains that "Uncas gave up nothing in the deal. He acquired for himself, however, English blessing to keep these lands—lands that he had acquired through 'conquest' of the Pequots and their former tributaries—clear of intruders" (89–90).

41 Cogley, *John Eliot's Mission*, chapter 8.

42 Bangs, *Indian Deeds*, 156. Evidence of Bourne's involvement in securing such deeds appears in his 1674 letter to Daniel Gookin, in which he declared, "There is a tract of land preserved for them and theirs forever, under hand and seal; the which is near ten miles in length, and five in breadth. There is the like done at Comassakumkanit, near Sandwich, and at Cotuhtikut: Our honored governour and magistrates being always very careful to preserve lands for them, so far as it is in their power to do it" (*Historical Collections of the Indians in New England*, in *MHSC* 1st ser., 1 [1792]: 198).

43 MAC 30:260a.

44 *MBR* 3:246. Likewise, the United Colonies commissioners granted land to the Pequot Indians under Harmon Garrett (MAC 30:111, 125). Daniel Gookin's explanation of the utility of Indians obtaining English grants for their own lands appears in *Historical Collections*, 179. See also Cogley, *John Eliot's Mission*, 142; and O'Brien, *Dispossession by Degrees*, 75–76.

45 MAC 30:136. For other examples, see *MBR* 4, part 2:94–95; and MAC 30:19, 19a, 21, 69.

46 Gookin, *Historical Collections*, 179. On the increased level of protection for Christian Indian lands, see Cogley, *John Eliot's Mission*, 233–37.

47 Jean O'Brien describes this approach in *Dispossession by Degrees*, 75.

48 While the laws were enacted in 1634, the colony did not publish its laws until 1648. See *The Colonial Laws of Massachusetts*, reprinted from the edition of 1672, with the supplements through 1680, William H. Whitmore, ed. (Boston, 1887), 74; and *MBR* 3:280. In conformance to this law, the deed to John Winthrop's three-thousand-acre farm excluded one hundred acres of "improved" Indian land (*MBR* 4, part 2:108); in another case, the Massachusetts General Court confirmed a land grant, "the just right of any Indian to any part of this land alwayes excepted" (*MBR* 3:189).

49 *RIR* 1:236, 404.

50 An example of this assertion of superior authority appears in a letter from Thomas Mayhew to John Winthrop Jr.: "I desire yow to resolve me if any man can possesse land that he doth purchase of the heathen, without the leave of the pattentees. . . . I suppose your sellfe can tell if any such liberty be to be taken or not, in a word or two, by any leave from his Majestie; to me it annyhilates patents" (*MHSC* 4th ser., 7:41).

51 *MBR* 3:233.

52 MAC 30:275a.

53 MAC 30:129; see also O'Brien, *Dispossession by Degrees*, 38.

54 MAC 30:279b.

55 SD 8:421.

56 Clark, ed., *Eliot Tracts*, 222.

57 MAC 30:260a.

58 On this incident see Jenny Hale Pulsipher, *Subjects unto the Same King: Indians, English, and the Contest for Authority in Colonial New England* (Philadelphia: University of Pennsylvania Press, 2005), 55–59; and Glover, *Paper Sovereigns*, chapter 5.

59 Pulsipher, *Subjects*, 28–32.

60 MAC 30:131, 132, 275a. For other examples of Indians using royal appeal, particularly in the eighteenth century, see Craig Yirush, "'Chief Princes and Owners of All': Native American Appeals to the Crown in the Early Modern British Atlantic," in Saliha Belmessous, ed., *Indigenous versus European Land Claims, 1500–1914* (New York: Oxford University Press, 2011).

61 W. Noel Sainsbury, ed., *Calendar of State Papers, Colonial Series (CSPC)* (Vaduz: Kraus Reprint, 1964 [1880]), 9:445, 22 Aug. 1676, #1023.

62 *CSPC* 9:242, #588–89.

63 Philip, sachem of the Wampanoags, complained that "now home [whom] the English had owned for king or queen thay wold disinheret, and make a nother king that wold give or seel them there land, that now thay had no hopes left to kepe ani land" (John Easton, "A Relacion of the Indyan Warre, by Mr. Easton, of Roade Isld., 1675," in Lincoln, ed., *Narratives of the Indian Wars*, 10–11.

64 *MHSC* 5th ser, 9:122–140.

65 Oberg, *Uncas*, 155–69, 205–14.

66 John Davis Papers, #38, Massachusetts Historical Society (MHS), Boston, Massachusetts.

67 Bangs, *Indian Deeds*, 40, 66.

68 In 1671, for instance, Plymouth confirmed the land Massasoit had earlier sold the colony, paying his son Philip an additional sixteen pounds (SD 7:272–73). See also Haynes to Winthrop, 1643, Ch. A. 1. 28, Boston Public Library, Boston, MA (printed in *MHSC* 4th ser., 6:355–56).

69 MAC 30:26. In response to the petition, the General Court ordered Rumneymarsh to provide twenty acres of land to Sagamore George.

70 Bangs, *Indian Deeds*, 158.

71 For a detailed account of John Wompas's land sales career, see Jenny Hale Pulsipher, *Swindler Sachem: The American Indian Who Sold His Birthright, Dropped Out of Harvard, and Conned the King of England* (New Haven, CT: Yale University Press, 2018).

72 Jeremy Bangs makes the argument that court cases prove the exceptionalism of fraud in his *Indian Deeds*, 222–23.

73 Winslow Papers, #35 [MS 33], MHS.

74 Connecticut Historical Society (CHS), Hartford, Connecticut, Manuscripts, Indian Deeds, First folder: Indians Documents, Misc. To appease the Indians,

the court ordered a payment of forty shillings, or two pounds, to one of the Native holders of the land, and gave two acres and a coat to two others.

75 The court ordered that Mamantoe retain two acres of the original plot of land (Manuscripts, Indian Deeds, First folder: Indians Documents, Misc., CHS).

76 For example, Daniel Gookin reported that the Okonnokamesitt Indians abandoned their apple orchard, which was located in the middle of the English town of Marlborough, "for it brings little or no profit to them, nor is ever like to do; because the Englishmen's cattle, &c. devour all in it, because it lies open and unfenced . . . and that was one cause of their removal" (*Historical Collections*, 220).

77 James D. Drake, *King Philip's War: Civil War in New England, 1675–1676* (Amherst: University of Massachusetts Press, 1999), 240, note 3; Evarts B. Greene and Virginia D. Harrington, *American Population before the Federal Census of 1790* (New York, 1932), 9–10.

78 Easton, "A Relacion," 10–11.

79 Eugene Aubrey Stratton argued that "exclusion of the Indians from the lands they had sold was not the only complaint the Indians had against the English, but it was the prime one" (cited in Bangs, *Indian Deeds*, 172). Cogley, *John Eliot's Mission*, 164–70. Virginia Anderson noted that Indian attacks on colonists' livestock increased when Massachusetts courts failed to solve the problem of English trespass on Native lands ("King Philip's Herds," 620).

80 Easton, "A Relacion," 10–11.

81 Randolph to William Penn, in Robert Noxon Toppan, *Edward Randolph, including His Letters and Official Papers*, 7 vols. (Boston: Prince Society, 1898), 2:80.

82 Drake, *King Philip's War*, 240–41, fn. 3–4.

83 Leavenworth, "Best Title," 296–97.

84 MAC 30:257; see also 30:301, 326a.

85 SD 12:297–99, 378–80.

86 Such assertions became widespread during the political upheavals of the last decades of the seventeenth century, when imperial officials such as Edmund Andros rejected the basis of the colonists' land claims. See, for example, the testimony of John Higginson, MAC 35:145.

87 Easton, "A Relacion," 10–11.

4

"Since We Came out of This Ground"

Iroquois Legal Arguments at the Treaty of Lancaster

CRAIG YIRUSH

Scholarship on the early modern world has begun to take the history of empires as seriously as it used to take the history of nation states. Historians of political thought now contend that many of the canonical thinkers of the seventeenth century—Grotius, Hobbes, Locke, among others—were closely involved in the activities of overseas trading companies, their ideas crafted in part to justify European expansion into the non-European world.[1] Legal historians have also shed their traditional preoccupation with the sovereign nation state in order to explore an early modern imperial world of divided sovereignty, legal pluralism, and jurisdictional complexity.[2] And scholars of early modern North America have begun to recognize the ways in which European settlers were engaged in an imperial project as they moved west, violating the rights of the African and indigenous inhabitants of North America, despite the republican idealism of 1776.[3]

Missing from this imperial turn has been any sustained attention to the ideas—legal, political, constitutional—of the indigenous peoples the Europeans encountered in the Americas.[4] Historians of early modern political theory have focused on the ideas the major European theorists used to justify European expansion, while legal historians have tried to understand the ways in which colonial officials and settlers employed these European discourses on the ground to justify their settlement against other Europeans and the indigenous peoples who were occupying the territory they coveted.[5] Yet in these encounters, Native Americans were not merely passive objects of European discourses. Rather, they responded to European claims with their own conceptions of law, rights, and political authority. The debate about the justice of European empire was thus a dialogue, not a monologue, and if we are to understand fully the intellectual dimension of these encounters, we need to listen to indigenous voices as they responded to European claims.[6]

It is a propitious moment to begin to take indigenous legal-political ideas seriously given the efflorescence of scholarly interest in Native Americans in the last generation. As the pioneering ethnohistorical work of James Axtell, Francis Jennings, Daniel Richter, James Merrell, and Colin Calloway (among many others) has shown, the world of the British settlers was shaped in important ways by the presence of Native peoples as traders, diplomats, and warriors.[7] Indeed, for most of the early modern period, the British settlers only controlled a small sliver of territory in eastern North America.[8] But if Native warriors, traders, and diplomats were in fact so central to the construction of Euro-American empires, then it becomes all the more urgent that we treat them as bearers of ideas, as participants in the debates about the justice of European empire.[9] Only when we do so will we have a full account of early modern debates about the legalities of empire, one that includes both indigenous and European arguments, and is open to the idea that they were mutually constitutive.

To get at these indigenous arguments, this chapter will look at an important 1744 treaty conference between the English and the Iroquois (or Haudenosaunee) Confederacy held at Lancaster, Pennsylvania. While what Natives said at treaty conferences has long been studied by scholars, they have usually done so to determine what their speeches can tell us about cultural contact, rather than for the ideas and arguments the speeches contain.[10] Yet treaties allow us access to an intellectual middle ground, where Natives were able to articulate their sense of justice in dialogue with Euro-Americans, in a forum that often took place on Native ground, and according to Native protocol, with English governors and negotiators using Native rituals and metaphors.[11] Given the consensual and deliberative traditions of Native communities, we can also take what their orators said at treaty conferences as representative of their nation's sense of the justness of their relationship with the newcomers rather than as the idiosyncratic position of one spokesperson.[12] By examining closely what was said at Lancaster, then, this chapter will explore the dialogue between indigenous and Anglo-American legal arguments, as both sides tried to work out who would control the valuable lands on the western side of the Appalachian Mountains. The outcome of these deliberations would, within a decade, play a part in precipitating a global war for empire.[13]

* * *

The nations that composed the Haudenosaunee, or People of the Long-house, came together gradually in a series of alliances sometime between 1400 and 1600 to form a League, putting an end to a period of chronic warfare.[14] Central to this League was a Grand Council of hereditary sachems who met regularly to keep the peace among the five Iroquois nations (from east to west, the Mohawks, Oneidas, Onondagas, Cayugas, and Senecas). The League's elaborate diplomatic rituals, which symbolized its people's deep commitment to peace, continued to shape their diplomacy into the era of European contact.[15] Although the League kept the peace, it was by all accounts a loose union, with the several nations of the Iroquois maintaining their autonomy.[16] Despite their fierce reputation in battle, war for the Iroquois was not primarily about the conquest of territory; rather, its purpose was to take captives, who were then incorporated into Iroquois society, assuaging the grief of the families of the dead, and replenishing the population.[17] In this sense, it was the counterpart to the Iroquois' diplomacy, as it ended, ideally, with the incorporation of conquered enemies as kin, thus expanding the zone of peace.[18]

With the arrival of Europeans in the seventeenth century, the Iroquois' world was transformed by the devastating impact of disease, and by the need to gain access to lucrative furs, which could then be traded for European goods (including weapons).[19] In their quest for furs and captives, the Iroquois, armed by the Dutch in the Hudson Valley, were able to defeat the Huron and other Indian nations to the north and west by the mid-seventeenth century. This earned them the enmity of the Hurons' allies, the French, who invaded Iroquoia in the 1660s. Although the Iroquois made peace with the French, they also entered into an alliance with the English colony of New York, which had conquered and displaced the Dutch. Known as the Covenant Chain, this alliance eventually encompassed Virginia, Maryland, and Pennsylvania as well as other Indian peoples.[20] However, when the English and French went to war in 1689, the Iroquois found themselves fighting the French with little help from their erstwhile English allies.

After a decade of punishing war, the Iroquois made simultaneous peace treaties with the French and the English in 1701, adopting a policy of neutrality between these European powers by playing one off against the other.[21] This policy of neutrality was orchestrated by the Iroquois Confederacy, which had emerged in response to contact with Europeans in the latter half of the seventeenth century, and which took the lead in foreign policy, leaving the hereditary League sachems to keep the peace internally.[22] In the early eighteenth century, another faction within the Iroquois Confederacy, composed of Senecas, Cayugas, Onondagas, and Oneidas, sought a counterbalance to the Mohawk-dominated alliance with New York by opening up diplomatic relations with Pennsylvania.[23] In return, Pennsylvania made the Iroquois the sole representatives for dealing with the indigenous peoples of the Delaware and Susquehanna Valleys, some of whom, like the Susquehannocks, had fought against the Iroquois in the previous century, and had then sought Iroquois protection when hostilities ceased in the late seventeenth century.[24]

This turn to Pennsylvania highlights the decentralized nature of both the League and the Confederacy, for the Mohawks had nothing to do with it; rather, this diplomatic initiative was made by the western Iroquois, who had been the ones trading and fighting in the south in the seventeenth century. The opening of Iroquois diplomatic and territorial claims to the south also facilitated the incorporation of the Tuscaroras as the Sixth Nation of the Confederacy in the early eighteenth century, after they fled north following defeat by the Catawbas and the English settlers in Carolina. This in turn led to raids by Iroquois war parties south through Maryland and Virginia, causing friction with settlers on the western edge of English settlement. All of these developments would be central to the deliberations at Lancaster.

* * *

On Friday, June 22, 1744, 252 Iroquois men, women, and children arrived in the small frontier town of Lancaster, Pennsylvania, for a treaty conference with the governor of Pennsylvania, and commissioners from Virginia and Maryland. Two years before there had been bloody clashes between Iroquois warriors heading south through Virginia to fight their enemies, the Catawbas, and Virginia's militia. Fearing a deadly border war, in 1743 Virginia had sent a delegation to Onondaga, the seat of both the Iroquois League and the Confederacy, for a meeting that laid the groundwork for the conference at Lancaster the following year.[25] To make matters worse, three English traders had also been killed by Delaware Indians, whom the Iroquois claimed as their tributaries, a matter that particularly exercised the Pennsylvanians at Lancaster. And at a treaty conference in Philadelphia in 1742, the Iroquois had complained to the governor of Pennsylvania of the encroachment of Maryland and Virginia on territory that they claimed was theirs, and that was now occupied by English settlers. The representatives of the English colonies at Lancaster were eager to deal with the grievances of the Iroquois in order to ensure the Six Nations' neutrality in the war with the French that had just begun (King George's War, 1744–1748).[26]

In attendance at Lancaster were representatives from the Onondagas, the Senecas, the Cayugas, the Oneidas, and the Tusacaroras. Apart from the Tuscaroras, these were the Nations of the Confederacy, who had begun dealing with Pennsylvania in the early eighteenth century. The Onondaga headman, Canassatego, was the principal Iroquois speaker at Lancaster.[27] Witham Marshe, the secretary for the Maryland commissioners, described him as "about 60 years of age" with "a manly countenance" and "a good-natured smile."[28] Like the other Iroquois leaders at Lancaster, Canassatego was not a League chief. Rather, he had most likely accrued his influence at Onondaga by shrewdness, political ambition, and a gift for oratory.[29]

Conrad Weiser, an adopted Iroquois who had represented Virginia at Onondaga in 1743, served as interpreter.[30] His job was crucial, for even though some of the Iroquois spoke English, proceedings at Lancaster would be conducted in Iroquois.[31] On their arrival, Weiser led the Indian delegation to vacant lots at the back of town where, according to Marshe, they erected cabins "according to the rank each nation of them holds in their grand council."[32] It was here that the Iroquois speakers could consult with their followers before replying to English arguments.

Two commissioners from Virginia were in attendance, and four from Maryland. Pennsylvania was represented by its governor, George Thomas, who had presided over the 1742 treaty with the Iroquois in Philadelphia.[33] Richard Peters, also of Pennsylvania, served as the conference's official scribe.[34] Peters was an Anglican clergyman, a member of the provincial council, and a defender of proprietary interests in the colony.[35]

Two issues were central to the negotiations at Lancaster in late June and early July of 1744—the Iroquois' claim to land in Maryland and Virginia, as well as the related question of the Iroquois' right of passage through the back country of Virginia; and Pennsylvania's demand for justice after the murder of Indian traders.

* * *

On June 25th, Governor Thomas of Pennsylvania, who was to play the role of mediator, opened the treaty conference by recalling Pennsylvania's meeting with the Six Nations in 1742, when the Iroquois had complained about "some Lands in the back Parts of" Maryland, "which they claim a Right to from their Conquests over the ancient Possessors, and which have been settled by some of the Inhabitants of that Government, without their Consent, or any Purchase made from them." Thomas added that the English had since discovered that the Iroquois were also claiming lands in Virginia. As well, there had been a skirmish "in the back Parts of Virginia" between the Six Nations and the Virginia militia, "with some Loss on both Sides." Both parties, though, had laid down their arms and agreed to Pennsylvania's mediation. Thomas hoped that this meeting between colonists and the "Deputies" of the Six Nations would result in "a firm Peace, Union and Friendship."[36]

Thomas also told the commissioners from Maryland and Virginia that it was imperative the English make peace with the Six Nations, as they had the power "of making cruel Ravages" upon the frontier; but if allied to the English, they would deny the French passage through their territories. Thomas noted that the Iroquois had been made worse off by "their Intercourse" with the English and by "our yearly extending our Settlements." Accordingly, he lectured the commissioners of Maryland and Virginia that they should relieve their plight with presents. As New York and Pennsylvania had learned, making peace with the Six Nations was less costly than going to war with them.[37]

Thomas then addressed the Six Nations, telling them that he was their "Brother" and "true Friend," and assuring them that Virginia and Maryland had come "to enlarge the Fire, which was almost gone out," and "to brighten the Chain which had contracted some Rust." They also wanted "to renew their Friendship with you," which they hoped would last "so Long as the Sun, the Moon and the Stars shall give Light." Thomas also told the Six Nations that the commissioners from Maryland and Virginia had powers derived from the English king, "your Father"; and he advised them to eschew the French, revive the Covenant Chain, and embrace the English as "Brethren," uniting with them "as one Body, and one Soul." The French, he said, hated them, while the English king had always protected them.[38]

Before replying, Canassatego repeated the substance of the governor's speech to the interpreter to make sure he understood it correctly, a practice that Peters, the official scribe, said was "a Method generally made use of by the Indians."[39] After taking the rest of the morning to procure a wampum belt in exchange for the one that Thomas had just given the Six Nations, Canassatego replied to the governor's speech. The English were their "Brethren," he insisted, and they wanted "to brighten the Chain of Friendship" between the two peoples, but not before the dispute over the lands now "possessed by them, which formerly belonged to us" was settled.[40]

Maryland's commissioners then addressed the Six Nations, calling them "Brethren," and presenting them with a "String of Wampum." After this conciliatory opening, the commissioners told the Iroquois that they had only recently heard their complaint that Maryland was occupying their land, and they accused the Iroquois of doing so in order "to terrify us." The commissioners warned the Six Nations that their accusations would dissolve "the Chain of Friendship subsisting, not only between us, but perhaps the other English and you," and they reminded them that the settlers in Maryland were numerous, courageous, and armed, and would not be "hurt in their Lives and Estates."[41]

Although they were willing to hear the Six Nations' claims, the commissioners insisted that Marylanders had been in possession of their province for "above one hundred years past," "undisturbed" by any claim from the Indians. What was more, they had obtained their land by signing a treaty with the "Susquahannah" more than ninety years earlier. The commissioners from Maryland also contended that the Six Nations had made themselves subjects of the king of England and given their land to him. Since Marylanders were also subjects of the king, who possessed their territory "by virtue of his Right and Sovereignty," the commissioners asked why the Six Nations were stirring up trouble between the two peoples, for they "are as one Man, under the Protection of that Great

King." The commissioners also claimed that Maryland and the Six Nations had signed a treaty sixty years ago, which had been "renewed and confirmed twice since that time." Despite being unsatisfied with the "Justice of your Claim to any Lands in Maryland," the commissioners told the Six Nations that they were eager to show "Brotherly Kindness and Affection" to them.[42]

Canassatego then rose to reply to the arguments of the Maryland commissioners. He said that since the commissioners had "gone back to old Times" he could not answer them immediately, but would take what they had said "into Consideration." The next morning, June 26th, Canassatego had a reply ready. He first reminded the Marylanders that, far from threatening them, the Six Nations had asked the governor of Pennsylvania "to write to the Great King beyond the Seas, who would own us for his Children as well as you, to compel you to do us Justice." Only after Maryland had failed to deal with their complaints had the Six Nations used "such Expressions as would make the greatest Impressions on your Minds"—the result of which was the meeting at Lancaster.[43] As for "the Affair of the Land," Canassatego gave a forceful rebuttal to Maryland's legal claims. The commissioners had told them, he said, that they had

been in Possession of the Province of Maryland above One Hundred Years; but what is One Hundred Years in Comparison to the Length of Time since our claim began? since we came out of this Ground? For we must tell you, that long before One Hundred Years our Ancestors came out of this very Ground, and their Children have remained here ever since. You came out of the Ground in a Country that lies beyond the Seas, there you may have a just Claim, but here you must allow us to be your elder Brethren, and the Lands to belong to us before you knew any of them.[44]

Canassatego then told a story about the Dutch arriving in Iroquois territory with goods to give them. This so pleased the Iroquois that they tied the Dutch ship "to the Bushes on the Shore." Desiring a stronger connection to the newcomers, they removed the rope from the tree and tied it to the bushes on the shore, then to a "big Rock," and, finally, to "the big Mountain" (which the interpreter said was a reference to "Onandago Country," while the rock symbolized "Oneido Country"). In return, the Dutch "acknowledged our Right to the Lands, and solicited us, from

Time to Time, to grant them Parts of our Country, and to enter into League and Covenant with us, and to become one People with us."[45]

When the English arrived, Canassatego continued, they became "one People with the Dutch." Since the English governor approved of the "great Friendship" between the Dutch and the Six Nations, he "desired to make as strong a League, and to be upon as good Terms with us as the Dutch were, with whom he was united, and to become one People with us." When the governor found out that "the Rope which tied the Ship to the great Mountain was only fastened with Wampum" and liable to perish, he gave "us a Silver Chain, which would be much stronger, and would last for ever." This the Six Nations accepted, fastening "the Ship with it, and it has lasted ever since."[46]

Canassatego conceded that there had been "small Differences with the English" and that some Englishmen had told the Six Nations that without English goods they "should have perished." Canassatego insisted that before the English arrived, the Indians had "Room enough, and Plenty of Deer," but are now "straitened," a condition he blamed on "that Pen-and-Ink Work that is going on at the Table (pointing to the Secretary)." To illustrate the duplicity of the English, Canassatego said that the governor of New York had sold "the Sasquahannah lands" to Onas (Pennsylvania) despite a promise to the Iroquois "that he would keep it for our Use." Canassatego added that once "our Brother Onas" learned of "how the Governor of New York had deceived us, he very generously paid for our Lands over again."[47]

Canassatego then turned to the question of the disputed land in Maryland. He said that the deeds of sale the colony had produced, which had been "interpreted to us," were valid; and that "the Conestogoe or Sasquahannah Indians had a Right to sell those Lands to you, for they were then theirs." "But," he added, "since that Time we have conquered them, and their Country now belongs to us." What is more, "the Lands we demanded Satisfaction for are no Part of the Lands comprised in those deeds." Rather, "they are the Cohongorontas Lands; those we are sure, you have not possessed One Hundred Years, no, nor above Ten Years, and we made our Demands so soon as we knew your People were settled in those Parts." These lands "have never been sold," he insisted, "but remain still to be disposed of"; and he said he was pleased that the colonists were now ready to offer goods for these "unpurchased Lands."[48]

The next day, June 27, Virginia's commissioners addressed the Iroquois. In 1736, they claimed, the Six Nations had informed Virginia that they wanted "Consideration" for some lands the colony occupied. The governor and the colony's Council then looked into old treaties and found "that you had given up your Lands to the Great King, who has had possession of Virginia above One Hundred and Sixty Years, and under that Great King the Inhabitants of Virginia hold their Land, so they thought there might be some Mistake." The commissioners then asked the Iroquois "what Nations of Indians you conquered any Lands from in Virginia, how long it is since, and what Possession you have had," adding that if there are any lands on our borders they "have a Right to, we are willing to make you a Satisfaction." After which, the commissioners laid down a string of wampum, told the Six Nations they had a chest of goods for them, and informed them that they were "our Brethren; the Great King is our common Father; and we will live with you, as Children ought to do, in Peace and Love." They also told the Six Nations that Virginia "will brighten the Chain, and strengthen the Union between us; so that we will never be divided, but remain Friends and Brethren as long as the Sun gives Light." To confirm this, they gave them a belt of wampum.[49]

Tachanoontia, an Onondonga warrior and diplomat, answered Virginia, telling the commissioners he was glad that Virginia and Maryland were "kindling this Fire" and confirming the "Treaties of Friendship" between the Six Nations and the English.[50] To Virginia's claim that the Six Nations had no right to the land in dispute, he replied that "[w]e have the Right of Conquest, a Right too dearly purchased, and which cost us too much Blood, to give up without any Reason at all, as you say we have done at Albany."[51] Indeed, he was certain that the Iroquois had never "relinquished our Right," for "[a]ll the World knows we conquered the several Nations living on Sasquahanna, Cohongoronta, and on the Back of the Great Mountains in Virginia." They all "feel the Effects of our Conquests, being now a Part of our Nations, and their Lands at our Disposal." Tachanoontia was willing to concede that the English may have conquered the Powhatans on the coast, "and drove back the Tuscarroraws, and that they have, on that Account, a Right to some Part of Virginia; but as to what lies beyond the Mountains, we conquered the Nations residing there, and that Land, if the Virginians ever get a good Right to it, it must be by us." Tachanoontia added that he was glad to hear that the Virginians had brought a big chest of goods with them in order to compensate the Iroquois for the loss of these lands; and he hoped that in the future "there may be no Dirt, nor any other obstacle in the Road between us."[52]

Having defended the Six Nations' land claims, Tachanoontia turned to the question of where the boundary was between the two peoples. He reminded the Virginians that twenty years ago at Albany they had taken "a Belt of Wampum, and made a Fence with it on the Middle of the Hill, and told us, that if any of the Warriors of the Six Nations came on your Side of the Middle of the Hill, you would hang them; and you gave us Liberty to do the same with any of your People." Tachanoontia desired that this treaty be "confirmed," pointing out to the commissioners that even though the Six Nations had "brought our Road a great deal more to the West, that we might comply with your Proposal," Virginians had never abided by the treaty. Instead, they "came and Lived on our Side of the Hill." Tachanoontia acknowledged that it was hard for the colonial government on the coast to control the back country, but he pointed out that because the settlers had encroached on the Six Nations' "new Road . . . our Warriors did some Hurt to your People's Cattle." The subsequent complaints from Virginia to the governor of Pennsylvania led the Six Nations to alter the road again, bringing it to "the Foot of the Great Mountain, where it now is." But, he insisted, "[I]t is impossible for us to remove it any further to the West, those Parts of the Country being absolutely impassable by either Man or Beast." For even after this concession, "your People came, like Flocks of Birds, and sat down on both Sides of it, and yet we never made a Complaint to you, tho' you must be sensible those Things must have been done by your People in manifest Breach of your own Proposal made at Albany." Tachanoontia added that this "Affair of the Road" must be settled before "the Grant of Lands." Either the Virginians must "remove more Easterly, or, if they are permitted to stay, that our Warriors marching that Way to the Southward, shall go Sharers with them in what they plant."[53]

On June 28, the commissioners of Maryland and Virginia asked the interpreter to inform the Iroquois that they would like to address them that afternoon. The commissioners of Maryland spoke first, telling the Iroquois that they could not admit "your Right" to "Lands now in our Province." They did, however, want to live in "Brotherly Love and Affection with the Six Nations," so "upon your giving us a Release in Writing of all your Claims to any Lands in Maryland, we shall make you a Compensation to the Value of Three Hundred Pounds Currency." The commissioners then called the Six Nations "good Friends" and "Brethren" and told them they wanted to be "as One Soul and one Body" with them. They also desired "a broad Road" between them that should always be kept clear, and hoped that "the Links of our Friendship" would never be "rusted." As a "Testimony" that "our Words and our Hearts agree," the commissioners presented the Six Nations with a belt of wampum.[54]

The Virginia commissioners then addressed the Iroquois' claims about "old Times," reiterating that they were unaware of any conquest the Six Nations had made over the Indians on the west side of the mountains, and thus could not understand how they could have "possessed" any lands there. On the contrary, the Virginians contended, "That Part was altogether deserted and free for any People to enter upon, as the People of Virginia have done, by Order of the Great King, very justly, as well as by an ancient Right, as by its being freed from the Possession of any other, and from any Claim even of you the Six Nations, our Brethren, until within these eight Years." The commissioners then reviewed the history of Virginia's diplomatic relationship with the Six Nations. The first treaty between the two had been seventy years earlier at Albany. It was, the commissioners claimed, a "Treaty of Friendship, when the first Covenant Chain was made, when we and you became Brethren." Fifty-eight years earlier, at the next treaty (also at Albany), the Iroquois declared themselves "Subjects to the Great King, our Father, and gave up to him all your Lands for his Protection." The commissioners also reminded the Six Nation that not only had they put their lands under the protection of the English king, but they had asked for and received his assistance against the French. As for the boundaries between their territories, the commissioners told the Six Nations that it was false to claim that the "white People, your Brethren of Virginia," were forbidden to pass to the west of the mountain. Rather, it was the Indians who were tributary to Virginia, as well as those who were tributary to the Iroquois, who were forbidden east of the mountains, while the settlers had an unlimited right to settle to the west of the mountains.[55]

As the commissioners concluded triumphantly—"what Right can you have to Lands that you have no Right to walk upon, but upon certain Conditions."[56]

The Virginia commissioners then underscored this history lesson with a lecture on the superiority of written over oral evidence. As they pointed out, the treaties "we rely on" are "in Writing" and thus "more certain than your Memory." And they reminded the Iroquois that "your Sachims and Warriors" signed treaties with Virginia after it had been "in Possession of these very Lands, which you have set up your late Claim to." So in the view of the commissioners, this was really not a dispute between the Six Nations and Virginia, but between the Six Nations and the king, "under whose Grants the People you complain of are settled." What was more, "Nothing but a Command from the Great King can remove them; they are too powerful to be removed by any Force of you, our Brethren." However, the commissioners assured the Six Nations that the king "will do equal Justice to all his Children," though they made it clear that this meant that Virginians "will be confirmed in their Possessions."[57]

As for the right of the Iroquois to pass through Virginia's territory, the commissioners told the Six Nations that the English had tried to end the wars between them and the southern tribes at Albany, but peace was not "long kept between you." The commissioners did say they would grant the Six Nations free passage through Virginia as long as the Indians were "orderly like Friends and Brethren." As for the contested lands, the commissioners told the Six Nations that they would settle with them for all the lands they claimed south of Maryland and Pennsylvania, though they added that "the Southern Indians claim these very lands that you do." The Virginians were willing to do so because they "are desirous to live with you, our Brethren, according to the old Chain of Friendship."[58]

The next day, Canassatego, while consulting "a Deal-board" with the geography of the contested territories inscribed on it, informed Maryland's commissioners that the representatives of the Six Nations had "deliberately considered" their claims about the land on "this Side" of the Potomac, and were ready to "release our Right and Claim thereto," adding that any English person who settled "beyond the Lands now described and bounded" would be free from disturbance by the Six Nations and their allies, and would be "our Brethren."[59] As a token of "Brotherly Kindness," he presented the commissioners with a belt of wampum.[60]

Gachradodow, a Cayuga warrior and orator,[61] then rose to inform the English that the two peoples had different conceptions of law and justice:

> The World at the first was made on the other Side of the Great Water different from what it is on this Side, as may be known from the different Colours of our Skin, and of our Flesh, and that which you call Justice may not be so amongst us; you have your Laws and Customs, and so have we. The Great King might send you over to conquer the Indians, but it looks to us that God did not approve of it; if he had, he would not have placed the Sea where it is, as the Limits between us and you.[62]

Turning to Virginia's claims about the treaties it had made with the Six Nations, Gachradodow replied that his people did not remember "that we were ever conquered by the Great King, or that we have been employed by that Great King to conquer others." He did, however, recall being employed by Maryland to conquer "the Conestogoes," after which they "carried them all off." As for the charge that the Iroquois were responsible for conflict with the "Cherikees" and Catawbas, Gachradodow told the Virginians that the Six Nations had made peace with the former, but the latter had been "treacherous," which meant the war would continue "till one of us is destroyed." He concluded his speech by lecturing the English on their treatment of the Indians: "You know very well, when the white People came first here they were poor; but now they have got our Lands, and are by them become rich, and we are now poor; what little we have had for the land goes soon away, but the Land lasts for ever."[63]

At a dinner the same day, Gachradodow was chosen by the "united Nations" to confer on Maryland the name of "Tocarry-hoganon, denoting Precedency, Excellence, or living in the middle or honourable place" between Pennsylvania and Virginia. The Iroquois did this to thank Maryland for inviting them there to "treat about their Lands, and brighten the Chain of Friendship."[64] The Maryland commissioners then told Conrad Weiser that a deed releasing the Six Nations' "Claim and Title" to certain lands in their colony was now on the table, following which Canassatego "made his Mark, and put his Seal" on it, as did "thirteen other Chiefs or Sachims of the Six Nations."[65]

In the afternoon, the Virginia delegation informed the Six Nations that their goods were ready to be delivered, in exchange for which the Virginians wanted them to "immediately make a Deed recognizing the King's right to all the Lands that are, or shall be, by his Majesty's appointment in the Colony of Virginia." After which, "The Indians agreed to what was said," though Canassatego added the caveat that they would "represent their Case to the King, in order to have a further Consideration when the Settlement increased much further back." The deed was then produced, the interpreter explained it to the Six Nations, and, according to "their Rank and Quality," they "put their Marks and Seals to it."[66]

* * *

At Lancaster, the Iroquois spokesmen offered several arguments as to why their claim to the disputed territories was superior to that of Maryland and Virginia. The first was that they had always been there, occupying the land on this side of the ocean.[67] As Canassatego put it in his response to Maryland, "[B]ut what is One Hundred Years in Comparison to the Length of Time since our claim began." That is, the Iroquois had been where the English now were "long before" the "One Hundred Years" that Maryland could boast of. Indeed, their "Ancestors came out of this very Ground, and their Children have remained here ever since." This was the basis for their "just Claim" to it. The Iroquois had then ceded some of their autochthonous territory to the English voluntarily by treaties as part of an alliance between sovereign peoples.

The Iroquois also claimed the disputed territory by right of conquest over its previous indigenous occupants. Although claims to territorial rights following a conquest were part of the contemporary European law of nations, the Iroquois' formulation of this argument at Lancaster appears to be a hybrid one, which retained the older idea of a mourning war leading to the incorporation of defeated foes as kin alongside the European idea of conquest rights to land.[68] As Tachanoontia told his Virginian interlocutors, the Indians the Iroquois claimed to have conquered were "now a Part of our Nations, and their Lands at our Disposal."[69] The Iroquois' assertion of conquest rights was also very specific. In reply to Virginia's query about who the Iroquois had conquered, Tachanoontia named four Indian peoples whom he claimed resided on the Susquehanna, the Cohongoranta (that is, the Potomac),[70] and "on the Back of the Great Mountains in Virginia."[71] Modern scholarship has identified three of them—the Conoys, who had lived along the Potomac in what is now Maryland, but who migrated north to the Susquehanna River Valley to live under Iroquois protection around 1700; the Kanawa, from the headwaters of the Potomac; and the Tutelos, who were from the southern Piedmont, but who also moved to the Susquehanna in the early eighteenth century.[72] The Iroquois did concede that the Virginians had a right, via conquest of the Powhatans on the tidewater as well as the Tuscaroras, to part of the territory they currently occupied, but not to the land west of the mountains.[73] The Iroquois' assertion of conquest right against Maryland was similarly fine-grained: they conceded that Maryland had been deeded land by the Susquehannocks, but they insisted that the Iroquois had since conquered them. And in any case, the land the Iroquois were claiming was not the same territory that Maryland had been deeded.[74] The specificity of the Iroquois' claims contrasts starkly with Virginia's more sweeping claims to land by conquest "Westward" to "the Great Sea."[75] The Iroquois demonstrated a similarly acute understanding of territorial boundaries in their negotiations with Virginia over a right of way to the south.

Nevertheless, the Iroquois' claim to territorial rights based on conquest has been treated with skepticism by some scholars.[76] We do know, however, that the western Iroquois Nations who were at Lancaster had gone to war with the Susquehannocks, an Iroquois-speaking people who, at various times in the seventeenth century, had occupied territory in both the Susquehanna River Valley and on the Potomac. By the mid-1670s, after decades of warfare, the Susquehannocks had been defeated and begun to disperse, though we do not know whether this defeat was by the English or by the Iroquois.[77] The consequence was that some of them moved north to live among the Iroquois, adopting the name Conestogas, and becoming one of several southern Indian nations who were adopted as "props" of the Longhouse.[78] The Susquenhannocks then assisted the Iroquois in raids on Maryland's tributary allies (the Piscataways and the Conoys) who had attacked them in 1675–1677, as part of Maryland's war on the Susqhehannocks. These raids took the Iroquois into Virginia as well, and so could be the basis for the Iroquois claims to have conquered the Conoys (among other peoples).[79]

The deliberations at Lancaster also allow us to observe the articulation of Anglo-American claims to property in dialogue with indigenous arguments. Maryland made its case against the Iroquois on the basis of long usage (they claimed to have been on their land for "above one hundred years past").[80] Maryland also invoked treaties signed with "the Susquahanna Indians" ninety years earlier, giving them the right to land on both sides of "the Great Bay of Chesapeak."[81] In addition, Maryland said that they were subjects of the "Great King's, and so we possess and enjoy the Province of Maryland by virtue of his Right and Sovereignty thereto."[82] Finally, Maryland contended that the Iroquois had submitted themselves to the king "near Sixty years ago," which had also involved a cession of their land rights.[83]

Missing from Maryland's array of legal arguments was any claim to conquest rights. Virginia, though, made conquest central to its rebuttal to the Iroquois, insisting that "the Great king holds Virginia by Right of Conquest, and the Bounds of that Conquest to the Westward is the Sea."[84] Virginia also advanced a claim to territory based on the fact that, by royal grant, they had occupied their territory for "above One Hundred and Sixty Years."[85] Like Maryland, the Virginians claimed that they had looked "into the old Treaties" and had concluded that the Iroquois had "given up your Lands to the Great King."[86] As to the lands in question on the west side of the mountains, Virginia's commissioners maintained that they were "altogether deserted," which meant that there were no Indians living there for the Iroquois to conquer, and thus the land was "free for any People to enter upon."[87] Finally, Virginia contended that they had "an ancient Right" to all land west of the mountains.[88]

* * *

Land rights was not the only contentious question debated at Lancaster. Governor Thomas and the Pennsylvanians also wanted justice for three Indian traders who had been killed by Delaware Indians. Two of the perpetrators had been seized by other Natives, but one had escaped. On June 28, Thomas informed the Iroquois that, according to English law, the murderer and all his accomplices must be tried, with the death penalty as the punishment if convicted. He added that two Pennsylvanians had recently been put to death for the murder of two Indians, which made it all the more pressing that the Iroquois find those who had murdered the traders and send them to Philadelphia for trial. He told the Iroquois that they could depute three Indians to be present at the trials to make sure there was no miscarriage of justice.[89]

A few days later, on July 2, Canassatego addressed Governor Thomas's complaint about the murder of the Indians traders. He told the governor that "[t]he Delaware Indians . . . are under our Power" and that "[w]e join with you in your Concern for such a vile Proceeding." But he then downplayed the gravity of the murders, telling Thomas that such violence happened frequently between English people and Indians. For example, "Three Indians have been killed at different times at Ohio, and we never mentioned any of them to you." The Iroquois did, however, have a conference with "our Cousins" the Delawares about the murder of the traders, and "reproved them severely for it." Canassatego then proposed that some of the Delaware chiefs take the two accused Indians to Pennsylvania for examination; however, he insisted that they would not go as prisoners. Having resisted Thomas's attempt to dictate the terms of the extradition, Canassatego complained to the governor on behalf of the Conoy Indians who had, he claimed, been forced off their lands by white people without compensation.[90]

Thomas replied to Canassatego with a warning: if the crimes were not punished, "there will be an End of all Commerce between us and the Indians, and then you will be altogether in the Power of the French." He also claimed to not have heard of the murder of the three Ohio Indians, but said that, if the claim was true, the perpetrators should have been executed. He then denied any knowledge of the harm done to the Conoy Indians, and demanded again that the accomplices be delivered to Philadelphia to be tried under English law. If they did not show up, he told Canassatego, he would assume that they were guilty; but if they submitted themselves to colonial justice and were acquitted, they would be set free.[91]

* * *

In the final two days of the conference, the parties discussed the onset of war with the French, as well as the need to renew old alliances. On July 3, Governor Thomas asked the Iroquois to share intelligence of French troop movements with the English, as well as to stop the French and their Indian allies from marching through Iroquois territory to attack the

English colonies. And he made it clear that Pennsylvania, Virginia, and Maryland "are ready to confirm our Treaties with your Nations, and establish a Friendship that is not to end, but with the World itself."[92] He then presented the Six Nations with wampum and goods in order to "confirm and establish the said Treaties of Peace, Union, and Friendship."[93] After warning the Iroquois that the Catawbas, though rash, "are also Children of the Great King,"[94] Virginia asked the Iroquois if they would send some of their children to live with the English in order to learn "the Religion, Language, and Customs of the White People" so that when Conrad Weiser was dead the English and the Iroquois could continue to communicate.[95] Maryland then presented its gifts to the Six Nations, telling them that the treaty would prevent "every future Misunderstanding between us," and promising to "bind faster the Links of our Chain of Friendship" and not let "the least Speck" of "Rust" make it unclean.[96]

Once again, Canassatego told the colonists that the Six Nations needed until the next day to answer them, for "your several Speeches . . . contain Matters of such great Moment" that "we propose to give them a very serious Consideration."[97] The next morning, on July 4, Canassatego told the English delegates that "you and we have but one Heart, one Head, one Eye, one Ear, and one Hand." He also promised to protect the English settlements and to tell the French governor, "our Father," not to come through Iroquois territory to fight the English. As well, he pledged the neutrality of the Indian allies of the French (whom he claimed the Iroquois controlled). Canassatego also informed the Virginians that the Six Nations would not be sending their children to them to be educated as "our Customs" differ "from yours." However, he added, "as the Dispute about the Land is now intirely over, and we perfectly reconciled, we hope, for the future, we shall not act towards each other but as becomes Brethren and hearty Friends." He also asked the Virginians if messengers from the Six Nations could continue to use the "old Road" to communicate with "the Tuscaroraes, who are our friends" (the Six Nations had opened "a new Road for our Warriors");[98] and he indicated that the Six Nations would be open to signing a peace with the Catawbas. His final request was that the Conoy Indians (who, he said, were relocating to be with the Six Nations) might be allowed free passage through Virginia. To Maryland, or "Tocarry-hogan," he agreed that no rust should tarnish "the Chain of Friendship" between the two peoples.[99]

As the treaty conference came to a close, Canassatego thanked the English delegates for the "very handsome Presents," and lamented that the Indians could not be equally munificent as "we are poor." For this, he blamed the "Indian traders among us," adding that "the White Peoples Cattle have eat up all the Grass, and made Deer scarce."[100] He then lectured the English delegates on the need for a union of all the colonies modeled on the Iroquois Confederacy: "Our wise Forefathers established Unity and Amity between the Five Nations; this has made us formidable; this has given us great Weight and Authority with our neighbouring Nations. We are a powerful Confederacy; and by your observing the same Methods our wise Forefathers have taken, you will acquire fresh Strength and Power; therefore whatever befals you, never fall out, one with another."[101]

The governor of Pennsylvania brought the treaty conference to an end by praising the Six Nations for their service to the English. He then reminded them that "[w]e are all Subjects, as well as you, of the Great King beyond the Water," and thus would always be inclined to live in friendship. Virginia assured the Six Nations that their messengers to Tuscaroras (as well as the Conoys) would have free passage through its territory. They also presented them with "a Paper, containing a Promise to recommend the Six Nations for further Favour to the King."[102]

Although the Iroquois appeared to have gotten what they wanted at Lancaster, the reality was different. Rather than ceding claims to lands in the Shenandoah Valley on the western border of Virginia, the deed they signed was interpreted by Virginia to include all the land claimed by the colony in its original charter—which meant all the land from the Ohio Valley to the Pacific![103] Within months, Virginia's governor had chartered a company to sell this land, which in turn led France to send troops into the Ohio Valley.[104] The subsequent war between the two European rivals for North America would be disastrous for the indigenous peoples east of the Mississippi.

* * *

Despite its dire outcome, the negotiations at Lancaster allow us to listen to a powerful articulation of indigenous legal-political ideas—ideas that were asserted in response to and in dialogue with English claims to property and sovereignty. As we have already discussed, at Lancaster the

Iroquois advanced two arguments about their territorial rights—first, that they had, literally, come "out of the ground," and thus had a better title to land on their side of the ocean than the recently arrived Europeans; and, second, that they had conquered Indian peoples to the south of Iroquoia and thus had a right to their former territories, which were now being occupied by settlers from Maryland and Virginia. Thus any land the English were to occupy legitimately had to be acquired voluntarily by a formally negotiated treaty. In their debates with Virginia and Maryland, the Iroquois also demonstrated a sophisticated awareness of exactly where their territories were and those of their tributaries, as well as where the English had legitimate claims.

The Iroquois also made it clear that they exercised sovereignty over the territories they occupied, which included a claim to jurisdiction over the tributary Indians whom they had incorporated into the Longhouse.[105] Their several nations also had the political capacity to form a "Union," and they lectured the delegates at Lancaster on the superiority of their confederated polity over the loose collection of English colonies that seemed unable to unite against the French. What is more, the Iroquois claimed the right, like all sovereign polities, to make alliances on their terms with both the English and the French. At Lancaster, they repeatedly addressed the English as "Brethren" and "Friends," words that denoted equality, and they invoked a number of metaphors (most prominently that of a "Chain") to describe their ability to make alliances with other polities like the English.[106] And though they referred to themselves as the "Children" of "the Great King beyond the Seas," they denied that this meant subordination to the English colonists. On the contrary, they told the colonists that they would appeal to the king "to compel you to do us Justice." They were also not willing to allow members of Indian nations tributary to them to be extradited to Philadelphia unilaterally, a sign that they saw their laws and polity as distinct from, and thus not subject to, the English. Nor were the Iroquois eager to be dragged into a war with the French, promising the English some aid, but otherwise insisting on maintaining an autonomous foreign policy.

The English at Lancaster also relied on long usage as a basis for claiming territory (so Virginia referred to its "ancient Right" to the lands in dispute), which is not surprising given the centrality of custom in their common law. Like the Iroquois, the Virginians also made conquest central to their territorial claims, though both were silent on what legitimated the conquest in the first place. Absent, though, from English claims at Lancaster was any sustained use of an argument from vacancy, or *terra* or *res nullius*, though the Virginians did make one claim that the disputed land was "deserted" and thus "free for any People to enter upon." Indeed, the English claim to land rights by conquest assumed the existence of a distinct people over whom the conquest was made.[107] Nor did any of the English representatives argue that they had a superior right to land in the New World because they, unlike the Indians, had labored on it. Absent too was any contention that the indigenous peoples across the conference table from them were savages or nomads or stateless people, lacking laws and government and systems of property. On the contrary, the minutes are replete with examples of the English recognizing Iroquois property and sovereignty by treaty, and embracing them as brothers and friends and allies, all of which cuts against the grain of much (though not all) of the recent work on Anglo-American arguments for empire in the early modern North America.[108]

The overlapping nature of the two sets of legal arguments at Lancaster is striking, but not perhaps surprising.[109] For the English and the Iroquois were not aliens, incapable of communicating with each other, even if, as the Iroquois speaker Gachradodow insisted, there remained deep differences between them on what constituted law and justice.[110] They both lived in loose confederations, with each colony or nation retaining a great deal of autonomy; and they both had a long history of making treaties with each other in order to deal with pressing questions about land, trade, and alliances. Even the tensions in the arguments of the Iroquois and their English interlocutors were similar in nature—for example, both claimed long usage or prescription alongside conquest as a basis for their territorial rights. Both peoples thus seemed less concerned to achieve the kind of coherence we associate with a formal legal treatise, and more interested in drawing on the full repertoire of arguments available to them as they debated the legitimacy of European settlement in the Americas.[111]

* * *

Studying the deliberations at Lancaster gives us a sense of what a fuller account of debates about the justice of early modern empire might look like, one that incorporates legal claims made by both indigenous and European peoples. Future research on indigenous legal arguments, however, will have to take seriously the fact that the Iroquois made treaties with other European powers. Their world, in other words, was not limited to the particular European empire that any one legal historian specializes in. So, for example, a fuller account of Iroquois legal ideas would require an examination of the arguments they made to the Dutch and the French as well as those they made to the English. Such a comparative study would allow us to determine whether there was a common set of Iroquois arguments across time and place, or whether the legal claims they made differed depending on who their interlocutors were. Scholars also need to relate Iroquois legal-political arguments to the rich metaphors—the talk of chains, and roads, and council fires, not to mention the imagery on the belts of wampum exchanged around the council fire—that structured the way that they and the English thought about their alliances. Scholars will also have to explore the relationship between Iroquois legal arguments and the myths about the origins of their League, the rituals of which structured diplomacy with both the English and other Native peoples.[112]

Future work on the legalities of early modern empire should also ask whether there was a common indigenous response to European empire, or whether different Native peoples held different conceptions of, say, property, or the justice of conquest.[113] For example, in their appeals to the crown in the eighteenth century, the Mohegans and other northeastern indigenous peoples made arguments about their political autonomy and property rights that were similar to those the Iroquois made at Lancaster. Unlike the Iroquois, however, they did not invoke conquest rights in these appeals.[114] Scholars also need to examine the arguments about law and justice that Natives made to each other, for intra-Native legal and diplomatic relations were often as important as their relationship with Europeans, if not more so.

This kind of fine-grained analysis should also be applied to scholarship on European legal arguments, which often reads as if there existed a consensus on the justice of dispossession, at least in the Anglo-American world, when in fact the evidence from the Lancaster treaty suggests a greater acceptance of indigenous legal rights among settlers and colonial officials.[115] In a similar vein, it would also be worth exploring whether

Anglo-Americans talked differently about the legal rights of a powerful confederacy like the Iroquois than they did about the weaker Native peoples on the eastern seaboard, most of whom had been conquered by the end of the seventeenth century. None of this is to suggest that we should abandon large-scale generalizations about law and justice in early modern European empires—just that they should be based on a wider range of encounters, attentive to the differences of time and place, and incorporate the indigenous legal arguments that were always in dialogue with European claims.

NOTES

1 The literature is large and growing. For a recent overview, see Jennifer Pitts, "Political Theory of Empire and Imperialism," *American Review of Political Science* 13 (2011), 211–35.

2 See the pioneering work of Lauren Benton, *Law and Colonial Cultures: Legal Regimes in World History, 1400–1900* (New York: Cambridge University Press, 2002); and *A Search for Sovereignty: Law and Geography in European Empires, 1400–1900* (New York: Cambridge University Press, 2010); as well as the essays in Lauren Benton and Richard Ross, eds., *Empires and Legal Pluralism: Jurisdiction, Sovereignty, and Political Imagination in the Early Modern World* (New York: NYU Press, 2013).

3 For a forceful argument along these lines, see Jack P. Greene, "Colonial History and National History: Reflections on a Continuing Problem," *William and Mary Quarterly* 64 (2007), 235–50. For the longstanding denial of indigenous rights in early American legal and political theory, see Craig Yirush, *Settlers, Liberty, and Empire: The Roots of Early American Political Theory, 1675–1775* (New York: Cambridge University Press, 2011).

4 To take but one example, Ken MacMillan's influential recent book on the use of Roman law to justify English settlement contains no discussion of indigenous rights, nor any consideration of the indigenous response to European claims. MacMillan, *Sovereignty and Possession in the English New World: The Legal Foundations of Empire, 1576–1640* (Cambridge: Cambridge University Press, 2006).

5 See for example the recent compilation edited by Sankar Muthu, which contains essays on the imperial thought of, among others, Machiavelli, Locke, Burke, and Mill, but relatively little on the indigenous response to these European theorists. Muthu, ed., *Empire and Modern Political Thought* (New York: Cambridge University Press, 2012).

6 For pioneering work on indigenous legal claims, see Jenny Pulsipher, *Subjects unto the Same King: Indians, English, and the Contest for Authority in Colonial New England* (Philadelphia: University of Pennsylvania Press, 2005); and the essays in *Native Claims* cited below. I have written about Native appeals to the

Crown as part of a larger project on indigenous arguments about empire, entitled *Chief Princes and Owners of All* (of which this chapter is also a part). See Craig Yirush, "Claiming the New World: Empire, Law, and Indigenous Rights in the Mohegan Case, 1704–1743," *Law and History Review* 29 (2011), 333–73; and Yirush, "'Chief Princes and Owners of All': Native American Appeals to the Crown in the Early Modern British Atlantic," in Saliha Belmessous, ed., *Native Claims: Indigenous Law against Empire, 1500–1920* (New York: Oxford University Press, 2011), 129–51.

7   On which see Daniel Richter, *Facing East from Indian Country: A Native History of Early America* (Cambridge, MA: Harvard University Press, 2001).

8   As Michael Witgen has recently argued, it was the Natives' new world as much as it was the Europeans'. Witgen, *An Infinity of Nations: How the Native New World Shaped Early North America* (Philadelphia: University of Pennsylvania Press, 2012).

9   The ethnohistorians cited above have carefully reconstructed Native culture and society, but have for the most part been less interested in the elucidation of their legal and political ideas. Scholars of indigenous peoples in colonial Latin America, however, appear more open to considering their ideas. See, for example, Gabriela Ramos and Yanna Yannakakis, eds., *Indigenous Intellectuals: Knowledge, Power, and Colonial Culture in Mexico and the Andes* (Durham, NC: Duke University Press, 2014); as well as the essays in this volume.

10 And to the extent that there has been a focus on the content of Native speeches, it has been for the quality of their oratory. For example, James Merrell, whose work on Indian treaties I am indebted to, says that the point of reading the minutes of these conferences closely is to "shed new light on Native American oratory," adding that if ethnohistorians are unable to do this they should hand the study of the speeches "over to intellectual historians and literary critics." James Merrell, "'I desire all that I have said . . . may be taken down aright': Revisiting Teedyuscung's 1756 Treaty Council Speeches," *William and Mary Quarterly* 63 (2006), 779, 817 (see also, 794, "the aim here is to begin a discussion of Teedyuscung's Easton oratory").

11 For the most recent accounts of English treaties with Native Americans, see Jeffrey Glover, *Paper Sovereigns: Anglo-Native Treaties and the Law of Nations, 1604–1664* (Philadelphia; University of Pennsylvania Press, 2014); and, for the eighteenth century (though it also contains discussion of the first century of treaty making), Colin Calloway, *Pen and Ink Witchcraft: Treaties and Treaty Making in American Indian History* (New York: Oxford University Press, 2013). According to Merrell, the treaties between the English and the Native Americans became bigger and grander affairs after about 1720. Merrell, *Into the American Woods: Negotiators on the Pennsylvania Frontier* (New York: Norton, 1999), 254.

12 The increasing numbers of Indians at treaty councils in the eighteenth century was a function of a desire for political consensus. See Merrell, *Into the American Woods*, 257.

13 On which, see Francois Furstenburg, "The Significance of the Trans-Appalachian Frontier in Atlantic History," *American Historical Review* 113 (2008), 647–77.

14 The literature on the Iroquois is large and sophisticated. On the origins of the League, see William Fenton, *The Great Law and the Longhouse: A Political History of the Iroquois Confederacy* (Norman: University of Oklahoma Press, 1998). The classic work on the Iroquois after the arrival of the French and English is Daniel Richter, *The Ordeal of the Longhouse: The Peoples of the Iroquois League in the Era of European Colonization* (Chapel Hill: University of North Carolina Press, 1992). On the Iroquois in the eighteenth century, see Richard Aquila, *The Iroquois Restoration: Iroquois Diplomacy on the Colonial Frontier, 1701–1754* (Detroit, MI: Wayne State University Press, 1983).

15 Timothy Shannon, *Iroquois Diplomacy on the Early American Frontier* (New York: Viking, 2008), 30.

16 Shannon, *Iroquois Diplomacy*, 50; and Richard Haan, "Covenant and Consensus: Iroquois and English, 1676–1760," in Daniel Richter and James Merrell, eds., *Beyond the Covenant Chain: The Iroquois and Their Neighbors in Indian North America, 1600–1800* (Syracuse, NY: Syracuse University Press, 1987), 53, 55–56.

17 Daniel Richter, "War and Culture: The Iroquois Experience," *William and Mary Quarterly* 40 (1983), 535–36.

18 Shannon, *Iroquois Diplomacy*, 34; and Francis Jennings, *The Ambiguous Iroquois Empire: The Covenant Chain Confederation of Indian Tribes with English Colonies from Its Beginnings to the Lancaster Treaty of 1744* (New York: Norton, 1984), 162–63 (on the Iroquois making war on those who refused to accept their peace). According to Mathew Dennis, the possibility that peoples outside Iroquoia might threaten their vision of peace meant that "the Five Nations were never pacifists." But however aggressive the Iroquois might have seemed to outsiders, "the Five Nations themselves had no program of military conquest; for the Iroquois these conflicts represented the frustration or failure of their vision, not its realization." See Dennis, *Cultivating a Landscape of Peace: Iroquois-European Encounters in Seventeenth-Century America* (Ithaca, NY: Cornell University Press, 1993), 97–98. Daniel Richter suggests that the Iroquois envisioned the diplomatic rituals of their League as an alternative to the mourning function of war. See Richter, "War and Culture," 536.

19 Richter, "War and Culture," 537–44.

20 On which see Haan, "Covenant and Consensus," 41–57; and Jennings, *The Ambiguous Iroquois Empire, passim*.

21 Gilles Harvard, *The Great Peace of Montreal: French-Native Diplomacy in the Seventeenth Century* (Montreal: McGill-Queen's University Press, 2001); and Aquila, *The Iroquois Restoration*, 85–128.

22 For the distinction between the League and the Confederacy, see Richter, "Ordeals of the Longhouse: The Five Nations in Early American History," in Richter and Merrell, eds., *Beyond the Covenant Chain*, 11–27. As Timothy Shannon points out, "the distinction between the Iroquois League and the Iroquois Confederacy

was never perfect," and most Europeans (who "had only the foggiest notion of what the Grand Council was") dealt with the Iroquois through "the framework of the improvised and expansive Confederacy, not the traditional League." See Shannon, *Iroquois Diplomacy*, 72–73. See also, Fenton, *Great Law and the Longhouse*, 493–94, on the supplanting of the hereditary chiefs in the eighteenth century by "headmen of achieved status" who "presided over the grand council, made embassies to Europeans, and signed treaties."

23 Richter, *Ordeal of the Longhouse*, 275.

24 On which, see Jennings, *The Ambiguous Iroquois Empire*, 113–71. For the Iroquois' claim to own all the lands in the Susquehanna River Valley (as well as the Shenandoah), see Aquila, *Iroquois Restoration*, 181.

25 See "Conrad Weiser's Report of His Journey to Onondaga on the Affairs of Virginia," in *A Journey from Pennsylvania to Onondaga in 1743* (Barre, MA: Imprint Society, 1973), 115–32.

26 The documentary record of the Lancaster conference is not extensive. I have based my account on Franklin's published version of the treaty minutes—*A Treaty Held at the Town of Lancaster, in Pennsylvania, by the Honourable the Lieutenant-Governor of the Province, and the Honourable the Commissioners for the Provinces of Virginia and Maryland, with the Indians of the Six Nations, in June 1744* (Philadelphia: Printed and Sold by B. Franklin, 1744). An identical version is in *The Minutes of the Provincial Council of Pennsylvania, from the Organization to the Termination of the Proprietary Government* (Harrisburg, PA: 1851), 4:698–737 (for Thomas's summation of the results of the treaty to the Provincial Council, see ibid., 739–40). The printer William Parks published another edition of the treaty minutes—*The Treaty Held with the Indians of the Six Nations, at Lancaster, in Pennsylvania, in June, 1744* (Williamsburg: Printed and Sold by William Parks). It is substantially similar to Franklin's edition, bar an introductory essay, "An Account of the First Confederacy of the Six Nations, Their Present Tributaries, Dependents, and Allies, and of Their Religion, and Form of Government," and copies of three agreements that the Iroquois made with the Virginia commissioners at Lancaster. The source for Parks's essay was Thomas Lee, one of the Virginia commissioners, who had become friends with Conrad Weiser, and to whom he put a series of questions about the Iroquois. The Williamsburg preface also appeared in the *American Magazine* of London in 1744. See Fenton, *Great Law and the Longhouse*, 434–38. The best account of the proceedings is the journal of William Marshe (cited below). William Black, the secretary for Virginia at Lancaster, also kept a journal, but it ends before the conference began. "The Journal of William Black," *Pennsylvania Magazine of History and Biography* 1 (1877), 117–32, 233–49. One of the Maryland commissioners, Edmund Jennings, wrote to Lord Baltimore about the treaty. See Calvert Papers, MSS 174, Maryland Historical Society. James Merrell has published a modern edition of the treaty, using Franklin's text. Merrell, ed., *The Lancaster Treaty of 1744 with Related Documents* (New York: Bedford St. Martins, 2008).

27 See William A. Starna, "The Diplomatic Career of Canasatego," in William A. Pencak and Daniel Richter, eds., *Friends and Enemies in Penn's Woods: Indians, Colonists, and the Racial Construction of Pennsylvania* (University Park: Pennsylvania State University Press), 144–63. In conformity with the text of the published treaty, I have spelled his name with an extra "s."

28 Marshe, "Journal of the Treaty Held with the Six Nations by the Commissioners of Maryland, and Other Provinces, at Lancaster, in Pennsylvania, June 1744," *Collections of the Massachusetts Historical Society*, 1st series, volume 7 (Boston: Samuel Hall, 1801), 179.

29 On Canassetego's status, see Starna, "The Diplomatic Career of Canasatego," 145. Fenton claims that none of the 127 Iroquois men at Lancaster held a hereditary League title. *Great Law and the Longhouse*, 425. According to Daniel Richter, "the key figures" in the emergent Confederacy's diplomacy with the French in the mid-seventeenth century "were village headmen and influential local orators, most of whom were evidently not League sachems." Richter, "Ordeals of the Longhouse," 21.

30 Paul Wallace, *Conrad Weiser, 1696–1760: Friend of Colonist and Mohawk* (Philadelphia: University of Pennsylvania Press, 1945).

31 On this point, see Merrell, ed., *The Lancaster Treaty*, 16. According to Fenton, Weiser translated from Onondaga to Mohawk and then into English at the Iroquois' treaty with Philadelphia in 1742. *Great Law and the Longhouse*, 414. Witham Marshe claimed that many of the Iroquois spoke English but that they refused to do so during treaty conferences. Marshe, "Journal," 180.

32 Marshe, "Journal," 179. See also, Fenton, *Great Law and the Longhouse*, 423. According to Mary Druke, Iroquois diplomacy, both with Natives and with Europeans, depended on building consensus via deliberation. Druke, "Linking Arms: The Structure of Iroquois Intertribal Diplomacy," in Richter and Merrell, eds., *Beyond the Covenant Chain*, 37. Leaders were not representatives in the European sense; rather, they depended on the explicit consent of their followers to make binding decisions.

33 *The Treaty Held with the Indians of the Six Nations, at Philadelphia, in July, 1742* (Philadelphia: B. Franklin, 1743).

34 The accuracy of English transcriptions and translations of Native speeches has been the subject of much debate. Daniel Richter argues that "the most valuable clues to Iroquois perspectives come from the speeches native leaders made during diplomatic encounters with Euro-Americans." Richter, *Ordeal of the Longhouse*, 5–6. Nancy Shoemaker notes that better "strategies for communication were . . . in place" by the eighteenth century, due in part to dictionaries, as well as greater numbers of colonists and natives who could speak and write multiple languages. Shoemaker, *A Strange Likeness: Becoming Red and White in Eighteenth-Century North America* (New York: Oxford University Press, 2004), 9–11 (quotation at 10). James Merrell argues that by using multiple accounts of treaty negotiations, scholars can find "genuine echoes of a long-forgotten native voice and native sensibility." Merrell, "'I desire all that I have said,'" 819.

35 On Peters's often malign role in Indian affairs, see Calloway, *Pen and Ink Witch-craft*, 67–68.
36 *A Treaty Held at the Town of Lancaster*, 4–5.
37 Ibid., 5.
38 Ibid., 6.
39 Ibid., 6.
40 Ibid., 6–7.
41 Ibid., 8.
42 Ibid., 8–9.
43 Ibid., 10.
44 Ibid., 11.
45 Ibid., 11.
46 Ibid., 12.
47 Ibid., 12. This is undoubtedly a reference to the land Charles II granted William Penn out of the territory he had earlier given his brother, the Duke of York.
48 Ibid., 13. Canassatego noted that the land had since been divided among Maryland, Pennsylvania, and Virginia.
49 Ibid., 14.
50 In his account of the Lancaster Treaty, Fenton refers to him as Tekanontie, "a noted war leader," "also known as 'the Black Prince.'" Fenton, *The Great Law and the Longhouse*, 418, 425, 428.
51 Tachanoontia also demanded to see the documentation and to be told who the interpreter was. Ibid., 15. Virginia claimed that the Six Nations had failed to make a claim to land in Virginia when specifically asked at Albany in May 1743. Ibid., 14.
52 Ibid., 15–16.
53 Ibid., 16–17.
54 Ibid., 18–19.
55 The Virginians are referring here to the terms of a 1722 treaty at Albany between their governor, Spotswood, and the Iroquois.
56 Ibid., 20–21.
57 Ibid., 21–22.
58 Ibid., 22.
59 Ibid., 22–23. The minutes say he was looking at "a Deal-board, where were some black Lines, describing the courses of the Potowmack and Susquehanna." A Deal-board is "a board made of pine or fur." Merrell, ed., *The Treaty of Lancaster*, 68.
60 *A Treaty Held at the Town of Lancaster*, 23.
61 The next day, Peters described him as one of the Six Nations "Chiefs," who gave a speech with "all the Dignity of a Warrior, the Gesture of an Orator, and in a very graceful Posture." *A Treaty Held at the Town of Lancaster*, 25.
62 Ibid., 23.
63 Ibid., 23–24.
64 Ibid., 25.

65 Ibid., 26. Those chiefs who had not signed the cession to Maryland earlier also did so on July 2nd.

66 Ibid., 29–30.

67 Or the "Great Water" as Gachradodow put it. Ibid., 23.

68 This is a hypothesis based on my reading of the relevant ethnohistories on the Iroquois. However, I could find no sustained discussion of Iroquois ideas of conquest in these works. Nor is there any in the standard reference books on the Iroquois. For example, Bruce Johansen and Barbara Mann, eds., *Encyclopedia of the Haudenosaunnee (Iroquois Confederacy)* (Westport, CT: Greenwood, 2000) contains no entry for "conquest" (or related terms like "warfare"). Timothy Shannon notes earlier Iroquois claims to land via conquest, most notably at the 1701 Montreal treaty. *Iroquois Diplomacy*, 59. For the European debates about conquest rights, see Tuck, *The Rights of War and Peace: Political Thought and the International Order from Grotius to Kant* (New York: Oxford University Press, 1999). For the use of conquest theory in English North America, see Yirush, *Settlers, Liberty, and Empire*, chapter 1.

69 Ibid., 16.

70 The official treaty minutes translated Cohongorontas as "Potomack." Ibid., 13.

71 Ibid., 16.

72 See Merrell, ed., *The Lancaster Treaty*, 59, note 12.

73 Ibid., 16–17. Merrell speculates that the Sachdagughroonaw, whom Tachanoontia says the Virginians had conquered, were on the tidewater when Jamestown was founded. Merrell, ed., *Treaty of Lancaster*, 59, note 13.

74 Ibid., 13. It is not clear from the minutes whether the Iroquois were claiming that the lands were on the Cohongorantas (that is, the Potomac), or were the lands held by a group of that name. Ibid., 16. The former seems more likely given the way that "Cohongorantas" was used in their former reply to Virginia, as well as in their cession of land to Maryland, where Canassetego referred to "the uppermost Fork of Potowmack or Cohongorantan River." Ibid., 23. It is also the case that in the seventeenth century the Susquehannocks had resided on the Potomac while they were fighting with the Iroquois.

75 Ibid., 20.

76 For skepticism, see Jennings, *The Ambiguous Iroquois Empire*, 135–36, 359–60. Jennings does concede that the Susquehannocks were "submerged politically in the tribal organizations of their hosts" (either the Delaware or the Iroquois) following a 1677 intertribal treaty at the Delaware village of Shackamaxon (155–56; quotation on 156). And he also notes that "[t]he Iroquois, as adopters of the bulk of the Susquehannocks, acquired a recognized right to the bulk of the Susquehanna Valley," though they then ceded it to New York, and they never claimed land to the south below the Falls (161). In contrast, Daniel Richter argues that the Iroquois-Susquehannock wars did lead to some of the latter, now known as Conestogas, being adopted by the Iroquois "with some coercion," and thus could be seen as the "equivalent to a mourning-war triumph." As such, the conquest claim, "while

not literally correct," has "some merit." The Susquehannock's lands might not have been "'wonn with the sword' (as some Iroquois would claim later), but they might as well have been." Richter, *Ordeal of the Longhouse*, 136.

77 George Hunt hypothesizes that the Susquehannocks, who were caught up in Bacon's Rebellion, suffered at the hands of militia from Maryland and Virginia and were then finished off by the Iroquois. See Hunt, *The Wars of the Iroquois: A Study in Intertribal Relations* (Madison: University of Wisconsin Press, 1940), 143.

78 On the conflict between the Iroquois and the Susquehannocks, see Jennings, *The Ambiguous Iroquois Empire*, 113–71; and Shannon, *Iroquois Diplomacy*, 68–69.

79 Jennings, *The Ambiguous Iroquois Empire*, 168–69.

80 *A Treaty Held at the Town of Lancaster*, 8. On the salience of territorial claims based on prescription in European jurisprudence, see Anthony Pagden, *The Burdens of Empire, 1539 to the Present* (New York: Cambridge University Press, 2015), 140–41.

81 Ibid., 9.

82 Ibid., 9.

83 Ibid., 9.

84 Ibid., 20.

85 Ibid., 14.

86 Ibid., 14. And see also, ibid., 20.

87 Ibid., 20.

88 Ibid., 20.

89 Ibid., 17–18.

90 Ibid., 26–28.

91 Ibid., 28–29.

92 Ibid., 30–31.

93 Ibid., 31–32.

94 Ibid., 32.

95 Ibid., 32–33.

96 Ibid., 33.

97 Ibid., 33.

98 On the new "Indian Road as agreed to at Lancaster," see William Parks's edition of the treaty, pages 75–76 (cited in note 26 above). It also contains the passes through Virginia that the Iroquois negotiated for the "Conoy Indians" and, on "the old Road," for the "Tuscaroros" (77–79).

99 Ibid., 34–37.

100 Ibid., 37.

101 Ibid., 38.

102 Ibid., 38–39.

103 Starna, "The Diplomatic Career of Canasatego," 155. The deed says that the "Sachims or Chiefs on behalf of the said Six Nations" "renounce and disclaim not only all the Right of the said Six Nations but also *recognize* and acknowledge the Right and Title to our Sovereign the King of Great Britain to all the land in

the said Colony as it is now *or hereafter may be peopled* and bounded by his said Majesty our Sovereign Lord the King his Heirs and Successors" (italics mine). Dinwiddie Papers, Virginia Historical Society, MSS 4. Starna claims that Canassatego either did not read or failed to understand the deed of cession.

104 On the use of treaties to dispossess Native Americans, see Dorothy Jones, *License for Empire: Colonialism by Treaty in Early America* (Chicago: University of Chicago Press, 1982); and Daniel Richter, "'To Clear the King's and Indian's Title': Seventeenth-Century Origins of European Land Cession Treaties," in Saliha Belmessous, ed., *Empire by Treaty: Negotiating European Expansion, 1600–1900* (New York; Oxford University Press, 2015), 45–77.

105 Though see Aquila, *Iroquois Restoration*, 160, on the independence of these tributaries.

106 On the Onondaga use of "brothers" to refer to "equals with reciprocal obligations," see Haan, "Covenant and Consensus," 48. Haan also claims that the metaphor of the chain was English in origin; the Iroquois spoke of "clasped hands" (45).

107 On which, see Merete Borch, "Rethinking the Origins of Terra Nulius," *Australian Historical Studies* 32 (2001), 222–39 (discussion of conquest being the opposite of a claim to vacancy or *terra nullius* on 227).

108 To take one representative example, David Armitage contends that "[f]rom the 1620s to the 1680s in Britain, and then in North America, Australia and Africa well into the nineteenth century, the argument from vacancy (*vacuum domicilium*) or absence of ownership (*terra nullius*) became a standard formulation for English, and later British dispossession of indigenous peoples." Armitage, *The Ideological Origins of the British Empire* (Cambridge: Cambridge University Press, 2000), 97. Legal historians have been more open to the argument that early modern English people recognized indigenous polities and territory. See Paul McHugh, *Aboriginal Societies and the Common Law: A History of Sovereignty, Status, and Self-Determination* (New York: Oxford University Press, 2004).

109 On parallel legal arguments between the English and the Powhatans in the early seventeenth century, see Andrew Fitzmaurice, "Powhatan Legal Claims," in Belmessous, ed., *Native Claims*, 85–106.

110 As the historian Nancy Shoemaker argues, there was "a bedrock of shared ideas." Shoemaker, *A Strange Likeness: Becoming Red and White in Eighteenth-Century America* (New York: Oxford University Press, 2004), 3. See also Daniel Richter's comparison of precontact North America and western Europe "as two great medieval agricultural civilizations," in Richter, *Before the Revolution: America's Ancient Pasts* (Cambridge, MA: Belknap Press, 2011), 41–42.

111 This is perhaps an instance of what the legal historians Lauren Benton and Benjamin Straumann call "the creative combination of legal arguments by imperial agents." Benton and Straumann, "Acquiring Empire by Law: From Roman Doctrine to Early Modern European Practice," *Law and History Review* 28 (2010), 31.

112 On the latter, see William Fenton, "Structure, Continuity, and Change in the Process of Iroquois Treaty Making," in Francis Jennings, ed., *The History and*

Culture of Iroquois Diplomacy: An Interdisciplinary Guide to the Treaties of the Six Nations and Their League (Syracuse, NY: Syracuse University Press, 1985), 3–36. For an attempt to link Native mythologies to Native legal conceptions, see Robert A. Williams Jr., *Linking Arms Together: American Indian Visions of Law and Peace* (New York: Routledge, 1999).

113 As Richard Haan argues, not all Iroquois peoples shared the same understanding of the Covenant Chain alliance with the English. Haan, "Covenant and Consensus," 45.

114 On these appeals, see Yirush, "Claiming the New World," and Yirush, "'Chief Princes and Owners of All'" (which considers the case of the Narragansetts and the Mashpee alongside that of the Mohegans).

115 Though Andrew Fitzmaurice has recently argued that, from the sixteenth century on, prominent European thinkers defended indigenous rights. Fitzmaurice, *Sovereignty, Property, and Empire, 1500–2000* (Cambridge: Cambridge University Press, 2014).

5

"*Ynuvaciones malas e rreprouadas*"

Seeking Justice in Early Colonial Pueblos de Indios

KAREN B. GRAUBART

In 1571 the Spanish jurist Polo de Ondegardo reported to his monarch, Philip II, "[T]here should not be considered two republics, of Indians and of Spaniards, but one" in Peru. Ondegardo, who as *corregidor* (royal magistrate) of Cuzco (1558–61, 1571–72) had been charged with producing justice for Indians, expressed his concern that the good practices of the Andeans were being forced out by emulation of Spanish ones, particularly litigation through the courts. His complaint was that the legal pluralism upon which Castilian governance was founded, characterized by protection of the *fueros*, or customary laws of Indians that did not contradict Crown or church law, was being undermined.[1] The reorganization of communities into *reducciones*, or concentrated towns, pulled them away from their dispersed resource bases. Spanish conquistadores replaced Andean lords as authorities. And rather than their customary social organization, Andean commoners turned to "*ynuvaciones malas e rreprouadas*" (bad and condemnable innovations).[2] Ondegardo argued that only respect for the ways that things had been done in the past would return prosperity to the struggling communities and thus to the imperial project. That stability would create greater *policía* (civility) among the Indians and their eventual full inclusion as Christian citizens.

Ondegardo, along with another Salamanca-trained lawyer, Juan de Matienzo, was an important advisor to Peruvian viceroy Francisco de Toledo (1569–81), selected by King Philip II to oversee colonial reforms during a time of economic, religious, and legal crisis. Indigenous populations were falling and, with them, the Crown's income. Conversion was not proceeding rapidly or securely. And even the grounds upon which the Spanish conquest was legitimated were under question. No longer readily predicated on the papal bulls of donation of 1493, which called for the conquest and evangelization of prepolitical societies, reformers had to explain how the Crown had *dominium* over complex, hierarchical empires in Mesoamerica and the Andes. By the late sixteenth century, Spanish rulers had conceded both territory and political authority to Indian republics, headed by natural lords (generally termed "caciques") but reorganized to embrace evangelization and *policia*.[3]

This was accomplished by recognizing the Andes as a plurijurisdictional society, composed of a variety of republics with allegiance to the Crown. But self-governing was not the same as autonomous or unchanged. Matienzo helped craft policies of *mita*, a forced labor rotation for staffing the silver mines at Potosí, on the model of an Inca practice for the state cultivation of corn. He advocated for the extension of the process of *reducción*, placing indigenous communities into concentrated towns on a gridded plan, to make Indians available for labor and evangelization but also to promote Spanish-style household organization and *policía*.[4]

Ondegardo's call to respect the *fueros* of the Indians, though, was a critique of Matienzo's and Toledo's policies. He was concerned that dislocating communities and introducing new political and economic ideas threatened their viability. Instead, he promoted a colonial ethnography, derived from his term among Cusqueño elites, which stated that Andeans held no private property but maintained land and animals collectively, reserving their produce for their overlords (once Incas and *kurakas*, now the Spanish crown and caciques) and their religion (once the Inca sun cult and their ancestors, now the Catholic Church), as well as for their own sustenance.[5] They divided up these obligations in such a way "that no one would receive injury," a justice that was now challenged by the alienation of once-collective lands and the creation of a new elite that was parasitic on the poor.[6] Maintaining the old divisions would create a flourishing society, properly connected to the Spanish crown through ties of tribute, protection, and evangelization.

But Ondegardo's ethnography was largely fictive, and his insistence that self-governance had to be tied to continuity with that fiction was shortsighted. The Andes was a large and diverse territory, and while Ondegardo's ethnography was drawn from conversations with interested Inca elites, it said little about regions like the north, the coast, or the Amazon, whose tenure under Inca domination had been short and contested. *Reducción*, as he predicted, further reorganized communities, cutting off distant kin or assimilating patches of migrants, and adding or subtracting kin groups (known as *ayllus*) to produce a unit size that met Spanish rather than Andean expectations.

For all these reasons it could be convenient to embrace Ondegardo's cynicism: colonial rule stripped communities of collective action and culture, of their justice. But historians have demonstrated that this was not true, that Andeans continue to express collective identities into the present, connected by long histories and ongoing relationships to territory and ancestors.[7] This continuity was facilitated, in part, by the colonial emphasis on republics and indigenous governance. But collective action did not necessarily require rejection of Spanish ideas. Instead, indigenous authorities sought strategies that reinforced their notions of justice in a changing world, even when they borrowed from the entangled law of legal pluralism. Because they were subject to aggressive acts of legal dispossession, they rapidly learned the new legal language. But they did not simply adopt Spanish legalisms, nor replace their own legal language with another. Instead, they created a flexible and heterogeneous approach to colonial political economy, one that reflected shared values rather than structural brittleness.

It is difficult to identify community decision making in Andean archives. Some Mesoamerican communities maintained internal records during this period, in part because their preconquest record keeping had continuity with colonial literacy, and in part because they were not ordered, as Andeans were, not to keep records.[8] In the Andes, indigenous *cabildos* (Spanish-style town councils) kept few records other than notarial documents like wills and contracts, which offer little discussion of collective justifications.

In this absence I look for evidence of community strategies and use these as proxies for collective decisions. I focus upon the Rimac River Valley, the coastal area around the city of Lima, towards the end of the sixteenth and beginning of the seventeenth centuries. Evidence comes from two kinds of sources: the records of the Spanish *corregidor de indios*, who oversaw certain restricted economic activities; and wills from indigenous valley residents, which offer details about inheritance and economic activities. Because so much of this evidence comes from notarial records, which overemphasize property and economic relations, my argument focuses upon land use, labor relations, the assertion of differential privilege, and collective economic strategies. But by examining the processes that Polo de Ondegardo alluded to in the 1560s—decisions that small communities took to defend their commonwealth, utilizing a heterogeneous assortment of legal approaches—we can see not only that the republics continued to self-govern but that they insisted upon their own justice in the face of colonial rule.

Local Jurisdiction: Governing Pueblos de Indios

Indigenous elites sought and received jurisdictional privileges to confirm their status as local rulers. In the most dramatic example, following upon the wars of conquest in central Mexico, the Tlaxcalan allies who had helped secure that victory sent a delegation to Spain to ask the Crown to remunerate his new Christian subjects. Charles V granted them what they wanted: Tlaxcalans would not be given in *encomienda* by Spanish officials, a relationship that required indigenous communities to produce tribute for Spanish grantees, becoming instead free vassals of the Crown. Their nobles had first-instance legal jurisdiction "such that they keep for their subjects their ancient customs for the conservation of that Province, City and Republic."[9]

Tlaxcala was an extreme case of a common variant, the generation of *pueblos de indios*, particular indigenous republics. These polities were ruled over by their caciques, though subordinate to the Crown and the Catholic Church. Caciques, however, were potentially treacherous: their recalcitrant idolatry was a barrier to Christian evangelization, and they were characterized as petty tyrants with a tendency to usurp community property. Like the Castilian aristocrats who had long been a thorn in the monarchy's side, they had to be countered by political towns with elected leaders who were directly under the purview of the Crown.[10]

The solution was the *reducción*, or the centralized and hispanized indigenous town, widely imposed in Peru beginning around 1570. In addition to its economic and missionary aspects, the *reducción* had political requirements: each *pueblo de indios* would be recognized as a republic, with a *cabildo* and Spanish-style elected officers and a notary. Their jurisdiction would be limited: "only to make inquiries, take prisoners, and bring delinquents to the jail in the Spanish town of the district, though they may punish Indians who fail to attend Mass on feast days, or get drunk or some other error, with a day of imprisonment, and six or eight lashes."[11]

These officers were intended to sideline the hereditary elite, caciques, who were now theoretically limited to organizing labor for tribute and *mita*, though in many communities they continued to exercise power and were even elected to *cabildo* offices. The instructions given by outgoing Governor Lope García de Castro to the incoming Viceroy Francisco de Toledo in 1568 walked the line between supporting and undermining hereditary elites: while some caciques "use great tyranny," García de Castro wrote, it is not our intention to "divide up their Indians," but rather to assure that "the natural lords and caciques have their Indians restored to them."[12] At that same time, he urged, "[L]et there be, among the Indians, *alcaldes* [magistrates], which the *audiencia* [high court] or, if the *audiencia* is too far, the *regidores* [of the Spanish *cabildo*] should appoint; and these *alcaldes* should be knowledgeable about small issues that arise among these Indians. And they should also adjudicate or punish small crimes, and these cases may be appealed to the *corregidor* of their district."[13]

Exactly how and what this small corpus of elected officials governed is difficult to say, although it is easier to identify the limits of their jurisdiction. They could not render judgments on serious crime within their community, as this was reserved to Spanish authorities; they could not impose judgments on outsiders, including members of another indigenous community. They could also have difficulty enforcing practices, such as inheritance or contracts, when the Catholic Church or Spanish law was engaged. They were subordinate to the royal *corregidor de indios*, who received tribute, issued licenses for restricted activities, and monitored relationships between indigenous and Spanish individuals and institutions.[14] In these and other ways, the jurisdiction of indigenous authorities was proscribed.

Yet there remained significant space for collective action within indigenous communities. Communities had to distribute the burden of tribute among themselves. Tlaxcala's *cabildo* records show that they chose to tax themselves progressively in the sixteenth century, requiring nobles to contribute far more than the poor, despite the Spanish headtax model with exemptions for nobles.[15] Leaders might encourage some forms of labor and discourage others, including wage labor outside the pueblo. Communities had collective responsibilities that had to be overseen: maintaining irrigation systems and public works, constructing homes, caring for shared and assigned agricultural fields and animals. Civil conflicts that might have seemed minor to royal authorities loomed large over pueblos knit together from different kin groups. Deciding who had access to privileges, or who had harmed another's property or reputation was central to maintaining community peace, and fell to indigenous leaders. These would have been resolved internally and mostly without paperwork, but they surely mattered to indigenous justice.[16]

Entangled Jurisdictions in the Lima Valley

The coastal city of Lima was founded in 1535 to support the Spanish conquest and occupation of highland Inca territories. This caused numerous changes to a site that, while not a major population center, had hosted an autochthonous Ychsma polity headed by the cacique Taulichusco, as well as an important oracle and pilgrimage center. Surrounding Taulichusco's community were other polities spread across three river valleys: Rimac, Lurín, and Chillón. As Spaniards created a massive political center in Lima, they relocated communities and negotiated political relationships.[17]

It was founded on a failure of intelligibility: Taulichusco (perhaps temporarily) endowed Francisco Pizarro with the lands for the city's settlement, and then found himself not only expropriated but now held in *encomienda* by Pizarro.[18] Pizarro relocated the community to Chuntay, just west of the Spanish settlement. In 1557 the Viceroy Marqués de Cañetere moved them again, joining them to other communities in the parish of Magdalena.[19] By the 1570s, all the valley polities were relocated to settlements that joined together multiple *ayllus* to become the *reducciones* of Magdalena, Surco, Late, Lurigancho, Carabayllo, and Pachacamac (see figure 5.1). These towns provisioned the city and were required to supply temporary laborers (*mitayos*) to work for the Spaniards in a variety of occupations.

These communities were under constant threat from Lima's citizenry, who viewed the valleys as an engine for urban expansion and personal enrichment. Spaniards sought to purchase, rent, and expropriate valley lands, and to usurp any available indigenous labor. While they would not realistically dominate property in the valley for another century,

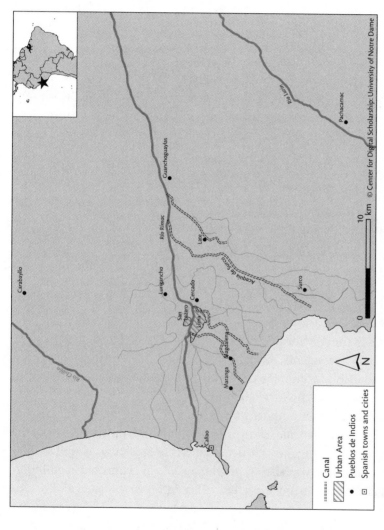

Figure 5.1: Pueblos de Indios in the Lima Valley in the sixteenth century.
Credit: Matthew Sisk, Center for Digital Scholarship, University of Notre Dame.

even by the middle of the sixteenth century they were making strong inroads.[20] Don Gonzalo Taulichusco, the son of the Yschma lord who conceded to Pizarro, wrote a will in 1562 lamenting his illegal and foolish sales of his community's lands (and those of caciques subject to him, over whose lands he had no rights) to Spaniards at unjust prices.[21] As Spanish administrators warned, caciques responded favorably to the incentive to sell lands.

The Crown recognized these incursions as a threat to the communities' ability to produce tribute, as well as a means for Spaniards to accrue inordinate power. It disallowed private sales of indigenous lands to Spaniards, and created its own monopoly in 1591 with the introduction of *composiciones de tierras*, auctions of indigenous lands deemed underused, which issued official titles to individuals and communities who could prove ownership and need and sold to Spanish clients those lands determined excessive.[22]

Indigenous men and women also moved to Lima, both those who homesteaded during their work rotations, and permanent immigrants, attracted by wage labor and tribute evasion. While *mitayos* were accompanied by their elites, permanent immigrants had no indigenous leadership. By 1570, the viceroy had erected a walled urban *reducción* right outside the city, called Santiago del Cercado, where the Jesuits would exercise pastoral power over *mitayos* and other residents.[23] The Cercado eventually formed its own indigenous *cabildo*, to govern some eight hundred residents, but at least two thousand more indigenous men and women lived within the city limits and operated autonomously of an explicit indigenous political community.[24]

The main Spanish authority for Indians in the region was the *corregidor de indios del Cercado*, charged beginning in 1565 with protecting the welfare of Indians against the depredations of Spaniards as well as their own caciques. He was also to provide justice in claims between indigenous and nonindigenous parties, either in the first instance or on appeal from another body. He was supposed to limit Spanish interventions into indigenous communities, but also to encourage and manage certain "innovative" norms around indigenous property, labor, and resources, if they were considered beneficial to the community's finances.[25]

The *corregidor de indios* carried out summary justice for indigenous clients with the assistance of a court-appointed lawyer and a notary. Little

paperwork from his court remains beyond a handful of litigation proceedings and a short run of notarial documents.[26] These few records,
however, reveal how communities deployed heterogeneous forms of
property to regulate their own justice.

During 1612–13, the office was held by Don Josephe de Ribera, with the
assistance of notary Cristóbal de Piñeda. Piñeda's extant notarial registers
(January 1612–April 1613) include the documents resulting from his daily
tasks.[27] The demographics of the notary's clientele are explanatory: of
some 107 documents drawn up in those sixteen months, twelve were
contracts between Spaniards, especially royal officials. Another fourteen were contracts between two or more indigenous parties or were
instruments drawn up for a single indigenous party, such as a will. The
vast majority, eighty-one, were contracts between at least one indigenous
and at least one Spanish party. Thus, the docket of the *corregidor* in 1612–
13 was dominated by situations where indigenous community members
left the jurisdiction of their cacique or Indian *cabildo*. In that sense, the
corregidor did not redefine justice in internal community matters.

However, his actions affected the distribution of resources and assign-
ment of property under indigenous authority. Indigenous wills from the
same period demonstrate a prolific entanglement of legal discourses.
Those wills reveal multiple conceptualizations of labor, property, and
resource management, drawing upon a variety of Spanish and pre-
conquest Andean practices. Taken together, they show that indigenous
communities attempted to find just ways to alleviate colonial stresses by
experimenting with new legal norms alongside older ones. The production of just outcomes for communities and individuals depended heavily
upon this flexibility.

Rural Land Tenure and Management

The valley's *reducciones* faced crucial questions regarding the use of their
agricultural lands, the largest source of wealth as a productive resource
and a potentially alienable good. Communities had to balance their new
needs for cash and their commitment to holding property in various
forms. Pre-Hispanic forms of tenure and ownership across the Andes
were complex and heterogeneous. Like Polo de Ondegardo, sixteenth-
century Spanish officials often characterized Andean communities as

unfamiliar with private property, instead dividing property each year according to family size and need and working most of the land in common. This was a simplification of practices in the highlands, where land was not permanently possessed but considered *sapsi*, or common-wealth.[28] Usufruct rights in the highlands were assigned by relationship, and the product of those lands was distributed proportionally among the kin groups, Inca authorities, local authorities, use for ritual purposes (both local and Inca), and care for the community's incapacitated. Institutional distribution was recast by Spanish theorists as ownership, such that the Catholic Church could claim any lands assigned to support Inca religious authorities, and the Crown anything reserved to support the Inca state.[29]

On the central coast, however, no discussion of proportionality and *sapsi* appears in the documentary record. Instead, coastal caciques were said to own their communities' lands, renting plots to their subjects in exchange for tribute, and colonial documents often refer to indigenous usufruct right rather than outright ownership.[30] Early colonial wills, like that written by Magdalena's cacique, Don Gonzalo Taulichusco, in 1562, describe heterogeneous claims: private ownership of large estates, lands tied to office, communal labor on lands not tied to particular owner-ship.[31] Indeed, Don Gonzalo's will left what appear to be his private ani-mal herds to the community for the purpose of paying tribute, perhaps creating ex nihilo a form of *sapsi*. Like early modern Spaniards, who were more likely to use collective than private property, colonial Andeans drew upon a flexible range of forms of use and proprietorship, including those of their ancestors and those of their conquerors.[32] This flexibility meant that as Spaniards encroached on property and courts presented new forms of titling and designating lands, communities could draw on a variety of means to defend needed resources and ascertain that they were justly distributed.

The creation of *reducciones* removed many communities from the lands they had previously tended, sometimes also disconnecting them from the forms of tenure they had applied. Declining populations also made it easy for Spanish officials to argue that communities had too much land, removing large estates with *composiciones* and selling them to the highest bidder.[33] What remained had to be distributed, titled, and managed by individuals, *ayllus*, and larger political units according to mutually acceptable social systems.

The *corregidor*'s office thus acted to protect its own notion of justice, which required that communities had enough land to produce food for themselves and the city, and enough money or crops to pay tribute. A solution to Spanish demand and indigenous poverty was to disallow Spaniards from purchasing indigenous lands but to facilitate leases. From the *corregidor*'s records, it is evident that communities found this attractive: over the eighteen-month period, fifty-two Spaniards approached him to contract leases from indigenous landowners. Indigenous agents found it advantageous to seek formal Spanish-language contracts in these cases: the courts could be called upon to enforce them, where their own authorities might not succeed.

The communities' assertive use of the *corregidor* as an agent to oversee land rentals was a pushback against the already massive expropriation of indigenous property. As the redistribution of coastal property to ecclesiastic institutions and individuals created haciendas to be worked by wage and enslaved labor, communities requested Spanish oversight of new revenue streams from rentals.[34] While some of the rentals were extensive, as when Antonyo de Clavijo rented twenty *fanegas* of land from the community holdings of Late, they presumably felt like a wall against permanent incursions.[35]

Wills from the period reveal the strains that led to such decisions. Widowed women, in particular, spoke to their strategies. Magdalena Picona of Late noted in 1630 that she owned eleven *fanegadas* of lands in that valley, purchased from the *encomendero* Don Lorenzo de Ulloa. She noted that "I can no longer cultivate the eleven *fanegadas* of land as I am single and widowed," and had long rented them to a Spaniard, Jorge Márquez. But even those payments no longer supported her, and Márquez paid her advances and small loans to cover the costs of her "necessities in illness and to feed and dress myself."[36] Similarly, Doña Ana Collon of Magdalena rented nearly eight *fanegadas* for many years to the Spaniard Pedro Ximenez Menacho. She no longer required Ximenez to sign annual leases, and he was also paying her in advance and above the rent. In the will, she left him a small piece of the land with her gratitude.[37]

But if rentals provided some relief, it was short-lived. Haciendas grew larger, and grazing animals required expanding turf, placing more pressure on land.[38] And it might be difficult to remove tenants, who sometimes claimed ownership and took heirs to court. The decision to rent unused assets to produce a revenue stream was a double-edged sword: while it temporarily staved off incursions, it also placed land in the market and within the *corregidor's* purview.

In contrast, almost no contracts were drawn up for rentals between two indigenous parties, which would fall within the jurisdiction of the community. There were three exceptions.[39] In two cases parties from different communities used the *corregidor* to write up an extra-community contract. In the last case, the contract was between members of different *ayllus* reduced to the town of Magdalena. The two men were subject to different leaders, even if their republic was represented by one cacique and *cabildo*. Thus communities retained control over internal property transfers, but they did so in ways that reflected how they functioned. The colonial republic did not replace local political structures, at least not in the first century of Spanish rule.

Wills from the period demonstrate how local governance mattered to land practices, producing heterogeneous types of holdings. This heterogeneity suggests that indigenous communities continued to control the distribution of some land, even though it increasingly meant accommodating to new legal languages to do so.

For example, in 1596, Costança Ticlla, the widow of a commoner in the Taulli *ayllu* of Surco, distinguished among a variety of kinds of property in her will.[40] She owned residential houses in the town of Surco, which she had inherited from her late husband and left to her grandson. She also owned two pieces of farmland inherited from her father, which were titled to her during a *composición* in the 1590s; she left them to a Catholic confraternity to support charitable acts. But she also referred to the town's community pastures, probably serving a community herd. Her will thus describes multiple forms of ownership and provenance, including direct private inheritance, colonial private titling, official community holdings, holdings given over to the church, and new urban plots associated with the centralized dwellings of the *reducción*. These definitions coexisted, and the forms of property transformed into one another almost ambivalently, as "family" land could be turned into church property in a will and then placed on the market for rental or sale. This multiplicity must have created new headaches for community leaders, but the heterogeneity of definitions offered flexible ways for communities to divide resources, reward elites, and hold off Spanish incursions.

In short, agricultural properties were a resource under terrific pressure in the century after conquest, but they were still largely governed by indigenous leadership. Communities faced complex decisions, and the evidence demonstrates, albeit indirectly, that they approached the problem strategically. Individuals and communities made short-term rentals to Spaniards, producing a revenue stream that supported collective tribute and individual wealth. In the short run, this could benefit the community and keep land under its control, but in the longer term it probably facilitated its transfer to Spanish hands. But much property remained within the community, to be used and distributed according to local mores. Even without much knowledge of land tenure and use on the central coast before Spanish contact, we can see multiple forms coexisting by the turn of the seventeenth century. In particular, we see the adoption of new property relations alongside older norms, aimed at finding space between the tense pressures of tribute payment and land expropriations. Communities retained their right to adjudicate and enforce those strategies; the fact that so little leaked out to appeals courts and *corregidores* is evidence that they did so with success.

Urbanization

Indigenous communities did have to address one entirely new form of property: private urban residences. On the model of Spanish towns, every *reducción* was drawn up to include a small plaza surrounded by a church, public buildings, and new residences for the pueblo's citizens. The concentration of residences was an unfamiliar practice for Andeans, and the officials with jurisdiction over them were faced with creating and enforcing rules for their distribution and management. Accordingly, they provide an important landscape for determining whose justice predominated in different circumstances.

The *corregidor* had jurisdiction over property relations involving indigenous parties within Lima itself, whose total population of about twenty-four thousand in 1619 included nearly equal numbers of Spaniards and Africans, but only fifteen hundred permanent indigenous residents. The latter lived throughout the city (with many more at the city's edges and another eight hundred in the Cercado), often in informal housing considered dangerously overcrowded and poorly constructed.[41]

Indigenous subjects who lived in Lima were largely required to accept the rules given by Spanish authorities. Eighteen indigenous clients approached the *corregidor* in 1612–13 to receive licenses to rent homes and workplaces in the city. Diego de Mexia, a mestizo, and his indigenous wife Leonor Mendes rented out a house that they had built themselves in San Lázaro parish to a Spaniard named Juan de Bertis in a nine-year lease; an Indian tailor named Juan de Alonso rented a small store in the *plazuela* of Santa Ana from a Spanish resident for a year.[42] In these cases, indigenous city residents utilized the *corregidor*'s office to enforce the civil law imposed by royal jurisdiction.

But they also, occasionally, attempted to bend the rules by utilizing strategies available to them. For example, royal law restricted Indians, who were classified as *miserables* or wretches requiring legal protection, from selling the homes they owned within the city.[43] However, Francisco Gómez requested special permission to sell his house in the city's parish of San Lázaro to another indigenous man.[44] Gómez's appointed lawyer advised the *corregidor* that the transaction would be "useful and opportune" as his client had no funds to maintain it. Gómez, who was infirm and planning to return to his natal home in Jauja, had allowed the house to fall into ruin while he lived elsewhere. The building's condition was so bad that his neighbor had replaced a shared wall and was now suing him. Witnesses testified to the dilapidated state of the property, Gómez's poverty, and the social disaster that would come of abandonment. The *corregidor* granted the license "given the utility that he has proven of selling the house," and drew up the contract.

In contrast, the Cercado operated in a curious framework. While literally at the city's edge, as a *reducción*, it was guided by the Jesuit order and governed by its own diverse indigenous leadership. Built on a large parcel at the city's edge in 1568–71, the Cercado was intended to corral temporary *mita* laborers during their labor rotations, and to force them to attend mass and catechism. The town's lots were originally sold to the far-flung communities that sent *mitayos* to the city, but residents rapidly erected shacks and houses, cultivated gardens, and planted fruit trees, making longer-term claims. As a community of immigrants who did not share customary law and now lived under the Jesuits, its law was sui generis. Learning from their Limeño neighbors, those residents treated their constructions as their own, selling them to other indigenous men and women or leaving them as inheritance to family members.

The Cercado thus came to be not simply a transitory space for *mita* workers but a permanent town. As such, its new functions threatened to overrule its original purpose. While houses were built and sold, and gardens were fenced in and their produce declared private property, the rights to the subsoil were understood to be vested with the communities whose treasuries had purchased the rights to house their workers back in the 1570s. These rights were articulated by the town's Indian *alcaldes*, by the *corregidor*, and occasionally by the Real Audiencia: a case settled in 1653 expropriated the lands purchased by an indigenous militia captain, for which he had received title from royal authorities, and returned them to the community of origin, which had largely abandoned them.[45] In the seventeenth century, community officials, reinforced by Spanish authorities, continued to evict permanent residents and even purchasers of sites in favor of retaining group access to the land.[46] Within the Cercado, the Catholic Church and royal officials enforced indigenous customary law, as they defined it: as collective rights against private claims.

In the Lima valley's rural towns, however, these new residential centers were imbued by their indigenous leadership with a sense of social hierarchy. While pre-Hispanic Andean settlements were generally quite dispersed—some over hundreds of miles and vastly different landscapes— each new *pueblo de indios* founded in the 1570s was centralized around a plaza, with a church, *cabildo* offices, often a jail, and lots distributed to residents (see figure 5.2). According to Spanish theory, the residential lots should be arranged according to "the qualities of the persons."[47] In a Spanish city, the most prominent citizens were placed closest to the plaza, so that social status could be assessed by geographic location.[48] While in the Cercado the *corregidor* and the Jesuits had decided upon the distribution of property, in the valley's pueblos communities created and distributed the residential symbols of social order on their own.

The initial distribution of these lots was made by caciques and *cabildos*, using their own notion of social hierarchy and space.[49] While little evidence of the original acts remains, there are clues in documents from Santiago del Surco, the town attached to the *encomienda* of Surco, which became a *reducción* in 1570 under Viceroy Toledo. It was the largest of the indigenous towns of the region, and composed of four or five separate

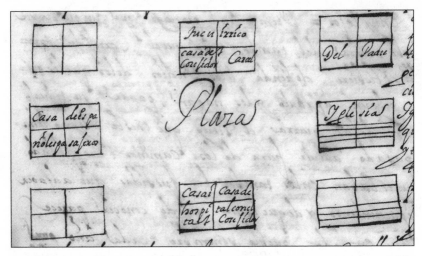

Figure 5.2: Plan for central plaza of a *reducción*. From Juan de Matienzo, Gobierno del Perú (1567) f. 38r. Reprinted with permission of Obadiah Rich collection. Manuscripts and Archives Division. The New York Public Library. Astor, Lenox, and Tilden Foundations.

ayllus or kin groups. The *reducción* included an urban settlement around the church of Santiago de Surco, with a building for the *cabildo* and permanent houses for its residents. Three wills left by its residents in 1596 allude to homes in the pueblo and burial in its church.[50] The *reducción* required a political process wherein new spaces could be invented and distributed, and property could be recognized.

Litigation over the inheritance of a lot and house brought to Lima's Real Audiencia in 1603 offers a rare glimpse of the distributional process in Surco.[51] At its founding, Surco's leaders distributed lots by *ayllu* such that members lived together, allowing *ayllu* leaders to collect tribute and distribute tasks and obligations easily. When a member of one *ayllu* died and a relative from another *ayllu* tried to inherit his residence, community leaders had ruled against the claimant, arguing that she was trying to elude obligations to her cacique by moving to another's jurisdiction. The claimant appealed to the *corregidor* and then to the *audiencia*, both of which upheld the community's ruling. The *audiencia* established the original distribution as Surco's customary law, limiting direct inheritance to kin within the *ayllu*, with no gesture to property law elsewhere.

Urban property was a new phenomenon in the Andes, and the way that indigenous officials treated it in the Cercado and in Surco reveals something of the vision of justice behind the act of distribution. While urban property in Lima was largely alienable, once distributed by the Crown or *cabildo*, in Surco and the Cercado this was not always the case. *Ayllu* membership, through the bonds of fictive kinship and the demands of reciprocal obligations, was more important than Spanish lines of inheritance or legal contract. Because the indigenous republics were entitled to their law, higher Spanish authorities enforced these rules, allowing us to glimpse something of local justice.

Labor

Labor was another resource under great stress. Adult indigenous men were required to produce tribute, in commodity or coin, and perform labor turns on a scheduled basis. Caciques were required to monitor this obligation, and face fines if they fell short. But with falling populations on the coast, traditional agriculture was inadequate to meet demands. Seeking wage labor, either on other agricultural sites or in urban settings, could be an individual or collective strategy. While individuals sought to escape their obligations, communities might encourage members to leave temporarily in order to send remittances. While out-migration eventually threatened pueblo stability, in the face of falling populations and inflexible demands, it could have been a collective strategy.

While most labor arrangements were informal, the *corregidor*'s office was supposed to oversee work contracts between Spanish and indigenous parties in the valley. As with land arrangements, these corresponded to new legal and organizational forms. Five men came in 1612–13 to draw up documents setting out employment or joint venture terms with another party. One was Francisco Perez, an "*yndio de china*" (Filipino) who contracted as a butcher to a Spanish cattle merchant.[52] Another was Juan Tomás, an indigenous native of Lima. Diego de Ocampo hired him to work in his Potosí store, where he would live with Ocampo for three years, making "instruments of the office of *vigolero* [luthier] which I know and understand, day and night, as is customary."[53] Ocampo would provide the tools and wood and pay an annual salary and a fifty-peso advance. Here the *corregidor* was charged with making sure that Spanish employers respected regulations governing compensation and labor practices for indigenous *miserables*. The existence of a legal contract meant that both parties were aware of legal constraints and protections governing their relationship.

The contracts also hint at changing labor arrangements within rural communities. Spaniards lacked the labor necessary to cultivate the lands they were acquiring. Antonyo de Clavijo had rented large parcels in Late in March 1612, and returned to the *corregidor* that August with two indigenous men from that town to form a partnership to cultivate them. Clavijo contributed the land, burros, and ploughshares, while Pedro Parrana and Agustín Llacsa provided the seed, their labor and that of other workers they would hire.[54] This was another step towards the hacienda system, wherein a small group of individuals accumulated large land parcels and hired wage laborers to work it. Even Indians who owned their own land might rent it out and then contract to cultivate another's fields.[55] Indigenous labor was supplemented by that of enslaved Africans. As Frederick Bowser points out, the massive rush for agricultural properties in the late sixteenth century was fueled by the increased flow of enslaved Africans to Peru.[56] The *corregidor*'s documents are a window into that changing logic of labor and compensation.

Wills, however, indicate that communities were not simply bleeding laborers, but were actively managing new and old economies to preserve their vitality. Communities continued to maintain both individual and collective parcels, suggesting that local labor norms, probably organized around preconquest notions of reciprocity and group labor, still had force.[57] *Ayllu* organization, as observed in Surco, was structured around mutual obligations between members, including reciprocal labor in large-scale agriculture. Other obligations, like cleaning the irrigation systems (*acequias*), or personal service to caciques, were distributed among the population according to principles of reciprocity. *Mita* labor had to be distributed among tributaries, and that decision lay with caciques, according to practices that retained a sense of legitimacy among the dwindling population groups. Before the Spanish conquest, labor was organized collectively as well as within families; colonial rule now introduced outright wage labor to this palette.[58]

But community treasuries required more income to support tribute, religious expenses, and other demands. Communities turned to new collective options, including subcontracting *tambos,* former Inca waystations now operating as inns for the many travelers on valley roads. While communities could generate income by running the *tambos* themselves, the capital and labor costs could be prohibitive. Many *tambos* were subcontracted to Spaniards, and the rents became part of the community's treasury, or *sapsi.*

Another revenue-producing project might have been the mass production of *chicha* (corn beer) for market, as is indicated by contemporary wills. María Capan of Surco, who testated in 1596, asked her executors to collect a debt from a Spaniard named Diego de Carabajal for a large amount of *chicha* he had purchased on credit from her.[59] But selling *chicha* could be a substantial project. Costanza Ticlla's 1596 will lists, as part of her estate in Surco, "a large pot in which *chicha* is made, holding three *arrobas,* which is in this town's tavern, and also two small pots, one of which holds two *arrobas* and the other one *arroba,* also in the tavern." She had even larger containers in her home, as well as seven small bottles scattered between her home and the homes of her clients.[60]

Ticlla's business was part of the community's larger project of supporting a tavern, which was founded on land belonging to the *ayllu* of Ydca.[61] The commodification of the *chicha* industry—formerly mass produced at imperial administrative sites or by specialists within communities, or simply within the household—and its association with street vendors as well as *tambos* and taverns, shifted the meaning of the drink. In the pre-Hispanic world, *chicha* fulfilled symbolic functions of reciprocity (lubricating relationships between work parties and leaders) as well as spiritual functions (feeding the ancestors). Colonial authorities sought to stop caciques from distributing *chicha* to workers and from brewing *chicha* for ritual use because of associations with drunkenness and idolatry. But they simultaneously regulated its mass production and sale to a multiethnic urban population. As Jane Mangan notes, *chicha* was "colonial business": in 1603, residents of the city of Potosí were said to have consumed 1.6 million bottles of the cheap drink.[62]

Given the scale of *chicha* consumption—which required extensive inputs, labor, and space—the business could take on political dimensions. In Carabayllo in the 1580s, the *corregidor* Hernán Vázquez delivered raw corn to one group of Indians under his jurisdiction to produce *chicha*, which he used to compensate a second group he required to cultivate wheat.[63] Wills indicate that many indigenous women in the communities around Lima brewed and sold *chicha* in their communities and in Lima. The case of Surco suggests another possibility: a community *chichería*, whose profits might be allocated towards tribute payment or other community functions, and whose management might be collective rather than private. Indigenous *cabildos* would have placed matters relating to *chicha* production, sale, and consumption on their agendas.

Even with the introduction of private lands and labor contracts, communities still maintained common herds and fields, for tribute as well as sustenance. They also invested in new practices and strategies, from subcontracting *tambos* to mass-producing *chicha* for market, to meet their increasing financial obligations. The income from these practices functioned as a community fund, which not only allowed caciques to meet tribute obligations but also provided resources for accomplishing tasks to shore up their own authority, including litigating against other communities and Spanish agents or promoting ostentatious Catholic practices.[64] Indigenous authorities led these strategies, distributing the labor and resources still under their control in ways that allowed them to produce just outcomes with some independence from Spanish authorities.

Slavery and Status

Perhaps the most unusual documents emanating from *corregidor* Ribera's office in 1612–13 were petitions for licenses for an economic activity that was explicitly prohibited to indigenous actors. Eight indigenous parties approached the *corregidor* in order to purchase or sell an African slave. Royal orders excluding indigenous ownership of African slaves were often ignored, and in special cases the authorities explicitly granted licenses.[65]

Three of the petitions were from indigenous men and/or women purchasing an African slave from a Spanish merchant. Another four involved indigenous agents selling African slaves to a Spanish party, as when Juan de Herrera sold a male slave to the priest of the church of San Lázaro, a notably multiracial Lima parish.[66] When indigenous actors sold slaves to Spaniards, they explicitly verified their ownership of the enslaved person; thus Hernando Quispe of Guaylas declared that he had purchased Juliana of Angola "to earn a wage, and I got and bought her from Juan de Salazar in the presence of . . . Rodrigo Baeza His Majesty's scribe, on March 16 of 1607, which paper I have presented as title of the said slave."[67] While the sale of valuable property before a notary often required the recital of provenance, this was particularly crucial for indigenous sellers, who were suspected of illegal transactions.

Perhaps unsurprisingly, most of the indigenous masters who owned slaves lived in Lima or the Cercado. The only rural indigenous purchaser in 1612–13 was Don Esteban Guaca, the scribe of Maranga, who purchased a twenty-four-year-old African man from a Spanish merchant.[68] African men and women would have been a common sight in the valley haciendas. But Spanish law prohibited Africans from entering indigenous towns, claiming they were a danger to Indians.[69] Indigenous masters did not generally use African slaves for agricultural labor, but either hired them out for a wage, or wielded them as a status good.

Indeed, the attraction of African slaves for indigenous men and women in Lima had less to do with labor concerns than with changes in the way that status was communicated.[70] Justice within the indigenous, as in the Castilian, community could hinge upon the appropriate distribution of privileges and status. The reorganization of political centers around the Lima valleys meant that former lines of aristocratic privilege were often broken, and they were supplemented or supplanted by new offices within the *cabildo* and the church. Moments such as the distribution of residential plots around recently constructed plazas in *reducciones* would have made those political tensions concrete, cementing the status of certain families in the form of large parcels and prestigious building sites. Viceroy Toledo in 1569 urged his inspectors to "plan out the house of the cacique principal, which should be wider and somewhat more authoritative than that of common Indians."[71]

Conquest and colonial rule also changed the kinds of privilege available and the criteria for receiving them. Indigenous authorities had formerly depended upon the interchange of symbolic goods with Inca elites to underwrite their own legitimacy. Now indigenous elites as well as upwardly mobile commoners struggled to reinscribe their status under new terms. While caciques largely remained wealthy and powerful as a hereditary aristocracy, they were challenged by the emergence of new power brokers as well as by the increasing demands of the colonial regime. Elites across the Andes complained indignantly that they, who had been largely exempted from paying tribute under the Inca, now all contributed.[72] The old ways of asserting status were rapidly eroded.

Compensation for leaders took new forms: salaries from the colonial government, skimming of community treasuries, goods available through relationships with Spanish merchants and bureaucrats. Older status markers, like *indios de servicio*, or the personal service of a group of one's subjects, were prohibited by colonial authorities, but more important, labor was probably scarce: in communities with diminishing populations, providing a full-time staff to take care of the cacique's household, herds, and crops would be impossible.

It is no surprise that those who aspired to power coveted the ownership of African slaves. In the rural pueblos, where seventeenth-century wills still enumerated Andean woven textiles rather than imported silks, and animals, tools, and raw materials rather than fine jewelry and housewares, there are few references to enslaved Africans as status goods. Some indigenous elites did own slaves: Don Gonzalo Taulichusco, the cacique of Magdalena, mentioned slaves in his 1562 will, and Doña María Llatan, the wife of Magdalena's cacique in 1631, owned six slaves purchased with her previous husband, a nobleman himself. Magdalena's proximity to Lima and its nobility's strong connections to Lima's elites probably made slave ownership both more desirable and more attainable.[73]

Caciques' ownership of slaves points to their new place as a status good, replacing the old "personal service" of one's subjects. Agustín de Gamarra and his wife Doña María Atayanqui applied for a license from the *corregidor* to purchase an African slave in March 1613.[74] Gamarra was a commoner from Cajamarca, living in Lima with his wife, a member of Magdalena's nobility. Their petition claimed that, despite her lineage, "they have no domestic service whatsoever." The *corregidor* agreed that she deserved the remedy of buying a servant to maintain her position, and issued the license so that the couple might purchase an unnamed, unbaptized woman "recently arrived from Guinea" from a Spanish merchant for 525 pesos. The purchase was partly funded by the rental of doña María's family lands in Magdalena to a Spaniard a few weeks earlier.[75]

The distribution of wealth and resources within indigenous communities was a central question of justice. Indigenous communities drew upon both old and new forms of status goods to reward their elites and differentiate them from their subjects, including property, labor, and ritual. But in urban centers like Lima and the Cercado, where different regimes governed the distribution of these goods, indigenous elites (and those hoping to supplant them) turned in particular to the new traffic in African slaves. Even the city's *corregidores* recognized this as a legitimate function of the indigenous claimant's status.

Conclusions: Innovations and the Space for Indigenous Justice

As Polo de Ondegardo noted in 1571, innovations had rapidly come to indigenous communities in Peru: Andeans found much of Spanish culture and law intelligible, and borrowed readily from them. This was nowhere so true as in the Lima valleys, where an expanding Spanish settlement first pushed indigenous communities out of their precontact homes, and then reached out to incorporate their lands and labor into colonial wealth production. Yet Ondegardo was wrong to assert that these innovations inherently threatened native polities and their self-governance, at least in the short run. While indigenous-controlled territories and labor forces were shrinking, and new forms of land and labor were being introduced, communities continued to take collective action with heterogeneous tools.

Andeans learned new legal languages to express their histories, their belief systems, and their use of and tenure over resources. Ironically, this facility has largely rendered their activism invisible to us, leaving a generation of ethnohistorians to write mostly of colonial accommodation. But colonial documents, particularly wills, restore collective struggles over justice to us, as they reveal communities searching for a variety of solutions to colonial problems. It is within that heterogeneity that we can see risk taking, argumentation, and experimentation, all aimed at preserving communities' sense of balance. Justice was not tied to a proportional division of land, or a refusal of private property: it seems, rather, to have emphasized kin-based access to resources and power, but also to collective choices about facing colonial challenges. Local justice within indigenous communities became interdependent with decisions made by Spanish jurists. In this sense, justice was transculturated or entangled, and was created at a number of levels: the individual and family, the larger community, and the leadership, both hereditary caciques and elected *cabildo* officers.

Indian justice in the Lima valley, then, consisted of the active management of heterogeneous norms partially defined outside the community's grasp but corresponding to requirements at home. It emerged not only from proactive behavior on the part of communities but also from Spain's long-held assumption that law came from many sites, including the customary law of the incorporated subjects. The embrace of "innovation," however, was double-edged: while renting agricultural land to Spanish tenants might have sustained communities and individuals in the short run, that limited access was surely preface to the larger invasion that would ultimately narrow indigenous control over the valley. But the source of the conflict was not a competing definition of property nor the willingness to recognize Spanish jurisdiction as part of a constellation of political practices. Our archives, carefully read, definitively demonstrate that indigenous elites and the communities they managed continued to seek ways to sustain their independence and to promote changing forms of indigenous justice. But the colonial system's voracious appetite for indigenous labor and production that would be consumed outside their local borders and for the benefit of others left communities inherently vulnerable.

REFERENCES

Abercrombie, Thomas A. *Pathways of Memory and Power: Ethnography and History among an Andean People*. Madison: University of Wisconsin Press, 1998.

Baber, R. Jovita. "The Construction of Empire: Politics, Law, and Community in Tlaxcala, New Spain, 1521–1640." PhD dissertation, University of Chicago, 2005.

Benton, Lauren. *Law and Colonial Cultures: Legal Regimes in World History, 1400–1900*. Cambridge: Cambridge University Press, 2001.

Benton, Lauren, and Richard J. Ross. *Legal Pluralism and Empires, 1500–1850*. New York: NYU Press, 2013.

Borah, Woodrow. *Justice by Insurance: The General Indian Court of Colonial Mexico and the Legal Aides of the Half-Real*. Berkeley: University of California Press, 1983.

———. "Juzgado General de Indios Del Peró O Juzgado Particular de Indios de El Cercado de Lima." *Revista Chilena de Historia Del Derecho* 6 (1970): 129–42.

Bowser, Frederick P. *The African Slave in Colonial Peru, 1524–1650*. Stanford, CA: Stanford University Press, 1974.

Castillero Calvo, Alfredo. *Fundación y orígenes de Natá*. Panamá: Instituto Panameño de Turismo, Dirección de Turismo Histórico, Social e Interno, 1972.

Charney, Paul. *Indian Society in the Valley of Lima, Peru, 1532–1824*. Lanham, MD: University Press of America, 2001.

Cobo, Bernabé. *Monografías históricas sobre la ciudad de Lima*. Lima: Librería e Imprenta Gil, 1935.

Coello de la Rosa, Alexandre. *Espacios de exclusión, espacios de poder: El Cercado de Lima colonial (1568–1606)*. Lima: Instituto de Estudios Peruanos: Pontificia Universidad Católica del Perú, 2006.

Cushner, Nicholas P. *Lords of the Land: Sugar, Wine, and Jesuit Estates of Coastal Peru, 1600–1767*. Albany: State University of New York Press, 1980.

De la Puente Luna, José Carlos. "That Which Belongs to All: Khipus, Community, and Indigenous Legal Activism in the Early Colonial Andes." *Americas* 72, no. 1 (2015): 19–54.

Diez de San Miguel, Garci, Waldemar Espinoza Soriano, and John V. Murra. *Visita hecha a la Provincia de Chucuito por Garci Diez de San Miguel en el año 1567*. Lima: Casa de la Cultura del Perú, 1964.

Flores-Zúñiga, Fernando. *Haciendas y pueblos de Lima: historia del valle del Rímac: de sus orígenes al siglo XX*. Lima, Perú: Fondo Editorial del Congreso del Perú, Municipalidad Metropolitana de Lima, 2008.

Garofalo, Leo J. "La Bebida del Inca En Copas Coloniales: Los Curacas del Mercado de Chicha del Cuzco, 1640–1700." In *Elites Indígenas En Los Andes: Nobles, Caciques Y Cabildantes Bajo El Yugo Colonial*, edited by David Cahill and Blanca Tovias, 175–212. Quito, Ecuador: ABYA YALA, 2003.

Graubart, Karen B. "Competing Spanish and Indigenous Jurisdictions in Early Colonial Lima." In *Oxford Online Encyclopedia in Latin American and Caribbean History*. New York: Oxford University Press, 2016.

——. "Learning from the Qadi: The Jurisdiction of Local Rule in the Early Colonial Andes." *Hispanic American Historical Review* 95, no. 2 (May 2015): 195–228.

——. "So That They Would Be Safe: The Walled Community of Santiago Del Cercado, Lima, and the Protection of Customary Law. In *Containing Law within the Walls: The Protection of Customary Law in Santiago del Cercado, Peru*, edited by Bain Attwood, Lauren Benton, and Adam Clulow, 129–46. Cambridge: Cambridge University Press, 2017.

——. "The Bonds of Inheritance: Afro-Peruvian Women's Legacies in a Slave-Holding World." In *Women's Negotiations and Textual Agency*, edited by Mónica Díaz and Rocío Quispe-Agnoli. New York: Routledge, 2017.

Hanke, Lewis, and Celso Rodríguez. *Los Virreyes españoles en América durante el gobierno de la Casa de Austria: Perú*. Vol. 280. Biblioteca de Autores Españoles. Madrid: Atlas, 1978.

Herzog, Tamar. "Colonial Law and Native Customs: Indigenous Land Rights in Colonial Spanish America." *Americas* 69, no. 3 (January 2013): 303–21.

Lamana, Gonzalo. *Domination without Dominance: Inca-Spanish Encounters in Early Colonial Peru*. Durham, NC: Duke University Press, 2008.

Levillier, Roberto. *Gobernantes del Perú, cartas y papeles, siglo XVI; documentos del Archivo de Indias*. Madrid: Sucesores de Rivadeneyra (s.a.), 1921.

Lockhart, James, Frances Berdan, and Arthur J. O. Anderson. *The Tlaxcalan Actas: A Compendium of the Records of the Cabildo of Tlaxcala (1545–1627)*. Salt Lake City: University of Utah Press, 1986.

Lohmann Villena, Guillermo. *El corregidor de indios en el Perú bajo los Austrias*. Madrid, Ediciones Cultura Hispánica, 1957.

——. "Testamento Del Curaca Don Gonzalo Taulichusco (1562)." *Revista Del Archivo General de La Nación* 7 (1984): 267–75.

Lowry, Lyn Brandon. "Forging an Indian Nation: Urban Indians under Spanish Colonial Control, Lima, Peru 1535–1765." PhD dissertation, University of California–Berkeley, 1991.

MacCormack, Sabine. "'The Heart Has Its Reasons': Predicaments of Missionary Christianity in Early Colonial Peru." *Hispanic American Historical Review* 65, no. 3 (1985): 443–66.

Mangan, Jane E. *Trading Roles: Gender, Ethnicity, and the Urban Economy in Colonial Potosí.* Durham, NC: Duke University Press, 2005.

Matienzo, Juan de. *Gobierno del Perú.* Buenos Aires: Compañía sud-americana de billetes de banco, 1910.

Melville, Elinor G. K. *A Plague of Sheep: Environmental Consequences of the Conquest of Mexico.* Cambridge: Cambridge University Press, 1994.

Morgado Maurtua, Patricia. "Un Palimpsesto Urbano. Del Asiento Indígena de Lima a La Ciudad Española de Los Reyes." PhD dissertation, Universidad de Sevilla, 2007.

Mumford, Jeremy Ravi. *Vertical Empire: The General Resettlement of Indians in the Colonial Andes.* Durham, NC: Duke University Press, 2012.

Mundy, Barbara E. *The Mapping of New Spain: Indigenous Cartography and the Maps of the Relaciones Geográficas.* Chicago: University of Chicago Press, 1996.

Murra, John V. *Formaciones económicas y políticas del mundo andino.* Lima: Instituto de Estudios Peruanos, 1975.

———. "Litigation over the Rights of 'Natural Lords' in Early Colonial Courts in the Andes." In *Native Traditions in the Postconquest World*, 55–62. Washington, DC: Dumbarton Oaks Research Library and Collection, 1998.

Nader, Helen. *Liberty in Absolutist Spain: The Habsburg Sale of Towns, 1516–1700.* Baltimore, MD: Johns Hopkins University Press, 1990.

Ondegardo, Polo de. "Relación de los Fundamentos Acerca del Notable Daño Que Resulta de No Guardar a Los Yndios Sus Fueros [1571]." *Colección de Libros y Documentos Referentes a la Historia Del Perú* 3 (1916): 45–188.

Ortiz de Zúñiga, Iñigo, and John V. Murra. *Visita de la provincia de León de Huánuco en 1562.* Huánuco, Perú: Universidad Nacional Hermilio Valdizán, Facultad de Letras y Educación, 1967.

Osorio, Alejandra. "El Callejón de La Soledad: Vectors of Cultural Hybridity in Seventeenth-Century Lima." In *Spiritual Encounters: Interactions between Christianity and Native Religions in Colonial America*, edited by Nicholas Griffiths and Fernando Cervantes, 198–229. Lincoln: University of Nebraska Press, 1999.

O'Toole, Rachel Sarah. *Bound Lives: Africans, Indians, and the Making of Race in Colonial Peru.* 1st ed. Pittsburgh, PA: University of Pittsburgh Press, 2012.

Owensby, Brian. *Empire of Law and Indian Justice in Colonial Mexico.* Stanford, CA: Stanford University Press, 2011.

Pagden, Anthony. *Lords of All the World: Ideologies of Empire in Spain, Britain, and France c.1500–c.1800.* New Haven, CT: Yale University Press, 1998.

Premo, Bianca. *Children of the Father King: Youth, Authority, and Legal Minority in Colonial Lima.* Chapel Hill: University of North Carolina Press, 2005.

Ramírez, Susan E. *Provincial Patriarchs: Land Tenure and the Economics of Power in Colonial Peru.* Albuquerque: University of New Mexico Press, 1986.

———. *The World Upside Down: Cross-Cultural Contact and Conflict in Sixteenth-Century Peru.* Stanford, CA: Stanford University Press, 1996.

Rostworowski de Diez Canseco, Maria. "Dos Probanzas de Don Gonzalo, Curaca de Lima (1555–1559)." *Revista Histórica* 33 (1983): 105–73.

Rostworowski de Diez Canseco, María. *Costa peruana prehispánica.* Lima: Instituto de Estudios Peruanos, 1989.

———. *Señoríos indígenas de Lima y Canta.* Lima: Instituto de Estudios Peruanos, 1978.

Salomon, Frank. *The Cord Keepers: Khipus and Cultural Life in a Peruvian Village.* Durham, NC: Duke University Press, 2004.

Sarabia Viejo, Maria Justina. *Francisco de Toledo: disposiciones gubernativas para e virreinato de Peru.* Sevilla: Consejo Superior de Investigaciones Científicos, 1996.

Spain, Consejo de Indias (Spain), and Tribunal Supremo. *Recopilacion de leyes de los reinos de las Indias.* Madrid: Boix, 1841.

Spalding, Karen. *Huarochirí, an Andean Society under Inca and Spanish Rule.* Stanford, CA: Stanford University Press, 1984.

Vassberg, David E. *Land and Society in Golden Age Castile.* Cambridge: Cambridge University Press, 1984.

Vergara, Teresa. "Hombres, Tierras y Productos: Los Valles Comarcanos de Lima (1532–1650)." *Cuadernos de Investigación, PUCP* 2 (1995): 5–45.

Zuloaga, Marina. *La Conquista Negociada: Guarangas, Autoridades Locales e Imperio En Huaylas, Perú (1532–1610).* Lima: IEP-IFEA, 2012.

NOTES

1 On legal pluralism in the Iberian world, see Benton, *Law and Colonial Cultures*; Benton and Ross, *Legal Pluralism and Empires, 1500–1850*; Owensby, *Empire of Law and Indian Justice*; Graubart, "Competing Spanish and Indigenous Jurisdictions."

2 Polo de Ondegardo, "Relación de los Fundamentos Acerca del Notable Daño Que Resulta de No Guardar a Los Yndios Sus Fueros [1571]," 3:47, 60–61, 150; see also Lamana, *Domination without Dominance*, 187.

3 For the debate over *dominium* and legitimacy, see Pagden, *Lords of All the World*.

4 Mumford, *Vertical Empire*, 69–70; Murra, "Litigation over the Rights of 'Natural Lords' in Early Colonial Courts in the Andes."

5 The belief that Andeans did not know private property was generally accepted by Spaniards. Collective property and indigenous laziness were linked in Matienzo, *Gobierno del Perú*, 15–16. On the relationship between the civilizing mission, governance, and these behaviors, see MacCormack, "'The Heart Has Its Reasons.'"

6 Ondegardo, "Relación de Los Fundamentos."

7 For colonial examples, see Zuloaga, *La Conquista Negociada*; Abercrombie, *Pathways of Memory and Power.* A more modern ethnography that connects to the past is Salomon, *The Cord Keepers.*

8   For example Lockhart, Berdan, and Anderson, *The Tlaxcalan Actas.*

9   Spain, Consejo de Indias (Spain), and Tribunal Supremo, *Recopilación de leyes de Indias,* Libro VI, titulo I, leyes 39–40; Baber, "The Construction of Empire," 102–5.

10 On royal policy to create towns to undermine the nobility, see Nader, *Liberty in Absolutist Spain.*

11 From Philip III's ordinances of 1618, in Spain, Consejo de Indias (Spain), and Tribunal Supremo, *Recopilación de leyes de Indias,* Libro VI, título I, ley xvi.

12 Hanke and Rodríguez, *Los Virreyes españoles,* 280:82–83.

13 Ibid., 280:82.

14 In contrast, in the Mexican Audiencia, Indians had a Juzgado General de Indios, a "tribunal of sweeping jurisdiction in Indian cases," mostly at the level of appeals, whose judge was the viceroy. On the Mexican court, see Borah, *Justice by Insurance*; Owensby, *Empire of Law and Indian Justice.*

15 Lockhart, Berdan, and Anderson, *The Tlaxcalan Actas,* 37.

16 For an examination of a case where these questions can be seen, see Graubart, "Learning from the Qadi."

17 Flores-Zúñiga, *Haciendas y pueblos de Lima*; Vergara, "Hombres, Tierras y Productos." On Lima, see Morgado Maurtua, "Un Palimpsesto Urbano." The best study of the region's transformations remains Rostworowski de Diez Canseco, *Señoríos indígenas de Lima y Canta.*

18 On Taulichusco's acts and his regrets, see Rostworowski de Diez Canseco, *Señoríos indígenas de Lima y Canta*; Rostworowski de Diez Canseco, "Dos Probanzas de Don Gonzalo."

19 Morgado Maurtua, "Un Palimpsesto Urbano," chap. 3.

20 Charney, *Indian Society,* 43; Cushner, *Lords of the Land,* chap. 1.

21 Lohmann Villena, "Testamento Del Curaca Don Gonzalo Taulichusco (1562)."

22 Vergara, "Hombres, Tierras y Productos," 16–19. On the ways that requirements like titling radically changed indigenous relationships to land, see Herzog, "Colonial Law and Native Customs."

23 On the Cercado, see Coello de la Rosa, *Espacios de exclusión, espacios de poder*; Lowry, "Forging an Indian Nation."

24 Lima's Indians had access to other forms of community organization, including confraternities and militias. See Charney, *Indian Society.*

25 See Lohmann Villena, *El corregidor de indios.* For the Cercado's office see Borah, "Juzgado General de Indios Del Perú."

26 The litigation is filed in Archivo General de la Nación, Perú (hereafter AGN) Series Fácticas, Corregimiento de Santiago del Cercado (hereafter CSC), and includes other regions of Peru.

27 AGN Protocolos Notariales (hereafter PN) 1533 Piñeda (1612–13). A variety of registers and unpaginated loose documents are bundled or sewn together under this signature.

28 On *sapsi,* see de la Puente Luna, "That Which Belongs to All."

29 E.g., Ondegardo, "Relación de los Fundamentos Acerca del Notable Daño Que Resulta de No Guardar a Los Yndios Sus Fueros [1571]," 3:70. For a highland case, see Diez de San Miguel, Espinoza Soriano, and Murra, *Visita hecha a la provincia de Chucuito*. Modern debates over resource management include Murra, *Formaciones económicas y políticas del mundo andino*; Ramírez, *The World Upside Down*; de la Puente Luna, "That Which Belongs to All."

30 A possibility that sheds light on Taulichusco's understanding of his offer to Pizarro in 1535. Rostworowski de Diez Canseco, *Costa peruana prehispánica*, 33–35; Graubart, "Competing Spanish and Indigenous Jurisdictions."

31 "Testamento de Don Gonzalo Taulichusco," AGN, PN 83, Alonso Hernández (1562), ff. 605–11.

32 On the varieties of concepts of property in early modern Spain, see Vassberg, *Land and Society in Golden Age Castile*.

33 Vergara, "Hombres, Tierras y Productos," 12–13.

34 See Cushner, *Lords of the Land*.

35 "Arrendamiento," AGN PN 1533 Piñeda f. 43 (29 March 1612). A *fanega de sembradura* (or *fanegada* in the sixteenth century) was the amount of land that could be planted with 1.5 bushels of seed, or the equivalent of 7.16 acres; see Ramírez, *Provincial Patriarchs*, 279.

36 "Testamento de Magdalena Picona," AGN PN 1853 Tamayo, ff. 833–835v (11 September 1630).

37 "Testamento de Doña Ana Collon," AGN PN 1856 Tamayo, ff. 635–7 (July 1635).

38 Melville, *A Plague of Sheep*, chap. 4.

39 AGN PN Pineda 1533, f. 131 (7 May 1612); f. 13 (January 1613); 39v (2 January 1613).

40 "Testamento de Costança Ticlla," AGN Testamento de Indios (hereafter TI) leg 1 (1596).

41 Vergara, "Hombres, Tierras y Productos." On informal housing in Lima, see Osorio, "El Callejón de La Soledad: Vectors of Cultural Hybridity in Seventeenth-Century Lima."

42 "Licencia y arrendamiento," AGN PN Piñeda 1533, f. 4v-10 (15 January 1612); "Arrendamiento," AGN PN Piñeda 1533, f. 294 (15 October 1612).

43 The status of *miserables* gave Indians similar protective rights to minors, offering them free legal representation and differential sentencing for crimes. See Premo, *Children of the Father King*.

44 "Pleito," AGN PN Piñeda 1533, ff. 44–47v (24–30 January 1613).

45 "Autos que siguieron los indios Yauyos," Derecho Indígena (hereafter DI), leg. 9, cuad. 130, 1653, AGN.

46 Graubart, "So That They Would Be Safe."

47 Castillero Calvo, *Fundación y orígenes de Natá*, 60.

48 Lima's foundation is described in Cobo, *Monografías históricas*, chap. 2.

49 For maps showing evidence of this in Mexico, see Mundy, *The Mapping of New Spain*, 118–26.

50 "Testamento de Constança Ticlla," AGN TI leg 1, 1596; "Testamento de Elvira Coyti," AGN TI leg 1, 1596; "Testamento de María Capan," AGN TI leg 1, 1596.

51 AGN DI leg. 4 cuad. 47 (1603, Surco).

52 "Contrato," AGN PN Piñeda 1533, f. 50 (April 1612).

53 "Contrato," AGN PN Piñeda 1533, ff. 286–287v (10 September 1612).

54 "Compañía," AGN PN Piñeda 1533 ff. 236–236v (2 August 1612).

55 E.g., "Testamento de Pedro Huaman," AGN TI leg. 1 (Surquillo, 1632).

56 Bowser, *The African Slave in Colonial Peru, 1524–1650*, 88.

57 Spalding, *Huarochirí*, 25–32.

58 On reciprocity as the basis for social organization, see ibid., 25–32.

59 "Testamento de María Capan," AGN TI leg 1 (1596).

60 "Testamento de Costança Ticlla," AGN TI leg 1 (1596). An *arroba* was equivalent to about twenty-five pounds.

61 AGN DI leg 4 cuad 47 (1603), f. 13v.

62 Mangan, *Trading Roles*, 82. On the pre-Hispanic uses of *chicha*, see Garofalo, "La Bebida Del Inca."

63 "Expediente sobre el juicio de residencia . . . ," Biblioteca Nacional del Perú A537 (1586).

64 De la Puente Luna, "That Which Belongs to All."

65 The earliest orders in Peru seem to be those of Dr. Gregorio González de Cuenca in 1566, archived as Archivo General de Indias, Patronato 189, ramo 11; and the 1565 letter of García de Castro to the Crown, in Levillier, *Gobernantes del Perú*, 3:121.

66 The following were licenses granted for sale or purchase of a slave, all in AGN PN 1533 Piñeda: f. 23 (February 1612); f. 25 (20 February 1612); f. 27 (February 1612); f. 57 (2 February 1613); f. 212v (19 July 1612); f. 250 (17 August 1612); f. 369 (19 December 1612).

67 "Venta de esclava," AGN PN Piñeda 1533 f. 212v (19 July 1612).

68 "Venta de esclavo," AGN PN Piñeda 1533 f. 23 (19 February 1612).

69 For example, Sarabia Viejo, *Francisco de Toledo*, 1:197 and Archivo General de Indias, Seville, Spain, Patronato 187, ramo 14 (1550). On the rhetoric of African danger, see Bowser, *The African Slave in Colonial Peru, 1524–1650*.

70 For the case of free blacks purchasing enslaved blacks, see Graubart, "The Bonds of Inheritance."

71 Sarabia Viejo, *Francisco de Toledo*, 1:34.

72 E.g., Ortiz de Zúñiga et al., *Visita de la provincia de León de Huánuco en 1562*, 2:116.

73 "Testamento de doña María Llatan," AGN PN 1854 Tamayo, ff. 334–37 (26 May 1631).

74 "Piden licencia para comprar una esclava negra," AGN PN Piñeda 1533 f. 65v-68 (16 March 1613).

75 "Arrendamiento de chacara," AGN PN Piñeda 1533 f. 58v (7 Feb. 1613).

PART II

At the Boundaries of Differing Conceptions of Justice

6

"Darling Indians" and "Natural Lords"

Virginia's Tributary Regime and Florida's Republic of Indians in the Seventeenth Century

BRADLEY DIXON

I.

In the spring of 1646, the Powhatan leader Opechancanough sat in irons in a Jamestown jail. Even in his dotage—he was more than a century old at his capture—Opechancanough had eluded his pursuers for two years. Now, Virginia's governor, Sir William Berkeley, planned to take his enemy off in triumph to London. The path that brought Opechancanough to this pass was long and twisted. Decades before, his late brother, the *mamanatowick*, or paramount chief, Wahunsonacock, had offered the English a place in their chiefdom. He gave the English a choice to live peacefully as neighbors and abide by the laws of Tsenacommacah.[1] Throughout those early years, both sides, English and Powhatan, sought ascendancy as they "attempted to mutually civilize each other."[2] The English, meanwhile, endeavored to crown Wahunsonacock as a vassal of King James. Failing that, they tried to undermine his authority and draw his people to them. The newcomers neither lived harmoniously within the chiefdom nor fully satisfied Native expectations of exchange.[3] Exasperated, Opechancanough led campaigns in 1622 and again in 1644 to restrain Virginia. In defeat, he suffered a last indignity. A guard murdered the old man in his cell.[4]

The "conquest of Apechanckenough, & all his Indians" in 1646—an event Thomas Ludwell boasted "noe other English Governmᵗ in the West Indies" had rivaled—led to the greatest intervention in Native affairs since the days when Englishmen longed for an empire of Indian vassals to rival Spain's.[5] That October, Berkeley and the English made a treaty with Opechancanough's successor, Necotowance, who acknowledged that he held "his kingdom from the king's Majesty in England."[6] As a token of submission, the treaty stipulated that "Necotowance and his successors are to pay unto the king's governor the number of twenty beaver skins at the going away of geese yearly."[7] The king of England, for his part, promised to protect the "king of the Indians"—meting out justice to his new vassal.

In its infancy, the colony's leaders, steeped in the literature of the Spanish conquests, conceived of Tsenacommacah as an "empire" or "kingdom" to conquer and rule as a "Protestant Mexico."[8] Only at mid-century did they obtain the power to do so. Over the next decades, the House of Burgesses remade Virginia's laws to reduce the tributary Indians to civility and Christianity. Forged between 1646 and 1676, Virginia's tributary regime was the closest that the English colonizers in Virginia came to the Spanish ideal of incorporating Natives into the colonial polity.

After 1646, the process of "mutually civilizing" one another that had characterized relations between Indians and English colonists in Virginia gave way to a new contest over the norms of justice. Native arguments with colonists in this era took the form of assertions of the corporate rights they believed English law entitled them to. Contention between Natives and settlers was less a question of which of the two legal cultures would prevail in any given situation; instead, these contests took place increasingly within the idiom of English law. Commonly, it was the Indian tributaries who sought to uphold the letter of colonial laws and treaties and English settlers who were happy to ignore or circumvent them. By this means, Natives gave concrete meaning to their legal status in the three decades before Bacon's Rebellion.

Unlike in Spanish America, the Natives' status with respect to Virginia's colonial state was contingent. England's king felt little theological imperative to see Indians receive justice equally with the Crown's other subjects. Inclusion and justice, however limited, depended on a host of considerations such as fears of Indian war, the flow of tribute and peltry to colonial elites, and, yes, at times, an interest in evangelization.

To explore whether Virginia's tributary regime should be considered an anomaly, out of step with usual English practice, this essay will evaluate it against both the colony's early, Spanish-inspired visions of colonial rule and the experience of other Native people living in the Spanish empire. Spanish Florida, specifically the history of the Apalachee Indians, offers a useful comparison. The English effort to colonize Tsenacommacah coincided with the first efforts by Spanish Franciscan friars to establish missions among the Apalachee of western Florida. What one historian called "Sir William Berkeley's Golden Age," and the tributary regime's height, coincided with what another once called the "Golden Age of Florida's Missions."[9]

By the middle of the seventeenth century, Spanish Florida comprised two "republics"—one for the Spaniards and one for the Indians. The "Republic of Indians" and the "Republic of Spaniards" were separate, corporate "estates" but members of the same Church and vassals to the same king.[10] In Florida, the separation between the two republics was more pronounced than elsewhere as the Indian provinces lay well beyond the main center of Spanish settlement, San Agustín.[11] Throughout Spanish America, Indian vassals merited a claim on the special favor of magistrates and the monarch as *personas miserables*, or miserable persons.[12] The Spanish defined Indian legal status as a form of minority, not of age but of capacity.[13] The law protected Indians' communal lands and many of their customs. They rendered tribute in goods and labor either as part of grants of labor to Spanish families known as *encomiendas* or, as in Florida, through the *repartimiento* labor draft that serviced public works. What the English knew of this system encouraged the picture of what an Anglo-Indian polity might be. Or, as Camilla Townsend has put it, the Spanish offered a plan for "bringing a population of Indians 'into the fold.'"[14]

By contrast, most histories of seventeenth-century Anglo-America tend—understandably—to stress the exclusion of Indians. Religious conversion was of as little interest to most colonists as it was to most Natives. As Anthony Pagden put it, the conversion of Indians had little place in English colonies founded "for no religious purpose other than their own perfection."[15] The reform of Virginia's Indian laws during the 1650s and '60s has therefore proved an interesting problem for historians, an aberration in an otherwise steady story of exploitation and dispossession.[16] Historians have contended that the tributary regime was concerned mainly with the exploitation of subject Indians, providing valuable perquisites and profits—including from Indian slaves—to the colonial governor and his clique.[17] Given English colonists' exclusionary tendencies, extending to Indians the protection of law was controversial enough to encourage rebels like Nathaniel Bacon, who, as recent scholarship has argued, believed either that the tributaries were the equals of poor whites or that they were simply above the law.[18] Metropolitan aspirations for peaceful Indian relations clashed repeatedly with the demands of frontier colonists.[19] In Virginia, attacks against Indian "scapegoats" proved "cathartic," especially for the men who had been the "losers" during the colony's growth of the mid-seventeenth century.[20] These prevailing tendencies led Stitt Robinson to conclude that the tributaries' status "modifies" the "glib generalization" that in the English colonies "the only good Indian was a dead Indian."[21] As John Elliott has argued, the closest the English ever came to establishing something like the "Republic of Indians" was among the "praying towns" of Massachusetts Bay—far from Virginia in more ways than one.[22]

But the case of the "two republics" in Spanish America can help to clarify the place of Native Americans living as tributaries in British America. The comparison illuminates aspects of English law that one might otherwise overlook. Despite great differences, the tributary regime in Virginia and the "Republic of Indians" shared important characteristics. Underlying them both was the principle that Indians required protection from the abuses of grasping colonists. In return, protected Natives rendered valuable services. Tributary Indians in Virginia were also tribute-paying subjects, living in semiautonomous communities, subject to but separate from the English for their better exploitation and protection.[23] By the 1660s, the law in Virginia even singled out the "poor Indians" for special favors. In the eyes of the law, Indians in Virginia were in many respects miserable persons with a special claim upon English justice. The Virginia Assembly imagined that settlement on their communal lands, with guaranteed title, would both insulate Indians from English encroachments and prepare them for conversion. These tributary Indians were at once subject to the government of the English and apart from it, often retaining their customs. Although their efforts seem curious, Virginia did not abandon the kind of evangelizing mission that animated Florida. And above all, the tributary regime, much like the "Republic of Indians," attempted to rule Indians through nobles. Concentrating on their convergences and contrasts may make the issues at stake in Bacon's Rebellion clearer.

II.

"The Natives of America att this day are of three Sorts," according to an English report of 1665.[24] "The first that live most civilly, are them that live within the Government of the Spaniards after the same manner that they doe, in apparel, building, trades and Religion." Descending from those "that live most civilly" come the "second Sort," who "live under the Contribution of the English, Portugalls, Dutch, ffrench, & c. and these keep still their ancient Customes, religions, and manners." These Indians "under the Contribution" maintained their own "severall Governors, or Kings, and live in townes." The third sort were the most barbarous Indians "in the Spanish Dominions where there is the most of them," whom the report considered "Inhumane." In the English mind, the second and third, less civil sorts of Indians were so because they were not subject to the same degree of European law and oversight as those "within the Government of the Spaniards." Thus Indians "under the Contribution of the English" possessed a degree of freedom that metropolitan and other thinkers believed was much more capacious than in the Spanish domains.

The contrasts were sharp but overdrawn. The Spanish had in fact upheld the Natives' rights to their customs so long as they were not "contrary to the law of God"—a standard admittedly far higher than the one that English courts would later uphold.[25] Spanish Indian vassals and English subject Indians performed similar functions and held some comparable privileges despite other, often striking, differences in authority, status, law, demography, and religion.

Both the Spanish in Florida and the English in Virginia relied in their own ways upon the chiefly lineages of the Native peoples they colonized. Under Spanish legal theory, Native leaders like the Apalachee *holah-tas*—or caciques, as the Spanish called them—were *señores naturales*, or "natural lords" on whose authority and consent Spanish colonial claims rested.[26] Apalachee's caciques retained great prestige, leading by consensus in what John H. Hann called "oligarchical democracies."[27] The Southeast's English colonizers had also sought the consent and thus the authority of the country's "natural lords." As Jeffrey Glover has shown, English colonizers paid careful attention to the forms of Native politics in order to secure territorial claims that would stand in Europe.[28]

Like the Spaniards in La Florida who conducted "conquest by contract," the English negotiated agreements with theoretical unequals. Roman law recognized "*consensus ad idem*, a 'meeting of the minds' or voluntary agreement between parties, [that] served as proof that a claim was pacified, or under control."[29] In 1608, the same year the first friar entered Apalachee, Virginia Company officials crowned Wahunsonacock. John Smith mocked the proceedings but captured their import with the *mamanatowick*'s response: "If your king have sent me presents," Wahunsonacock declared, "I also am a king, and this my land."[30] Wahunsonanock stood on his rights as a natural lord. Wahunsonacock used the English gifts from King James I to enhance his spiritual power in Tsenacommacah.[31]

Making the Powhatans into English vassals was an important object of the Virginia Company's Indian policy before 1622. By 1609, company officials planned to draw away the loyalty and tribute of the peoples under Wahunsonacock's authority. Some peoples, like the Accomacs on the Eastern Shore, gladly accepted alliance with the newcomers in a move to regain their independence from the resented *mamanatowick*.[32] But the English held a different view of the matter. In 1612, the colony's secretary, William Strachey, fantasized about the Powhatans becoming like the "Cassiques" of colonial Peru—rich and well protected under a European sovereign.[33] The Powhatans "shall by pattents and Proclamations hold their landes as free burgers and Cittizens with the English and Subjectes to king James, who will give them Justice and defend them against their enemyes."[34]

In 1614, Ralph Hamor described the ceremony where the Chickahominies swore their fealty to King James I. The Chickahominies were fiercely independent, so their embrace of the English was probably a political gambit. But Hamor's description makes clear at least the English interpretation of the Indians' actions. The Chickahominies became "King James's noblemen"—vassals who could expect justice from the king and his deputy, the governor in Virginia.[35] The terms of the Chickahominies' "submission" were a model for an empire on the cheap, with Native incorporation occurring without the "expensive labors of conversion"—a fact with lasting significance.[36]

After the uprising of Powhatans in 1622, the company went bankrupt and the Crown revoked its charter. The uprising colored Indian affairs for decades until the second great assault under Opechancanough in 1644. After Opechancanough's defeat, the subsequent "articles of peace" in 1646, as Robin Beck recently put it, meant that "his Pamunkey Indian successors were the vassals of a foreign *Mamanatowick*, England's Charles I."[37]

After 1646, English governors claimed the power to appoint Indian *weroances*. The treaty of 1646 declared that Virginia's governor could appoint or confirm Indian leaders. The assembly of 1664–1665 denied tributary Indians the "power within themselves to elect or constitute their owne Werowance or theire Comander but the present hon[ble] Govern[r]. & his Successors from time to time shall constitute and authorize such person in whose fidelitie they may finde greatest cause to Repose a confidence to be the Commander of the respective Townes."[38] Not only did the government claim the power to name Indian leaders; it also vowed to defend them against all challengers. The treaty of 1646 pledged the English to uphold the power of Necotowance and his successors against "rebells."[39] The 1664–1665 act declared that should a town "refuse their obedience to or murther such person then that nation of Indians soe refuseing or offending [is] to be accompted enimies and Rebells and proceeded against accordingly."[40] The English hoped to increase Indian leaders' dependence upon the colony. If English boasts were serious about appointing tributary Indian leaders, in practice power reposed in the same people year in and year out. Cockacoeske, the queen of Pamunkey, led her people for thirty years.[41] In Apalachee, as in Tsenacommacah, the succession was hereditary and matrilineal—which, along with other Native political customs, the Spaniards typically honored.[42]

The privileges of Indian nobles commanded respect in Apalachee. During their periodic inspections of the province, Spanish officials carefully noted the ranks of leaders consulted in each visited town, commonly asking, as during the 1657 visitation of Ocuya, "whether any of their vassals had failed to respect them."[43] To hold their loyalty, the Spanish plied their Indian vassals with gifts paid for by the colonial *situado*, or payments the king made to maintain Florida's administrative expenses.[44] Nobles were exempt from the demands of manual labor. They enjoyed the same privileges as Spanish *hidalgos*—including the right to "wear swords and ride horses."[45] With their swords, Spain's Indian vassals in Florida fought for the colony and the Crown. By the mid-seventeenth century, the Spanish had organized Indians into militias under the leadership of their caciques. Some Indian militiamen received guns, food, uniforms, and even military pensions upon their old age.[46]

Tributary kings and queens had acquired something like a privileged standing in Virginia law. On 13 March 1660, the Virginia Assembly passed an act exempting the king of the Weanoaks from arrest for debt. Fresh from jail, the king had petitioned the assembly for relief. Declaring that by his recent imprisonment at the hands of creditors "much detriment hath accrewed to the publique," the assembly gave him a respite from arrest until "the first of March next," perhaps to reorder his affairs.[47] The 1662 act of the assembly "concerning Indians" prohibited anyone from arresting a tributary Indian ruler without a "spetiall warrant" from the governor and two members of the council.[48] The law's purpose was to keep the "making of peace and warre" in the hands of the governor and out of the "power of every individuall in the country."[49] Native American elites possessed recognized, if limited, legal privileges and participated in a Virginia politics that turned on the maintenance of peace.

Native elites as well as commoners used European law to hold onto their lands and possessions. In both places boundaries emerged. Policing the boundaries between the Republic of Indians and the Republic of Spaniards was an ongoing task. Regulations stipulated how long, for instance, Spaniards and *castas*—people of mixed blood—could remain among the Indians when on official business.[50] The Franciscan friars also struggled to segregate Indian women from Spanish men, mainly the soldiers who occupied the provinces in Florida.[51] In Virginia, legal separation between Indians and Englishmen was the product of mixed motives. The colony reeled after the two attacks in 1622 and 1644 and, until at least 1656, the law permitted an armed Englishman to shoot an Indian whether under the colony's "protection" or not.[52] The 1646 articles and subsequent enactments provided clothing and badges to distinguish tributary Indian messengers.[53] Laws against "entertaining" Indians posited separation out of fear; laws against "encroachment" on Native lands avowed separation for the sake of protection, much as in Florida. The challenges of colonial intrusion facing Natives in Florida and Virginia were similar, but their scale was greater in the English colony.

The demographic realities in Tsenacommacah and Apalachee were nearly mirror images of one another. Fray Martín Prieto, the first

Franciscan friar to visit Apalachee, reported to his superiors that the whole province had turned out for him—some thirty-six thousand souls.[54] In the same year as the first Franciscans entered Apalachee, Tsenacommacah consisted of around thirty separate polities of nearly fifteen thousand people.[55] The most dramatic differences were in European population. Few Spaniards dreamed of making a life along what historian Michael Gannon called the "rim of Christendom." Their numbers in Florida never much exceeded three thousand persons, with most living in San Agustín.[56] In Apalachee, the first garrison of seven or eight soldiers established themselves in a blockhouse in 1638.[57] After the Apalachee revolted in 1647, the number of soldiers increased. They brought families who lived alongside the Indians at the mission village of San Luis de Talimali. The Spanish presence strained relations with the Apalachee, especially near the end of the century, when the Spanish population in the province was at its highest. But there were never more than a few dozen Spaniards in a province full of Indians. In 1675, the bishop of Cuba estimated Apalachee's population at 10,520 souls—meaning that the province held over 80 percent of Florida's Natives.[58] In Virginia, on the other hand, tobacco lured migrants across the Atlantic who were hoping to establish themselves eventually on land of their own. Between 1629 and 1640, the English population rose from just twenty-six hundred people to eighty-one hundred.[59] By 1685 the English population was nearly ten times that of the Natives. War, dispossession, and disease took their toll as the century wore on. In Virginia, the influx of new settlers swarmed around what Helen Rountree has called "separate islands" of communal Indian lands.[60] A census of 1669 listed nineteen different tributary Indian polities within the jurisdictions of nine English counties.[61] By 1675, an estimated twenty-nine hundred tributary Indians lived within Virginia's purported boundaries.[62] The demography of the two colonies is undeniably different. But in Florida and Virginia, the law in both colonies pursued nominally the same ends—to prevent European encroachment on Indians' communal landholding claims.

Both European legal systems held Indians to be part of a special class. Indians in Spanish America—since at least 1501—were *vasallos*, or vassals of the Crown. Classification as *Indio* in Spanish law—with its "distinct civic status"—was coveted even for other non-Spaniards in the New World and elsewhere.[63] Spanish law dating to the Middle Ages defined vassalage as a mutual obligation between a superior lord and an inferior under his charge.[64] By the time the English colonized Virginia, the word "vassal" had become a pejorative term.[65] Historians, notably Francis Jennings, have regarded "vassalage" and its implication of reciprocal relationships between Englishmen and Indians with a skeptical eye.[66] But the term appeared in Native petitions during the Mohegan Land Case, signifying a reciprocal bond.[67] From the Indians' perspective, they performed vital services and expected considerable autonomy and favor in return. "Indian" certainly did not, in Virginia, come with a presumption against enslavement. Still, the sum of the various articles of peace, rulings from the Crown and the Lords of Trade, and a number of colonial statutes would together establish the tributaries—even after Bacon's Rebellion—in a sounder, more formal legal position than that of other Indians. By 1736, George Webb's handbook for Virginia justices of peace divided the law's treatment of tributaries into "Privileges and Restraints of Tributaries" on one hand and "Their Duty" on the other. The "Tributary Indians [were] entitled to Protection of the law in their Persons and Properties, equaly [sic] with English subjects."[68] The status of Indians within Virginia moved along a graduated scale. Of the tributaries, the law singled out the Pamunkeys, the Chickahominy, and the Eastern Shore Indians for privileges that set them apart from "Free Indians," Indian servants, and "Indian slaves."[69] The corporate rights of the three nations Webb listed had developed over time.

Among the privileges of tributary Indians in Virginia were those "of Oystering fishing and gathering Tuchahoe Cortenions, and other wild fruites by which they were wonted for a great part of the year to Subsist." The assembly originally enacted this provision in 1662 "for the better releife of the poor Indians whome the Seateing of the English hath forced from their wanted conveniencys."[70] The logic of Virginia's law for the relief of the "poor Indians" bears at least some resemblance to the Spanish legal category *personas miserables*. Some English travel writers were familiar with the principle. In 1572, Henry Hawks noted that in Mexico "the Indians are much favoured by the Justices of the Countrey and they call them their orphanes."[71] The provision of justice, Hawks believed, was the reason the Indians there were so civil.[72] In English law no such universal category existed. England's "poor Indians" were the creations of missionaries, objects, in Laura M. Stevens's words, of "imperial pity." Unlike its Spanish counterpart, "in English the term invoked no legal privileges, only emotion."[73] Yet, in Virginia, conquest—or as the law called it, the "Seateing of the English"—left the "poor Indians" in need of the law's special favor and added meaning to the category.

Virginia's government at times also claimed to protect Indians on account of another supposed incapacity—their ignorance of English law. After a spate of defaults to crooked English creditors, Virginia enacted a law voiding the debts of Indians and forbidding further loans to them on this basis.[74] In fact, tributary Indians showed they knew the law better than the English. Whether in the courthouse or in the council chamber, Indians in Virginia were quick to point out when Virginians violated their rights. The law became intelligible through common ceremonies. The annual payment of tribute reminded each side of the terms of their uneasy coexistence. Shortly after accepting the "articles of peace" of 1646, Necotowance met William Berkeley to deliver his tribute and reaffirm peace. Bearing "twenty Beaver-skinnes to be sent to King *Charles* as he said for Tribute," Necotowance pronounced a "long Oration" vowing never to "wrong" the English.[75] But the colonists often proved worse than forgetful. In 1685, the Rappahannock County Court considered "the Freedom of a Rappahanock Indian Woman." She had been "taken in the late Warr between the English & Indians and then sold for a Servant."[76] The court "debated the matter" but they lacked the "Articles of Peace [that had been] concluded w^th: the Neighbouring Indians after the late War; in w^ch: Articles this Court do conceive the time of service for Neighbouring Indians then taken, is Limited." When squatters began to swarm at the end of the century, the then queen of Pamunkey, probably "Mrs. Betty," complained "that severall English have Encroached vpon the Libertyes of her people, Contrary to the Articles of Peace, and Severall Orders of the Genll Court."[77] Queen Betty and the lords commissioner for trade and plantations in Whitehall were of the same mind. In January 1700, the lords ordered "[t]hat the Articles made with the Indians at Middle Plantation the 29th: of May 1677 be exactly observed: As likewise all other Treaties whatsoever."[78] Other than the employment of official interpreters, however, the English made few concessions to encourage the mutual intelligibility of the law. Raising the articles of peace and statutes, tributary Indians tried to hold English colonists to account despite colonial dismissals that they were ignorant of the law.

Natives' alleged incapacities did not lead Virginia lawmakers—or metropolitan authorities for that matter—to imitate Spanish America's elaborate Indian justice system. There were no special Indian courts like Mexico's *juzgado de indios*. Nor did the English often—except through various ad hoc arrangements in New England—appoint guardians or, in Virginia, "trustees," over Indian nations until the eighteenth century.[79] The regular outlet for Indian grievances in Apalachee was the *visita*, or visitation of the province. The most extensive of these inspection tours of Spanish officials through Indian towns happened in Florida about every six years with the term of each governor.[80] The visitations provided a forum where Indian caciques complained about infringements on the "Republic of Indians."[81] Under Spanish law, Indians, with their customs, leaders, and rights to self-government, constituted an entirely separate jurisdiction, or *fuero*, of their own.[82]

In Virginia, Indian complaints often received hearings in county courts where "local barons" held great sway. Some counties, like Rappahannock in 1656, even negotiated their own treaties with nearby Indians.[83] During the Berkeley years, Indians could testify in court and often did.[84] But the Indian jurisdiction in Virginia was divided. As the colony's secretary, Thomas Ludwell, put it in 1666, "[I]f they commit any offence against an Englishman, or hee against them, It is tryable in our Courts or before some of our Magistrates."[85] But their disputes with one another were "still left to y[e] Discision of their owne Customes."[86]

The two resources over which Indians and colonists clashed most often, whether in Florida or in Virginia, were labor and land. In Florida, the *encomienda* "did not take hold."[87] In other words, no Spanish *conquistadores* had divided Indian laborers among themselves. Members of the "Republic of Indians" still owed labor to the Spanish through the *repartimiento* system, but obligations varied according to an Indian's rank. Indian commoners' "labor reserves" provided food and serviced projects in the provinces and at the presidio, San Agustín.[88] Labor was ever in the minds of Virginians. But colonists followed other patterns to obtain it. Despite the urgings of figures like John Smith, who admired how the Spaniards had the Indians "doe all manner of drudgery worke," the Virginians never established anything like the *encomienda* system.[89] Instead, they took Indians as slaves or as indentured servants—not uncommonly for outrageously long terms. The closest to something like

a labor draft that the English attempted appeared in legislative enactments at midcentury. The assembly invited the Indians to send children
as hostages or, as the law put it, "gages of their good and quiet intentions
to vs."⁹⁰ In return, the English would "do their best to bring them vp
in Christianity, civillity and the knowledge of necessary trades." Native
children, unsurprisingly, were not forthcoming.

In Virginia, tribute came in forms other than labor. Within a few years
after 1646, as the Powhatan chiefdom finally broke apart, each constitu-
ent tributary Indian polity rendered its own quota of pelts, greatly increasing the number of these valuable commodities that became the
formal perquisite of the governor in 1686.⁹¹ In 1669, Virginia levied a
quota of wolves' heads on the tributary Indians commensurate with their
estimated fighting strength.⁹² Men appointed for each county court were
"to keep a just accompt of the number, and to present to the said court
such as are deficient." The "great man of the towne" was liable to appear
in court if his people had not met the quota.

In 1697, near the end of his tenure as governor of Virginia, Sir Edmund
Andros had inquired into the colony's past efforts to convert Indians.
Andros's report was brief. "No perticular means have bin used at any
tyme to convert yᵉ Indians to the Christian Religion."⁹³ "No perticular
means" perhaps, but evangelization was nominally a principle guiding
Virginia's Indian policy after 1646. Not since before 1622 had Virginia's
Indian policy possessed quite the same tenor. Then, the Virginia Company had planned to erect an Indian college at Henrico with the support
of private benefactions.⁹⁴ A theological imperative—however gradually
it was to work in practice—still influenced the colony's Indian law well
after the Powhatan uprising of 1622. But it was nothing like as strong as
the religious mission in Florida, where Indian evangelization became its
highest objective. With a dedicated body of Franciscan friars, the missions in Florida found consistent and able champions with powerful
connections across the Atlantic. This institutional difference between the
English colony and its southern, Spanish neighbor was glaring. But the
weakness of metropolitan commitment and the lack of hearty ministers
to live among the Indians did not mean that Virginia made no moves
toward converting Natives.

The burgesses of the Interregnum (1649–1660) believed that the
missionary ends of the colony in Virginia demanded attention. And

property was their main instrument—especially the Indians' communal lands. Having "humblye acknowledged themselves tributaryes to his Sacred Majestye, and that the Soverainitye of the land whereon they live doth belong to his most Excelent Majestye," colonial officials "granted" the Pamunkey "Commander" Totopotomoi "five thousand Acres of land adjacent to the place where he now liveth" for him and his people as part of the "Course for theire Reducement to Civillitye."[95] Other forms of property also counted. The English had often employed Indians to hunt the wolves that ravaged their livestock herds. By 1655, they had decreed that "for every eight wolves heads brought in by the Indians, The King or Great Man (as they call him) shall have a cow delivered him at the charge of the publick."[96] The burgesses declared that it would "be a step to civilizing them and to making them Christians." The law prompted Edmund Morgan's quip that "cows proved no more successful as missionaries than the few ministers who tried their hand at it."[97] But that the colonists bothered at all is suggestive. Property and Christianity joined together. The assembly declared that communal lands would "not be alienable by them the Indians to any man de futuro."[98]

The core of the legislative program passed in 1650 and again in 1658. Indians were "first served with the proportion of fiftye Acres of land for Each Bowman."[99] The tributary Indians would receive patents for their lands, and the "libertye of all Waste and unfenced Land for Huntinge."[100] In 1652 and again in 1658, the assembly cited the injuries the Indians suffered at English hands. The burgesses recounted how "many Complaints have been brought to this Assembly touching wrong done to the Indians." The English by their incursions were "fforceinge them into such narrow Streights, and places That they Cannot Subsist, Either by plantinge, or hunting, And for that it may be feared, that thereby they may be Justlye Driven to dispaire."[101] The burgesses declared it "Contrarye to Justice" for English colonists to encroach on the Indians' land. And they declared that such violations threatened "the true Intent of the English planters of this Countrey, Whereby the Indians might by all faire, and Just usage be reduced to Civilitye, and the true Worshipp of god."[102]

The Indians' souls were not the only ones at stake. "Intrenching" upon the Indians' land dishonored English religion. From "Divers Informations" the assembly also learned that unscrupulous Englishmen had "Corrupted some of the Indians to steale, and Conveigh away some other Indians Children."[103] The assembly passed an act demanding that Englishmen have the permission of the parents of any Indian servants they acquired. In 1660, the burgesses allowed one "John Beauchamp, merchant" to take "his Indian boy into England" on the condition that "at the county court in Charles Cittie Countie he make it appeare that he hath the consent of the said Indian boy's parents soe to doe."[104] The theft of Indian children was a "great Scandall of christianitye, and of the English nation," the law first passed in 1649 had thundered, "Renderinge Religion Contemptible, and the name of Englishmen odious."[105]

Not everyone agreed with the assembly's interpretation of God's will. As early as 1657, the Anglican clergyman Lionel Gatford reported that some Virginians claimed that they could seize the Indians' "lands and estates" on the principle of "*dominium fundatur in gratiae*"—that dominion is founded in grace.[106] "To justify . . . their matchless iniquities and impieties, especially their rapines, murthers, and all sorts of cruelties exercised upon the poor Indians," Gatford reported, "some of the Planters hav[e] usurped the office of publike preachers." From their makeshift pulpits the planters declared themselves "Saints" with a "just right to whatsoever the Indians call theirs; & may when they have opportunity and power, turn the Indians out of all their lands and estates, & take them into their own possession."[107]

In Apalachee, there was less pressure on the Indians' communal land rights. In Florida, Native lands served the colonial religious mission but in an altogether different way. An Apalachee field of maize, along with the labor to tend it, supported the friar who ministered to each of the mission villages in the province.[108] Spanish law provided much firmer guarantees of Indian *pueblos'* communal property in lands than Virginia law did, and in 1680, the general recapitulation of the Laws of the Indies, or *Recopilación de las leyes de los Reynos de las Indias*, reaffirmed the principle.[109] Most of Spanish officialdom long before had rejected arguments like those of Gatford's "Saints."

So had the Restored English monarchy. Early in his reign, Charles II charged the Council for Foreign Plantations to "consider how such of the Natives . . . may be best invited to the Christian Faith."[110] In practice, the Crown and colonial officials first extended Indians legal protection. Some Indian leaders interpreted the king's policy in these terms. Weunquesh, the daughter of the sachem Ninigret, petitioned Charles II in 1680, explaining that it was the king's "will and pleasure that vs the heathen and Natives of the Land: Should jnioy Common justice and Equiti as well as the Rest of your subiects in thees parts."[111] Affirming such principles of "Equiti" was the closest Whitehall came to a guiding Indian law to match the Spanish *Leyes de las Indias*. In keeping with Restoration policy, the Virginia Assembly recapitulated previous Indian law into a statute "concerning the Indians" in 1662. The act confirmed Indians' title to land, forbade Indian kings and queens from alienating any parcel of their territory, and punished English squatters. Indeed, the assembly laid the fault of past disorders with the Indians squarely on the "violent incursions of divers English made into their Lands."[112]

The arrangement between Virginia's government and tribute-paying Native American elites had largely kept the peace between them for thirty years. The Indian tributaries retained coveted land in Virginia. They enjoyed some profits from the peltry trade, exchanging valuable skins and furs for English goods. Should English settlers threaten their holdings—and they often did—the Indian elites could appeal for redress to the governor, the council, the courts, the assembly, and, in theory, to the king of England himself from whose power the law claimed they held their lands.

By the mid-1670s a substantial faction of colonists believed that the law too much favored elite tributary Indians like the king of the Weanoaks and the queen of Pamunkey. The surviving nobles of old Tsenacommacah had managed to keep both their lands and their religions. The persistence of a non-Christian, Native American nobility under the protection of the English Crown galled many Virginians. Lionel Gatford's fears in 1657 were prescient. Some Virginians resented the position of the defeated, non-Christian Powhatan nobles and refused them the protection of law. In the person of Bacon, their grumbles eventually caught the ear of a man bent on uprooting the indigenous elite once and for all.

III.

The "Republic of Indians" in Florida ostensibly rested upon Native consent. Without the blessing of the land's "natural lords," Spanish occupation in Apalachee would have been impossible. Virginia's early leaders for their part had sought Indian consent in order to make claims on territory that would stick in Europe. After 1646, the English even claimed the authority to appoint tributary *weroances*. In practice this meant colonial officials confirmed Native leaders who had succeeded according to their own customs, through heredity or election. Both colonial regimes tried to rule through Native chiefly lineages. But in Virginia—and indeed throughout British North America—the status of Native nobles was controversial. When Indian troubles along Virginia's frontiers broke out in 1675, a new migrant to Virginia aimed to end the debate by branding all Indians enemies, taking their lives and confiscating their property.

Nathaniel Bacon brought eighteen hundred pounds and a restless ambition with him to Virginia. Within a few months of his arrival in 1674, Bacon had accepted a seat on Virginia's council from Sir William Berkeley.[113] Bacon took his conciliar duties lightly, whiling away his time with other "new men" at Curles, his plantation on the Falls of the James River. Bacon set up a post not far from Curles where he hoped to profit in the lucrative Indian trade. In 1675 Bacon's plantation idyll ended. What began as a petty dispute between a party of "foreign" Doegs and an English planter over stolen hogs spiraled into a war with the powerful Susquehannocks—formerly Virginia's allies. The colony was already rife with dissension. Servants, itching to escape harsh conditions and the lengthening terms of their indentures, plotted to run away from their masters. Quakers and other religious nonconformists suffered severe persecutions under the Restoration regime in Virginia. The Indian troubles catalyzed opposition. The crisis humbled Sir William Berkeley and made Nathaniel Bacon "General by the Consent of the people" in an anti-Indian crusade. The choice of his targets, however, was neither indiscriminate nor merely convenient.

Bacon tried to destroy the Native American nobility that Virginia's government protected. Bacon and his crew attacked the most vulnerable segment of Virginia's landholders—the kings and queens of the tributary Indians. He objected to their lands, their property, and their legal status. In his 1676 "Manifesto" Bacon singled out the tributary rulers for condemnation, professing his "manifest aversion of all, not onley the Foreign but the protected and Darling Indians."[114] His wrath fell hardest on the Pamunkeys—Powhatan's, Opechancanough's, and Cockacoeske's people—Virginia's preeminent tributary Indians. The rebel leader disparaged the Pamunkey ruler's noble title, rejecting the claim that "both the Governour and Councell are . . . bound to defend the Queen [of the Pamunkeys] and Appamatocks with their blood."[115]

In mocking the royal titles the English gave indigenous leaders, Bacon tapped into a strain of colonial thought that equated Indians with a pretended nobility. Colonists all over criticized the Indians' purportedly aristocratic lifestyle. New Englander Thomas Morton noted that Indians "remoove for their pleasures . . . after the manner of the gentry of Civilized nations."[116] Another compared Indian wigwams with "gentlemen's 'Summerhouses in England.'"[117] Indian hunting grounds must have seemed like the deer parks of noblemen in England. Bacon's forces drove the Pamunkeys off their communal lands and into Dragon Swamp. Bacon averred that the behavior of the tributaries had long ago forfeited their right to land. He declared that "they have bin for these Many years enemies to the King and Country, Robbers and Theeves and Invaders of his Majesties' Right and our Interest and Estates."[118] For their alleged treacherous behavior, Bacon argued that "those neighbour Indians" were "wholly unqalifyed for the benefitt and Protection of the law."[119]

Religious thinking bolstered Bacon's legal argument. The paradox of why the government should protect, in Rebecca A. Goetz's memorable phrase, "hereditary heathens" fueled Baconian ire.[120] In a colony where, after 1667, baptism did not confer freedom to Africans and Indians, that the "Darling Indians," the tributaries, enjoyed a modicum of freedom must have truly rankled Bacon's partisans. When they asked, "[A]re not the Indians all of a Colour[?]" Bacon's followers meant that all Indians behaved treacherously.[121] In the 1670s behavior and belief were inseparable. Philosophers of the day disputed whether English sectarians were capable of being orderly subjects, let alone whether non-Christians could be. Bacon's "Declaration of the People" from 30 July 1676 made the point when it proclaimed that Berkeley had "sold his Majesty's Country and the lives of his loyall subjects to the barbarous heathen."[122] Crucial was Bacon's denial of the tributaries' loyalty and their status as legal "subjects." Berkeley's acceptance of "heathen" Indians as tributary subjects was tantamount to formal, legal religious toleration. Without the kind of missions and royal support that buttressed Spanish objectives for the "Republic of Indians" in Florida, not to mention Native interest in conversion, the tributary regime in Virginia stood on a shaky legal foundation from the perspective of the Baconites.

Seventeenth-century English philosophers generally agreed that Muslims, Jews, and pagans—whose ranks often included American Indians—were not subject to the persecutions of the civil magistrate. In North America, as elsewhere, the matter was of urgent, practical concern.[123] The philosopher John Locke, as an author of the 1669 *Fundamental Constitutions of Carolina*, had the chance to enact a policy of toleration for Native religions.[124]

But the England that Bacon had left behind was a persecuting, confessional state.[125] During the Restoration era, more than eleven thousand Quakers alone would languish in jails for refusing to conform to the established Church of England.[126] In Virginia, Protestant sectarians suffered fines, whippings, and banishment—especially Quakers, whose activities authorities often linked with the menace of Indians.[127] In England, Charles II had twice relaxed the persecution of Catholics and dissenting Trinitarian Protestants with declarations of indulgence in 1662 and 1672.[128] The king swiftly withdrew both edicts after protests from angry members of Parliament. But from Bacon's perspective, toleration for "heathens" in Virginia did not spring from the executive's mere motion but had found secure roots in the colony's statutes for thirty years. Bacon's rebellion was in part a revolt against Berkeley's protection for the non-Christian, tributary Indian leadership. Bacon might have found support for his policy in common law. To Bacon, even the tributary Indians were—as Coke concluded in "Calvin's Case" (1608)—"perpetual enemies for the law presumes not that they will be converted, that being *remota potentia*, a remote possibility."[129] Bacon had in effect put this principle to the test. Just a few years later, in fact, English courts would discard Coke's theory on the conquest of infidels. A 1683 decision concluded that conquered infidels could keep such customs as were inoffensive to "the law of God."[130]

The collapse of Bacon's Rebellion led to the Crown's reaffirmation of legal protection for Indians in a treaty that again embodied principles in common with the *república de indios* in Florida. The royal commissioners, whom Charles II sent to settle Virginia's affairs after the rebellion, established a comprehensive new treaty at Middle Plantation—modern-day Williamsburg—in 1677. On the date of Charles II's birth

and restoration, 29 May, the king's commissioners and the signa-
tory kings and queens of the Indians revived the tributary regime in
Virginia. The articles of peace—*"Founded upon the strong Pillars of
Reciprocal Justice"*—guaranteed the Indians' *"Just Rights"* and provided
means for *"Redress of their Wrongs and Injuries."* The tributaries again
affirmed their "Subjection to the Great King of *England*" and that in
return they would hold their lands "in as free and firm manner as others
His Majesties Subjects have and enjoy their Lands and Possessions."[131]
Against the encroachments and injuries of the English, the tributary
Indians would "be well Secured and Defended in their Persons, Goods
and Properties."[132] Redress would be open to them before the colony's
governor, who would, in the king's name, "Inflict such Punishment on
the wiful Infringers hereof, as the Laws of *England* or this Countrey
permit, and as if such hurt or injury had been done to any *Englishman*."[133] Equal justice for tributary Indians was "but just and reasonable,
they owning themselves to be under the Allegiance of His most Sacred
Majesty."[134] In a sign of how far-reaching were treaty makers' intentions, the eighteenth article required that conflicts "between any of the
Indians in Amity with the *English*" come before "His Majesties Governour, by whose Justice and Wisdom it is concluded such Difference shall
be made up and decided, and to whose final Determination the said *Indians* shall submit and conform themselves."[135] The treaty outlawed the
enslavement of tributaries.[136] And it recognized Cockacoeske's authority
as a paramount chief, signaling a commitment (at least by royal officials)
to try to rule through Native chiefly lineages.[137] Accepting the terms were
the queen of Pamunkey, a "faithfull Friend to an[d] Louer of the English"; her son, Captain John West, "a good brave young man" who had
"been very active in the Service of the English"; the stately queen of the
Weanoaks, who "had taken to her selfe the name of Queene Catherine
[of Braganza]" to mark the occasion; the king of the Nansemonds, "a
very friendly Indian and much conversant among the English"; and last,
the ancient king of the Nottoways, who "Governes his people with prudence and good Discipline."[138]

The commissioners requested raiment and ornaments proper to the
nobles' stations—since the Indians believed "gifts a kind of Sacred pledge
of ffriendshipp."[139] The commissioners also asked that "Silver Badges to
the number of Twenty wth the names of your Matie: and the Tributary

Princes inscribed might bee made, and sent over to bee worne for distinction by the Indians as by the former peace."[140] Once, such badges were simply a way to tell friend from foe—without one, an Indian was liable to be shot until the legal reforms of the 1650s. Now, the badges, along with robes and crowns, would inspire, in both Indians and Englishmen alike, the respect due to the kings and queens. By sending these tokens, King Charles II could not only "most inifinitly endeare your Royall name and memory amongst them, But begett a reverence to them from their own people as well as your Maties: Subjects in Virginia, when they shall see hereby that they are in your Royall Esteeme as well as Protection."[141] But the gifts that the commissioners requested for the restored monarchs also signified the supremacy of Charles II, who granted them. As the commissioners gushed in their report back to Whitehall, the Indian kings and queens "expressly owne to have their immediate dependence on, to owe all Subjection and allegiance, and to hold their Crowns of and from yor Matie: to whom they most justly give the name and Title of great King." This admission, claimed the commissioners—forgetting the articles of 1646—was "more then [sic] ever was Stipulated of, or ownd by them in any former Treaty had or made by them."[142]

IV.

On 18 October 1677, the treaty came before the Committee of the Privy Council for Trade and Plantations for review. Coming to the article that kept the English from seating within three miles from the Indians' towns, Major Robert Bristow, a merchant who had suffered the wrath of the Bacon rebels and earned the commissioners' good opinion, objected to it "as a thing very inconvenient and prejudiced to the English planters."[143] Bristow's observation presaged the struggles with colonists that lay ahead. Then, near of the end of their sitting, Thomas Lord Culpeper, soon to be the next governor of Virginia, asked one last question of the lords—"what manner the Indians are to bee treated, as well in Civil as in Criminal causes."[144] After a debate, the board answered Lord Culpepper's question. "It is agreed," the lords concluded, "that they ought to receive the same measure of Justice from the English, as the English, by law, expect from them."[145]

Bacon had lost the legal argument as far as Whitehall was concerned—or as one historian put it, Bacon's party had lost the "first round."[146] There were other rounds. During the early eighteenth century, Alexander Spotswood strengthened the tributary regime, encouraged new Native peoples to join it, and renewed efforts at Indian education with the enrollment of Indians at the College of William & Mary and the education of tributary Indians at Fort Christanna.[147] But problems remained, and tributaries continued to educate Englishmen on the law of the land. In August 1715, the Nottoway Indians petitioned the House of Burgesses, demanding "all our former Rights & priveledges and that wee may be admitted to live on and hold our Lands according to law." The Nottoways declared that they had "alwayes been true and faithfull tributaries to this Colony" but were now under such "great Restrictions and Hardships . . . never before felt by this Nation or any other tributarys."[148]

By then, the prospects of Indian tributaries were bleak. The eighteenth century saw many of Virginia's tributaries in deep poverty, their numbers dwindling. Other colonies, like North Carolina, where the tributary model was established, also witnessed a gradual decline in the fortunes of Natives living along or within colonial boundaries.[149] Eighteenth-century diminutions of Indian legal status reflected their consequent decline in political power. They were no longer a potential threat to the peace. Still, the treaties and laws of the seventeenth century had the cumulative effect of elevating Indian status slightly above that of enslaved Africans in the new, eighteenth-century racialized order.[150]

The contradictions of tributary status in the English colonies—the mixture of harshness with aspirations for "justice," the goal of separation with the hope of mutual benefit—defy easy comprehension. Examining them from the recent scholarly perspective that considers Iberian models normative in a vast "Spanish periphery" exposes sharp contrasts but also striking similarities with practice elsewhere in the Americas.[151] Although the tributary regime in Virginia never reached the heights of the colony's early Spanish-inspired fantasies, at times it promoted coexistence and in modern times, its treaty underpinnings have served to promote self-determination and sovereignty for Virginia Indians. Moreover, the case of tributaries in Virginia and other colonies, along with the work of scholars who have studied Natives of New England and their interactions with the law, suggests that Indians were constituents in a somewhat different English empire than we have come to expect.[152] Tributaries were both Indians and subjects who understood their legal rights—often better than the English—and in whom metropolitan and colonial officials took more than occasional notice.

Florida's "Republic of Indians" felt increasing pressure as the seventeenth century gave way to the eighteenth. English-inspired slave raids from the new colony of Carolina and its Indian allies decimated Florida's Indian provinces. Much like Bacon, the English raiders had little regard for any distinctions among their victims. By 1704, the Apalachee had abandoned their homeland. They scattered in a diaspora that took some east to the Spanish presidio and others far west into French Louisiana. Another group resettled for a time in Carolina, where some of their caciques seem to have pressed English authorities to honor values consonant with those they expected as members of Florida's "Republic of Indians."[153] Today, the Talimali Band of Apalachee Indians numbers around three hundred members mostly living in Rapides Parish, Louisiana.[154]

The Pamunkey Indians hold some of the same lands today that the "articles of peace" confirmed to them in 1646 and 1677. The modern-day Commonwealth of Virginia has long officially recognized the Pamunkey. And in July 2015, the Pamunkey became the 567th federally recognized tribe, after a long legal process.[155] Their legal claims rest in part on a treaty their leaders negotiated with a Stuart monarch in an age when American independence was a fantasy and Anglo-Indian coexistence was still a real—if fading—possibility.

NOTES

1   Tsenacommacah is the indigenous word for the Powhatan chiefdom. William Strachey: "The severall territoryes and provinces which are in chief commaunded by their great king Powhatan, are Comprehended vnder the denomynation of Tsenacommacoh." See William Strachey, *The Historie of Travell into Virginia Britania (1612)*, eds. Louis B. Wright and Virginia Freund (London: Hakluyt Society, 1953), 37.

2   Frederic W. Gleach, *Powhatan's World and Colonial Virginia: A Conflict of Cultures* (Lincoln: University of Nebraska Press, 1997), 3.

3   Daniel K. Richter, "Tsenacommacah and the Atlantic World," in *The Atlantic World and Virginia, 1550–1624*, ed. Peter C. Mancall (Chapel Hill: University of North Carolina Press, 2007), 29–65.

4 Gleach, *Powhatan's World*, 178; Warren M. Billings, *Sir William Berkeley and the Forging of Colonial Virginia* (Baton Rouge: Louisiana State University Press, 2004), 96.

5 Thomas Ludwell to Secretary Lord Arlington, 18 July 1666, UK National Archives, Kew, CO 1/20, No. 125.I, folio 220a.

6 William Waller Hening, ed., *The Statutes at Large; Being a Collection of All the Laws of Virginia from the First Session of the Legislature in the Year 1619* (New York: Bartow, 1823), 1:323.

7 Ibid.

8 April Lee Hatfield, "Spanish Colonization Literature, Powhatan Geographies, and English Perceptions of Tsenacommacah/Virginia," *Journal of Southern History* 69, no. 2 (May 2003): 245–82; Eliga H. Gould, "Entangled Histories, Entangled Worlds: The English-Speaking Atlantic as a Spanish Periphery," *American Historical Review* 112, no. 3 (June 2007): 769; Jorge Cañizares-Esguerra, *Puritan Conquistadors: Iberianizing the Atlantic, 1550–1700* (Stanford, CA: Stanford University Press, 2006); Camilla Townsend, *Pocahontas and the Powhatan Dilemma* (New York: Hill and Wang, 2004).

9 Ethan Schmidt, *Divided Dominion: Social Conflict and Indian Hatred in Early Virginia* (Boulder: University Press of Colorado, 2015), ch. 5; Michael V. Gannon, *The Cross in the Sand: The Early Catholic Church in Florida, 1513–1870* (1965, repr. Gainesville: University Presses of Florida, 1983), ch. 4.

10 Amy Turner Bushnell, "Ruling the 'Republic of Indians' in Seventeenth-Century Florida," in *Powhatan's Mantle: Indians in the Colonial Southeast*, eds. Gregory A. Waselkov, Peter H. Wood, and Tom Hatley (Lincoln: University of Nebraska Press, 2006): 195–213; Brian P. Owensby, *Empire of Law and Indian Justice in Colonial Mexico* (Stanford, CA: Stanford University Press, 2006), 24; Alejandro Cañeque, *The King's Living Image: The Culture and Politics of Viceregal Power in Colonial Mexico* (New York: Routledge, 2004), 241 and 253; Tatiana Seijas, *Asian Slaves in Colonial Mexico: From Chinos to Indians* (New York: Cambridge University Press, 2014), ch. 5.

11 Bushnell, "Ruling," 199.

12 Owensby, *Empire of Law*, 55–56.

13 Bianca Premo, *Children of the Father King: Youth, Authority, and Legal Minority in Colonial Lima* (Chapel Hill: University of North Carolina Press, 2005).

14 Townsend, *Pocahontas*, 43.

15 For the ideological basis of exclusion, see Anthony Pagden, *Lords of all the World: Ideologies of Empire in Spain, Britain, and France, c. 1500–c. 1800* (New Haven, CT: Yale University Press, 1995), 37.

16 Alfred A. Cave, *Lethal Encounters: Englishmen and Indians in Colonial Virginia* (Santa Barbara, CA: Praeger, 2011), 141; Gleach, *Powhatan's World*, 184–98.

17 Daniel K. Richter, *Before the Revolution: America's Ancient Pasts* (Cambridge, MA: Harvard University Press, 2009), 273–74; April Lee Hatfield, *Atlantic Virginia: Intercolonial Relations in the Seventeenth Century* (Philadelphia: University of

Pennsylvania Press, 2004), 35; James D. Rice, *Tales from a Revolution: Bacon's Rebellion and the Transformation of Early America* (New York: Oxford University Press, 2012), 220.

18 Wilcomb E. Washburn, *The Governor and the Rebel: A History of Bacon's Rebellion in Virginia* (Chapel Hill: University of North Carolina Press, 1957); Schmidt, *Divided Dominion*; Lauren Benton, *A Search for Sovereignty: Law and Geography in European Empires, 1400–1900* (New York: Cambridge University Press, 2010), 99.

19 Michael Leroy Oberg, *Dominion and Civility: English Imperialism and Native America, 1585–1685* (Ithaca, NY: Cornell University Press, 1999); Stephen Saunders Webb, *1676: The End of American Independence* (New York: Knopf, 1984).

20 Kathleen M. Brown, *Good Wives, Nasty Wenches, and Anxious Patriarchs: Gender, Race, and Power in Colonial Virginia* (Chapel Hill: University of North Carolina Press, 1996), 161; Helen C. Rountree, *Pocahontas's People: The Powhatan Indians of Virginia through Four Centuries* (Lincoln: University of Nebraska Press, 1990), 96–99; Edmund S. Morgan, *American Slavery, American Freedom: The Ordeal of Colonial Virginia* (New York: Norton, 1975), 257.

21 W. Stitt Robinson Jr., "Tributary Indians in Colonial Virginia," *Virginia Magazine of History and Biography* 67, no. 1 (Jan. 1959): 64.

22 J. H. Elliott, *Empires of the Atlantic World: Britain and Spain in America, 1492–1830* (New Haven, CT: Yale University Press, 2006), 85.

23 Owensby, *Empire of Law*, 24–26.

24 "Generall Description of America or the New World," 1665, CO 1/19, no. 147, 1, UK National Archives, Kew.

25 Amy Turner Bushnell, *Situado and Sabana: Spain's Support System for Florida*, Anthropological Papers, no. 74 (New York: American Museum of Natural History, 1994), 95–96.

26 Bushnell, "Ruling," 200.

27 John Hann, *Apalachee: The Land between the Rivers* (Gainesville: University of Florida Press, 1988), 100.

28 Jeffrey Glover, *Paper Sovereigns: Anglo-Native Treaties and the Law of Nations, 1604–1664* (Philadelphia: University of Pennsylvania Press, 2014).

29 Ibid., 3.

30 John Smith, "The Proceedings of the English Colonie in Virginia . . . (1612)" in *Captain Smith: Writings and Other Narratives of Roanoke, Jamestown, and the First English Settlement of America*, ed. James Horn (New York: Literary Classics of the United States, 2007), 73.

31 Richter, "Tsenacommacah," 54; Glover, *Paper Sovereigns*, 68.

32 See James D. Rice, "Escape from Tsenacommacah: Chesapeake Algonquians and the Powhatan Menace," in *Atlantic World and Virginia*, 101–2.

33 William Strachey, "From the Historie of Travell into Virginia Britania (1612)," in *Captain John Smith*, 1074.

34 Strachey, "Historie," in *Captain John Smith*, 1074.

35 Ralph Hamor, *A True Discourse of the Present Estate of Virginia* . . . (London: John Beale, 1615), 13–14.

36 Glover, *Paper Sovereigns*, 93.

37 Robin Beck, *Chiefdoms, Collapse, and Coalescence in the Early American South* (New York: Cambridge University Press, 2013), 102.

38 Virginia acts, UK National Archives, Kew, CO 5/1376, p. 19.

39 Hening, *Statutes at Large*, 1:323.

40 Virginia acts, UK National Archives, Kew, CO 5/1376, p. 19.

41 Martha W. McCartney, "Cockacoeske, Queen of Pamunkey: Diplomat and Suzeraine," in *Powhatan's Mantle*, 245.

42 Hann, *Apalachee*, 103.

43 See, for instance, the troubled 1657 visitation of Governor Rebolledo (who had disrespected the chiefly privileges of the Timucua). John H. Hann, ed. and trans., *Florida Archaeology* no. 2 (1986), 97.

44 Bushnell, *Situado*, 108–10.

45 Bushnell, "Ruling," 201.

46 Ibid., 205.

47 Hening, *Statutes at Large*, 1:547.

48 Hening, *Statutes at Large*, 2:141.

49 Ibid.

50 Bushnell, "Ruling," 199.

51 Bushnell, *Situado*, 106.

52 Hening, *Statutes at Large*, 1:415–16.

53 Robert Beverley, *The History and Present State of Virginia* . . . (London: 1705), 23–24.

54 Hann, *Apalachee*, 10–11.

55 Helen C. Rountree, *Pocahontas, Powhatan, Opechancanough: Three Indian Lives Changed by Jamestown* (Charlottesville: University of Virginia Press, 2005), 13.

56 John E. Worth, *The Timucua Chiefdoms of Spanish Florida*. Vol. 1, *Assimilation* (Gainesville: University Press of Florida, 1998), 77.

57 Hann, *Apalachee*, 3.

58 Ibid., 166.

59 Rountree, *Pocahontas's People*, 78–79.

60 Ibid., 87.

61 Hening, *Apalachee*, 2:274–75.

62 Peter H. Wood, "The Changing Population of the Colonial South: An Overview by Race and Region, 1685–1790," in *Powhatan's Mantle*, 64.

63 Seijas, *Asian Slaves*, 5.

64 Owensby, *Empire of Law*, 257–58.

65 "vassal, n. and adj." OED Online. Oxford University Press. www.oed.com, accessed 30 August 2015.

66 Francis Jennings, *The Invasion of America: Indians, Colonialism, and the Cant of Conquest* (Chapel Hill: University of North Carolina Press, 1975), 105–27.

67 Paul Grant Costa, "The Last Indian War in New England: The Mohegan Indians v. the Governour and Company of the Colony of Connecticut, 1703–1774" (Yale University, unpublished Ph.D. dissertation, 2012), 173–74.

68 George Webb, *The Office and Authority of a Justice of Peace . . .* (Williamsburg, VA: 1736), 184–85.

69 Ibid., 184.

70 Virginia acts, 1661/2, UK National Archives, Kew, CO 5/1379, Folio 22a.

71 Henry Hawks, "A relation of the commodities of Noua Hispania, and the maners of the inhabitants, written by Henry Hawks merchant, which liued fiue yeeres in the sayd country, and drew the same at the request of M. Richard Hakluyt Esquire of Eiton in the county of Hereford, 1572," in Richard Hakluyt, *Principall Navigations . . .* , vol. 3 (London: 1600), 468.

72 Ibid.

73 Laura M. Stevens, *The Poor Indians: Missionaries, Native Americans, and Colonial Sensibility* (Philadelphia: University of Pennsylvania Press, 2004), 19–20.

74 Act XIX, "An Act concerning the Trusting of Indians," March 1660, Hening, *Statutes at Large*, 1:541.

75 *Virginia: Being, A full and true Relation of the present State of the Plantation . . .* (London: 1649), 13.

76 5 March 1685, (Old) Rappahannock County, Orders (No. 1), 1683–1686 Transcript, Orders, 1686–1692, pp. 77–78, Reel 13, Library of Virginia, Richmond.

77 12 May 1699, in H. R. McIlwaine, ed., *Legislative Journals of the Council of Colonial Virginia*, 3 vols., ed. H. R. McIlwaine (Richmond, VA: 1918), vol. 1, 262–63.

78 Letter to Francis Nicholson, 4 January 1700, CO 5/1359, p. 377, UK National Archives, Kew.

79 Helen C. Rountree, "The Termination and Dispersal of the Nottoway Indians of Virginia," *Virginia Magazine of History and Biography* 95, no. 2 (Apr. 1987), 193–214.

80 Hann, *Apalachee*, 114.

81 Bushnell, "Ruling," 200.

82 Owensby, *Empire of Law*, 25.

83 Oberg, *Dominion*, 186.

84 Rountree, *Pocahontas's People*, 142.

85 Thomas Ludwell to Lord Arlington, "A Description of the Government of Virginia," 18 July 1666, CO 1/20, no. 125.i, folio 221, UK National Archives, Kew.

86 Ibid.

87 Bushnell, *Situado*, 31.

88 Worth, *Timucua* 1:151.

89 John Smith, "The Generall Historie of Virginia . . . Divided into Six Books," in *Captain John Smith*, 484.

90 Hening, *Statutes at Large*, 1:395.

91 Rountree, *Pocahontas's People*, 91.

92 Hening, *Statutes at Large*, 2:274–76.

93 Edmund Andros to the Board of Trade, UK National Archives, Kew, CO 5/1309, folio 24a.

94 Margaret Connell Szasz, *Indian Education in the American Colonies, 1607–1783* (Lincoln: University of Nebraska Press, 2007), ch. 3 passim.

95 Warren M. Billings, "Some Acts Not in Hening's 'Statutes': The Acts of Assembly, April 1652, November 1652, and July 1653," *Virginia Magazine of History and Biography* 83, no. 1 (Jan. 1975): 65–66.

96 Hening, *Statutes at Large*, 1:394.

97 Morgan, *American Slavery, American Freedom*, 232.

98 Hening, *Statutes at Large*, 1:395.

99 Billings, "Some Acts," 68; Hening, *Statutes at Large*, 1:456–57.

100 Billings, "Some Acts," 68; Hening *Statutes at Large*, 1:457.

101 Billings, "Some Acts," 72; Hening *Statutes at Large*, 1:467.

102 Billings, "Some Acts," 72; Hening *Statutes at Large*, 1:467.

103 Hening, *Statutes at Large*, 1:481.

104 Hening, *Statutes at Large*, 1:546.

105 Billings, "Some Acts," 64–65; Hening, *Statutes at Large*, 1:481.

106 [Lionel Gatford], *Publick Good without Private Interest; . . .* (London: 1657), 8.

107 Ibid.

108 Bushnell, *Situado*, 111.

109 España, *Recopilación de las leyes de los reynos de Las Indias . . . , tomo Segundo* (En Madrid: pro Iulian de Paredes, 1681), 199.

110 King to Council for Foreign Plantations, 1 December 1660, UK National Archives, Kew, CO 1/14, folio 143b.

111 Narragansett Sachems and "Squa Queen" of the Narragansetts, UK National Archives, Kew, CO 1/44, no. 49.

112 Virginia acts, 1661/2, UK National Archives, Kew, CO 5/1379, Folio 21b.

113 Numerous accounts of Bacon's life exist. For a helpful summary, see Warren M. Billings, "Bacon, Nathaniel (1647–1676)," *Oxford Dictionary of National Biography* (New York: Oxford University Press, 2004; online edition, Oct. 2007), www.oxforddnb.com, accessed 1 September 2014.

114 "11. Bacon's 'Manifesto,'" in Warren M. Billings, ed., *The Old Dominion in the Seventeenth Century: A Documentary History of Virginia, 1607–1689* (Chapel Hill: University of North Carolina Press, 1975), 278.

115 Ibid.

116 Quoted in James Axtell, *The Invasion Within: The Contest of Cultures in Colonial North America* (New York: Oxford University Press, 1985), 138.

117 Ibid.

118 "11. Bacon's 'Manifesto,'" in *Old Dominion*, 278.

119 Ibid., 279.

120 Rebecca Anne Goetz, *The Baptism of Early Virginia: How Christianity Created Race* (Baltimore, MD: Johns Hopkins University Press, 2012).

121 Quoted in Rice, *Tales*, 44.

122 Quoted in Washburn, *The Governor and the Rebel*, 71.
123 Richard W. Pointer, "Native Freedom? Indians and Religious Tolerance in Early America," in *The First Prejudice: Religious Tolerance and Intolerance in Early America*, eds. Chris Beneke and Christopher S. Grenda (Philadelphia: University of Pennsylvania Press, 2011), 169–94.
124 Article 97, *The Fundamental Constitutions of Carolina* (London: 1670), 21; [John Locke], *A Letter concerning Toleration . . .* (London: 1689), 34–35.
125 Rice, *Tales*, 148–51.
126 John Marshall, *John Locke, Toleration, and Early Enlightenment Culture: Religious Intolerance and Arguments for Religious Toleration in Early Modern and "Early Enlightenment" Europe* (Cambridge: Cambridge University Press, 2006), 105.
127 Goetz, *Baptism*, 128.
128 Tim Harris, *Restoration: Charles II and His Kingdoms* (London: Penguin, 2005), 63.
129 "Calvin's Case," in *The Reports of Sir Edward Coke, Knight: In Thirteen Parts*, vol. 4 (London: Butterworth, 1826), 29.
130 Craig Yirush, *Settlers, Liberty, and Empire: The Roots of Early American Political Theory* (New York: Cambridge University Press, 2011), 44.
131 King of Great Britain, *Articles of Peace between the Most Serene and Mighty Prince Charles II . . . and Several Indian Kings and Queens . . .* (London: 1677), 5.
132 Ibid., 7–8.
133 Ibid., 8.
134 Ibid.
135 Ibid., 14.
136 Ibid., 13.
137 See McCartney, "Cockacoeske," 254.
138 "Retvrne of His Majesty's Commissioners for Virginia," 1677, UK National Archives, Kew, CO 5/1371, p. 266, folio 135b; CO 5/1371, p. 357, folio 181a.
139 "Names and characters of & Prisints to ye Indians &c.," 1677, UK National Archives, Kew, CO 5/1371, p. 270.
140 Ibid.
141 Ibid., pp. 270–71.
142 "To the Kings Ma:ᵗʸ most humble proposalls on behalf of the Indian Kings &c.," UK National Archives, Kew, CO 5/1371, pp. 265–66 and folios 135a–135b.
143 Minutes of the Board of Trade, 18 October 1677, UK National Archives, Kew, CO 391/2, pp. 130–131; for more on Bristow, see Michael Leroy Oberg, ed., *Samuel Wiseman's Book of Record: The Official Account of Bacon's Rebellion in Virginia, 1676–1677* (Lanham, MD: Lexington Books, 2005), 284 and n. 58.
144 Minutes of the Board of Trade, 18 October 1677, UK National Archives, Kew, CO 391/2, p. 131.
145 Ibid.
146 Rice, *Tales*, 183.
147 See Szasz, *Indian Education*, 68–73.

148 Petition of the Nottoway Indians to the House of Burgesses, 4 August 1715, Mss1 L51 661 Lee, Lee Family Papers, Virginia Historical Society, Richmond.

149 Michelle LeMaster, "In the 'Scolding Houses': Indians and the Law in Eastern North Carolina, 1684–1760," *North Carolina Historical Review* 83, no. 2 (Apr. 2006): 193–232.

150 Brown, *Good Wives*, 242–43.

151 Gould, "Entangled Histories," 768.

152 Craig Yirush, "Chapter 6: 'Chief Princes and Owners of All': Native American Appeals to the Crown in the Early-Modern British Atlantic," in *Native Claims: Indigenous Law against Empire, 1500–1920*, ed. Saliha Belmessous (Oxford: Oxford University Press, 2011), 129–51; Jenny Hale Pulsipher, *Subjects unto the Same King: Indians, English, and the Contest for Authority in Colonial New England* (Philadelphia: University of Pennsylvania Press, 2005).

153 For the best treatment of the Apalachee diaspora, see Hann, *Apalachee*, ch. 13.

154 Tony Horowitz, "Apalachee Tribe, Missing for Centuries, Comes out of Hiding," *Wall Street Journal*, March 9, 2005, A1.

155 "A Renowned Virginia Indian Tribe Finally Wins Federal Recognition," *Washington Post*, July 2, 2015, www.washingtonpost.com, accessed 30 June 2016.

7

Covering Blood and Graves

Murder and Law on Imperial Margins

NANCY O. GALLMAN AND ALAN TAYLOR

In eighteenth-century North America, natives and newcomers frequently mingled in settings that combined alcohol and weapons, and they occasionally quarreled, fought, and killed. After a killing, the responses by native chiefs and colonial authorities determined whether the violence could be contained short of war. To preserve peace, chiefs and officials needed to communicate that a particular killing was an isolated event regretted by the killer's people. A violent death had to be mutually categorized and demarcated as a murder, so that it would not become the first casualty of a war. But whose law—colonial or Indian—should bring closure to an intercultural murder?

Imperial officials belonged to a hierarchical culture wherein government claimed an exclusive power to investigate, adjudicate, and punish murder. For colonial officials, only another death could bring proper closure to a murder; only the government could legitimately kill in revenge; and it could do so only after a formal, public, and adversarial process known as a trial. A government's authority became publicly manifest whenever and wherever it could try and punish criminals and could, thereby, exclude the operation of private vengeance. Colonial officials regarded trials and executions as proof that they dwelled in a civilization rather than in savage anarchy.[1]

Natives, however, defended their independence by adhering to customary law in which only the ceremonial delivery and acceptance of presents could avert revenge killings. Natives called these ceremonies "covering the grave" or "covering the blood," which meant setting aside the pursuit of vengeance. Prior to the nineteenth century, no native group possessed or wanted the state apparatus and legal culture collectively to arrest, try, convict, and punish murder. They had no police, no courts, no jail, and no gallows. In the event of a murder, revenge belonged to the male relatives of the deceased. They lost face as cowards if they failed to secure blood revenge, for no spirit of the murdered could rest or give his or her kin peace until avenged.[2]

When possible, the vengeful tracked down and dispatched the actual killer, who might flee but was expected to submit when found. In western Pennsylvania, a missionary, David McClure, saw a confronted murderer calmly sit down to sing his death song while the avenger smoked a pipe for twenty minutes before plunging a tomahawk into the killer's skull. If the original killer proved elusive, the kin of his victim might take revenge on a member of his clan and nation. Such killings, however, perpetuated a bloody cycle of further revenge.[3]

No chief had any legitimate power to try and punish murderers. Indeed, anyone who so interfered became a party to the blood feud. The authority of the chiefs depended upon their prestige and persuasive abilities—which in turn hinged upon their restraint in the exercise of any force, especially over nonrelatives. Rather than execute a murderer, chiefs sought to restore harmony without further bloodshed. To curtail the cycle of violence, they persuaded the relatives of the dead to accept presents from the kin of the murderer, all formally delivered to "cover the grave" (or "the blood"). Acceptance meant forfeiting the right to seek revenge.[4]

In contrast to colonial law, native groups entrusted judgment to the kin of the killer and the killed. Native justice called for death as an option in a complex process of negotiation, not as a mandate. These negotiations assumed the weight of law because they involved acts of persuasion central to native political identity. By persuading clans to cover a death without further bloodshed, chiefs reinforced the organizing principle of kinship in native groups. Compensation nurtured the core relationships that ordered native clans, towns, and nations.

Murders involving a killer and killed from different nations were especially dangerous and called for special exertions by the chiefs of both peoples. Otherwise, the feud between families could escalate into a war between nations. Natives insisted that their legal customs should govern their relationship with the colonists. In regions where natives remained powerful and potentially threatening, colonists usually, but grudgingly, accepted native customary law in cases of intercultural murder, wherein natives killed, or were killed by, nonnatives.

In this essay, we examine and compare two regions, during the eighteenth century, where native customary law encountered imperial attempts to enforce formal, colonial law. In both cases, the imperial need for native allies complicated the push for legal jurisdiction over resisting Indians. To the north, during the 1750s and 1760s, British officials dealt with the Haudenosaunee (or Iroquois) confederation, also known as the Six Nations: Mohawks, Oneidas, Onondagas, Tuscaroras, Cayugas, and Senecas. They dwelled between the British colony of New York, along the Hudson and Mohawk Rivers, and the French colony of Quebec, in the St. Lawrence River valley. Essential to British diplomacy with natives further north and west, the Haudenosaunee could demand primacy for their legal customs in cases of intercultural murder. To the south in East Florida, Spanish officials, during the 1780s and 1790s, had to incorporate growing numbers of Anglo-American settlers who threatened to subvert the colony's northern border. To counter that threat, colonial officials tried to reconcile their hierarchical legal and political system with the superior power of the region's natives, Lower Creeks and Seminoles, whom the Spanish needed as allies in the event of war with the Americans.

In both encounters, we find an overt clash between imperial and native law, a clash with high stakes for the balance of power between colonies and their native neighbors. But we also find considerable resilience to native law. In addition, both settings featured clashing interests and legal cross-currents within those colonial polities as some officials made a virtue of necessity by adhering to a legal plurality that contradicted the ideology of their imperial superiors. The interplay of categorical legal imperialism with pragmatic local pluralism slowed the expansion of imperial jurisdiction over native peoples in eighteenth-century North America.

Haudenosaunees

During the fifteenth century, the Haudenosaunee peoples had formed a Great League to avert war by discouraging revenge killings. Rather than try murderers, the league established ritual procedures and experts to help the killers atone by covering graves. During the 1750s, the Haudenosaunee maintained an uneasy alliance with the British settlers who had moved into the Mohawk Valley of New York. In return for access to British trade goods, the Haudenosaunee provided land to settlers and alliance in war against the French and their native allies.[5]

To preserve their autonomy and the alliance, the Haudenosaunee needed to draw the British into their legal customs in cases of intercultural murder. The occasional killing compelled colonial officials and native chiefs to renew their mutual understanding. In 1757 a colonial fur trader, Thomas Smith, found two Oneida warriors helplessly drunk after breaking into his storehouse to consume his rum. Infuriated, Smith clubbed both to death. One of the victim's brothers was a prominent chief, Nickus, who angrily confronted the British superintendent for Indian affairs, Sir William Johnson. Nickus "stripped off a Scarlet Laced Coat, a Gorget, Laced Hat & everything Sir William had given him . . . & threw them all down at his Feet & said he would not keep or wear them any longer." By publicly and angrily shedding his gifts, Nickus conveyed the rupture of his people's alliance with the colonists in the valley, who thereafter could expect killings in revenge for Smith's murders.[6]

To avert revenge killings and war, Johnson performed the traditional Haudenosaunee condolence ceremony with the Oneida chiefs on July 9, 1757. Johnson ritually offered a belt of wampum and gifts—seven silk handkerchiefs, ten shirts, and ten black strouds—to "cover the Graves of the Deceased so as to hide them from your sight." This mollified Nickus and the other Oneida chiefs, who restored their alliance with the colonists.[7]

Even when Haudenosaunee killed colonists, colonial authorities had to accept presents rather than try, convict, and execute the native suspects. Prior to 1759, British officials feared alienating the Haudenosaunee, lest they assist the Canadian French, the enemies of the British Empire in North America. Recognizing the limits of their power, New Yorkers never judicially executed any Haudenosaunee—despite several murders of colonists. And the natives sought no revenge on the colonists who killed natives. Instead, both sides preserved their alliance, known as the Covenant Chain, by ceremonially covering the graves with presents for the kin.[8]

Even when a settler killed an Indian, chiefs favored covering the grave. Averse to capital punishment, they refused to cooperate with judicial process, urging clemency instead. In 1722 in the neighboring British colony of Pennsylvania, the governor offered to execute two colonists for murdering an Indian. Preferring to receive presents, Haudenosaunee chiefs replied, "[O]ne life is enough to be lost." Needing their goodwill, the governor suspended the prosecution, liberated the killers, and covered the grave. In 1757, Johnson pressed the Mohawks to reveal a colonist suspected of treasonous speech, but "it was, to no purpose, as they said the Man might be hanged." Johnson later noted, "The Indians are so universally averse to our modes of Capital punishment that they would never stand to their Information even against an Enemy, much less a secret friend, from an Apprehension that the Parties must Suffer death." Indians hated the coercive instruments of colonial power—the jail, whip, and gallows—even when exercised on colonists. Sir William Johnson's nephew, Guy Johnson, noted, "They are by no means fond of Punishment, and often beg our People, and the soldiers off for offenses committed against them." A Moravian missionary concluded, "The whole system of the laws of the white people appear [sic] to all free Indians (those not incorporated among white people) to be intolerable, not to say tyrannical. The very word law is odious to them."[9]

Natives felt threatened by colonial legal proceedings. Although they executed enemies and suspected witches (categories that lacked or defaulted on kinship ties), Haudenosaunees balked at assisting any formal trial and execution by their colonial allies—even if the culprit had killed an Indian. Surely, natives reasoned, the offended relatives of the executed man would seek revenge; or perhaps the process was a trick meant to provoke a war. The Indians also anticipated that such executions would set ominous precedents, inviting colonial authorities to execute any Indian who killed a colonist. In 1728, after hanging two colonists for murdering natives, the governor of Pennsylvania boasted to a Haudenosaunee delegation: "We & you are as one People; we treat you exactly as we do our own People." Although meant to reassure, these words appalled Indians, who most assuredly did *not* want to be treated under law like colonists. Indeed, the imposition of colonial law in cases of intercultural murder measured the demise of Indian autonomy. In sum, natives saw nothing to gain and everything to lose if the colonizers substituted executions for covering the grave.[10]

War

Resident in the Mohawk Valley since 1738, Johnson was a pragmatist who learned Haudenosaunee ways. He recognized that the British empire needed to accept the plural legal cultures of a frontier setting where natives were too important as allies to alienate as enemies. But he often had to defend these adaptations to distant superiors and newly posted military commanders from Britain. Ideological imperialists longed to assert the supremacy of colonial over native law. When and where imperial officials felt sufficiently powerful, some longed to impose their will on natives by mandating a new order where colonial trials would determine, and colonial executions would conclude, cases of intercultural murder. Testing their own power, colonial officials demanded that Indian chiefs arrest suspects for surrender to colonial justice. But any chief who succumbed to imperial pressure and arrested fellow Indians for colonial execution became, in native eyes, accessory to a new murder and subject to assassination by kinsmen of the executed.[11]

As a result, colonial demands for murderers threatened to rupture Indian societies, obliging them to choose between civil strife and external war. In southern New England, this colonial insistence and Indian resistance provoked the Pequot War (1637) and King Philip's War (1675–1676), which crushed native independence in that region. Thereafter, the New England colonies routinely (indeed, disproportionately) subjected the surviving Indians to trial and execution for murder.[12]

Similarly, in 1759 a Cherokee war erupted over the demand by South Carolina's governor that Indians surrender suspects accused of killing intruding settlers. The Cherokee chiefs had proposed the traditional alternative: to compensate every settler death with a scalp or prisoner taken from their mutual enemies, the French. The governor abruptly rejected that offer, for he wanted dead Cherokees rather than more dead Frenchmen. His intransigence appalled the Cherokees, who recognized that submission would sacrifice their independence to colonial jurisdiction.

The impatient Carolinians seized and executed twenty-two natives who had visited the colony to negotiate, which provoked a massive war along the Carolina frontier.[13]

After initial victories in 1760, the Cherokees suffered severely in 1761, when British and colonial invaders destroyed their towns and growing crops, sentencing the survivors to hunger and land cessions. Far to the north, Johnson noted that the Cherokee war occasioned "great Suspicion and Jealousy thro' all [the] Nations." He feared a native uprising provoked by the confrontational policies of Sir Jeffrey Amherst, the British military commander in North America.[14]

Too proud of his empire, Amherst sought to subordinate natives to the British law of murder. In April of 1759 Amherst insisted upon trying Thennewhannega, a Cayuga warrior, for murdering a trader named John McMickel. Johnson advised accepting a traditional alternative: that the Cayuga take and deliver French scalps to the British to cover McMickel's grave. But the doctrinaire Amherst refused to budge. Johnson apparently induced the Cayuga chiefs to deliver up Thennewhannega by suggesting that Amherst would then pardon him—as French officials did in murder cases, saving face for both sides. Defying Johnson's arrangement, Amherst employed a court-martial to try and convict Thennewhannega. In a small concession to native sensibilities, Amherst executed by firing squad, rather than hanging, a slower and ignoble death that Indians especially despised.[15]

Amherst's handling of Thennewhannega anticipated the new legal regime that he sought to impose after conquering French Canada in 1760. With French imperial competition eliminated, Amherst believed that he could dictate to the Indians, who felt appalled. Long-time French allies, the Great Lakes nations were especially uneasy at the transfer of the French forts to British garrisons. But even the Haudenosaunee rued the French defeat because they lost clout without the capacity to play one empire off against another. General Thomas Gage explained, "They saw us sole Masters of the Country, the Balance of Power broke, and their own Consequence at an End. Instead of being courted by two Nations, a Profusion of Presents made by both, and two Markets to trade at, they now depend upon one Power."[16]

In 1762–1763, native conditions deteriorated as abusive traders and intrusive settlers poured into Indian country. Most of the traders were

newcomers who cheated Indians for short-term gain rather than cultivate long-term relationships as the French traders had done. Settlers also
rushed into the upper Ohio Valley, driving out native peoples and transforming the habitat into farms.[17]

Adding insult to injury, Amherst cut costs by curtailing the traditional
diplomatic delivery of presents to Indian chiefs. He deemed these gifts
a waste of money given the removal of French competition. If obliged
to acquire their goods exclusively from traders, the Indians would, he
reasoned, work harder, leaving less time to plot against British domination. A categorical, imperious man, Amherst equated his will with
perfect justice: "The Indians may be assured I shall always use them as
they Deserve: Reward them as far as is in my power, if they merit it, &
punish them if they Deserve it." Indians, however, considered presents
as marks of respect due to people who accepted forts in their country, so
they regarded the revocation of diplomatic gifts as showing a menacing
contempt.[18]

In conquering French Canada, Amherst mistakenly thought that
he had also conquered the Indian country. Amherst overestimated the
power of his overstretched forces—about eight thousand men scattered
over half a continent—to impose imperial dictates in the vast Indian
country and on the confusing tangle of relationships involving diverse
villages, contentious traders, and intruding settlers. Unmoved by Indian
complaints, Amherst insisted, "I would have the Indians know that we
will be Masters at these posts, and that they are to behave in an orderly
manner when they come to them."[19]

Johnson worried that Amherst's measures would provoke a massive
Indian war. Johnson noted that the Indians interpreted the new policies
and settler invasion "as the first steps to enslave them and invade their
properties." The catalytic issue that ignited a massive and bloody uprising was Amherst's confrontational handling of two cases where Indians
murdered colonists.[20]

In September 1762, Amherst learned of the murder near Detroit in
August of a colonial trader, John Clapham, by two Indian slaves, known
as Panis, who belonged to nearby Ottawas, an Algonquian-speaking nation. The British commander at Detroit, Major Henry Gladwin, secured
their arrest and confinement, pending Amherst's determination. Seeking
"the most Exemplary punishment," Amherst ordered executions "with

the utmost rigor and in the most publick manner." He boasted that his execution of Thennewhannega in 1759 had achieved "the desired Effect." But this time he wanted the culprits "hanged . . . as I think that manner of Death is most Suitable to Such Infamous Wretches."[21]

Amherst's order angered natives, who claimed the exclusive power to kill their own slaves (who lacked the protection of kinship). Rather than seeking pardons for the two accused Panis, the Ottawas wanted to execute the culprits in a traditional manner—by burning to death—to assert their power and thereby preclude the British from conducting their own ritual execution by hanging. The Indians feared losing their autonomy and sovereignty. Similarly understanding the stakes, Amherst directed the hanging to proceed. One Pani, a man, escaped by breaking his leg irons, but the other Pani, a woman, suffered a public hanging in April 1763.[22]

Two weeks later the Ottawa, led by a chief named Pontiac, attacked the British at Detroit. Although Gladwin's garrison narrowly survived, other native nations surprised and destroyed the smaller British posts around the Great Lakes in an uprising that the British misnamed "Pontiac's Rebellion." As autonomous nations, the natives were neither rebels nor did Pontiac lead most of them. Despite the lack of any unified command, the rebellion coalesced from common grievances, similar tactics, and prior communications. Until far too late, Amherst ignored the warning signs of trouble. On May 29, 1763, at New York City, Amherst wrote to Johnson, dismissing rumors of an Indian uprising, "as it certainly is not in their Power to Effect any thing of Consequence against Us."[23]

A second murder controversy escalated the war by spreading it eastward to involve the Chenussios. The westernmost Haudenosaunees, the Chenussios were a branch of the Seneca nation dwelling in the Genesee Valley. In October 1762 near Kanadasega, a village at the foot of Seneca Lake, two Chenussios shot and killed a trader and his servant. Amherst vowed, "I am Determined that the Murderers shall be Delivered up, or I Will give Immediate Orders for the March of a Body of Men to take Revenge on the Nation, or Village, to which they belong."[24]

Johnson felt compelled to demand the murderers from the Chenussio chiefs, but they rejected the ultimatum, citing the usual excuse that the suspects had fled to parts unknown. In the spring of 1763 other Haudenosaunee chiefs met with Johnson and insisted they could not "deliver up the Murderers, having no Laws for that Purpose." Teyawarunte invoked "the antient Custom of our Forefathers and Yours," who believed "that it was better to Accomodate Matters already bad enough, than to shed further Blood thereon." Surprised by Johnson's apparent support for Amherst's new legal policy, Teyawarunte speculated, "[W]e cannot help being of opinion [that] You have some other cause for pushing us so much in this affair & that we have reason to think [it] is for our Lands which the great Spirit gave us." He warned Johnson to "look back to the Old Covenant & abide by it."[25]

Formerly so masterful in native diplomacy, Johnson suddenly seemed out of touch as he pushed Amherst's provocative policy. Perhaps Sir William was playing a double game, posturing in public for Amherst's consumption while sending conciliatory messages in private to the chiefs. If so, the Chenussios missed the winks and nudges, for they acted as if they faced an imminent British attack for their defiance. Making a preemptive strike in June 1763, the Chenussios joined the uprising by attacking British garrisons and settlements in northwestern Pennsylvania. On September 14, they ambushed British teamsters and troops at the portage around Niagara Falls, the critical supply line for Detroit to the west. By closing the portage, the Chenussio attacks threatened the Detroit garrison with starvation.[26]

By the fall, the uprising had killed about four hundred British soldiers and eight hundred colonists, destroying most of the posts and pushing the settlement frontier back by two hundred miles as survivors fled eastward. Enraged by the uprising, Amherst fantasized about inflicting genocide. "It Behooves the Whole Race of Indians to Beware," for he planned to "put a Most Effectual Stop to their very Being." Reality defied Amherst's fantasies, for his eight thousand British regulars were scattered from Florida to Nova Scotia and from New York City to Detroit. Amherst could scrape together only about two thousand to cope with the rebellion: half as many as the hostile warriors.[27]

The uprising dismayed Amherst's superiors, who recalled him to London in late 1763. They entrusted the North American command to a more flexible commander, Thomas Gage, who placed greater trust in Johnson's expertise in Indian affairs. By July 1764, many of the natives were running low on ammunition and receptive to meeting Johnson for a diplomatic council at Fort Niagara. About two thousand natives attended, drawn from the Great Lakes nations as well as the Haudeno-saunee. The attending Chenussios still refused to surrender the sus-pected murderers, claiming that one had died and the other had fled to the Ohio country. Stymied, Johnson agreed to accept a land session from them: four miles wide on both banks of the Niarara River.[28]

But Johnson had to pay lip service to the legal ideology of his superiors by writing clauses into his treaties committing the natives to surrender-ing future murder suspects. Johnson acted cynically, for he knew, as did other pragmatic officers, that his empire lacked the means to enforce those treaties short of another frontier war. A British captain explained, "If they are hanged, the savages will look upon it as murder in cool blood, & revenge will ensue."[29]

Imperial pretensions also suffered from the inability of colonial of-ficials to control their own settlers, who murdered natives with im-punity. Colonial magistrates arrested some settlers for murdering natives, but few were convicted and punished. Either mobs broke open jails to free the suspects or jurors acquitted in the belief that the murder of an Indian should be rewarded rather than punished. Pennsylvanians said that "killing an Indian . . . was the same thing as killing a wild beast!" In August of 1766, Johnson counted twenty mur-dered Indians during the preceding six months—but only two mur-derers had been convicted and executed: both in New Jersey. Johnson concluded, "Neither our Laws, nor our People are much Calculated for redressing Indians."[30]

Unable to enforce the law of murder on his fellow colonists, Johnson had to cover graves, mollifying natives with ceremony and presents. This became so routine that Johnson defined the practice for Gage's benefit in December of 1765: "A parcel of black Strouds are to be given for Mourn-ing as well as for covering the Graves of the deceased. Several Belts of Wampum are also necessary, besides presents to the Familys that Suf-fered & to the Chiefs, the Whole expence of which may amount to about £100. Less will make no appearance." After covering the grave for some Haudenosaunee, Johnson reported that "they expressed some satisfac-tion, but told me that we often upbraided them for not keeping their people in order, which they were sorry to see, was too much our own case." Murderous settlers exposed as hollow the colonial claim to superi-ority over Indians in keeping law and order.[31]

Unable to hang their own people, British officials could not hang Indians. Obliged to cover Indian graves, officials had to accept Indian wampum to cover colonial graves. During the next ten years, Indians continued to kill British subjects, usually traders or their servants deep in Indian country. To bridge the gap between official ideology and the reality of limited power, imperial officials persuaded chiefs to surrender suspects on the tacit understanding that they would receive quick pardons from Gage rather than trials in court. As a further inducement, Johnson rewarded cooperative chiefs with presents when the prisoners returned home. At the return ceremony, however, the Indians had to listen to a pompous speech declaring, in the words of George Croghan, that they benefited from "the Humanity and Clemency of the British Nation," which had the "Power to punish any Nation who dare Offend us," and that in the future, "we would punish with death, every Offender." But that future never arrived until after a revolution ousted the British empire from most of North America.[32]

These compromises avoided war without resolving the fundamental conflict between native law and British common law. That enduring conflict rendered Johnson indispensable as the one British official able to persuade the general to pardon and the Indians to trust in that promise. Embarrassed by two Pottawatomies held in Detroit for killing a trader, in 1769 Gage concluded, "Sir William Johnson must endeavor to make the best of it, and attribute our Releasing of them, to our Wish of conciliating their Affections by fair means."[33]

Where Amherst had insisted upon subjugating all Indians to British military might and legal jurisdiction, Johnson imagined a composite empire: a coalition of peoples, albeit of unequal status and varying roles. According to Johnson, the empire *needed* some Indians as allies: as semi-autonomous peoples with a distinct warrior ethos, rather than as subjects and certainly not as enemies. Allies required regular consultation and generous presents from a well-financed superintendent.

But invading settlers threatened Johnson's arrangements by killing Indians faster than he could cover their graves. In the midst of a new Indian war in the Ohio Valley, Johnson died in 1774 and his empire soon followed as the British failed to suppress an American Revolution that embraced settler expansion. Far to the south, the new and ambitious

United States would affect Spanish efforts to sustain their own alliance with native peoples in East Florida.[34]

East Florida

The gap between imperial pretensions and colonial reality was especially stark in East Florida during the 1780s and 1790s. Only two thousand in number, the Spanish sustained only a few colonial enclaves, primarily at St. Augustine, in a native-dominated region. Consequently, the Spanish needed native allies to fend off potential invasion from the north in Georgia, where a large and growing American population coveted Florida. By allying with the Spanish colony, the Lower Creeks and Seminoles sought to secure access to trade goods and obtain assistance against American settlers. But natives bristled if treated as vassals of the Spanish king. Colonial officials could ill afford to alienate the Lower Creeks and Seminoles by demanding a submission to imperial law. Yet, that law expressed ideological imperatives essential to Spanish official identity.[35]

Spanish law upheld a Catholic social hierarchy organized by class and race. At the hierarchy's highest point sat the king, followed by aristocrats, archbishops, and bishops, and common people below them. In the Americas, Native, African, and African-descended peoples ranked at the bottom, beneath those considered of pure Spanish blood. Regarding society as vulnerable to collapse into anarchy, Spanish officials valued social inequality as creating chains of patronage and clientage binding superiors to inferiors, thereby sustaining social control and stability. As colonizers, Spaniards sought to subordinate natives within that social hierarchy.[36]

Colonial authorities were supposed to enforce this hierarchy through a complex system of colonial law, known as *derecho indiano*. The king issued orders, known as *cédulas*, and circulated them to colonial officials through the principal administrative body of Spain's American colonies, the Council of the Indies. In the next rung of imperial authority, *viceroys* and *audiencias* oversaw local governors, *corregidores*, *alcaldes mayores*, and *cabildos*, who supplemented royal dictates with colonial statutes—subject to royal confirmation. Following Roman legal tradition, the king ruled through an array of local laws and officials, who struggled to balance legal centralization with local heterogeneity.[37]

The Crown appointed the governor of East Florida and his subordinates, including a council of local notables. The governor also received supervision from the governor of Cuba and the viceroyalty of New Spain. Distant from the ultimate centers of Spanish governance at Madrid and Cádiz, Florida's governors exercised significant discretion to execute law in the colony. They issued local ordinances regulating public conduct, trade, the status of slaves and free blacks, and access to land. They also superintended civil suits and conducted criminal investigations and trials.[38]

In murder cases, each governor supervised an elaborate and lengthy criminal proceeding that functioned as both an investigation and a trial. The case began when an official or common subject formally accused someone of killing another. The governor opened an investigation over which an official, known as the *asesor militar*, presided. The investigation presumed guilt, which defendants rarely overcame. Taking and recording testimony under oath, the *asesor militar* questioned witnesses, including the accused. The evidence and legal argument informed sentencing decisions more than questions of guilt. Conforming to Roman legal practice, colonial trials lacked juries. Upon conviction, the governor passed sentence, and the case became subject to review by colonial officials in Havana or the Supremo Consejo de la Guerra in Madrid.[39]

Criminal law in Spanish St. Augustine officially featured a highly structured and hierarchical apparatus grounded in normative legal principles that favored executive power. Governors exercised broad prosecutorial authority in every case, leading to discretionary, often discriminatory, sentencing with minimal oversight from the Crown. Regardless of race and social position, individuals had legal representation and could testify under oath—an expression of Spain's attempts to incorporate colonized peoples into its empire, but always as subordinate peoples at the bottom of the social hierarchy designed to preserve order. By imposing punishment unequally and unevenly among white and nonwhite defendants, colonial governors used law to assert an imperial ideology that arranged people into social strata and defined social change as disorder. The Spanish imperial vision relied on cultural, racial, and class distinctions. Paternalistic, the Spanish vision promised Crown protection of the properties of the lowest in society from predation by the most powerful colonists.

In contrast to Spanish law, the Lower Creeks and Seminoles sought justice without submitting to a statist hierarchy. Social and political organization instead rested on principles of kinship, uniting in clans individuals who believed they shared a blood relationship deriving from a founding ancestor and descended in a matrilineal line. Clan membership determined virtually all the rights and responsibilities of a native village—from marriage to trade relationships to the rules governing murder and war. Each village usually had several resident clans, each with its own headman, who looked to a head chief only for coordination of collective discussions and decisions. Social cohesion derived from the collective expectations of clan members, not from a coercive authority theoretically derived from an absolute ruler at the top of a hierarchy.[40]

Operating through the shared governance of clan and village, native customary law relied on decentralized authority and rule by consensus. Enforcement of norms derived not from a coercive institutional authority but from the shared fear of social disgrace. The combined threats of public disapproval or ridicule, withdrawal of town support or protection, and private sanctions regulated unacceptable behavior and promoted peace. Southeastern Indians idealized social harmony achieved through voluntary consent as a primary goal of law. Seeking consensus within a village, natives relied on a prolonged process of discussion and persuasion to reach compromise. Rather than impose decisions and sentences, the village chief could only coordinate and guide a discussion among the many clan chiefs.[41]

As in the Northeast, in cases of murder the victim's kin could seek revenge on the killer or his relatives, but that could expand and prolong a spiral of retaliation. Consequently, clan chiefs usually encouraged the kin to accept gifts of deerskins or trade goods from the killer's relatives to "cover the blood" of the deceased and end the sorrow short of retribution. When the killing crossed clan lines, the aggrieved clan could demand, instead, that the killer's clan execute him, which would contain the contagion of revenge.[42]

As with the Haudenosaunee, the Lower Creeks and Seminoles preferred negotiation rather than additional killing, when Europeans took Indian lives. In 1803, the crew of a Spanish fishing boat killed the brother of Seminole chief Kinache and two other Indians near Tampa Bay. Rather than seek revenge for the murders, Kinache preserved the alliance and its trade by accepting a Spanish investigation that concluded that the crew had killed the Indians in self-defense.[43]

In this borderland, rum, tempers, and firearms often mixed, leading to violence between colonists and natives. When colonists and Indians accused each other of murder, Spanish formalism clashed with Native custom, making it difficult for them to resolve to their mutual satisfaction murder cases that threatened their alliance and mutual security. For if either group considered the death a general threat, rather than an isolated incident, war would ensue.[44]

To manage that risk of war, in 1784 the Spanish governors of Louisiana and West Florida negotiated a treaty with Lower Creek and Seminole chiefs. East Florida's governor then adopted that treaty for his colony. Article Twelve stipulated,

> To maintain the order required for reason, equality and justice, core principles of this Congress and on which we depend for our lives and property, as well as the tranquility of our People: it is provided that in the event an individual of our Nation commits the horrible and detestable crime of murder of a subject of the King of Spain, we are obliged to deliver the head of the aggressor. In like manner, I, the interim Governor and respective Commanders of these Provinces commit, when subjects of the King of Spain do the same, that we will punish the delinquent according to the Law of our Kingdoms, in the presence of the aggrieved Chief.

The Lower Creeks and Seminoles agreed to put to death any Indian who killed a Spanish subject, and colonial officials committed to execute any Spanish subject who killed an Indian. This accord served as mutual assurance that local disputes did not spiral into large-scale violence that could disrupt the alliance and thereby expose East Florida to attacks from north of the border. The treaty disentangled killing from war by defining murder as a question of law—but it left intact the different forms of law sustained by the colony and the natives. Neither side conceded the primacy of the other's culture or jurisdiction for providing justice in cases of intercultural killings. Particular killings obliged chiefs and officials to confront the tensions between their modes of law and justice.[45]

But Spanish officials complicated the regional geopolitics by welcoming hundreds of Anglo-Americans as settlers placed strategically along the St. Marys River: the northern border with Georgia. Lacking Hispanics willing to colonize that fertile but dangerous borderland, Spanish officials hoped that generous land grants and oaths of allegiance could convert Anglo-Americans into loyal subjects able to defend the colony against their counterparts in Georgia. In effect, the Spanish tried to build a settler firewall to keep away more hostile settlers from the American orbit. But those settlers distrusted the Indian allies of the Spanish and coveted their lands. Consequently, these new subjects despised the legal pluralism essential to the alliance that defended the colony.[46]

The alliance threatened to unravel in 1793 when someone killed and scalped a settler named Juan (or John) Houston as he was hunting deer along the St. Marys River. Angry and fearful, the other settlers blamed Indians and demanded war. Instead, Governor Juan Nepomuceno de Quesada initiated an investigation that, on flimsy grounds, identified one Lower Creek, named Micko Ketocksey, as the presumed killer. By narrowing the suspects to one supposed murderer, the governor avoided demanding the collective retribution of war. But the investigators overlooked contrary evidence that three American horse thieves had recently crossed the border and clashed with Houston. Nonetheless, the governor called upon Lower Creek and Seminole chiefs to execute Ketocksey in accordance with the treaty of 1784. "It now becomes necessary for me to require from your Justice," the governor wrote, "requisite Satisfaction for the said murder, according to the 12th Article of the treaty held at Pensacola, ten winters ago, between the Indian Nations & the Subjects of the Great King of Spain." But the chiefs declined, apparently unwilling to kill one of their own.[47]

In frustration, Quesada escalated the crisis by demanding that the chiefs deliver up Ketocksey for criminal prosecution under Spanish law. Giving priority to mollifying the new settlers, the governor threatened to alienate his native allies. The natives called the governor's bluff by responding only with vague promises to look for Ketocksey while they consulted with one another. The governor had to drop the matter, while the settlers seethed.[48]

The case of Juan Houston reveals the tensions among Spanish colonial law, native justice, and the ambitions of borderland settlers. Governor Quesada conceded that Ketocksey had recently suffered an assault by a settler whom Quesada had not punished. Seeking vengeance, the governor reasoned, Ketocksey killed Houston. By dropping his calls for satisfaction, Quesada deferred to native law, recognizing the futility of even the 1784 treaty to impose Spanish reciprocity on native lives.[49]

In the northern borderland of Florida, Spanish officials, settlers, and Indians vied to assert sovereignty through law. Whether killed by whites or Indians, Houston had been hunting deer in defiance of native claims along the St. Marys River. Despite settler demands for punitive action, Quesada pursued prolonged negotiations with Indian chiefs that fell far short of the Spanish formalities of prosecution, imprisonment, and execution. At the same time, he eschewed accepting the native practice of covering the blood with gifts in lieu of another death. Like Sir William Johnson with the Haudenosaunee, Governor Quesada made a show of demanding compliance with a treaty that he could not enforce against native wishes. In 1793 in East Florida, the Spanish empire had even less clout with Indians than the British had during the 1760s along their settler frontier. Because multiple legal regimes overlapped in East Florida, the Spanish had to accept a legal pluralism that prolonged Native sovereignty by limiting the reach of colonial law.

Ultimately, the Spanish could not halt settler pressure from Georgia to the north. Unable to repel American raids on their Seminole and Lower Creek allies, the Spanish sold East Florida to the United States, which took possession of the colony in 1821. Dispensing with a native alliance, the victors sought to subordinate and dispossess Florida's natives, provoking wars that endured into the 1850s. Ultimately, however, American settlers claimed the land and imposed their legal system premised on white supremacy and private property.

Empires sustained plural legal systems to manage killings on frontiers so long as colonial officials could manage an equipoise of power between their settlers and the natives. Savvy officials, like Sir William Johnson and Governor Quesada, seized opportunities to make a show of their devotion to imperial ideologies of their superior and inclusive legal order. But they also recognized the hollowness of their pretensions, looking the other way or pardoning supposed culprits rather than put those ideologies to a test that could only discredit them. When making these concessions, officials deferred to native justice despite not fully understanding its meanings. In cases of intercultural murder, native principles of crime and punishment trumped those of the colonial order. The priority of sustaining the alliance made native law intelligible to colonial officials, who had to restrict the scope of imperial authority over borderland violence and native peoples.

Along New York's frontier with Haudenosaunee peoples, the clash between imperial imperatives and local legal pluralism divided distant rulers from pragmatic officials on the ground. In East Florida, similar debates became more complex as the Spanish tried to incorporate and subordinate some Anglo-American settlers, who longed instead to dominate and dispossess the native allies of the colonial regime. The interplay between three notions of justice—Spanish, Anglo-American, and Lower Creek—complicated the alliance essential to the colony's security from invasion. Without that alliance, Americans might conquer Florida and impose a system that removed Indians from the land as it denied the legitimacy of their modes of law.

In the short run, pragmatic colonial officials lived with plural systems that upheld native autonomy. As colonial law became intelligible to native peoples, they had to assert their own autonomy by reiterating their own mode of seeking justice. The Haudenosaunee insisted on covering the grave, whether the victim was native or colonist. In Florida, native chiefs could invoke colonial process when it served their interests, as when Chief Kinache sought to avoid a prolonged confrontation between his people and the Spanish. Instead of dominating native peoples, colonial law became one tactical resource occasionally tapped by native peoples—so long as their own modes of justice could demand colonial restraint. In New York and East Florida, mutual intelligibility preserved native autonomy during the eighteenth century. During the next century, however, along the American frontier, north and south, settler numbers and aggression would subordinate natives in part by imposing a law of murder that demanded trials and executions rather than the covering of blood and graves with presents.[50]

NOTES

1 Richard L. Bushman, *King and People in Provincial Massachusetts* (Chapel Hill: University of North Carolina Press, 1992), 55–60; Gordon S. Wood, *The Radicalism of the American Revolution* (New York: Knopf, 1992), 11–77; Colin M. MacLachlan, *Criminal Justice in Eighteenth-Century Mexico: A Study of the Tribunal of the Acordada* (Berkeley: University of California Press, 1974), 21–26.

2 Warren Johnson, "Journal, 1760–1761," in Dean R. Snow, Charles T. Gehring, and William A. Starna, eds., *In Mohawk Country: Early Narratives about a Native People* (Syracuse, NY: Syracuse University Press, 1996), 254; Sir William Johnson to Arthur Lee, Feb. 28, 1771, in Edmund B. O'Callaghan, ed., *The Documentary History of the State of New York*, 4 vols. (Albany, NY: Weed, Parsons, 1849–1851), vol. 4: 434; Milton W. Hamilton, ed., "Guy Johnson's Opinions on the American Indian," *Pennsylvania Magazine of History and Biography* 77 (July 1953): 322; Wilbur R. Jacobs, *Wilderness Politics and Indian Gifts: The Northern Colonial Frontier, 1748–1763* (Lincoln: University of Nebraska Press, 1966), 75; John Phillip Reid, *Patterns of Vengeance: Crosscultural Homicide in the North American Fur Trade* (Pasadena, CA: Ninth Judicial Circuit Historical Society, 1999), 31–38; John Phillip Reid, *A Law of Blood: The Primitive Law of the Cherokee Nation* (Dekalb: Northern Illinois University Press, 2006), 73–84.

3 Franklin B. Dexter, ed., *Diary of David McClure, Doctor of Divinity, 1748–1820* (New York: Knickerbocker Press, 1899), 69–70; *New-York Journal*, July 2, 1788.

4 Leslie R. Gray, ed., "From Fairfield to Schonbrun—1798," *Ontario History* 49 (Winter 1957): 83; Walter Pilkington, ed., *The Journals of Samuel Kirkland* (Clinton, NY: Hamilton College, 1980), 355; Donald K. Kent and Merle H. Deardorff, eds., "John Adlum on the Allegheny: Memoirs for the Year 1794," *Pennsylvania Magazine of History and Biography* 84 (Oct. 1960): 471–72; *Albany Gazette*, Sept. 6, 1787; Reid, *Patterns of Vengeance*, 101–17.

5 Daniel K. Richter, *The Ordeal of the Longhouse: The Peoples of the Iroquois League in the Era of European Colonization* (Chapel Hill: University of North Carolina Press, 1992), 30–49; Anthony F. C. Wallace, *The Death and Rebirth of the Seneca* (New York: Knopf, 1970), 39–44.

6 Sir William Johnson, Indian Journal, July 7–11, 1757, in James Sullivan et al., eds., *Papers of Sir William Johnson* (*PSWJ* hereafter), vol. 9: 796–98 ("stripped off"); Sir William Johnson, speech, July 7, 1761, *PSWJ*, vol. 3: 434.

7 Sir William Johnson, "Journal of Indian Affairs," July 7–11, 1757, and Johnson to Peter and Elizabeth Wraxall, July 17, 1757, in Sullivan et al., eds., *PSWJ*, vol. 9: 796–98 and 799; Johnson to Jeffery Amherst, June 21, 1761, in Sullivan et al., eds., *PSWJ*, vol. 10: 292. A "stroud" was a heavy woolen cloth in great Indian demand.

8 New Yorkers could dominate the smaller, weaker Indian nations of Long Island and the Hudson Valley, who were outnumbered by the newcomers by 1700, but New Yorkers recognized the limits of their power beyond the Hudson Valley. For the want of colonial executions of Haudenosaunee, see Daniel Allen Hearn,

The Legal Executions in New York State: A Comprehensive Reference, 1639–1963 (Jefferson, NC: McFarland, 1997), 5–14. The colony did execute an Indian in 1708, but he was an indentured Long Island Indian.

9 Hamilton, ed., "Guy Johnson's Opinions," 322; Sir William Johnson, "Journal of Indian Affairs," July 5, 1757, in Sullivan et al., eds., *PSWJ*, vol. 9: 795 ("to no purpose"); Johnson to Earl of Dartmouth, May 2, 1774, in Sullivan et al., eds., *PSWJ*, vol. 8: 1146 ("universally averse"). For the Pennsylvania 1722 episode, see James H. Merrell, *Into the American Woods: Negotiators on the Pennsylvania Frontier* (New York: Norton, 1999), 120–21; and Eric Hinderaker, *Elusive Empires: Constructing Colonialism in the Ohio Valley, 1673–1800* (New York: Cambridge University Press, 1997), 123–24. For the Moravian missionary (Benjamin Mortimer), see Elma E Gray and Leslie Robb Gray, *Wilderness Christians: The Moravian Mission to the Delaware Indians* (Ithaca, NY: Cornell University Press, 1956), 165.

10 Ogista (Seneca), speech, June 16, 1765, MG 19 F35, Series 1 (Papers of the Superintendent of Indian Affairs), Library Archives Canada (LAC hereafter). For the quotation of Governor Patrick Gordon, see Hinderaker, *Elusive Empires*, 123–24.

11 Lauren Benton and Richard J. Ross, "Empires and Legal Pluralism: Jurisdiction, Sovereignty, and Political Imagination in the Early Modern World," in Benton and Ross, ed., *Legal Pluralism and Empires, 1500–1850* (New York: NYU Press, 2013), 1–20.

12 Yasuhide Kawashima, *Puritan Justice and the Indian: White Man's Law in Massachusetts, 1630–1763* (Middletown, CT: Wesleyan University Press, 1986), 233–39; Neal Salisbury, *Manitou and Providence: Indians, Europeans, and the Making of New England, 1500–1643* (New York: Oxford University Press, 1982), 123–24, 186–87, 215–28; Jill Lepore, *The Name of War: King Philip's War and the Origins of American Identity* (New York: Knopf, 1998), 21–47, 182–85.

13 Ian K. Steele, *Warpaths: Invasions of North America* (New York: Oxford University Press, 1994), 228–29.

14 Steele, *Warpaths*, 228–34; Richard White, *The Middle Ground: Indians, Empires, and Republics in the Great Lakes Region, 1650–1815* (New York: Cambridge University Press, 1991), 260; Sir William Johnson to Daniel Claus, Mar. 10, 1761, in Sullivan et al., eds., *PSWJ*, 3: 356.

15 Sir William Johnson, Canajoharie Council Minutes, Apr. 13, and 16,1759, in O'Callaghan, ed., *New York Colonial Documents*, vol. 7: 380–81, 386; Peter Wraxall to Johnson, June 8, 1759, in O'Callaghan, ed., *Documentary History of the State of New York*, vol. 2: 788; Hearn, *Legal Executions in New York*, 14. For the French mode, see White, *Middle Ground*, 246. For Cayuga resentment (and the warrior's name), see Johnson, Indian Journal, Dec. 12, 1763, in Sullivan et al., eds., *PSWJ*, vol. 10: 962.

16 Milton W. Hamilton, *Sir William Johnson: Colonial American, 1715–1763* (Port Washington, NY: Kennikat Press, 1976), 283–84, 294; Sir William Johnson, "Review of the Trade and Affairs of the Indians in the Northern District of

America," Sept. 22, 1767, in O'Callaghan, ed., *New York Colonial Documents*, vol. 7: 958; Thomas Gage to Lord Halifax, Jan. 7, 1764, in Clarence Edwin Carter, ed., *The Correspondence of General Thomas Gage with the Secretaries of State, 1763–1775*, 2 vols. (New Haven, CT: Yale University Press, 1931), vol. 1: 10–11.

17 White, *Middle Ground*, 263–65; Sir William Johnson, "Review of the Trade and Affairs of the Indians in the Northern District of America," Sept. 22, 1767, in O'Callaghan, ed., *New York Colonial Documents*, vol. 7: 960–61; George Croghan to Johnson, July 25, 1761, and Johnson to Sir Jeffrey Amherst, July 29, 1761, in Sullivan et al., eds., *PSWJ*, vol. 10: 316–17, 320–22; Fred Anderson, *Crucible of War: The Seven Years War and the Fate of Empire in British North America, 1754–1766* (New York: Knopf, 2000), 523–26, 532–34.

18 Sir Jeffrey Amherst to Sir William Johnson, July 11, 1761, Amherst to Johnson, Aug. 9, 1761, Johnson to Major William Walters, Apr. 29, 1761, Daniel Claus to Johnson, Dec. 3, 1761, and George Croghan to Johnson, May 10, 1762, in Sullivan et al., eds., *PSWJ*, vol. 3: 506, 515, 575–76, 727, 733; Walters to Johnson, Apr. 5, 1762, in Sullivan et al., eds., *PSWJ*, vol. 10: 427; Johnson, "Journal to Detroit," Oct. 19, 1761, in Sullivan et al., eds., *PSWJ*, vol. 13: 270.

19 George Croghan to Johnson, Jan. 25, 1760, in Sullivan et al., eds., *PSWJ*, vol. 10: 134; White, *Middle Ground*, 256–57; Amherst to Johnson, July 6, 1762, in Sullivan et al., eds., *PSWJ*, vol. 3: 825.

20 Sir Jeffrey Amherst to Sir William Johnson, Aug. 9, 1761, in Sullivan et al., eds., *PSWJ*, vol. 3: 515; Johnson, "Journal to Detroit," July 20, 1761, in Sullivan et al., eds., *PSWJ*, vol. 13: 221; Teyawarunte, speech, May 28, 1763, in Sullivan et al., eds., *PSWJ*, vol. 10: 683–84; Johnson to Lords of Trade, Nov. 13, 1763, in O'Callaghan, ed., *New York Colonial Documents*, vol. 7: 577 ("first steps"); Gregory Evans Dowd, *War under Heaven: Pontiac, the Indian Nations, and the British Empire* (Baltimore, MD: Johns Hopkins University Press, 2002), 52–53.

21 Capt. Donald Campbell to Sir Jeffery Amherst, Aug. 4, 1762, Major Henry Gladwin to Sir Jeffrey Amherst, Oct. 26, 1762, and Amherst to Major Henry Gladwin, Sept. 15, 1762, MG 13, War Office 34 (Amherst Papers), Reel B-2664, vol. 49: 99, 126, 313, LAC; Amherst to Sir William Johnson, Sept. 19, 1762, in Sullivan et al., eds., *PSWJ*, vol. 10: 520–21.

22 Sir William Johnson to Sir Jeffrey Amherst, Oct. 1, 1762, and Amherst to Johnson, Oct. 10, 1762, in Sullivan, et al., eds., *PSWJ*, vol. 3: 87; Major Henry Gladwin to Amherst, Jan. 26, and Apr. 20, 1763, in MG 13, War Office 34 (Amherst Papers), Reel B-2664, vol. 49: 146, 177, LAC; Dowd, *War under Heaven*, 65–66.

23 Sir Jeffrey Amherst to Sir William Johnson, May 29, 1763, in Sullivan et al., eds., *PSWJ*, vol. 10: 689; Anderson, *Crucible of War*, 538–40, 544.

24 Sir William Johnson to Sir Jeffrey Amherst, Nov. 12, 1762, and John Johnston to Johnson, Dec. 1, 1762, in Sullivan et al., eds., *PSWJ*, vol. 10: 568–69, 582; Amherst to Johnson, Nov. 21, 1762, in Sullivan et al., eds., *PSWJ*, vol. 3: 941–42 ("Determined").

25 Guy Johnson, Journal, Dec. 6–7, 1762, Teyawarunte, speech, Mar. 16, 1763, Sir
    William Johnson, speech, Mar. 16, 1763, Johnson to Sir Jeffery Amherst, Mar.
    18, 1763, and Teyawarunte, speech, May 26, 1763, in Sullivan et al., eds., *PSWJ*, vol.
    10: 590–95, 629–630, 630–31, 623–25, and 678–79; Johnson to Amherst, June 6,
    1763, in O'Callaghan, ed., *New York Colonial Documents*, vol. 7: 522–23.

26 Anderson, *Crucible of War*, 540–41, 550–51; Dowd, *War under Heaven*, 127–30,
    137–38; Sir William Johnson, Indian Journal, July 9, and Oct. 6, 1763, RG 10
    (Indian Affairs), vol. 9: 338, 376–77, LAC; Johnson to Amherst, Oct. 6, 1763, Major
    William Browning to Johnson, Oct. 22, 1763, and Jean Baptiste de Couagne to
    Johnson, Nov. 11, 1763, in Sullivan et al., eds., *PSWJ*, vol. 10: 867, 906, 921.

27 Sir Jeffrey Amherst to Sir William Johnson, June 22, July 9, July 16, Aug. 14,
    and Aug. 20, 1763, in Sullivan et al., eds., *PSWJ*, vol. 4: 151, 167, 172, 189, and 193;
    Amherst to Johnson, Aug. 27, 1763, in RG 10 (Indian Affairs), vol. 9: 423 ("It
    behooves" and "put a most effectual stop"), LAC; Amherst to Johnson, Sept. 30,
    1763, in O'Callaghan, ed., *New York Colonial Documents*, vol. 7: 568–69. For casu-
    alties, see Anderson, *Crucible of War*, 552. For the distribution of British troops,
    see Dowd, *War under Heaven*, 117.

28 Sir William Johnson to Thomas Gage, June 29, 1764, and Johnson, c. July
    1764, enumeration of Indians at the Niagara council, c. Aug. 1764, Johnson to
    Gage, Aug. 5, 1764 and Aug. 22, 1764, in Sullivan et al., eds., *PSWJ*, vol. 11: 245, 276,
    324–26, 337; Johnson to Earl of Halifax, Aug. 30, 1764, and "Articles of Peace with
    the Chenussio Indians and other Enemy Senecas," Aug. 6, 1764, in O'Callaghan,
    ed., *New York Colonial Documents*, vol. 7: 647, 652–53.

29 Treaty of Peace with the Delaware Nation, May 8, 1765, and Sir William John-
    son, speech, July 24, 1765, in O'Callaghan, ed., *New York Colonial Documents*, vol. 7:
    739, 856; Thomas Gage to Johnson, Dec. 14, 1767, in O'Callaghan, ed., *Documentary
    History of the State of New York*, vol. 2: 890; Capt. James Stevenson to Johnson, Dec.
    18, 1770, in Sullivan et al., eds., *PSWJ*, vol. 7: 1041 ("If they are hanged").

30 White, *Middle Ground*, 344–46; John C. Heckewelder, *History, Manners, and Cus-
    toms of the Indian Nations Who Once Inhabited Pennsylvania and the Neighboring
    States* (Philadelphia: Historical Society of Pennsylvania, 1876), 337 ("killing"); Sir
    William Johnson to Thomas Gage, June 27, 1766, in Sullivan et al., eds., *PSWJ*,
    vol. 12: 115 ("Neither"); Johnson to Lords of Trade, June 28 and Aug. 20, 1766, in
    O'Callaghan, ed., *New York Colonial Documents*, vol. 7: 837, 852; Gage to Lord
    Shelburne, Oct. 10, 1767, in Carter, ed., *Correspondence of General Thomas Gage*,
    vol. 1: 152–53. For the murder of the two Indian women, see "A Horrid Murder,"
    Pennsylvania Gazette, July 10, 1766; "Court of Oyer and Terminer," *Pennsylvania
    Journal*, Aug. 7, 1766.

31 Sir William Johnson to Cadwallader Colden, Jan. 27, 1764, and Johnson to Gov.
    John Penn, Feb. 9, 1764, in Sullivan et al., eds., *PSWJ*, vol. 4: 306–7, 323 ("they
    expressed"); Johnson to Gage, Dec. 21, 1765, in Sullivan et al., eds., *PSWJ*, vol. 11:
    983 ("A parcel").

32 White, *Middle Ground*, 349–50. For such an episode at Fort Pitt in 1765, see
    Ogista, speech, June 16, 1765, Lt. Col. John Reid, speech, June 17, 1765, Gage to
    Johnson, July 8, 1765, and Johnson to Gage, July 20, 1765, in Sullivan et al., eds.,
    PSWJ, vol. 11: 791, 792, 834, 862. For Johnson's release of two Pottawatomies who
    had killed two soldiers near Detroit in 1766, see Johnson, speech, July 24, 1766,
    in O'Callaghan, ed., *New York Colonial Documents*, vol. 7: 855–56. For another
    episode near Detroit in 1767, see Johnson to Gage, July 11, Aug. 6, and Aug.
    21, 1767, in O'Callaghan, ed., *Documentary History of the State of New York*, vol. 2:
    858, 861, 862; Johnson, Indian Journal, Sept. 14, 1767, in Sullivan et al., eds., *PSWJ*,
    vol. 12: 364; George Croghan, speech, Nov. 22, 1767, in Sullivan et al., eds., *PSWJ*,
    vol. 13: 441 (quotations).

33 Thomas Gage to Lord Hillsborough, Aug. 12, 1769, in Carter, ed., *Correspondence
    of General Thomas Gage*, vol. 1: 234; Farrell Wade to Johnson, Nov. 24, 1770, and
    Johnson to Capt. John Brown, Dec. 29, 1770, in Sullivan et al., eds., *PSWJ*, vol. 7:
    1019, 1052.

34 Hinderaker, *Elusive Empires*, 190–92; White, *Middle Ground*, 354–64.

35 Paul E. Hoffman, *Florida's Frontiers* (Bloomington: Indiana University Press,
    2002), 238–39.

36 Alfredo Jiménez, "Who Controls the King?" in Jesús F. de la Teja and Ross Frank,
    eds., *Choice, Persuasion, and Coercion: Social Control on Spain's North American
    Frontiers* (Albuquerque: University of New Mexico Press, 2005), 1–2; Jane Land-
    ers, "Social Control on Spain's Contested Florida Frontier," in Teja and Frank, eds.,
    Choice, Persuasion, and Coercion, 27–48.

37 John Jay TePaske, *The Governorship of Spanish Florida, 1700–1763* (Durham,
    NC: Duke University Press, 1964), 23–24; Charles R. Cutter, *The Legal Culture of
    Northern New Spain, 1700–1810* (Albuquerque: University of New Mexico Press,
    1995), 31–43; MacLachlan, *Criminal Justice in Eighteenth-Century Mexico*, 3–4,
    14, 21.

38 TePaske, *Governorship of Spanish Florida*, 58–76; M. C. Mirow, "Law in East
    Florida, 1783–1821," *American Journal of Legal History* 55, no. 1 (January 2015):
    89–118; Duvon Clough Corbitt, "The Administrative System in the Floridas,
    1783–1821, II," *Tequesta* 1, no. 3 (1943): 5767; Cutter, *Legal Culture of Northern
    New Spain*, 31–43, 69–82.

39 MacLachlan, *Criminal Justice in Eighteenth-Century Mexico*, 42, 55, 71; *Las Siete
    Partidas*, Partida VII, Title VIII, Laws I–XV, trans. Samuel Parsons Scott (Chi-
    cago: Commerce Clearing House, 1931), 1342–50.

40 Reid, *Law of Blood*, 35–48; James W. Covington, *The Seminoles of Florida* (Gaines-
    ville: University Press of Florida, 1993), 5–9; Charles Hudson, *The Southeastern In-
    dians* (Knoxville: University of Tennessee Press, 1976), 184–257; Claudio Saunt, *A
    New Order of Things: Property, Power, and the Transformation of the Creek Indians,
    1733–1816* (New York: Cambridge University Press, 1999), 11–37; Robbie Ethridge,
    Creek Country: The Creek Indians and Their World (Chapel Hill: University of
    North Carolina Press, 2003), 92–119.

41 William Bartram, "Travels through Georgia and Florida, 1773–74: A Report to Dr. John Fothergill," annotated by Francis Harper, *Transactions of the American Philosophical Society* 33 (Nov. 1943): 150, 160. Reid, *Law of Blood*, 231, 241–44; Ethridge, *Creek Country*, 107–8; Saunt, *New Order of Things*, 11–37.

42 Reid, *Patterns of Vengeance*, 31–74, 101–17; Reid, *Law of Blood*, 73–84; Kathryn E. Holland Braund, *Deerskins and Duffels: The Creek Indian Trade with Anglo-America, 1685–1815* (Lincoln: University of Nebraska Press, 2008), 154; Ethridge, *Creek Country*, 228–38; Lisa Ford, *Settler Sovereignty: Jurisdiction and Indigenous People in America and Australia, 1788–1836* (New York: Cambridge University Press, 2010), 35.

43 Governor Enrique White to Jacob Dubreuil, Jan. 25 and Feb. 7, 1803, and Dubreuil to White, Oct. 26, 1803, Records of East Florida, Reel 43, Library of Congress.

44 Ethridge, *Creek Country*, 195–238; Braund, *Deerskins and Duffels*, 139–63; Saunt, *New Order of Things*, 46–50; Covington, *Seminoles of Florida*, 22; Kathleen DuVal, *The Native Ground: Indians and Colonists in the Heart of the Continent* (Philadelphia: University of Pennsylvania Press, 2006), 110–15.

45 "Artículos de Convenio," May 31, 1784, and June 1, 1784, in Miguel Gómez del Campillo, ed., *Relaciones Diplomáticas Entre España y los Estados Unidos, Según los Documentos del Archivo Histórico Nacional* (Madrid: Consejo Superior de Investigaciones Científicas Instituto Gonzalo Fernando de Oviedo), vol 1: 412–19.

46 Kathleen DuVal, *Independence Lost: Lives on the Edge of the American Revolution* (New York: Random House, 2015), 320–22; David J. Weber, *The Spanish Frontier in North America* (New Haven, CT: Yale University Press, 1992), 278–81; Susan R. Parker, "Men without God or King: Rural Settlers of East Florida, 1784–1790," *Florida Historical Quarterly* 69 (Oct. 1990): 135–55; Gov. Vicente Manuel de Zéspedes to Bernardo de Gálvez, July 16, 1784, in Joseph Byrne Lockey, ed., *East Florida, 1783–1785: A File of Documents Assembled, and Many of Them Translated* (Berkeley: University of California Press, 1949), 230–36.

47 Richard Lang to Carlos Howard, Nov. 26, 1793, and Dec. 7, 1793, Howard to Juan Nepomuceno de Quesada, Nov. 27 and Dec. 9, 1793, Quesada to Howard, Nov. 30 and Dec. 18, 1793, Quesada to Chief Juan Canard, Jan. 18, 1794, Cusita King, Coweta Warrior, Usitches Far Off Warrior to Governor of Florida, c. Jan. 1794, Records of East Florida, Reel 43, Library of Congress.

48 Juan Nepomuceno de Quesada to Diego de Vegas, Nov. 18, 1794, and "A Talk from the Hallooing King of the Cowetas and Little Warrior of the Broken Arrow by order of the Chiefs of the Lower Creeks assembled at the Broaken [sic] Arrow," Apr. 19, 1795, Records of East Florida, Reel 43, Library of Congress.

49 Carlos Howard to Richard Lang, Nov. 27, 1793, Howard to Juan Nepomuceno de Quesada, Nov. 27 and Dec. 9, 1793, Quesada to Howard, Dec. 18, 1793, Records of East Florida, Reel 43, Library of Congress; Quesada to Luis de Las Casas, Jan. 2, 1794, Records of East Florida, Reel 9, Library of Congress.

50 Ford, *Settler Sovereignty*, 17–25, 30–42, 55–71, 183–96; Alan Taylor, *The Divided Ground: Indians, Settlers, and the Northern Borderland of the American Revolution* (New York: Knopf, 2006), 317–22, 327–28, 341–42, 381–83.

8

"Sovereignty Has Lost Its Rights"

Liberal Experiments and Indigenous Citizenship in New Granada, 1810–1819

MARCELA ECHEVERRI

In the province of Santa Fe, at the core of the viceroyalty of New Granada, in July of 1810, creoles (American-born Spaniards) expelled the viceroy from the city of Santa Fe and created a Junta Suprema. Aligning itself with other rebel autonomist projects across Spanish America, the Santa Fe Junta did not recognize the authority of the Regency, the peninsular government that sought to rule in the name of King Fernando VII in the critical context of the Napoleonic invasion of the Iberian Peninsula (see map 8.1).

Experimenting with self-rule, the Junta of Santa Fe published a constitution in April 1811. A year later, in April 1812, it declared itself an independent republic. In a radical gesture, the Santa Fe Junta also reinvented itself by adopting the name "Cundinamarca." The recourse to a pre-Hispanic name loudly signaled the interest of its founders in symbolically appropriating the territory by connecting the emergent polity with the native population's ancient rights.[1] Simultaneously, however, the legislative framework set up by the Santa Fe Junta and reinforced by the Republic of Cundinamarca attempted to change—in fact, dismantle—indigenous rights.

In September of 1810, immediately after declaring its independence from the Regency, the Santa Fe Junta Suprema had announced a comprehensive law that abolished the category of Indians and made them equal to other citizens.[2] Soon after, in late 1810 and 1811, protests across New Granada's central highlands—for example, in the Indian towns of Chipaque and Cocuy—revealed natives' understanding of the profound imperial-wide crisis of sovereignty as a context that allowed them to gain greater freedom while they held on to their pacted rights as Indians. In other words, the protests exposed a divergence between what legislators saw as the means of consolidating egalitarian and inclusive polities under their leadership and Indians' willingness to embrace the opportunity to act autonomously, guarding their difference, yet also demonstrating that once the sovereignty of the Crown was in crisis, they had no less right than creoles to define the terms of any social or legal transformation. Judging from their actions between 1810 and 1819, indigenous people's contentious reactions to the creole government's projects of radical innovation pivoted around three issues: the authority of the creole Junta to issue legislation; the Indians' right to political protection and legal representation; and the relation between tribute payment, land rights, and Indians' autonomous jurisdiction.

New Granada Indians' continued pursuit of their ethnic interests destabilized the creole project, leading it to failure by 1814 when Fernando VII returned to his throne. During the juncture of the monarchical restoration (1814–1819),[3] Spain repressed the American independentist juntas and imposed an absolutist government mainly through military agents. In that context, indigenous people became allies of the monarchical regime and actively and consistently upheld their colonial rights to representation and autonomy, grounding these in their duty to pay tribute.

In this essay I explore how Indians' responses to the monarchical crisis, the liberal reforms, and the 1814 monarchical restoration impacted regional politics throughout New Granada between 1810 and 1819.[4] I do so by contextualizing the conflicts between indigenous people and the creoles' attempts to found independent republics within two broad dimensions: one, the temporal depth of Bourbon reformism, which refers to the way redefinitions of the monarchy during the eighteenth century and up to the early nineteenth century affected the Indians' position within the empire and in relation to the creoles. Second, focusing on the 1810–1819 cycle of shifts from absolutism to liberalism and back, I will draw comparisons between the liberal experiment in Santa Fe and the creation and implementation of changes to indigenous peoples' rights in the Cádiz imperial project of liberal reform, which developed simultaneously and in a dialectical relationship to the creole autonomist projects.

The 1812 Cádiz Constitution was put into practice in some areas of New Granada (and Spanish America more broadly) that remained under royalist control, such as the southwestern city of Pasto. Seen in contrast to what happened across the insurgent territories in the central highlands—where the Cundinamarca and Tunja republics had been erected—in Pasto the royalist authorities' policy of negotiating with indigenous people, something they had been doing since the beginning of the monarchical crisis, produced a relatively more stable environment between 1810 and 1819. This seems to be due to the fact that the source of legitimacy for the alliance between the royalists and the indigenous communities in Pasto was the king's sovereignty. Thus, while the liberal reform and the war also generated conflicts across the royalist regions, these conflicts were of a different nature than those that emerged from the liberal legislation around Santa Fe, where what was in question and at stake was precisely the allegiance of indigenous people to the political projects of the creoles. In other words, in southwest New Granada, the Indians sought a productive engagement with liberalism in the context of royalist rule during this period, and in the region around Santa Fe, indigenous people identified the creole government as an insurgent, illegitimate government, and thus challenged most of its attempts at transformation.

This study of indigenous peoples' engagement with early Hispanic liberalism in New Granada speaks to various historiographical debates. First, the essay is a contribution to rethinking the history of liberalism in Spanish America by beginning in the early nineteenth century, instead of with the traditional decades of 1820–1850 that are generally chosen as a starting point from which to explore this subject. The widespread constitutional experiments across Spanish America between 1810 and 1814 contain relevant clues for understanding the complex history of Hispanic liberalism in its broadest sense. Significantly, New Granada was a place where constitutions were produced very early, even earlier than in Cádiz.

Though historians up until now may have thought of "liberalism" as the guiding principle that both the Santa Fe and Cádiz liberal projects shared, on closer inspection it is clear that liberalism was different within each of the two unequal institutional frameworks that were being developed on each side of the Atlantic at this time: the national-imperial frame that deputies in Cádiz were seeking to create and the anticolonial republican form being introduced by the local New Granadan constitutional experiments.

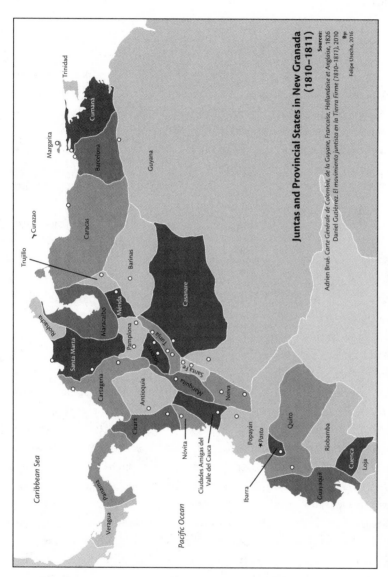

Map 8.1: Juntas and Provincial States in New Granada (1810–1811).

Thus, this study argues that liberalism's history must be understood as changing over time and in different social settings. Building upon the historiography that advocates for an understanding of European liberalism as plural, I go further and expand the study of liberalism to include the New Granadan experiments, and Indian politics in that context, in the study of Hispanic liberalism and Atlantic liberalism more broadly. That is to say, historians today recognize that Hispanic liberalism can be distinguished from other European variants. Here I will show that Hispanic liberalism can itself be understood in plural fashion by recognizing the different emphases between peninsular and American versions.[5]

Moreover, the particularity in each context of liberal reform produced substantial differences in the ways in which indigenous people perceived changes. Historians of Latin America have begun to explore the Indians' interpretations of and participation in the monarchical crisis and the rise of independent polities, together with the conceptions they had of their rights in each of these transformative processes.[6] Yet, in the broader field of studies about Hispanic liberalism, in the last five decades the Cádiz Constitution has received overwhelming attention while it is only recently that the pioneering cases of constitution making in places like New Granada have become an object of serious study.[7] And the few authors who have produced works dealing with this theme have not looked at the role that indigenous people and indigenous rights played in these early liberal experiments.[8]

The developments in New Granada illustrate the particular paths of Spain and Spanish American polities in the turbulent eighteenth- and nineteenth-century Atlantic world. One of the aspects of the Spanish empire's plural legal ground since the fifteenth century was that Indian vassals inhabited a separate legal category and a particular condition as minors. That is, Hispanic rule was based on the background of a judicial system that presupposed inclusiveness (furthered by Catholic discourse and institutions) while relying on a differential definition of indigenous people—one couched in corporate terms.[9]

Granting citizenship to Indians was an Enlightenment idea that had emerged in the context of Spanish imperial and monarchical reformist projects of the eighteenth century, and it was linked to political processes in the colonial context. During the eighteenth century an impulse to deepen the process of Indians' economic integration—a crucial precedent to Hispanic liberalism—intensified old and produced new tensions. Indigenous peoples' ongoing political engagement with earlier, longstanding discourses and practices of justice and rights proved to be conflictive factors in this transformative context. In other words, Indians' visions of justice and their effective engagement with it shaped— and sometimes even hampered—the application of ideas about, and the creation of new institutions and relations that responded to, the liberal vision of reformers on both sides of the Atlantic.

From the perspective of contrasts among the British and Spanish Atlantic empires, a significant specificity of the latter was that indigenous people shared the legal framework of the monarchy with colonial officials and other Spanish subjects. Indeed, in areas of consolidated colonial rule, by the turn of the nineteenth century, Indians were not outsiders of the colonial world.[10] Up to the nineteenth-century monarchical crisis, the Spanish empire's innovation in the treatment of indigenous people deepened the differences with the British empire and the United States, both of which excluded Indians as subjects or citizens, respectively. That is to say, Hispanic liberalism on both sides of the Atlantic implied—at least in theory—the dissolution of corporate bodies in favor of Indians' inclusion as citizens while, after the American Revolution, Indians in North America lost their place in the British empire and by the nineteenth century, in the United States, they were considered "foreign nations" outside of the body politic.[11]

The changes developing in New Granada between 1810 and 1819 as a case study show why and how local and regional jurisdictional tensions involving indigenous people articulated to the critical shift in the Spanish empire's legal framework.[12] Ultimately, in that period the liberal reforms' attempt to undermine plural legal institutions was more intellectual and discursive than an applicable radical innovation. Yet it is important to look at how natives and creoles envisioned sovereignty and equality and to what extent, on what terms, and by what means they were willing to embrace change given the highly volatile context. Though the legal reforms trialed during the monarchical crisis implied a search for social homogeneity, Indians experienced them through the lens of their particular identities, which led them to challenge liberalism. All throughout the period studied in this essay, they instrumentalized a legal framework—the judicial system—that they knew in practice. They did so in the context of a crisis of Spanish imperial sovereignty, albeit using the very channels, means, and arguments that the empire had granted them and that they had continually revitalized for centuries.[13]

Difference and Integration in New Granada

Native people had played a foundational role in the process of colonization and in the formation of the New Kingdom of Granada, especially in the highland areas with high population density at the time of the Conquest. The natives' sociopolitical organization in *cacicazgos*, or chiefdoms, also had facilitated their incorporation into the colonial administrative structure. In the central highlands located on the eastern cordillera (in the *altiplano cundi-boyacense*, or plateau encompassing Santa Fe and Tunja) where the Spanish established the central government of New Granada, Indians were still a significant part of the population by the turn of the nineteenth century. Also in the southwestern province of Popayán, bordering the Kingdom of Quito, the Indian populations in the jurisdiction of Pasto were some of the most resilient native communities to survive and adapt to Spanish rule (see table 8.1).

In the process of being integrated into the imperial edifice of the monarchy, these native societies had changed. They had become "Indians," vassals of the king who had a particular legal status that hinged upon their corporate or communal organization. Two of the most significant rights accorded to the indigenous communities were the possession of land grants (called *"resguardos"* in New Granada) and semi-autonomous self-governments headed by native *Alcaldes*, or mayors. In exchange, natives paid a head tax called *tributo*, or tribute, which was collected by the other two authorities in charge of governing them: the caciques, or ethnic authorities, and the *corregidores*, or Spanish magistrates.

The *Recopilación de las leyes de Indias*, a compendium of laws for Spanish America published in 1680, was the legal baseline through which Indians came to understand and defend their rights. Produced during Habsburg rule, the *Recopilación* was a detailed outline of regulations in all matters of government for the Indies and it was foundational for indigenous people as they became adept in using legal tools. In book 6, the

TABLE 8.1

Population Distribution in New Granada, Pasto, Santa Fe, and Tunja
(Late Eighteenth Century)

	New Granada*		Pasto*		Santa Fe*		Tunja**	
Indians	461,501	35.95%	14,101	46.45%	31,561	36%	36,186	14%
Free People Of All Colors	432,314	33.67%	2,000	6.58%	30,239	34.5%	112,469	43%
White	320,323	24.95%	14,141	46.58%	24,569	28%	103,376	40%
Slaves	69,590	5.42%	113	0.37%	1,174	1.3%	6.047	2.3%
Total Population	1,283,728		30,355		87,543		258,078	

* The years of these statistics vary: New Granada (1778), Santa Fe (1796), Pasto (1797). Source: Hermes Tovar, *Convocatoria al poder del número. Censos y estadísticas de la Nueva Granada, 1750–1850* (Bogotá: Archivo General de la Nación, 1994), 69–73, 319.

** The year of this Tunja census is 1776. Source: Diana Bonnett, *Tierra y comunidad un problema irresuelto. El caso del altiplano cundiboyacense (Virreinato de la Nueva Granada) 1750–1800* (Bogotá: ICANH, Universidad de Los Andes, 2002), 166.

Recopilación specifically addressed all issues pertaining to Indians, such as the organization of Indian towns, tribute payment and collection, and legal representation in the figure of the *"protector de indios."*[14]

In this framework, Spanish justice thus allowed Indians to benefit from special "privileges," which shaped the Indians' engagement with politics. Legal protection and representation were one joint aspect of Indians' corporate identity that came attached with the fiscal duty to pay tribute (the tributary pact secured Indians' rights). Because the essence of the legal category of "Indian" implied minority, which, in turn, supposed the natives' need for legal protection, legal institutions and channels as well as hierarchies were crucial mechanisms of government and political action. The *protector de indios* was a core figure in the formal recognition of Indians as a class whose interests had to be defended. The right to representation by the protector guaranteed Indians' protection vis-à-vis more powerful agents, such as creoles. Ethnic elites also had the responsibility to represent the communities, and their knowledge of the law secured their position as authorities.

Tribute, which was a fiscal institution that cut across the category of Indian vassals, was an arena of ongoing contention for a simple reason: it allowed natives across class lines to balance their rights and duties vis-à-vis the Crown and local colonial officials, as well as within the communities. Throughout the colonial era, tribute payment and collection acquired changing meanings as they were exposed to local negotiation but also to the processes of imperial transformation.

By the turn of the nineteenth century, from the Indians' perspective, the terms of Spanish justice (and justice's political potential) were under the specific pressures that the Bourbon Crown's attempt to reform the monarchy and increase its revenues had brought to bear on the mechanisms of tribute collection. This change affected native authorities and Indian commoners differently; in fact, it could potentially benefit the caciques if they collaborated with the *corregidor*, though at the risk of losing legitimacy in the eyes of the community.

On the other hand, since the sixteenth century indigenous people had been losing control of the lands that the Crown had granted them. People of mixed ancestry (*mestizos, mulatos*) and creoles had been progressively encroaching on indigenous territories. While indigenous people continued to claim their rights as tribute-paying vassals to the Crown's protection of their lands, the increasing pressure over Indian lands, along with shifts in the mentality about productivity in the higher echelons of the monarchical government (and among some creoles, as we will see), led the Crown to consider the possibility of dividing the *resguardos* and granting land to the people who were eager to exploit it.

The eighteenth-century project of imperial reform went as deep as to attempt an overhaul of the institutions and categories of rule, including justice and the role of the economy and politics. The indigenous peoples were a central part of the discussions about the best way to put the Spanish American territories at the heart of development by creating processes that would allow them to adapt to and participate in the new circumstances.[15]

Since the eighteenth century, creoles had been deeply involved with the project of transforming the monarchy to maximize production and well-being, yet at the same time resenting some aspects of the Bourbon state's approach to ruling and reform. For example, Pedro Fermín de Vargas, a creole who was in the Enlightenment intellectual revolution of the late eighteenth century, which in New Granada produced important work in the fields of botany and geography, wrote two treatises of political economy: *Pensamientos Políticos* and *Memoria sobre la Población del Nuevo Reino de Granada.* Vargas penned these texts around 1789, in the aftermath of the Comunero Rebellion that he had witnessed first-hand.[16] Among other subjects, these treatises reflected specifically on the place of indigenous people in New Granada and also discussed why it was necessary—in fact, ideal—to transform them into citizens and property holders enjoying the same social status as other nonindigenous people. Significantly, Vargas suggested that the common lands that the Crown had granted to the Indians represented only an "illusory freedom" (*libertad ilusoria*), one that forced them to remain attached to the Crown. Vargas affirmed that Indians (as well as blacks) were all interested in becoming mestizo or white. He added that the natives abhorred Spain and were seeking to free themselves from the yoke of oppression that had begun with the violent dispossession of the Conquest. Most interestingly, Vargas discredited Spanish policy for having had the effect of making Spanish subjects "stupid." In addition, he used the example of the alliance among creoles, Indians, and other *castas* during the Comunero Rebellion to argue that they were unanimously against Spanish rule.[17]

Vargas's written work is an illustration of the background preceding the New Granadan creoles' approach to social and political transformation of indigenous people in the years 1810–1816. Indeed, while his writings do not have to be interpreted as expressing a pre-independence national feeling or identity, they did find an echo in the legislation that the Santa Fe Junta developed in the first years of experimenting with autonomous rule. That is to say, while some creoles held a belief in the need to free indigenous people from their state of servitude, they also assumed that indigenous people were seeking that liberation, and they saw making Indians equal citizens as a foundational gesture toward a more socially solid and economically viable Santa Fe.

Thus, when in 1810 Santa Fe deputies were acting to create a new framework for the social and economic transformation of the region, they expressed a belief that the legal, fiscal, and ethnic category of "Indian" was no longer necessary or desirable for the new government that they were founding. By "freeing" the indigenous population of the tax burden that tribute represented, the law promised to bring equality. Indeed, in coupling the two radical measures—abolishing tribute and dividing *resguardos*—lawmakers in Santa Fe revealed how their thinking aligned with the colonial logic according to which tribute payment and land possession were two sides of the same coin.[18]

At the same time, New Granadan legislators were overtly critical of "Bourbon despotism" in a public campaign disseminated through periodicals. Creoles produced and published a narrative that questioned the legitimacy of the peninsular government and moreover deromanticized Cádiz's legal measures based on promises of uniting the Hispanic community from both hemispheres in a Spanish nation.[19] Yet, as we have seen, the steps taken by the Santa Fe Junta Suprema in 1810 (and the Cundinamarca state in 1811 and 1812) to turn indigenous people into equal citizens had roots in the changes in political philosophy and administration that had been initiated, but for the most part had failed, during Bourbon rule.

Native-creole relations had been mediated by the Crown's protection of Indians' rights and, for that reason, the creoles' republican project that took shape during the monarchical crisis pivoted around two goals. First, the provincial governments that evolved into independent republics were taking sovereignty into their own hands. Second, in that process, the republican governments were entering into a new relationship with the indigenous people whereby the Indians, although nominally being equal to other citizens, would be a population under the creole governments' control. Creoles sought Indian collaboration in their anticolonial project in the context of military conflicts between the emergent republics and representatives of Spanish rule across New Granada. Thus the legislation also became a means for trying to win indigenous people over to the insurgent faction and prevent them from defending the peninsular government.

Contrasting Views of Authority, Community, and Equality in New Granada and Cádiz

In the fluid context of the monarchical crisis beginning in 1808, Indians as much as creoles confronted an unprecedented instability in the judicial framework that had until that moment regulated relations between Spanish American subjects and the Crown as well as among them. What was at stake was the very nature of the social organization of Spanish America, in relation both to the peninsula and to the evolution of the philosophical perspectives on political economy and the understanding of the nature of political communities that developed during the revolutionary era.[20] When the men in government positions attempted to bring to life their liberal ideas and revamp institutions, they had to contend with the powerful presence of indigenous people—not just as objects but also as subjects—whose understanding of those same processes mediated the liberal reform and shaped the reach of the liberal experiments in New Granada.[21]

Between 1810 and 1815, the creole governments in Santa Fe and neighboring Tunja who were heading the new political communities that included Indians as citizens adapted their approach toward the indigenous populations as a result of a series of revolts in the Indian towns that these governments were now seeking to govern. The revolts taught the creoles that they could not assume that the Indians would accept and comply with the legal changes that the new republics were imposing upon them.

One of the earliest revolts to take place was in September 1810, the same month in which the Junta Suprema of Santa Fe passed a comprehensive law that aimed to design a New Granada–wide policy of liberalization and also to appeal to the indigenous population with the offer of new rights of citizenship. The priest of Chipaque, an Indian town in the province of Santa Fe, denounced disturbances among the Indian population that were motivated by rumors that were circulating "that there is no king." "Disastrously mistaken," he said, "they imagine that there are no judges to govern them, and reject any authority that might attempt to control them."[22]

The news that indigenous people in Chipaque had affirmed that "there [was] no king" suggests that they were well aware of the monarchical crisis. And their reaction to "reject any authority that might attempt to control them" was, interestingly, not all that different from the path taken by the Santa Fe municipal council (*cabildo*); in fact, this rebellion might have spurred the Indians in Chipaque to question the *cabildo*'s self-proclaimed authority to rule in the absence of the monarch.[23]

Ten months later, in July 1811, the priest José Andrés Moya was still complaining about the situation in Chipaque, where things had turned even more serious: Indians were spreading their conspiratorial ideas and "contaminating everyone else" beyond Chipaque, and they had "scandalously insulted by word and deed the town's mayors, breaking their staffs (*varas*)." Staff breaking was not uncommon. It was often a prelude to an argument about whether the precepts of justice were being violated. In this case, breaking the mayors' staffs was a sign that the Indians refused to recognize the authority of those who held them. Though it is not clear whether the mayors were in this case Indians or not, it is possible that the circumstances were also unleashing a crisis within the communities and structures of the Indian government. Transformations in discourses of governance impacted the very foundations upon which "Indianness" was grounded, generating conflicts within the communities themselves. In any case, with those actions the Indians loudly questioned the power of the creole Junta to legislate.[24]

North of Chipaque, in June 1811, right after Cundinamarca proclaimed the first constitution, Josef Santiago Crespín y Pérez, the priest of Cocuy (in Tunja Province), denounced the "perverse interpretation the Indians had of the proclamation published, sent from the capital [Santa Fe], about having been declared equal (*igualación*) to whites."[25] The priest requested that officials in the capital follow up on the proclamation by clarifying the legitimate purpose of the law and explaining to the Indians that they should not use the changes in legislation as an argument for disturbing public order.

What exactly did the priest Crespín y Pérez mean by "perverse interpretation"? To the creoles the law was an instrument for exercising control over the Indians. To the Indians, the law that declared them "equal to whites" was, much the opposite, an indication that they did not have to accept the creoles' pretention to govern them. As in Chipaque, Indians in Cocuy framed their interpretation of the law's proclamation within the context of the absence of the king, which called the legitimacy of the creole rebel governments' legislative sovereignty into question. Rather than accept creole legislation, indigenous people were generating their own responses to the monarchical crisis.

The creoles, on the other hand, took very seriously their duty to emancipate indigenous people by ridding them of the payment of tribute, which they called an "unjust and ignominious pension," and by dissolving the communal lands, the latter a means of universalizing the basic right to individual property. In 1810 the Santa Fe Junta professed "paternal sentiments" towards the inhabitants of New Granada, especially the Indians. The first step toward the goal of extending to the indigenous population the "benefits that until this moment they have not had" was to abolish tribute payment and declare that Indians should from that moment on be taxed on the same terms as other citizens.[26] The law did not stop there. As part of "elevating" Indians to the new status of citizens on equal terms with the others, the law included a project to divide Indian lands and provide each family with a plot of land of its own. Furthermore, this material equality arrived with the promise that public schools were to be created in every territory previously considered a *resguardo,* or reservation.[27]

This suggests that, rather than expecting indigenous people in Chipaque and other towns in Santa Fe's jurisdiction to understand the law in the same way as did the creoles who produced it, the uprisings had made it clear that the Junta needed to make an effort to educate the Indians on both the purpose and the implications of the law making Indians citizens. The desired consequence of explaining the law's benefits ideally would be not only to put a halt to the uprising and make the Indians "obedient to the authorities" but also, and more importantly, to guarantee the Indians' loyalty to the "new generous liberal government in the capital."[28]

Published at the height of the military confrontations between Santa Fe and the representatives of Spanish authority (and also in the midst of diplomatic tensions among juntas in New Granada), for the purpose of gaining indigenous people's support and keeping them as potential military allies, the law thus had used a paternalist tone to establish liberal measures. Indeed, the Junta declared its goal to be to bring happiness to "those men and peoples who decide to be part of its government."[29]

Yet, three years after the start of the revolution and just a couple of months before the monarchical restoration, in mid-March 1814, an article about the debate around the plan to pair legal equality with the dissolution of the Indians' common lands appeared in the *Gaceta Ministerial de Cundinamarca*—the official paper of the Republic of Cundinamarca. The article cited the words of Manuel Bernardo Alvarez, the president of the chamber of senators in Santa Fe, who said, "We have stated publicly to the world that our political transformation is naturally just. But if we now take the *resguardos* from the Indians, will the public response then not be to say that we are more tyrannical than the Conquistadors who, in spite of their inhumanity, granted them some specified territory?"[30]

Comparing the creole republic's measures to the tyranny of Spain was a severe judgment. It subverted the spirit of the republic's ongoing efforts to separate from Spain on the basis of an anticolonial discourse that discredited Spanish rule. And those words had a specific effect of delegitimizing the liberal framework that had so powerfully inspired the plan to abolish communal landholding as a necessary corollary to making Indians citizens. In light of the actual and potential consequences of such a radical innovation, Alvarez was open to giving colonial law a more moderate reading, one that justified the history behind the Indians' legal privileges. In broad terms, what Alvarez was saying signaled the imminent failure of the creole project of liberal reform.

Moreover, as war intensified between the regions under royalist control and those that were forming independent polities, the creole elites saw a need to court indigenous people, which included appealing to their interests via sound legislation. Indeed, indigenous people proved to be strategic allies of the independence cause as much as they were of the royalists in places like Pasto or Santa Marta. For instance, when in 1813 Antonio Nariño led the Cundinamarca military campaign against the Popayán royalists, he traveled with an Indian called Astudillo, who had some influence with the people in Tierra-Adentro and who supported Nariño by granting him some Indians to help transport artillery.[31]

In the debate published in the *Gaceta Ministerial de Cundinamarca* in mid-March 1814, Manuel Bernardo Alvarez added to his concerns by asking the following question: "Calambás, the Indian who is currently fighting against Sámano's [royalist] forces, will he not be shocked to find out that as a reward for his valor he has lost his lands?"[32] Alvarez's criticism suggested that the creole liberal legislative proposal was an inappropriate—and dangerous—reward for those indigenous people who had, up to that point, supported the independence cause.

The Junta Suprema of Santa Fe and the state of Cundinamarca had initially abolished tribute and legislated to have communal lands divided as a departure from colonial law. Yet the ambiguous positions of the legislators themselves made the legal process inconclusive at the moment of the monarchical restoration in 1814. And the foundations for establishing the citizenship rights of indigenous people were tenuous due to another crucial factor that shook the bases of the republican project: the ways in which the Indians had reacted to the political process that had been underway since 1808. Though the creole project had attempted to attract the Indians with its promises of equality, it had, in fact, alienated them.

As a counterpoint, it is important to consider the parallel, intertwined, but also contrasting developments in Cádiz and its impact on indigenous politics in the regions where the imperial constitution was applied. The Santa Fe Junta's expedited legal reform was competing explicitly with the first experiment with constitution writing in the Iberian Peninsula. During the absence of King Fernando VII, Spanish liberals sought to transform legal categories and practice everywhere in Spain and Spanish America. Between 1810 and 1814, the deputies in Cádiz embarked on a project to dismantle seigniorial institutions in the monarchy and to create an imperial nation. Similar to the New Granadan insurgent juntas and confederations, albeit on an imperial scale, the laws that emanated from the peninsula included a proposal to transform the status of the Indians. Among other reforms, the resulting 1812 Cádiz Constitution developed a new definition of citizenship that for the first time encompassed Spaniards and Indians on equal terms.[33]

The intersection between the Cádiz Constitution and the New Granadan legislative projects as regards a liberal approach to Indian citizenship must be understood in the context of the precedent that they shared of the Bourbon vision of an empire-wide policy to transform indigenous rights. In the juncture of the monarchical crisis, the dialectic between the two constitutional processes that were to define the legal aspects of Indianness took place sequentially, on both sides of the Atlantic.[34] If we consider the issue of tribute, for example, the Regency (the peninsular government preceding the Cortes) abolished it on March 26, 1810. By September, the Junta Suprema of Santa Fe had also abolished tribute. Then, in Mexico on October 5, Viceroy Francisco Xavier Venegas decreed the abolition of tribute as a reaction to Hidalgo's revolt, which also proposed changes in this tax. It was not until a year later, on March 12, 1811, that the Cortes in Cádiz abolished the payment of tribute.[35]

The corollary to abolishing tribute that stipulated that lands should be divided and distributed individually among the Indians was also discussed in Cádiz. The idea was not, however, to strip communities of their entire *resguardos* of communal property but to take the land that seemed to be un- or underused and make it productive. This resembled the Bourbon vision that had been developed in the previous century.

Although constitution making in Cádiz and in Spanish America revolved around similar themes, and the integrationist policy that became central to constitutional and legal changes in New Granada was an influential factor in determining the Cortes's decision to develop parallel laws, the specific circumstances, as well as the legal consequences, of the debates that took place in Cádiz were nonetheless very different from the ones that took place in Santa Fe.[36]

The imperial scope of the Cádiz Constitution, and the nation it sought to represent, explains the fact that deputies in Cádiz sought to reconcile liberalism with the earlier social structures and administrative practices of the Spanish monarchy. This project regarded the corporative society that made up the Spanish territories, in the Peninsula, the Americas, and the Philippines, as the ground upon which to develop new institutions. Indeed, the multiplicity of entities, territorial dimensions, and interests that the Cádiz constitutional project had to embrace gave way to very specific legislative decisions.

The constitutional monarchy did not attack local powers but, rather, sought to articulate both the imperial and the local spheres. Instead of an outright disqualification of precedent, for instance, deputies in the peninsula wanted to find a balance between the innovations that they saw as necessary and the historical definitions of sovereignty, rights, and authority that had characterized the Spanish monarchy up to that point. Moreover, justice continued to be recognized as a tool for protecting particular privileges.[37]

The liberal constitution originating in Cádiz was unevenly received and applied across the empire, due to the context of the monarchical crisis and the rise of anticolonial warfare in the American kingdoms. And in the territories that continued under Spanish rule participating in the configuration of a constitutional monarchy, there were varied reactions to the Cádiz Constitution. Yet in all royalist regions, such as New Granada's southwestern city of Pasto, it impacted how indigenous people conceived of their rights.[38]

In New Granada's Southwest, the conflict began when Quito declared an autonomist junta in 1809. Popayán governor Miguel Tacón associated with the Indian communities in the Pasto highlands on the basis of a negotiation of the tribute that Indians would have to pay. Tacón considered the Indians' military participation in the defense of the region and, more generally, their loyalty, crucial to the success of the royalist military mission. Thus he rewarded it with a reduction in the tribute quota, a *gracia* (dispensation) that was meant to lower their burden during the exceptional circumstances of the war.

Therefore, in Pasto, where indigenous people consistently supported the royalist government against encroachments from rebel juntas across New Granada between 1809 and 1816, the Cádiz liberal reform was articulated to earlier political dynamics around the issue of tribute within Indian communities. After 1812, the Indians of the commoner class who sought to have their tribute reduced in exchange for their military service also appealed, with the support of the *protector de naturales* Juan Díaz Gallardo, to the laws arriving from the peninsula to justify their claims.

But that action went against the interests of the caciques, who saw any potential changes in tribute collection as a threat to their positions as ethnic authorities. In other words, the priorities of indigenous people and their understanding of the legal changes and opportunities brought about by the war were relative to their position within Indian communities. The definitions of loyalty and Indianness espoused by the caciques and by Indian commoners in Pasto turned out to be in contradiction. And while the period of liberal government seems to have benefited the commoners, in their alliance with the protector, the caciques found the restoration a favorable context in which to regain their strength.[39]

Taken together, the experiences of indigenous people with both strands of liberal reform contrast mainly in the fact that in Pasto liberalism intensified conflicts across class lines while in the central highlands around Santa Fe the antagonism seems to have revolved around the opposition of the Indian communities versus the creoles. But Indians did not exclusively reject the notions of liberalization emanating from Cádiz and from the Cundinamarca Constitution. They could also see its potential for abolishing the practices that sustained unequal and abusive relations affecting them as Indians. This explains why, for example, throughout New Granada, both in the Santa Fe region under autonomist rule and in royalist Pasto, the liberal context and, in particular, the category of citizenship became a tool for some Indians to protest their submission to the priests. The fact that the consequences were similar once the relations between indigenous people and church authorities were exposed to liberal reform suggests that Indians' relationship to priests constituted another node of the politics inherent to all indigenous people in New Granada.[40]

Indian Politics, Sovereignty, and the Monarchial Restoration in New Granada

Both the Cádiz and Santa Fe experiments at liberal reform were short lived, interrupted by the return of the king to the throne in 1814. The consequences of the monarchical restoration were immediate: in Spain, Fernando revoked the constitution and made every effort to reinstitute absolutist rule, repressing and eradicating liberal institutions. Then he sent an army to pacify the American rebels. Pablo Morillo was the military leader of the expedition in charge of pacifying Venezuela and New Granada, and his army successfully brought the New Granadan rebels under monarchical control by June 1816.

At the moment when the armies of Morillo arrived in the New Granada highlands, the legal framework of the empire was once more, as in the context of the monarchical crisis, in flux. Military authorities represented the king and attempted to enforce the return to absolutism. Yet at every step they also had to negotiate the return of Spanish rule. In this context, indigenous people once again saw opportunities to reverse the changes underway in the previous years. A look at this process in the area surrounding Santa Fe yields further information about the politics of the Indians, particularly regarding legal representation, tribute, and the defense of native jurisdiction.

Precisely because the *protector de indios* had been at the core of the justice system in the Spanish monarchy, making available to Indians the legal advocate that could defend Indians' interests in court, along with its project to eradicate the category of "Indians," the Cundinamarca creole government had actually abolished the institution of *protector de indios* across the central highlands.[41]

Yet in September 1814, on the eve of the monarchical restoration, Luis José García, a civil fiscal agent, informed the Cundinamarca government that

[a]lthough from the beginning of the political transformation our system has worked incessantly to emancipate Indians from their unhappy state of abjection and dependence in which they have remained since the Conquest, it was never possible to establish by law (*fijar*) the rights of this wretched group of people; even worse, *we have had to constantly extend*

all the privileges that suppose and are proof of their inferiority. . . . One of these [privileges], *perhaps the one they consider most valuable,* is the institution of protector of the Indians [*Protectoría*], granted to them by the previous laws.[42]

These words resonate with Manuel Bernardo Alvarez's statement reproduced in the *Gaceta Ministerial de Cundinamarca* in March that same year, which expressed doubt about the legitimacy of the liberal laws in the eyes of indigenous people. Yet García's words went further. He accepted the failure of the "political transformation" the creoles had set out to achieve. And, unlike Alvarez, who questioned the liberal reform's absolute moral value as "just," García continued to uphold a view of the indigenous people as victims of Spanish domination. That is, García lamented the republic's incapacity to change the social reality with laws, and he significantly tied that incapacity to the Indians' rejection of the new laws, due to their attachment to the privileges they were granted, such as the institution of protector. Indigenous people had reclaimed powers for their legal representation in the courts and successfully limited the applicability of the republican changes at their heart.

Just as questions of legal representation expressed Indians' interest in defending their privileges, from the indigenous peoples' perspective, preserving autonomy (including maintaining their access to communal lands) hinged upon tribute payment. In the province of Mariquita, which had been incorporated into Cundinamarca in 1811, in the town of Coyaima the indigenous authorities and the priest in the towns of Coyaima and Natagaima were the most interested in defending tribute. After Fernando VII was restored to his throne, in 1816 they strategically defended the importance, for the Crown, of protecting indigenous communities by stating that these were the source of tribute and tribute was an institution that, first and foremost, benefited the king.

The goal of the Indian authorities' plea was to justify the need of undoing some of the most radical and corrosive reforms of the "intrusive government" (meaning the Cundinamarca Republic), which had abolished the institutions of *corregidor*, tribute, and the monopoly on cane-rum (*aguardiente estanco*).[43] Other changes instituted by the revolutionaries, like having white mayors (*alcaldes*) governing Indian towns, had already been declared illegal by Viceroy Francisco de Montalvo after the monarchical restoration. The Indians complained and had had to denounce on July 8, 1816, that "the government had hidden [the viceroy's] order," yet by 1817 the governor of the province of Neiva was still continuing to appoint government officials. The Indians claimed that this went against their right to elect their own authorities, those who would govern them, and who would collect tribute, which "we pay to the sovereign."[44] Professing their will to pay tribute as a practice that entitled them to the right of autonomy, the Indians in Coyaima were thus posing the question of who was to be the sovereign over them, insisting on their uneasiness with the creole republic's intention to govern them. Most importantly, their gesture to advocate for tribute was a way of performing and materializing the king's sovereignty while at the same time guaranteeing their own sovereignty in Coyaima.

In 1817 the complaints continued, now directed to Viceroy Juan Sámano, and denounced the transformation of Indian towns into *"parroquias de blancos,"* or white parishes. The Indian authorities wrote in their letter to the viceroy that Indians were leaving their towns, something that, of course, had a negative effect on the king's fiscal interests because "without the Indians no tribute would be paid." This, they stressed, brought about an even more worrisome result: "the king has lost his rights."[45] Here, too, recognizing the Crown's sovereignty went in tandem with a claim to communal sovereignty.

The indigenous authorities and the priest crafted an argument that downplayed self-interest. The presence of white people in the town was directly detrimental to the king. To justify the need to stop whites from settling in the town and "expel them from our land," and to give legitimacy to their plea, the Indian authorities also referred to a document of 1721 produced during the inspection (*visita*) of Fernando Saavedra, who had ordered Spanish people and mestizos to keep out of Indian territory. Further, they wrote, "[T]he law prohibits them from coming close to the Indians because they are troubled men leading dissolute lives (*hombres inquietos de mala vida*)." Offering to be loyal vassals, and reproducing the representation of non-Indians as dangerous to the colonial order based on a reference to the 1721 *visita* and the law of the *Recopilación*, the Indian authorities requested support for preventing the situation from getting worse and for enforcing the law.[46]

These conflicts illustrate the long-lasting impact of the change in government during the years when Cundinamarca had abolished Spanish rule and attempted to make Indians equal to the rest of the population. For indigenous people seeking to reverse or at least stop these consequences, earlier Spanish legislation—the 1680 *Recopilación*—continued to be a valuable legal ground for trying to receive attention and support from the restored monarchical authorities in New Granada.

The appeals also suggest that the Indian authorities who had lost their power over and control of the indigenous populations as a result of the revolution were attempting to reclaim these prerogatives during the years of the monarchical restoration. Their reference to eighteenth-century precedents was strategic because it allowed the Indian authorities to articulate their concerns—in representation of the community—with the interests of the government in restoring colonial rule. The Indian authorities were defending the institution of tribute as being in the best interests of the royal treasury and in their own interests as loyal vassals. In addition, the *corregidor* was presented as the legitimate authority for ensuring the proper collection of tribute for the king, with these funds also being a source of income for caciques and priests. Indeed, because a portion of tribute did not leave local communities and went to fund the construction of local churches, Indian authorities allied with priests to advocate in favor of its collection.[47]

A final case suggests the way in which tribute was central to the defense of indigenous communities and the terms of their reincorporation into the monarchical regime. Cocuy, one of the Indian towns that, as we have seen, revolted in 1811, later had been integrated into the jurisdiction of the Republic of Tunja and had accepted the Tunja constitution.[48] But in 1816 the Cocuy community declared loyalty to the royal authorities that, supported by an army, had arrived to restore absolutist rule. It may seem logical that the Indians swiftly acquiesced to the restoration and turned their backs on the republican project. After all, Morillo's armies were ruthlessly imposing the king's rule, and, to a certain extent, the association between the Indians in Cocuy and the royalist government after 1816 must have come into being with a certain degree of coercion. But at the same time, to guarantee their appeal, the royalists made promises of rewards to the Indians in exchange for their support.

This juncture in fact turned out to be favorable for the Indians in Cocuy (and others throughout the *corregimiento* of Chita)[49] in their efforts to restore their communal identities and press the royalists to recognize their significance as loyal vassals. The Indians had built a road between Cocuy and Los Llanos, that is, from the snow-covered mountain range where Cocuy is located to the eastern plains, a strategic location that connected New Granada with Venezuela, where the royalist armies of Morillo needed to establish a solid base for their pacification of rebels in both regions. These actions justified the Indians' request for an exemption from the payment of tribute. Indians argued that their efforts to support the royalist army with goods and labor were putting unbearable stress on their economies, making it impossible for them to add the tribute payment to their other contributions.[50]

But, significantly, indigenous people—in Cocuy as elsewhere—did not advocate for the abolition of tribute. They negotiated a reduction in the amount they would be required to pay or forgiveness of their unpaid tribute, but the abolition of the head tax that characterized them as a separate legal corporation of "Indians" was not part of their position. This was not about challenging tribute as such, but about recognizing that it had to be proportionate, just. As had been the practice based on the laws of the Indies, tribute payments might be modified if other circumstances supervened, such as the building of roads.

Indigenous people in New Granada's central highlands in the changing context of 1810–1819 defended tribute payment with the goals of protecting their territorial autonomy and the communal sovereignty of indigenous authorities and securing the rights of Indian commoners to legal protection on the basis of the legal framework that guaranteed them.

Conclusion

Following Napoleon's invasion of the Iberian Peninsula in 1807–1808, unrest grew in Spain's American territories. The initial reaction of most municipal councils to the need to defend the king's sovereignty against France was replaced in some places by a rejection of the authority of the resistance government that was attempting to maintain its grip on the transatlantic empire. Both in Spain and in Spanish America, liberalism became the language of rebellion and independence—against France in the first case and against Spain in the latter case. The goals of each of these projects of resistance led to the creation of different polities, an imperial nation and a group of republics, yet in both spaces constitution writing and the "constitution" of the new polities went hand in hand with reimagining the place of indigenous people within those experimental liberal societies. Though equality for all was a core value of the legal reforms in both Spain and New Granada, equality as it pertained to Indians had different meanings on either side of the Atlantic.

As we have seen, the Indians' diverse interpretations of the changing legal situation hinged upon the way indigenous rights had been construed and negotiated at the intersection of local and imperial contexts in earlier centuries. In this sense, neither the Cundinamarca nor the Cádiz legal reforms were radical breaks. Mapping out the connections between the legal changes and the concept of justice requires understanding local contexts and temporal backgrounds that explain the depth of Indians' impact on the regional politics across New Granada.[51]

In the territories governed by Cádiz and in those under the control of insurgent juntas, the conception and implementation of these legal reforms were halted by the return of Fernando VII to the throne in 1814. A look at the rise and fall of the liberal experiment in Santa Fe, in particular, has allowed us to get a grasp on the radical tensions that had emerged from the efforts to transform Indians into citizens. These tensions were at the core of the instability of the constitutional project, resulting from the ways in which indigenous people were interpreting the legal transformations imagined and in process of implementation.

Moreover, the Indians, on one hand, and the legal reformers in New Granada, on the other, misconstrued each other's conceptions of justice in this fluid context. At least in discourse, New Granadan legislators attempted to serve the interests of indigenous people by turning them into citizens. The Indians' recourse to protest and their engagement with the politics of the law during the war signaled a different understanding of the context and shaped the possibility for social change.

The reactions of indigenous people who lived in royalist and insurgent regions to the liberal reforms suggest that, taken as a whole, indigenous communities in New Granada were more adaptable to the Cádiz strand of liberalism than to the liberal experiments led by creoles. Indigenous people were less keen to accept the creoles' pretension to subsume them into a polity that granted sovereignty effectively to the creoles, while their own forms of communal sovereignty were coming into attack and faced elimination from those same creoles who claimed to represent them. Indeed, the Spanish liberals and the royalists across the Americas seem to have succeeded in introducing the Cádiz Constitution as a document that upheld the sovereignty of the monarch and, as such, created more opportunities for them to defend their communal rights.

A comparative view that puts the case of New Granada in a hemispheric context shows important contrasts. In North America, the United States did not view liberalism or republicanism as a project that entailed the integration of indigenous people as citizens. Another case in Spanish America, Peru, shows that Indians rejected tribute as an exploitative extraction in the context of the war before 1812. This was the case in part because they resented the pressure exerted over the communities by officials trying to expand revenue to sustain the royalist army. Aside from the regional histories of indigenous politics at the base of each of these different cases, an important particularity of Peru lies in the incidence of the military forces coming from Buenos Aires to the Peruvian highlands with their own project for tribute abolition. This generated one more crack within the social structure and created space for indigenous people to radicalize to the point of materializing an anticolonial struggle that instead of defending tribute, as in New Granada, rejected it.[52]

In the cases studied here, from 1810 onward in the monarchy's crisis, through the independence wars, and after the monarchical restoration, tribute's material and symbolic power was potentialized, as it was put to the test of being at the center of two opposing forces. On one hand, Indians were in favor of withholding tribute as a means of defending Indian identity, claiming rights to state protection, and preserving territorial autonomy. This was common both to the royalist and to the insurgent regions; even when Indian commoners and caciques were divided on their interests, or when Indians negotiated the amount to be paid, tribute as an institution that legitimated Indians' particular rights was not in question.

On the other hand, in Santa Fe, creoles viewed tribute as a pernicious institution that perpetuated Indian inferiority, and their project was to dissolve it in favor of equality and integration. This contention did not end either with the monarchical restoration or with independence. Once creoles founded the Republic of Colombia in 1819, they, again, began a campaign to outlaw tribute. Yet the research presented here illustrates why it is important to treat the period 1810–1819 in its own terms and not simply as a prelude to independence.[53] The conflicts that emerged in that decade, which developed at the local level and in conjunction with legal transformations of imperial and regional scale, were crucial for the understanding that indigenous people and creoles had of Indianness and of the limits and potentials in reinventing the institutions upon which it was founded.

ACKNOWLEDGMENTS

Many thanks to Magali Carrillo, Daniel Gutiérrez, Francisco Ortega, Brian Owensby, Txema Portillo, Richard Ross, Clément Thibaud, Sinclair Thomson, and Isidro Vanegas for their generous engagement with me on the themes developed in the essay.

NOTES

1 The Cundinamarca Constitution—Art. 1, Tit. 1—preserved its "primitive and original" name in the act of recovering rights that it maintained had been dormant for three hundred years. Daniel Gutiérrez, *Un Nuevo Reino. Geografía política, pactismo y diplomacia durante el interregno en Nueva Granada (1808–1816)* (Bogotá: Universidad Externado de Colombia, 2010), 247–48. María Teresa Calderón and Carlos Villamizar, "El sistema adoptado en la Nueva Granada: 'Liberal' como concepto durante la consolidación del orden republicano (1808–1850)," in *La aurora de la libertad*, ed. Javier Fernández Sebastián (Madrid: Marcel Pons, 2012), esp. 190–91. This process of replacing colonial names with indigenous names was widespread across Spanish America during this same period and later on when the independent republics were founded. See Rebecca Earle, *The Return of the Native: Indians and Mythmaking in Spanish America, 1810–1930* (Durham, NC: Duke University Press, 2007), esp. ch. 2.

2 Archivo General de la Nación de Colombia (hereinafter AGNC), Archivo Anexo, Historia 11, ff. 221–23.

3 The most recent reinterpretation of the events following Fernando's return to the throne, including the military campaign against insurgents and its legacies in the independence of Colombia, is Daniel Gutiérrez, *La Restauración en la Nueva Granada (1815–1819)* (Bogotá: Universidad del Externado, 2016). Gutiérrez argues that for New Granada, the years 1815–1819 are the ones that define this period, previously known as the "Reconquista," or reconquest.

4 I generally use the term "Indians," referring to a legal category that encompassed the descendants of native peoples across Spanish America, at times referring to them as "natives" to translate the word *naturales* when it is used in archival documents.

5 Gabriel Paquette, "Introduction: Liberalism in the Early Nineteenth-Century Iberian World," *History of European Ideas* 41, no. 2 (2015), DOI: 10.1080/01916599.2014.914312. See also, Brooke Larson, *Trials of Nation Making: Liberalism, Race, and Ethnicity in the Andes, 1810–1910* (New York: Cambridge University Press, 2004).

6 The historiography includes Cesáreo de Armellada, *La Causa Indígena Americana en las Cortes de Cádiz* (Caracas: Universidad Católica Andrés Bello, 1979); Karen Caplan, "The Legal Revolution in Town Politics: Oaxaca and Yucatán, 1812–1825," *Hispanic American Historical Review* 83, no. 2 (2003), 255–93; Jordana Dym, "'Our Pueblos, Fractions with No Central Unity': Municipal Sovereignty in Central America, 1808–1821," *Hispanic American Historical Review* 86, no. 3 (2006), 431–66; Marcela Echeverri, "Race, Citizenship, and the Cádiz Constitution in Popayán (New Granada)," in *The Rise of Constitutional Government in the Iberian Atlantic World: The Impact of the Cádiz Constitution of 1812*, eds. Scott Eastman and Natalia Sobrevilla Perea (Tuscaloosa: University of Alabama Press, 2015), 91–110; Claudia Guarisco, *Los indios del valle de México y la construcción de una nueva sociabilidad política, 1770–1835* (Zinacantepec: El Colegio Mexiquense, 2003); Claudia Guarisco, *La reconstitución del espacio político indígena: Lima y el Valle de México durante la crisis de la monarquía española* (Castelló de la Plana: Universitat Jaume I, 2011); Federica Morelli, *Territorio o Nación. Reforma y disolución del espacio imperial en Ecuador, 1765–1830* (Madrid: Centro de Estudios Políticos y Constitucionales, 2005); Scarlett O'Phelan, "Ciudadanía y etnicidad en las cortes de Cádiz," *Elecciones* 1 (2002), 165–85; José M. Portillo, "Proyección historiográfica de Cádiz. Entre España y México," *Historia Crítica* 54, no. 3 (2014), 49–74; Jaime Rodríguez, "Las primeras elecciones constitucionales en el Reino de Quito, 1809–1814 y 1821–1822," *Revista Procesos* 14 (1999), 13–52; Jaime Rodríguez, "Ciudadanos de la nación española: los indígenas y las elecciones constitucionales en el Reino de Quito," in *La mirada esquiva: Reflexiones históricas sobre la interacción del estado y la ciudadanía en los Andes (Bolivia, Ecuador y Perú), siglo XIX*, ed. Marta Irurozqui (Madrid: Consejo Superior de Investigaciones Científicas, 2005), 41–64; Maria Luisa Soux, "Tributo, insurgencia y movimientos sociales," in *El complejo proceso hacia la independencia de Charcas (1808–1826). Guerra, ciudadanía, conflictos locales y participación indígena en Oruro* (La Paz: Instituto Francés de Estudios Andinos, 2010), 219–83; Martha Terán, "Los tributarios de la Nueva España frente a la abolición y a la restauración de los tributos, 1810–1822," in *Los indígenas en la Independencia y en la Revolución Mexicana*, eds. Miguel León-Portilla and Alicia Mayer (México: UNAM/INAH/Fideicomiso Teixidor, 2010), 250–88.

7 See Isidro Vanegas, *El constitucionalismo fundacional* (2nd ed; Bogotá: Ediciones Plural, 2014); Gutiérrez, *Un Nuevo Reino*; María Teresa Calderón and Clément Thibaud, *La magestad de los pueblos en la Nueva Granada y Venezuela, 1780–1832* (Bogotá: Taurus, Instituto Francés de Estudios Andinos, Universidad Externado de Colombia, 2010). Francisco Ortega writes about the importance of the New Granadan constitutions in "Ariadne's Thread: Navigating Postcolonial Spanish America's Labyrinth through Constitution Building in New Granada (1809–1812)," in *Constitutionalism, Legitimacy, and Power: Nineteenth-Century Experiences*, eds. Kelly L. Grotke and Markus J. Prutsch (Oxford: Oxford University Press, 2014), 225–40. Around one hundred provincial constitutions were created across Spanish America in the nineteenth century. Other examples of Spanish American constitutions are the constitutions of Venezuela, Chile, and Quito. See Víctor Uribe-Urán, "Insurgentes de provincia: Tunja, Nueva Granada, y el constitucionalismo en el mundo hispánico en la década de 1810," *Historia y Memoria* 5 (2012): 30; Marta Lorente and José M. Portillo, *El momento gaditano. La constitución en el orbe hispánico (1808–1826)* (Madrid: Congreso de los Diputados, 2011), 88.

8 An exception for New Granada is Elizabeth Karina Salgado Hernández, "Indios, ciudadanía y tributo en la independencia neogranadina. Antioquia (1810–1816)," *Transhumante. Revista Americana de Historia Social* 4 (2014): 26–43. For Mexico, see Brian Owensby, "Comunidades indígenas y gobierno en la época de la independencia. Reflexiones sobre antecedents virreinales y transformaciones decimonónicas," in *Declaraciones de independencia. Los textos fundamentales de las independencias americanas*, eds. Alfredo Avila, Jordana Dym, and Erika Pani (Mexico: El Colegio de México/Universidad Nacional Autónoma de México, 2013), 81–108.

9 Legal pluralism was a general trait of governance in early modern empires. As Richard Ross and Philip Stern argue in "Reconstructing Early Modern Notions of Legal Pluralism," in *Legal Pluralism and Empires, 1500–1850*, eds. Lauren Benton and Richard Ross (New York: NYU Press, 2013), 110, "legal pluralism [w]as essential to the social organization of politics." See also Jack Greene, "Negotiated Authorities: The Problem of Governance in the Extended Polities of the Early Modern Atlantic World," in *Negotiated Authorities: Essays in Colonial Political Constitutional History* (Charlottesville: University Press of Virginia, 1994), ch. 1; Jane Burbank and Fred Cooper, "Rules of Law, Politics of Empire," in *Legal Pluralism and Empires*, ch. 11.

10 Some native people continued to live at the margins of the empire, engaging partially with the colonial state and in a range of relations—sometimes of superiority—with the Spanish colonists. A paradigmatic case in South America are the Mapuche, who lived in the territories that later became Chile and Argentina. In New Granada the Guajira Peninsula, where the Wayuu people live, is an example of a frontier. See Forrest Hylton, "'The Sole Owners of the Land': Empire, War, and Authority in the Guajira Peninsula, 1761–1779," *Atlantic Studies* 12, no. 3 (2016): 315–44.

11 Jane Burbank and Fred Cooper, *Empires in World History: Power and the Politics of Difference* (Princeton, NJ: Princeton University Press, 2010), 258–63.

12 Lauren Benton and Richard Ross, "Empires and Legal Pluralism: Jurisdiction, Sovereignty, and Political Imagination in the Early Modern World," in *Legal Pluralism and Empires*, 12.

13 As Burbank and Cooper argue in "Rules of Law, Politics of Empire," in *Legal Pluralism and Empires*, 285, "The idea of universal law—that laws are to be exactly the same for every subject—is itself a creation and one that 'contradicts' the inequalities everywhere present in social life at all times." In the New Granada case, indigenous people were actively defending their right to parity *and* social difference, a stance that not only questioned the legitimacy or applicability of the liberal reform's underlying goal of equality but also, most importantly, suited their interests.

14 See *Recopilación de las leyes de los reynos de las Indias* ([1681, Madrid: Viuda de Joaquín de Ibarra, 1791] Madrid: Facsimile reprint, 1941), Book 6, Title 4: "De las reducciones y los pueblos," Title 5: "De los tributos y tazas de los indios," and Title 6: "De los protectores de indios."

15 Brian Owensby, "Between Justice and Economics: 'Indians' and Reformism in Eighteenth-Century Spanish Imperial Thought," in *Legal Pluralism and Empires*, 143–69. Tamar Herzog shows why and how in this period links between negative underlying assumptions about collective use and backwardness justified "undermining rights of certain sectors." See Herzog, "Did European Law Turn American? Territory, Property, and Rights in an Atlantic World," in *New Horizons in Spanish Colonial Law: Contributions to Transnational Early Modern Legal History*, eds. Thomas Duve and Heikki Pihlajamäki (Frankfurt: Max Planck Institute for European Legal History, 2015), 89–91.

16 On the 1781 Comunero Rebellion, see John L. Phelan, *The People and the King: The Comunero Revolution in Colombia* (Madison: University of Wisconsin Press, 1978).

17 Pedro Fermín de Vargas, *Pensamientos Políticos Siglo XVII y XVIII* (Bogotá: Nueva Biblioteca Colombiana de Cultura, 1986), 168–95. The historiographical consensus today is critical of earlier assessments of the eighteenth century as the moment of the emergence of a national identity that would lead toward independence. See, for example, Jeremy Adelman, "Iberian Passages: Continuity and Change in the South Atlantic," in *The Age of Revolutions in Global Context, c.1760–1840*, eds. David Armitage and Sanjay Subrahmanyam (New York: Palgrave Macmillan, 2010), 59–82. Aside from denouncing the Spaniards as "intruders," Vargas also claimed that the Indians were the original owners of the land, an argument that potentially conflicted with his own position as a creole. Simón Bolívar expressed this tension clearly in his 1815 Jamaica Letter: "We are, moreover, neither Indian nor European, but a species midway between the legitimate proprietors of this country and the Spanish usurpers. In short, though Americans by birth we derive our rights from Europe, and we have to assert these rights against the rights of the natives, and at the same time we must defend ourselves against the invaders."

18 AGNC, Archivo Anexo, Historia 11, ff. 221–23.

19 Already in January of 1809 the peninsular authorities had declared the equality of all parts of the monarchy. Clément Thibaud, "Un Nouveau Monde de républiques. De l'empire aux Etats sans roi en Colombie et Venezuela, 1790–1820" (unpublished manuscript), ch. 5, explores the negative portrayal of the Cádiz liberal reforms in the New Granadan press.

20 José M. Portillo describes the late eighteenth century as a period of a search to transform the Spanish Catholic monarchy into an imperial state, and he studies the impact of the realization of that goal on indigenous people in Tlaxcala. See *Fuero Indio: Tlaxcala y la identidad territorial entre la monarquía imperial y la república nacional, 1787–1824* (Mexico D.F.: El Colegio de México, 2014).

21 This, of course, is not exclusive to New Granada.

22 AGNC, Archivo Anexo, Historia 11, doc. 15, f. 187R.

23 Enslaved people in New Granada's Pacific Lowlands also formed juntas in this juncture. See Marcela Echeverri, *Indian and Slave Royalists in the Age of Revolution: Reform, Revolution, and Royalism in the Northern Andes, 1780–1825* (New York: Cambridge University Press, 2016), 169–70.

24 AGNC, Archivo Anexo, Justicia T. 9, carpeta 1, ff. 78V, 85R-V. In response to this last request by the priest, in August the fiscal ordered the capture of those who had been accused of being involved in the disturbances.

25 AGNC, Archivo Anexo, Historia 12, doc. 9, f. 542.

26 AGNC, Archivo Anexo, Historia 11, ff. 221–23.

27 AGNC, Archivo Anexo, Historia 11, ff. 221–23.

28 AGNC, Archivo Anexo, Historia 11, doc. 15, f. 187R.

29 AGNC, Archivo Anexo, Historia 11, f. 225. On conflicts among provincial juntas in New Granada, see Gutiérrez, *Un Nuevo Reino*.

30 *Gaceta Ministerial de Cundinamarca* no. 163 (March 17, 1814), 127.

31 José María Espinoza, *Memorias de un abanderado. Recuerdos de la Patria Boba. 1810–1819* (Bogotá: El Tradicionalista, 1876), 33–34.

32 *Gaceta Ministerial de Cundinamarca* no. 163 (March 17, 1814), 127.

33 Before 1812, citizenship had been linked to *vecindad* and vassalage; being a *vecino* or citizen had a local connotation that linked people to a particular city or town. Tamar Herzog, *Defining Nations: Immigrants and Citizens in Early Modern Spain and Spanish America* (New Haven, CT: Yale University Press, 2003), chs. 2 and 7. Cristóbal Aljovín, "Monarquía o república: 'ciudadano' y 'vecino' en Iberoamérica, 1750–1850," *Jahrbuch für Geschichte Lateinamerikas* 45 (2008), 31–55; Marta Irurozqui, "De cómo el vecino hizo al ciudadano y de cómo el ciudadano conservó al vecino. Charcas, 1808–1830," in *Revolución, independencia y las nuevas naciones de América*, ed. Jaime Rodríguez (Madrid: Fundación MAPFRE TAVERA, 2005), 451–84. Article 18 of the constitution read as follows: "Those are Spanish citizens who are born of Spanish parents in any part of the Spanish dominions, and reside in the said dominions." Chapter 4, "On Spanish Citizens," article 18 in *Constitution of the Spanish Monarchy* (Philadelphia:

Palmer, 1814), 6. In Spanish the article says, "Son ciudadanos aquellos españoles que por ambas líneas traen su origen de los dominios españoles de ambos hemisferios y están avecindados en cualquier pueblo de los mismos dominios." The constitution used "Spanish" to refer to all because the Cortes had prohibited the use of any denomination other than Spanish or Spanish American. In practice, however, the term "Indian" continued to be used in various contexts (as well as in the Cortes).

34 The news of the beginning of the Cortes sessions in Cádiz in September 1810 did not arrive in Cartagena until January 1811. Clément Thibaud has also referred to this dialectical relationship between the New Granadan and Cádiz constitutional processes in "Un Nouveau Monde de républiques," 213–19. Josep Fradera, *La nación imperial (1750–1918)* (Barcelona: Edhasa, 2015), xvii, stresses simultaneity and develops the argument in the following way: "The idea of political rights that made all individuals equal, profoundly revolutionary and foundational to the modern world, was a discovery—almost simultaneous—of people in the metropolis and in the colonies."

35 "Bando del virrey, publicando el de la Regencia de la Isla de León, libertando del tributo a los indios," in *Colección de documentos para la historia de la guerra de independencia en México de 1808 a 1821*, Tomo II, coord., Virginia Guedea and Alfredo Avila (México D.F.: Universidad Nacional Autónoma de México, 2007), 2. Marie Laure Rieu-Millan, *Los diputados americanos en las Cortes de Cádiz* (Madrid: Consejo Superior de Investigaciones Científicas, 1990), 117. The Cortes also discussed the abolition of the *mita* and *yanaconazgo*.

36 Rieu-Millan, *Los diputados americanos*, 121.

37 Portillo, *Fuero Indio*, 68.

38 In Caribbean New Granada, the royalists continued to rule in Santa Marta and Riohacha, also in Panama, and in the Kingdom of Quito, including Pasto.

39 Archivo Histórico Nacional de España, Consejos 21674, exp. 1, doc. 5. See Echeverri, *Indian and Slave Royalists*, ch. 4.

40 De Armellada, *La causa indígena Americana*, 13–14; Echeverri, *Indian and Slave Royalists*, 145–50; Guillermo Sosa, *Representación e independencia, 1810–1816* (Bogotá: Instituto Colombiano de Antropología e Historia, 2006), 108.

41 In contrast, in Pasto the protector Gallardo was a crucial mediator for furthering the transformations of indigenous peoples' rights within liberal reform. Echeverri, *Indian and Slave Royalists*, ch. 4.

42 AGNC, Archivo Anexo, Gobierno T. 25, f. 520. Emphasis added.

43 AGNC, Archivo Anexo, Gobierno T. 29, f. 952r-v. Gutiérrez, *Un Nuevo Reino*, 254–58.

44 The interesting wording in the document is "que pagamos a la soberanía." AGNC, Archivo Anexo, Gobierno T. 35, f. 516v-517r.

45 AGNC, Archivo Anexo, Gobierno T. 35, f. 517r-v.

46 AGNC, Archivo Anexo, Gobierno T. 35, f. 519r.

47 See *Recopilación de las leyes de los reynos de las Indias*, Book 6, Title 5: "De los tributos y tazas de los indios," Ley xxxj, p. 213.

48 Nubia Fernanda Espinoza Moreno, "La cultura política de los indígenas del norte de la provincia de Tunja durante la reconquista española," *Anuario Colombiano de Historia Social y de la Cultura* 37, no. 1 (2010), 126, 140.

49 Chita included the following towns: Boavita, Guacamayas, Chiscas, Cocuy, Güicán, and la Salina.

50 AGNC, Colonia, Tributos, T 60, 22, d. 26, f. 553. Espinoza Moreno, "La cultura política de los indígenas del norte de la provincia de Tunja," 121–48.

51 On precedents to the liberal reform in Bolivia, see Rossana Barragán, "'Indios esclavos': en torno a la mita minera y la igualdad, 1790–1812," in *L'atlantique Revolutionnaire: Une Perspective Ibéro-Américain*, eds. Clément Thibaud, Gabriel Entin, Alejandro Gómez, and Federica Morelli (Paris: Perséides, 2013), 151–78.

52 David Klassen, "'Governed Only by Their Liberty': Indigenous Rebellion in Huánuco, 1812" (unpublished manuscript).

53 Tristan Platt studied the rise of creole-liberalism in independent Bolivia, arguing that communities invested in the pact of reciprocity as a defense of what he terms "ethnocidal liberalism." Platt's argument does not see the pact of reciprocity as enshrined in a legal framework, however. See *Estado Boliviano y ayllu andino: tierra y tributo en el Norte de Potosí* (Lima: Instituto de Estudios Peruanos, 1982); Tristan Platt, "Liberalism and Ethnocide," *History Workshop Journal* 17 (1984): 3–18.

PART III

Concluding Perspectives

9

In Defense of Ignorance

Frameworks for Legal Politics in the Atlantic World

LAUREN BENTON

In 1834, in a place the English called Brisbane Water, on the edge of New South Wales, a large group of Aborigines attacked the house of settler Alfred Jacques and carried off most of its contents, in the process injuring Jacques's convict servant. It was reported that one of the Aborigines declared that they, and not whites, would be "master now." One defendant stated at trial that the raiders "had a right to steal what they thought proper," and their defense lawyer suggested a motive: the whites were squatters on Aboriginal land. In analyzing this episode, Bruce Kercher concluded that the Aborigines were performing a legal act, one that another historian of Aboriginal Australia characterized as "judicial violence."[1] Aborigines were looting the Brisbane Water house in part to proclaim their authority over the area. The raid fit within a broader pattern of frontier violence in which attacks by Aborigines against whites responded to settler incursions and answered specific acts of white violence. The attack was punitive, in other words: an assertion of jurisdiction.

The Brisbane Water case, unfolding far from the Atlantic arena of Iberian-English-Indian law that is the subject of this volume, helps to highlight two points. The first is the dubious value and methodological challenges of historical questions about when and how mutual understanding of legal behavior developed. We can speculate that Aborigines and settlers failed to understand each other's law, but the evidence also suggests the work of studied ignorance—for Aborigines, a purposeful disregard for settler sovereignty and for settlers, a willful refusal to recognize Aboriginal claims to local authority. Historians of frontier violence in New South Wales have turned toward sketching the legal logic of encounters and away from the goal of recovering elusive and some-times purposefully hidden Aboriginal or settler legal understandings.[2]

The second point is that legal interactions in the Americas developed in the context of a chronologically longer and geographically wider phenomenon of interpolity law.[3] Indians as well as Europeans were engaged in interpolity interactions framed by law well before, and well after, their encounters in the early modern Atlantic world. It is important to consider continuities, as well as to evaluate how interpolity relations in the Americas may have influenced broader patterns in the Atlantic world, and beyond.

This essay takes up both themes. I suggest that "intelligibility" is not the same as "understanding," and that it is possible to glean evidence of the first without speculating about the second. A legal landscape can be "intelligible" to actors when only some of its features become knowable through experience and the application of analogy. After exploring this perspective, I evaluate some alternatives to a search for understanding of law, ultimately returning to the comparative context of European-indigenous legal interactions.

It may seem churlish to comment on a volume about legal intelligibility by suggesting that we ought to jettison a search for legal "understanding." But I think it is important not to assume that historical actors were "straining to understand each other's notions of justice" and to trace instead when and how they were able to read the legal landscape, often fairly well, and often with other goals in mind.[4] As the rich and varied chapters in this volume show, legal interlocutors were maneuvering for advantage, in the process creating new discourses and approaches to law even as they cited tradition and angled for continued autonomy. The chapters' evidence slips around the edges and through the cracks of the frame of legal understanding and moves towards some wider implications for the study of the structured legal politics of colonial encounters.

The Trouble with Understanding

Historians are very aware of the difficulties of characterizing "understanding"—what historical actors believed, thought, perceived, or knew. The sources we have are not just a little insufficient to the task; they are in most cases startlingly inadequate. We can tell something about what people did if we are lucky enough to have fairly good sources; if we have extraordinary sources, we can tell a little about what they claimed to be thinking, or about what they claimed others were thinking. Even then, most historians will admit, we cannot with any degree of confidence represent what historical actors understood. We know this in part because we are familiar with the challenges of characterizing "understanding" in the present, when more varied and extensive sources are far more accessible. Further, we know that even seemingly virtuoso legal performances might not accurately reflect legal understanding. Historical actors sometimes sought advantage through feigned mastery, choosing for effect to perform demonstrations of legal acumen with a degree of bluster.

It is even more difficult still to describe an *absence* of understanding. It is often impossible to discern whether social actors miss cues because they hold strong beliefs about the way things ought to be; because they are simply unable to interpret signs correctly; or because they find it more advantageous to pretend that they are naïve, or even stupid. Like feigned mastery, studied ignorance is a familiar and often favored legal strategy. As Bourdieu argued, studied ignorance is not just something that individual actors may find valuable to adopt as a posture. The legitimacy of repeating social interactions may *require* studied ignorance on the part of participants. The example Bourdieu gives is the role of studied ignorance in gift exchange; ignoring the reciprocal nature of the exchange over the long run is essential to performing and recognizing such cultural attributes as generosity, deference, and good taste.[5] Accounting for the relative value of gifts and foregrounding the obligation to give would undermine the lived experience of gift exchange as a spontaneous sign of sociability and friendship.

Just as anthropologists regard culture as practice and the contents of culture as knowable only in the doing, legal anthropologists insist that law evolves through practice. This means that norms make spectacularly bad objects of analysis. Even though legal actors refer to norms as immutable, their views of norms emerge through conflicts and social interactions. This is not to say that law does not have special characteristics, or that it is impossible (or uninteresting) to trace legal change through the study of pronouncements about fundamental values or doctrines. But an emphasis on law as culture points us away from both the study of "black letter" law and the quest to characterize various groups' understanding of law. It urges instead the close analysis of patterned strategic behavior that is simultaneously cultural and, through its repetition, institutional in effect. The anthropologist Lawrence Rosen puts it this way:

> In each instance, law is so inextricably entwined in culture that, for all its specialized capabilities, it may, indeed, best be seen not simply as a mechanism for attending to disputes or enforcing decisions, not solely as articulated rules or as evidence of differential power, and not even as the reification of personal values or superordinate beliefs, but as *a framework for ordered relationships*, an orderliness that is itself dependent on its attachment to all the other realms of its adherents' lives.[6]

Rosen points to the importance of studying "institutional structures" that develop deep associations with specific "orientations" guiding improvised legal strategies.[7]

This approach takes us back to an appreciation of feigned mastery and studied ignorance in legal interactions. Just as in gift exchange participants want the gift to stand for friendship rather than signal an economic transaction, in legal interactions, historical actors placed a high value on the appearance of justice and displayed a formal tolerance for unjust outcomes—even rather a lot of them. Studied ignorance about the fact that legal processes were stacked against one group, in other words, was often key to the recognition of legal authority as legitimate.[8] At the same time, because we are not talking about law as sets of norms or rules but rather law as practice, the legal framework becomes subject to change. Routine acts may lose legitimacy over time; jurisdictional boundaries may shift, creating new sources of legitimate legal authority; and seemingly fixed attachments by a group to a particular way of doing law may give way to adaptation and importation of legal processes that only a few years before would have appeared impossible.

Historians have already applied this perspective in a number of key studies of plural legal politics in the Atlantic world.[9] As Jenny Pulsipher notes in her chapter in this volume, one of the most influential histories of European-Indian interactions, Richard White's *Middle Ground*, offered a possible, if flawed, solution to the analytical challenges of knowing what historical actors did or did not understand about one an-other's law. Analyzing French and Indian interactions in a zone where neither side held a monopoly on violence, White characterized certain rapprochements as arising from "creative . . . misunderstandings." He as-serted that groups of French traders and Indians found ways to man-age law across political communities even though they appeared to have little comprehension of each other's law. For example, when a group of Algonquian Indians killed two Frenchmen, the Algonquians wanted to give the French Indians as slaves to compensate other Frenchmen for the loss. The French, in contrast, demanded punishment of all partici-pants in the murder. What followed was a negotiated resolution that defied legal logic on both sides: two Indians who may or may not have taken part in the attack were executed. That result clashed with French ideas of punishment as ideally restricted to guilty parties, and it also contrasted sharply with Algonquians' view that the most appropriate re-sponse to the crime was restitution, not punishment.[10]

A number of the chapters in this volume provide examples that match White's account of arrangements arising not from understanding but from negotiations and improvised accommodation. Nancy Gallman and Alan Taylor, for example, detail instances when Iroquois killed settlers and "colonial authorities had to accept" presents as restitution rather than "try, convict, and execute native suspects."[11] Craig Yirush discusses a case in which Pennsylvanians were seeking a way to find and pun-ish the perpetrators of a murder of three traders; the Indians suggested compensation instead.[12] In these cases, as in the Pays d'en haut encoun-ters analyzed by White, the inability of one group to assert power consis-tently over others created the conditions for creative compromise.

These examples appear to move beyond White's emphasis on cre-ative misunderstanding to the extent that the authors do not imply, as his analysis does at times, that there were insiders who had a clear un-derstanding of the law. In the settings White analyzes, we would need to be persuaded that there was a clear "French" or "Indian" way of doing justice, as well as that individual Frenchmen and Indians present had a well-developed sense of what "their" law required. For Europeans, we know that ideas circulating on the edges of empire were often very vague. Most expedition commanders or settlement heads were not law trained, and they administered law very often on the basis of what they could recall about legal practices at home, what they had heard from others about law, and what they imagined the expectations of their superiors to be. They did not simply improvise to create variants from a baseline set of legal practices and standards; they often gestured only vaguely at precedents they thought they knew.[13]

Uncertainty did not flow from simple ignorance of the law. In most cases, there was actually no clearly defined body of legal doctrine or practice for historical actors to master and attempt to reproduce. We must thus be very careful about characterizing "English and Spanish notions of justice" or referencing more specific legal knowledge, such as a "Portuguese understanding of authority."[14] The point I am making comes across clearly in recent studies of English colonial law that emphasize the diversity of colonies' timing in adopting English common law. Whereas earlier studies sought to gauge how the law of English colonies differed from law in England, historians now recognize that much of English legal history remains opaque, and that no seventeenth-century colonist possessed a fulsome knowledge of "English law."[15] Yirush agrees, noting the fallacy of scholarship that "reads as if there existed a consensus on the justice of dispossession . . . in the Anglo-American world."[16] It may be tempting to assert that there was no such uncertainty in Spanish America, where the Laws of the Indies were supposed to be applied everywhere and where the crown dictated certain institutional consistencies in colonial courts. Yet regional variations in the administration of law were in fact striking, and they flowed from different local political conditions as well as from flexibility built into Spanish institutional designs.[17] Karen Graubart reminds us in her chapter in this volume that diversity was not just a condition of "Spanish" law but an ideology of rule in a composite polity that recognized "that law came from many sites, including the customary law of the incorporated subjects."[18]

More broadly, neither colonists nor Indians composed a monolithic group in interpreting law. As the articles in this volume show, legal encounters in the Americas were driven by a diversity of factions on both sides. As Brian Owensby and Richard Ross put it, "the term 'community' implies a misleading stability." Gallman and Taylor emphasize that colonial officials had to represent the scope of their jurisdiction as greater than it in fact was when they were writing home or crafting treaties that would be sent home. They operated within the confines of "the reality of limited power." Bradley Dixon, also in this volume, catalogs the array of arrangements of Indians with the English colony of Virginia. Emerging from these accounts is a portrait of a fluid, plural legal order encompassing multiple European and Indian polities, a complex jurisdictional field that was in continual flux.[19]

The chapters confirm, too, a broader finding in the literature that Indians and Europeans in most cases learned very quickly to recognize the legal routines of their interlocutors, however foreign they may have seemed, and to size them up in crafting legal strategies. Jenny Hale Pulsipher, for example, traces adjustments by both the English and the Indians in practices around the sale of rights to land and observes that "Native and English land laws and practices became mutually intelligible fairly soon after contact." Yirush shows that adjustments took place on both sides, with Indians sometimes insisting on Indian protocol, and "English governors and negotiators using Native rituals and metaphors." Graubart finds that Indians "rapidly learned the new legal language" without giving up their own legal forms. Rather than representing corrosive and irreversible legal change, such adaptations often extended the autonomy of Indian polities and provided them with a wider array of tools for deflecting settler encroachments.[20]

Taken together, these findings recommend a clear distinction between "intelligibility," defined by the ability to act strategically in a shifting legal field, and "understanding," defined by the capacity to grasp legal concepts. The chapters present clear and convincing evidence of flexible adjustments to quickly perceived legal constraints, with or without evidence of a grasp of principles or norms behind those constraints. It seems clear that we can appreciate the speed and sophistication with which interlocutors came to read the contours of one another's legal systems without speculating about the degree to which their resulting strategies reflected genuine understanding. Gallman and Taylor arrive at a similar conclusion and argue that "officials deferred to native justice despite not fully understanding its meanings."[21]

It is easy to slip into language that conflates understanding with strategic reading of others' legal behavior or assumes the existence and discoverability of underlying norms. Herzog appears to adopt a perspective of law as informed by flexible conventions and shaped by legal strategy in her emphasis on actors' "expectations" of what was "legitimate and possible," and she uses this lens to illuminate the way Portuguese represented interactions with Indians as signs of alliance and vassalage, and to identify Indians' pursuit of other ends. But in framing her case study, Herzog also collapses conventions into "rules" that were "silently operating in the background" to give legal actions their meaning and establish ways of defining justice. This is a leap, or at least a large hop. As we see in Portuguese and Indian recognition of alliance and protection as categories of legal interaction (more on these categories below), there was often nothing culturally proprietary or morally scripted about conventions. In any case, historians have dull tools with which to uncover supposedly determinative "normative structures" operating in deep background to legal behavior and utterances.[22]

Owensby and Ross wander a bit off course in a similar way when they state that "law became intelligible as historical actors began to appreciate the values and history behind a legal idea." For them, understanding necessarily preceded mutual intelligibility, while intelligibility was a precondition for jurisdictional politics and strategic engagements with law. Their overview of European-indigenous legal interactions begins with a phase of misunderstanding, moves toward deepening understanding through repeated interactions, and resolves in an imperfect understanding by groups of the "other's legal commitments and interventions." This framework contrasts rather markedly with the analysis of strategic interactions and adaptive legal strategies described elsewhere in the first chapter, and in the volume more generally, as constituting what we might call intelligibility-through-practice.[23]

A number of the chapters, too, explicitly turn on its head the notion that understanding is a precondition or accompaniment to intelligibility. Social actors are instead shown to engage in legal behavior while holding what we can only assume to be a wide variety of levels of understanding. As they developed legal strategies, they began to use the language, rituals, and routines of interlocutors' law, and these improvisations generated novel legal forms. Pulsipher calls these creations the result of "hybrid" legalities. Graubart refers to the "prolific entanglement of legal discourses" in the Andes. And Marcela Echeverri remind us that Indians in the late eighteenth century used "the very channels, means, and arguments that the empire had granted them and which they had continually revitalized for centuries."[24] The chapters place on bright display an array of compelling evidence that historical actors not only utilized the legal discourses and categories of other polities in sophisticated ways but did so, ironically, in the service of a conservative aim of avoiding change and preserving legal autonomy.

Cultivated Ambiguity

We might leave things here, with a cautionary note about the difficulties of studying understanding and norms, and an exhortation to disconnect "intelligibility" from a genealogy of "conceptions of justice." But it is possible to say more, and to point with more precision at categories of analysis that may work better, alongside a view of "intelligibility" that operates without requirements of understanding law. A now well-established framework for analyzing colonial legal interactions informs some of the chapters in the volume: a focus on jurisdictional politics. Many of the chapters also throw light on another cross-polity connection, a shared discourse about protection. Conflicts over jurisdiction and protection have in common their appeal as legal processes imbued with enormous ambiguity. Like feigned mastery and studied ignorance, cultivated ambiguity was strategically very useful to actors across the legal order.

Consider jurisdiction. In referring to plural legal orders, the authors acknowledge that the legal orders they study were layered, composite frameworks in which continual jockeying over the legitimate reach of various legal authorities was endemic. Conflicts over what to do about murders on the frontier, as we know from Lisa Ford's work, encompassed jurisdictional jockeying that at times resulted in very significant institutional shifts.[25] Gallman and Taylor echo this approach in their account of the "expansion of imperial jurisdiction over native peoples in eighteenth-century North America" as the outcome of jurisdictional politics rather than the simple result of inexorably growing power. Attention to jurisdiction activated local politics, but its import was also broader, and more systemic. Gallman and Taylor point to the stakes of colonists' defining Pontiac and his warriors as "rebels"—that is, as insiders challenging legitimate authority—against a different jurisdictional map in which Indian polities were "autonomous nations" and possessed legitimate legal authority independent of colonists.[26]

The engine that heated up this politics was the potential for ambiguity in any jurisdictional arrangement. Precisely because every polity was itself multijurisdictional, it was possible to represent jurisdictional complexity as a condition both of "inside" legal politics and of "outside," or interpolity, relations.[27] This ambiguity was often an aid to political and legal maneuvering in fast-changing circumstances. It helped colonists who claimed dominance but lacked enforcement power, and it helped Indians who asserted their autonomy while parrying increasingly virulent threats.

Nowhere is the value of ambiguity more clear than in the politics surrounding arrangements of protection.[28] References to protection pervaded the Americas in the period covered in this volume and, indeed, the early modern world. Protection framed mutual security pacts between polities and figured frequently in setting the terms for agreements about alliances. This "basic currency of interpolity relations" also had an inside register, in which rulers sought and established legitimacy by touting their capacity to protect subjects and dependents.[29] Ubiquitous as it was, "protection talk" was often very imprecise.[30] Two parties could claim to be protecting each other, simultaneously casting the other as the weaker entity. A polity with growing power could cite protection as a rationale for aggression across borders, a political possibility that persists into the present. At the same time, treaties and other written agreements referenced protection as if it had a secure meaning and recognized it as a crucial element of interpolity ordering.[31]

References to protection were commonplace in European-Indian relations. New England Indians utilized the language of protection to appeal to the English crown for shelter from "the incursions of the Massachusetts English."[32] Colonists, in turn, referenced protection in reminding the Iroquois that at Albany they had made themselves "Subjects to the Great King, our Father, and gave up to him all your Lands for his Protection."[33] Tributary Indians in Virginia were promised "Protection of the law in their Persons and Properties."[34] In Spanish America, the crown pledged protection for Indian customary law, and royal appointees, *protectores de Indios*, advocated for Indians in colonial courts.

The most striking element of protection arrangements was their ambiguity. A pact of mutual protection formed the basis for alliances, in turn memorialized through gift giving. The equality of alliances and the reciprocity of gifts could give way, slowly or quickly, to unequal relationships and the payment of tribute.[35] Pulsipher traces the way reciprocal gift giving in New England held within it the possibility of English dominance, as settlers advanced a view of gifts as payments for land.[36] At the same time, ambiguity served Indians who continued to assert claims to tribute from the English and extract multiple gift payments for the same land. In Virgina, as Dixon shows, the government embraced the idea of Indian ignorance of English law and on that basis asserted their duty to protect Indians—by extending authority over them.[37] Playing with the toggle point between alliance and dominance, Amherst manipulated the symbolism of the gift exchange to assert English mastery.[38]

The flexibility of protection arrangements made the borders between polities very porous. This point is important because it calls into question one of the familiar generalizations of comparative studies of English and Iberian relations with Indians. Owensby and Ross repeat this generalization in the first chapter when they ask, "[H]ow does it matter that indigenous people and settlers in Ibero-America were considered part of a single social order, while in British America they were virtually always considered distinct nations?"[39] In this volume, several chapters call that generalization into question. Dixon highlights the persistence of tributary arrangements in Virginia in which Indians were simultaneously outside and inside the legal order of the colony as tributary polities within English jurisdiction.[40] Graubart shows how Andean Indians maneuvered to maintain their autonomy well after Spanish justice supposedly had incorporated them within the colonial legal order.[41] The point is not that there were no differences across English and Iberian spheres. Rather, these rich counterexamples affirm the value of identifying legal frameworks (jurisdiction, protection) recognized across polities and imbued with flexibility.

These familiar entanglements created constraints that guided further institutional change. Gallman and Taylor suggest that imperial quests for alliance building made it harder to push for jurisdiction over Indians. Echeverri reports on varieties of liberalism driven by a similar critique of "Bourbon despotism," with some focused on turning indigenous people into citizens of the empire. She traces how in New Granada, Indians sought advantage in a liberal pledge of protection that would guarantee their right to remain outside, or at least on the edges, of colonial government. Yirush points out that contemporaries certainly were acutely aware of the presence of other powers, both multiple Indian polities (not "stateless," as some might assume) and multiple European powers.[42] The effect of these flexible arrangements of interpenetrating jurisdictions and fluid pledges of protection across the early modern world was to generate various kinds of interpolity formations, some of which persisted over decades if not centuries and brought autonomous or semi-autonomous polities into close relation.[43]

Here, in other words, is legal intelligibility turned into institutional feature of pluri-political settings. Interpolity formations emerged and persisted as actors, some with strikingly different cultural experiences, recognized similar kinds and purposes of legal behavior. The languages of jurisdiction and protection framed legal interactions in ways that lent some stability (though not necessarily peace) to what were often cluttered and chaotic regions.

Conclusion

It may be useful to return to the events at Brisbane Water. The parallels between this episode and some European-Indian colonial engagements in the Americas are striking. Turning rebellion into garden-variety criminal acts (or, as with Pontiac, turning warfare into rebellion) did not flow from lack of understanding.[44] Studied ignorance about indigenous peoples' possession of legal authority provided cover for the "lawfare" of colonial polities.[45] And Europeans did not have a monopoly on studied ignorance. Just as Aborigines disregarded settlers' claims, Indians in the Americas at times strategically ignored evidence that whites sought not just usage but ownership over lands over which they gained control through ambiguous ceremonies and contracts.

These parallels suggest that we can insert the legal interactions probed in this volume in a larger context of interpolity law that must in turn be framed capaciously. Rubrics such as jurisdiction and protection had clear referents within the substantively very different legal systems of what were also culturally different groups of interlocutors.[46] To argue this point is not to propose the existence of some sort of universal law that spanned early modern polities but to follow the structural logic of complex political engagements to reasonable conclusions. If they originated only in political theory, such conclusions might be difficult to trust. But we find engagement in jurisdictional politics and negotiations over protection in a very wide array of circumstances and encounters. Evidence of the operational force of such frameworks extends across the Americas and to zones of interaction involving agents from all the major European empires and from multiple Indian political communities, regardless of the length of time of contact. Specific tools of legal strategy might have been learned in colonial encounters, but the capacity for legal strategy was longstanding and ubiquitous.

This perspective reveals sets of interactions that in any one case may appear to happen off-stage. This volume focuses on English and Iberian imperial agents, but we also know that French and Dutch ventures yielded similar jockeying over jurisdiction and protection.[47] Studies of Indian diplomacy and extraction of gifts or tribute from Europeans in North America have established that Indians, too, were sophisticated actors in legal processes that were legible to them, though they might not have grasped the full intent or more subtle meanings of European legal pronouncements—also poorly understood by most Europeans.[48] In short, we find more points of commonality than contrast in the plural legal orders of the Atlantic world.

Recognizing shared frameworks opens the way to analyzing an array of interpolity formations. Whether present or not, European and Indian rivals served as audiences for local legal conflicts. For Europeans, the idiom of claims making was important, not least of all because imperial agents hoped and expected to bid again for royal patronage. For Indians, shows of strength and mastery before European agents could substantially bolster power vis-à-vis other Indian polities or other European powers, while the opposite was also true: stories of weakness traveled fast, sometimes with dangerous and destructive consequences. Moreover, the coexistence of multiple polities recognizing similar modes of legal interaction had far-reaching spatial and political effects. Networks of alliances, regional legal regimes, and interimperial micro-regions are among various formations that have begun to replace the more generic "borderlands" label as ways of describing complex interpolity patterns.[49]

This perspective has relevance for comparative analysis, too, as standard generalizations about the contrasting character of Iberian-Indian and English-Indian relations come into question. One such

generalization is that North American Indians in or near English settlements were not accepted into the empire's body politic as vassals,
whereas in Spanish America, legal institutions were designed precisely
with the goal of incorporation. I have already discussed the exceptions
to these patterns contained in just this volume; one wonders how many
exceptions it might take to unsettle this generalization. A second often-
repeated point of contrast stacks the centralized nature of Spanish imperial law against the supposedly decentralized development of English
colonial law. Surely, there is something to this. But as the chapters in this
volume show, all legal politics was local, even when it referenced metropolitan instructions, and similar structures of delegated legal authority
in legally different empires created jurisdictional similarities. Perhaps
the most troubling generalization, not mentioned much in this volume
but with great staying power, is that Spaniards governed through control
of people and the English through control of land. But jurisdictional
conflicts on the edges of both empires encompassed both categories, as
several articles in this volume make clear. Land-hungry Spanish settlers
and Englishmen trading in Indian slaves maneuvered much like their
counterparts through similarly complex jurisdictional orders to preserve
their prerogatives and promote the protection of their property.

None of these statements requires judgments about when and how
much Europeans and Indians understood the other's law. Understanding is overrated, both as a legal capacity and as an object of historical
inquiry. Abilities to "read" political-legal constraints and to engage in
legal practices with even basic competence, in contrast, brought enormous dividends. In the pluri-political Americas between 1600 and 1825,
legal intelligibility gave rise to interlocking, plural legal orders that were
made and remade through plotted and spontaneous conflicts at law.

NOTES
1 Bruce Kercher, "White Fellow Eat Bandicoots & Black Snakes Now: Aborigi-
   nes, Law, and Resistance in the Supreme Court of New South Wales under
   Francis Forbes," paper presented at the World History Association meeting,
   Victoria, Canada, 1999; Henry Reynolds, *The Other Side of the Frontier: Ab-
   original Resistance to the European Invasion of Australia* (Sydney: University of
   New South Wales Press, 2006 [1981], 83); Kristyn Harman, *Aboriginal Convicts:
   Australian, Khoisan, and Māori Exiles* (Sydney: University of New South Wales
   Press, 2012), 52–67; R v Long Dick, Jack Jones, Abraham, and Gibber Paddy

1835; and R v Monkey and Others 1835, *Decisions of the Superior Courts of New South Wales, 1788–1899,* Bruce Kercher (ed.), Division of Law, Macquarie University, Sydney, www.law.mq.edu.au. On frontier violence as contests over jurisdiction, see especially Lisa Ford, *Settler Sovereignty: Jurisdiction and Indigenous People in America and Australia, 1788–1836* (Cambridge, MA: Harvard University Press, 2011).

2   See for example Lisa Ford, *Settler Sovereignty.*

3   The term "interpolity law" is introduced in Lauren Benton and Adam Clulow, "Legal Encounters and the Origins of Global Law," in Jerry Bentley, Sanjay Subrhahmanyam, and Merry Wiesner-Hanks (eds.), *Cambridge World History* (Cambridge: Cambridge University Press, 2015), vol. 6, part 2, 80–100.

4   The phrase is from Brian P. Owensby and Richard J. Ross, "Making Law Intelligible in Comparative Context," in this volume.

5   Pierre Bourdieu, *Outline of a Theory of Practice* (Cambridge: Cambridge University Press, 1977), 6: "If the system is to work, the agents must not be entirely unaware of the truth of their exchanges . . . while at the same time they must refuse to know and above all to recognize it."

6   Lawrence Rosen, *Law as Culture: An Invitation* (Princeton, NJ: Princeton University Press, 2006), 7. Emphasis added. On cultural patterns as institutions, see also Lauren Benton, *Law and Colonial Cultures: Legal Regimes in World History, 1400–1900* (New York: Cambridge University Press, 2002), chapter 7.

7   Rosen, *Law as Culture,* 130.

8   See my discussion of this point in Lauren Benton, *Law and Colonial Cultures,* chapter 7.

9   For an overview, see Lauren Benton and Richard Ross, "Empires and Legal Pluralism: Jurisdiction, Sovereignty, and Political Imagination in the Early Modern World," in *Legal Pluralism and Empire,* ed. Lauren Benton and Richard Ross (New York: NYU Press, 2013), 1–20.

10   Richard White, *The Middle Ground: Indians, Empires, and Republics in the Great Lakes Region, 1650–1815* (Cambridge: Cambridge University Press, 1991), x, 76–81.

11   Nancy O. Gallman and Alan Taylor, "Covering Blood and Graves: Murder and Law on Imperial Margins," in this volume.

12   Craig Yirush, "'Since We Came out of This Ground': Iroquois Legal Arguments at the Treaty of Lancaster," in this volume.

13   This point is well developed with regard to European imperial agents' knowledge of the legal basis for the acquisition of territory in Lauren Benton and Benjamin Straumann, "Acquiring Empire by Law: From Roman Doctrine to Early Modern European Practice," *Law and History Review* 28:1 (2010): 1–38.

14   The first quotation is from Owensby and Ross, this volume; the second, from Tamar Herzog, "Dialoguing with Barbarians: What Natives Said and How Europeans Responded in Late-Seventeenth- and Eighteenth-Century Portuguese America," in this volume.

15 William Nelson, *The Common Law in Colonial America*. Vol 1, *The Chesapeake and New England, 1607–1660* (New York: Oxford University Press, 2008), 4–6; and see Lauren Benton and Kathryn Walker, "Law for the Empire: The Common Law in America and the Problem of Legal Diversity," *Chicago-Kent Law Review* 89:3 (2014): 937–56.

16 Craig Yirush, this volume. It is worth noting, too, that even if and when doctrines about possession and occupation were well known by Europeans, the doctrines themselves did not provide a primer for performance and claims making, only a guide to those elements of proof that might support claims to the control of territory. On this point see Ken MacMillan, *Sovereignty and Possession in the English New World: The Legal Foundations of Empire, 1576–1640* (Cambridge: Cambridge University Press, 2006); Benton and Straumann, "Acquiring Empire by Law"; and Lauren Benton, "Possessing Empire: Iberian Claims and Interpolity Law," in *Native Claims: Indigenous Law against Empire, 1500–1920*, ed. Saliha Bellmessous (New York: Oxford University Press, 2011), 19–40.

17 An example is the early history of the Inquisition in the empire, and the controversies about the inclusion of Indians and the question of who was authorized to preside over Inquisition trials.

18 Karen Graubart, "'Ynuvaciones malas e rreprouadas': Seeking Justice in Early Colonial Pueblos de Indios," this volume.

19 Owensby and Ross, this volume; Gallman and Taylor, this volume; Bradley Dixon, "'Darling Indians' and 'Natural Lords': Virginia's Tributary Regime and Florida's Republic of Indians in the Seventeenth Century," this volume.

20 In this volume: Jenny Hale Pulsipher, "Defending and Defrauding the Indians: John Wompas, Legal Hybridity, and the Sale of Indian Land"; Yirush; and Graubart.

21 Gallman and Taylor, this volume.

22 Herzog, this volume.

23 Owensby and Ross, this volume.

24 Marcela Echeverri, "'Sovereignty Has Lost Its Rights': Liberal Experiments and Indigenous Citizenship in New Granada, 1810–1819," in this volume.

25 Lisa Ford, *Settler Sovereignty*.

26 Gallman and Taylor, this volume.

27 For discussions of the tension between "inside" and "outside" registers in law and political thought, see Annabel S. Brett, *Changes of State: Nature and the Limits of the City in Early Modern Natural Law* (Princeton, NJ: Princeton University Press, 2011); R. B. J. Walker, *Inside/Outside: International Relations as Political Theory* (Cambridge: Cambridge University Press, 1993); and Lauren Benton and Lisa Ford, *Rage for Order: The British Empire and the Origins of International Law, 1800–1850* (Cambridge, MA: Harvard University Press, 2016), chapter 7.

28 This paragraph and the next draw from Lauren Benton and Adam Clulow, "Empires and Protection: Making Interpolity Law in the Early Modern World," *Journal of Global History* 12 (2017): 74–92. See also Lauren Benton, Adam Clulow, and Bain

Attwood, eds., *Protection and Empire: A Global History* (Cambridge: Cambridge University Press, 2017).

29 Benton and Clulow, "Empires and Protection," 74; Annabel Brett, "Protection as a Political Concept in English Political Thought, 1603–1651," in Benton, Chulow, and Attwood, eds., *Protection and Empire*.

30 The phrase comes from an analysis of protection in the early nineteenth-century British empire, in Benton and Ford, *Rage for Order*, 115.

31 Lauren Benton and Adam Clulow, "Webs of Protection and Interpolity Zones in the Early Modern World," in Benton, Atwood, and Clulow, eds., *Protection and Empire*.

32 Pulsipher, this volume.

33 Yirush, this volume.

34 Dixon, this volume.

35 On the toggling from alliances to conquest using the language of protection, see Lauren Benton, "Shadows of Sovereignty: Legal Encounters and the Politics of Protection in the Atlantic World," in *Encounters Old and New: Essays in Honor of Jerry Bentley*, ed. Alan Karras and Laura Mitchell (Honolulu: University of Hawaii Press, 2017).

36 Pulsipher, this volume.

37 Dixon, this volume.

38 Gallman and Taylor, this volume.

39 Owensby and Ross, this volume.

40 Dixon, this volume.

41 Graubart, this volume.

42 Yirush, this volume; cf. Eliga H. Gould, *Among the Powers of the Earth: The American Revolution and the Making of a New World Empire* (Cambridge, MA: Harvard University Press, 2014), 12.

43 Benton and Clulow, "Webs of Protection." The perspective adds a dimension to the analysis of "borderlands" regions by recognizing patterns of interpenetration and overlap, sometimes over long periods of time, of corridors and enclaves claimed by different powers. Lauren Benton, *A Search for Sovereignty: Law and Geography in European Empires, 1400–1900* (Cambridge: Cambridge University Press, 2010), 37.

44 Gallman and Taylor (this volume) make this point regarding Pontiac.

45 David Kennedy, "Lawfare and Warfare," in *Cambridge Companion to International Law*, ed. James Crawford and Martti Koskenniemi (Cambridge: Cambridge University Press, 2012).

46 Benton and Clulow, "Legal Encounters and the Origins of Global Law."

47 One analysis of Dutch-Indian politics of protection is Timo McGregor, "Protection, Violence, and the Practice of Authority in New Netherland, 1624–1664," paper presented at the Atlantic History Workshop, New York University, December 9, 2014. Rushforth's approach to French-Indian relations also fits well with this framework. See Brett Rushforth, *Bonds of*

Alliance: Indigenous and Atlantic Slaveries in New France (Chapel Hill: University of North Carolina Press, 2012).

48 For example, Gregory Evans Dowd, "'Insidious Friends': Gift Giving and the Cherokee-British Alliance in the Seven Years' War," in *Contact Points: American Frontiers from the Mohawk Valley to the Mississippi, 1750–1830*, ed. Andrew R. L. Cayton and Fredrika Teute (Chapel Hill: University of North Carolina Press, 1998); Andrew R. L. Cayton, "'Noble Actors' upon 'the Theatre of Honour': Power and Civility in the Treaty of Greenville," in Cayton and Teute, *Contact Points*, 235–69; and of course Daniel Richter, *Facing East from Indian Country: A Native History of Early America* (Cambridge, MA: Harvard University Press, 2001).

49 Rushforth, *Bonds of Alliance*. Benton and Ford, *Rage for Order*, chapter 6; 2015. Lauren Benton and Jeppe Mulich, "The Space between Empires: Coastal and Insular Microregions in the Early Nineteenth-Century World," in *The Uses of Space in Early Modern History, 1500–1850*, ed. Paul Stock (New York: Palgrave, 2015), 151–71. Pekka Hämäläinen, "The Shapes of Power: Indians, Europeans, and North American Worlds from the Seventeenth to the Nineteenth Century," in *The Contested Spaces of Early America*, ed. Julianne Barr and Edward Countryman (Philadelphia: University of Pennsylvania Press, 2014), 31–68.

10

Intelligibility or Incommensurability?

DANIEL K. RICHTER

"How and to what extent," Brian P. Owensby and Richard J. Ross ask, "did settler law and its associated notions of justice become intelligible—tactically, technically, and morally—to Natives and vice versa?"[1] This is an excellent question, to which the thoughtful essays in this volume provide an answer: indigenous and European peoples were perfectly capable of making the other's legal systems intelligible when it was in their mutual interests to do so. The problems arose when there was no such mutuality. Perhaps, then, the fundamental issues revolve less around "the Negotiating of Legal Intelligibility" than what we might term the negotiating of legal incommensurability. The few scholars who have pondered the concept of legal incommensurability define it narrowly in terms of "the absence of a scale or metric" for choices for which "no ranking of the options in the order of their comparative worth is possible."[2] While on some meta-level, it may be true that Native people dealing with empires in the Americas often had no good choices, the point here is not whether one regime was better than another or whether some choice could be made between them. Instead, it is the fundamentally incompatible aims that indigenous and colonizing peoples often sought through their legal systems, the profoundly different scales of value they assigned to otherwise mutually intelligible terms like "justice" and "rights." When legal systems lacked such common standards of measurement, intelligibility only made incommensurability more plain.

* * *

"Incommensurability" is not quite the same as "incomparability." Legal philosopher Ruth Chang prefers to "reserve the term 'incommensurable' for items that cannot be precisely measured by some common scale of units of value and the term 'incomparable' for items that cannot be compared." As she explains, "[R]ecent discussions of incommensurability have revolved around its putative significance for the valuation of goods, maximizing theories of right action." Hence the emphasis is usually on narrow questions of finding a scale for cost-benefit calculations or of determining monetary compensation for hard-to-compare injuries. But such legal issues can almost always be resolved in some way, "for *precise* measurability of items by a single unit of value is not essential," as long as some agreement on a system of value exists. "Comparability, however, is essential" for Chang. "How could things be valued in terms of trade-offs between costs and benefits if costs and benefits are incomparable? How could value be maximized if its instances cannot be compared?"[3]

Incomparabilities abound in this volume, not least in what the essays say about the basic assumptions of Iberian and British imperial legal regimes. As Brian Owensby and Richard Ross describe it, "the Spanish expected most Natives to be enveloped within their empire while settlers lived off indigenous labor and tribute, evangelized Indians, reordered their towns, invited or drove them into imperial tribunals, and tried to partially 'Hispanicize' their customs and governance." For the most part, the English did none of these things, and so their "colonial legal system did not calibrate and enforce the extraction of work, money, and goods from indigenous peoples."[4] This is another way of saying that the Iberians engaged in what historian Nancy Shoemaker calls "imperial power colonialism," while the British tended toward settler colonialism. As theorist Patrick Wolfe puts it, "[S]ettler colonies were not primarily established to extract surplus value from indigenous labour," but rather they were "premised on displacing indigenes from (or *re*placing them on) the land." And, as Walter Hixon writes, imperial power colonialism dealt "as little as possible with land seizure or internal governance, seeking instead to find and work through reliable indigenous partners" to achieve its exploitative ends. By contrast, "[S]ettlers came not to exploit the indigenous population for economic gain, but rather to remove them from colonial space."[5]

At least in the abstract, therefore, imperial power and settler colonial regimes could not have been more incomparable, and their legal cultures more incommensurable in their metrics of value. To the Spanish, and to a lesser extent the Portuguese, indigenous peoples were vassals: integral, if inferior, parts of the imperial polity, fully subject, at least in theory, to its legality. To the English, indigenous peoples were outsiders: independent, if not entirely sovereign, communities, external to a legal system designed to remove them from the landscape. To the Spanish, Natives were *personas miserables*, deserving protection. To the English, Natives were *savages*, deserving exclusion. For the Iberians, indigenous peoples were subject to the law and the rights and responsibilities that came with vassal status and the emphasis on "justice" that dominated the colonizers' legal culture. For the English, indigenous outsiders were at best subject to something like international law, which required no acknowledgment of the validity of Native legal customs with respect to English discourses of rights and liberties. For the Iberians, indigenous peoples, like other subjects and vassals, were dealt with through courts, decrees, legislation, and crown officials. For the English, indigenous peoples, like other foreign powers, were engaged through negotiations, treaties, and warfare. For the Iberians, despite the mild warnings of legal theorists who insisted on Native possessory rights, the land of indigenous vassals almost unquestionably belonged to the crown. For the English, despite the *terra-nullius* fantasies of legal theorists and settlers alike, the land of indigenous people in practice almost always belonged to Natives, until purchased or conquered from them.[6]

There were of course many exceptions to these generalizations about whether Native peoples were inside or outside colonial legal regimes and about the degree to which those legal regimes exercised a cynical instrumentalism. No European polity was purely either imperial or settler in its nature, and one could seldom see anything as clear-cut as a "settler state [that] practised lawfare against the tribes."[7] But to the considerable extent that the generalizations were true, Native peoples dealing with Iberian and English legal regimes faced incomparable dilemmas. To survive, indigenous peoples and leaders whom the Spanish deemed vassals *had* to make Spanish law intelligible to themselves on a daily basis—except when, as Karen B. Graubart's Andean peoples (and their would-be protector Juan Polo de Ondegardo) were adept at doing, it behooved them to decry *ynuvaciones males e rreprouada* that were incomprehensible to Native traditions. By contrast, indigenous people and leaders asserting their independence from the English, and later the British, empire had every incentive *not* to confess the intelligibility of foreign legalities—unless, as Jenny Hale Pulsipher shows for Native land speculator John Wampus and Craig Yirush for Onondaga orator Canassatego at the Treaty of Lancaster, it was in their interest to mobilize their adept understanding of English legal ways.[8]

The multiplicity of those legal ways—what Christopher Tomlins and Bruce Mann label "The Many Legalities of Early America"—provide another apparent source of incomparability. We are now used to thinking in terms of "legal pluralism" in early modern European empires. What Graubart says for the Andes may as well have applied everywhere in Iberian spheres of influence: people lived in "a plurijurisdictional society, composed of a variety of republics with allegiance to the Crown."[9] The editors' first chapter, along with Marcela Echeverri's essay, stresses the further complication of change over time in imperial legal regimes, from the sixteenth through the early nineteenth centuries, and before and after U.S. and Latin American independence. The multiplicity of legalities, the many local variations, and the varied temporal realities of legal encounters cannot be overstressed. There was no single Spanish, Portuguese, or English legal language for Native peoples to find intelligible. This was especially true for British North America, with its multiple polities and its multiple variations on contests between settlers and Native peoples. That those settlers came not just from England but from Ireland, Scotland, German-speaking principalities, the Netherlands, and elsewhere, while creating slave-based economies exploiting captives transported from Africa (and from Native North American communities) further complicates comparability. So too does the competition between multiple imperial powers— French and Spanish as well as British before 1763; Spanish, British, and U.S. after 1776. The kinds of complicated imperial relations outlined in Herzog's and in Gallman and Taylor's essays were the norm, not the exception, for North American Native peoples in the seventeenth and eighteenth centuries. The extent to which that norm applied to Meso- and South America deserves further exploration.

And what of the extraordinary diversity of Native peoples' own legal cultures throughout the Americas? Many Andeans and Meso-Americans traced their heritages to extremely hierarchical societies based on indigenous imperial conquests. Some North Americans lived in relatively hierarchical chiefdoms such as the Powhatans and the Wampanoags, others in more egalitarian confederacies such as the Haudenosaunee, still others in complicated multiethnic polities such as the Creeks or what Michael Witgen terms the "shape-shifting" egalitarian communities of the Anishanabeg. In the Southeast and elsewhere, communities often had separate leadership structures—indeed perhaps even separate "structural poses"—for war and for peace, or distinguished "red towns" from "white towns" associated with those two legalities. Within all this diversity, peoples traced their kinship matrilineally, patrilineally, or bilaterally, recounted their moral and legal traditions through countless origin stories and oral traditions, and understood the meanings of war and peace in multiple ways. Everywhere, disease and warfare forced peoples to migrate, combine, and recombine their traditions, which in no cases were ever historically static. And, while it is true that, for the most part, indigenous legalities in North America stressed the compensation of victims rather than the European insistence on punishment of perpetrators, these trends played out in myriad ways.[10] With such an array of local and temporal complexity, the difficulties of comparison seem insurmountable.

Until, in the chapters by Tamar Herzog, Jenny Hale Pulsipher, and Bradley Dixon, the bases for comparison across all the diversities become clear. Each of their essays explores an exception to the generalizations supposed to hold for Iberian imperial powers and British settler colonies. And each reveals incommensurability to be more significant than intelligibility. Herzog finds indigenous people in the Amazon basin seeking "trade and protection" that "did not necessarily entail political subjection." This Native strategy would have been more familiar to British than to Iberian colonizers, who persistently tried to create vassals rather than allies. In this incommensurate context, intelligibility was not the real problem. Certainly "the dialogue between the Portuguese and the natives was compromised by the different legal conceptions each held" and "a true cacophony took place." Yet the noise "did not happen because the members of rival groups did not understand one another." Instead, it "was the consequence of the diverse expectations each party had as to the results."[11] The Portuguese rivaled the Spanish for national dominion over all indigenous peoples; particular Native communities sought economic relationships with particular Portuguese individuals. The two sides lacked a common metric, not a common vocabulary. Incommensurabilty trumped intelligibility.

Pulsipher conveys a comparable lesson in a seemingly incomparable context. John Wompas was the product of the kind of Native vassalage system that English colonizers were not supposed to have tried to impose. But recent historiography suggests that what historian James Drake calls the "covalent" political system that enmeshed mid-seventeenth-century Massachusetts Bay, Plymouth, and Connecticut with Wampanoags, Narragansetts, and Mohegans in many ways resembled the Spanish model of a *república de españoles* and a *república de indios*.[12] This literature, says Pulsipher, shows that "Native and English land laws and practices became mutually intelligible fairly soon after contact." Her essay "trace[s] the development of legal intelligibility from an initial phase of 'creative misunderstanding' to a time when both Natives and English effectively used legal hybridity, drawing on each other's land ways to legitimize purchase of Native land and defend their possession." This hybridity—this mutual intelligibility—however, only reinforced the incomensurabilty of aims, "and the dominance of the English increasingly meant that the benefits of legal hybridity accrued to the English, not the Indians." Native people legally and, in colonizers' eyes justly, received scandalously low prices for their land, and, "by the end of the seventeenth century, one of the main uses of legal hybridity was English colonists asserting the validity of their own land purchases based on the proper consent of sachems, elders, and traditional Native holders."[13]

If mid-seventeenth-century New England Native people understood all too well their place in an incommensurate legal regime, much the same could be said for surviving components of the Powhatan paramount chiefdom dealing with English Virginia. Dixon argues that Virginia's policies toward tributary Indians "were the closest that the English colonizers . . . came to the Spanish ideal of incorporating Natives into the colonial polity." Cockacoeske, the queen of Pamunkey, along with her counterparts, thoroughly understood Virginia's rights-based legal discourse and insisted on "the corporate rights they believed English law entitled them to." Repeatedly, "in fact, tributary Indians showed they knew the law better than the English." English Virginians who were not part of Governor William Berkeley's inner circle understood all too well the mutual intelligibility of the legal system that made a place for what Nathaniel Bacon called "the protected and Darling Indians." Using familiar rights-based English legal discourse, Bacon's Manifesto "declared that 'they have bin for these Many years enemies to the King and Country, Robbers and Theeves and Invaders of his Majesties' Right and our Interest and Estates,'" rendering tributaries "'wholly unqalifyed for the benefit and Protection of the law."'[14]

The violence of Bacon's Rebellion, which nearly destroyed Virginia's tributary Indians (and the ferocity of King Philip's War, which similarly ravaged the indigenous communities that rose up against New England's attempt to make them vassals), reveals an important aspect of English legal pluralism: the incommensurable metrics of rights and justice embraced by three, not just two, legalities that understood each other all too well. Ignoring what historian John Mack Faragher calls the "ternary model of relations among metropolitans, colonial settlers, and aboriginal peoples" elides "the important distinction between settlers on the ground and the elites at the level of the state or metropole and prevents a full understanding of the dynamics of settler colonialism."[15] In many ways, the most incommensurate of metrics were those deployed by settlers and their elite metropolitan or provincial governments. Two episodes during the early days of Bacon's Rebellion reveal such a ternary relation in action.[16]

When Governor William Berkeley, primary architect of the tribute system, refused to issue a commission for Nathaniel Bacon to lead troops against the tributaries and other Native peoples, Bacon surrounded the statehouse with musketeers in order to get his way. "Berkeley utterly refused, and rising from his chair of judicature came down to Bacon, and told him to his Face and before all his men that hee was a Rebell and a Traytor etc. and should have noe commission, and uncovering his naked Bosome before him, required that some of his men might shoot him, before ever he would be drawn to signe or consent to a commission for such a Rebell as Bacon." Then,

all the answer Bacon gave the Governor was, "Sir, I came not, nor intend to hurt a haire of your honor's head, and for your sword your Honor may please to putt it up, it shall rust in the scabboard before I shall desire you to drawe it. I come for a commission against the Heathen who dayly inhumanely murder us and spill our Brethren's Blood, and noe care is taken to prevent it," adding, "God damne my Blood, I came for a commission, and a commission I will have before I goe," and turning to his soldiers, said "Make ready and Present [arms]," which they all did. Some of the

Burgesses looking out at the windows and seeing the soldiers in that posture of Firing cry'd out to them, "For God's sake hold your handes and
forebear a little, and you shall have what you please."[17]

Bacon did get what he pleased, and Berkeley, still proclaiming him a
traitor, waged war against him for it. The governor and loyalists in the
House of Burgesses turned for help to the queen of Pamunkey, who,
like Bacon before her, showed up at the legislature to respond in person.
She, too, had many grievances, not least the memories of a disastrous
Virginia war against nontributary Indians a few years earlier, in which
her husband Tatapamoi and dozens of other men perished. When sum-
moned to Jamestown, Cockacoeske

entred the Chamber with a Comportment Gracefull to Admiration, bringing on her right hand an Englishman Interpreter, and on the left her Son
a Stripling Twenty Years of Age, She having round her head a Plat of
Black and White Wampum peage Three Inches broad in imitation of a
Crown, and was Cloathed in a Mantle of dress't Deerskins with the hair
outwards and the Edge cut round 6 Inches deep which made Strings re-
sembling Twisted frenge from the Shoulders to the feet; Thus with grave
Courtlike Gestures and a Majestick Air in her face, she Walk'd up our
Long Room to the Lower end of the Table, Where after a few Intreaties
She Sat down; th' Interpreter and her Son Standing by her on either side
as they had Walked up, our Chairman asked her what men she would
Lend us for Guides in the Wilderness and to assist us against our Enemy
Indians. . . . She after a little Musing with an earnest passionate Countenance as if Tears were ready to Gush out and a fervent sort of Expression
made a Harangue about a quarter of an hour, often interlacing (with a
high shrill Voice and vehement passion) these Words, *Tatpatamoi Che-
piack, I. e.* Tatapamoi dead . . . ; for which no Compensation (at all) had
bene to that day Rendered to her wherewith she now upbraided us.

   Her Discourse ending and our Morose Chairman not advancing one
cold word towards asswaging the Anger and Grief her Speech and
Demeanour Manifested under her oppression, nor taking any notice of all
she had Said. . . , He rudely push'd againe the same Question "What
Indians will you now Contribute" etc.? of this Disregard she Signified her
Resentment by a disdainfull aspect, and turning her head half a side, Sate

mute till that same Question being press'd, a Third time, She not return-
ing her face to the board, answered with a low slighting Voice in her own
Language "Six," but being further Importun'd She sitting a little while
Sullen, without uttering a Word between Said "Twelve," tho' she then had
a hundred and fifty Indian men in her Town, and so rose up and gravely
Waked away, as not pleased with her Treatment.[18]

The legal cultures and legal languages on display in these two scenes
were profoundly incommensurate. Berkeley spoke a metropolitan vocabulary of imperial honor and authority against a disreputable rebellious
traitor; Bacon voiced a settler-colonial profanity of indigenous extir-
pation; Cockacoeske, in her chiefly regalia and dignified Algonquian
words, expressed disillusioned grief. No one, however, misunderstood
the others and their incommenserate aims. And no one understood more
fully what was at stake than Cockacoeske. Shortly after her appearance
in the House of Burgesses, Bacon's forces sacked the main Pamunkey
town, killed an unidentified number of people, enslaved forty-five others, and plundered wampum, furs, imported cloth, and "divers sorts of
English goods (which the Queene had much value for)." Cockacoeske,
accompanied by a ten-year-old boy, fled "into wild woodes where shee
was lost and missing from her owne People fourteen dayes, all that
tyme being Sustained alone onely by gnawing sometimes upon the legg
of a terrapin, which the little Boy found in the woods and brought her
when she was ready to dye for want of Foode."[19]

Whatever vindication Cockacoeske may have gained on the English
king's birthday in 1677, when she was restored to her tributary status
in the Treaty of Middle Plantation, neither she nor anyone else misunderstood the ternary power relationships in which she was enmeshed.
Linguistic divides, cultural differences, alphabetic versus wampum litera-
cies, punishment of offenders versus compensation of victims—none of
these rendered the incommensurablity of imperial, settler, and Native
legal objectives unintelligible. Wise Natives and wise metropolitans fully
understood the three-way incommensurability. "A governor of Virginia
has to steer between Scylla and Charybolis, either an Indian or a civil
war," concluded colonial governor Alexander Spotswood a generation
later. "Bacon's Rebellion was occasioned purely by the governor and
council refusing to let the people go out against the Indians who at that

time annoyed the frontiers."[20] That settler colonists regarded Native peoples as an annoyance is an understatement.

The efforts of British governors and Native leaders to steer between Scylla and Charybolis in the early eighteenth century produced the era's greatest accomplishment in North American legal intelligibility, the elaborate intercultural protocols that structured the events known as treaty conferences. Hundreds of people—the vast majority of them Native—would gather for days or even weeks of speeches, gift exchanges, public and private negotiations, all in ritual contexts that blended European and, mostly, Native legal traditions. Native people encoded their most important messages on wampum belts; English people wrote things down in formal documents sent to offices in the metropole. Native orators delivered metaphorical speeches in formal idiom that only the adept, even among Native auditors, could fully understand. People addressed each other in carefully calibrated kinship terms and by traditional council names evoking historical experience. Interpreters of varied linguistic skills struggled to translate the speeches into something Europeans could understand and, conversely, to transmute English documents into a form that Native people would not ridicule. One product of such efforts was the seemingly oxymoronic phenomenon of the "written talks" that circulated among Europeans and Natives in the North American Southeast. As countless scholars have pointed out, the opportunities for miscommunication, deliberate or otherwise, were legion. And the deliberate forms of miscommunication ranged from the kind of "creative misunderstanding" that allowed each side to come away satisified to the kind of outright fraud that could lead to war.[21]

Yet for all the misunderstandings, miscommunications, and misdirections, on a fundamental level there was no inherent problem with intelligibility. As historian Jeffrey Glover has shown, a working intelligibility characterized even the earliest days of English North American colonization, when the Virginia Company secretary Gabriel Archer carefully described for a London audience the Chesapeake Algonquian rituals that sealed a treaty with the newcomers.[22] From those days henceforth, throughout the colonial period, everyone knew what the stakes were: keeping the peace, maintaining coalitions against imperial and Native rivals, peaceful expropriation of land, negotiating solutions to crimes of the sort discussed by Gallman and Taylor. Each side understood perfectly well what the other hoped to gain by its own standards of legality and tried to manipulate those standards to its best advantage. That the aims were incommensurate did not mean they were unintelligible. Indeed, as voices quoted throughout this volume attest, it was precisely when Europeans failed to live up to their own professed standards of legality that Native people became most incensed. A long-time veteran of treaty councils, the Delaware leader Teedyuscung expressed this attitude eloquently in 1754, when he explained to Pennsylvanians why his people had opened hostilities in what came to be known as the Seven Years War. "The Land is the cause of our Differences that is our being unhappily turned out of the land is the cause, and thô the first settlers might purchase the lands fairly yet they did not act well nor do the Indians Justice for they ought to have reserved some place for the Indians." What he meant by "justice" was based, on the one hand, in a thorough understanding of the professed legal methods by which the British claimed to purchase Native territories, and, on the other hand, in a deep recognition of the incommensurability of settler interpretations of that word. "If regular Methods had been formerly taken for an habitation or residence for the poor Indians in this Land," he lamented, "this would not have come to pass."[23]

By Teedyuscung's day, North American Natives more and more came to embrace the legal otherness that the eighteenth-century British ascribed to them. Among the earliest articulations of this kind of constructed unintelligibility occurred in the 1690s, when a Mohawk leader exaggerated to the governor of New York that his people had "no forcing rules or laws amongst us."[24] It had not always been thus. Native and European legal cultures had never been neatly bounded things, incapable of absorbing other ideas and practices or reacting to them in strategic ways, nor did indigenous and European actors inherently lack frameworks for common understanding. Even in the early seventeenth century, a period when we might expect the most profound unintelligibility, Shoemaker finds, "under the metal armor and beards, face paint and tattoos, . . . a bedrock of shared ideas" that allowed mutual comprehension. Only over time, when the incommensurability of European and Native legal aims, particularly regarding sovereignty and land, became clear did the two sides construct respective walls of unintelligibility. "European acquisition of North American land and resources at the expense of the continent's native residents," writes

Shoemaker, "was the root cause behind the rising conviction that Indians and Europeans were, certainly by custom and probably by nature, opposite peoples." In the late eighteenth century, when settlers north and south threw off the metropolitan imperial yoke and ternary relationships became binary, the wall of unintelligibility solidified.[25]

* * *

"How and to what extent did settler law and its associated notions of justice become intelligible—tactically, technically, and morally—to Natives and vice versa?"[26] The word "settler" in Owensby and Ross's question is crucial, and for Teedyuscung, as well as Cockacoeske and countless other Native people—as well as their metropolitan governors—those notions were nearly always all too intelligible. As Marcela Echeverri shows, indigenous people in New Granada came to that intelligibility as soon as creole settlers attempted to establish independent liberal regimes in the early nineteenth century. When the Santa Fe Junta Suprema abolished the legal category of "Indian" in the name of liberal equality of citizenship, it engaged a common settler-colonial project that rhetorically erased indigenous communities from the landscape.[27] Like Teedyuscung, whom they almost certainly had never heard of, indigenous peoples in towns such as Chipaque and Cocuy evoked a thoroughly intelligible arsenal of "channels, means, and arguments that the empire had granted them and which they had continually revitalized for centuries." These means included resisting the complete abolition of the tributary "head-tax that characterized them as a separate legal corporation of 'Indians.'" The issue, Echeverri concludes, "was not about challenging tribute as such, but about recognizing that it had to be proportionate, just." For creoles, however, any form of tribute payment was "'unjust and ignominious.'"[28] "Just" was a term utterly intelligible to all sides, but everyone understood that its meanings could be utterly incommensurate. Metropolitans and indigenous peoples sometimes found a common metric for "justice." Natives and settlers seldom could.

NOTES

1 Owensby and Ross essay in this volume.

2 Matthew Adler, "Law and Incommensurability: Introduction," *University of Pennsylvania Law Reveiw* 146 (1998), 1170–71.

3 Ruth Chang, *Making Comparisons Count* (New York: Routledge, 2002), xvii–xviii.

4 Owensby and Ross essay in this volume.

5 Nancy Shoemaker, "A Typology of Colonialism," *Perspectives on History* 53, no. 7 (October 2015), 29–30; Patrick Wolfe, *Settler Colonialism and the Transformation of Anthropology: The Politics and Poetics of an Ethnographic Event* (London: Cassell, 1999), 1–8 (quotation from p. 1); Walter L. Hixson, *American Settler Colonialism: A History* (New York: Palgrave Macmillan, 2013), 1–22 (quotation from p. 4).

6 According to Tamar Herzog, Iberians developed a practical theory "that after Indians contracted with Europeans rather than becoming partners or allies, both they and, most important, their lands became the property of the crown." In a sense, then, native people, not their land, became "the true *terra nullius*, which they hoped to possess" (*Frontiers of Possession: Spain and Portugal in Europe and the Americas* [Cambridge, MA: Harvard University Press, 2015], 95, 132). On the English, see Daniel K. Richter, "The Strange Colonial North American Career of *Terra Nullius*," in Bain Attwood and Tom Griffiths, eds., *Frontier, Race, Nation: Henry Reynolds and Australian History* (Melbourne: Australian Scholarly Publishing, 2009), 159–84. For a thoughtful yet hard-headed overview of the complexities of "premodern" common law on indigenous land rights, see P. G. McHugh, *Aboriginal Societies and the Common Law: A History of Sovereignty, Status, and Self-Determination* (Oxford: Oxford University Press, 2004), 61–116.

7 McHugh, *Aboriginal Societies and the Common Law*, 5 (quotation); Mark D. Walters, "Histories of Colonialism, Legality, and Aboriginality," *University of Toronto Law Journal* 57 (2007), 819–32.

8 Graubart, Pulsipher, and Yirush essays, in this volume.

9 Graubart essay in this volume (quotation); Christopher L. Tomlins and Bruce H. Mann, eds., *The Many Legalities of Early America* (Chapel Hill: University of North Carolina Press, 2001); Lauren Benton and Richard J. Ross, eds., *Legal Pluralism and Empires, 1500–1850* (New York: NYU Press, 2013).

10 Margaret Holmes Williamson, *Powhatan Lords of Life and Death: Command and Consent in Seventeenth-Century Virginia* (Lincoln: University of Nebraska Press, 2003); Kathleen J. Bragdon, *Native People of Southern New England, 1500–1650* (Norman: University of Oklahoma Press, 1996); Daniel K. Richter, *The Ordeal of the Longhouse: The Peoples of the Iroquois League in the Era of European Colonization* (Chapel Hill: University of North Carolina Press, 1992); Joshua Piker, *Okfuskee: A Creek Indian Town in Colonial America* (Cambridge, MA: Harvard University Press, 2013); Michael Witgen, *An Infinity of Nations: How the Native New World Shaped Early North America* (Philadelphia: University of Pennsylvania Press, 2012); Charles Hudson, *The Southeastern Indians* (Knoxville: University of Tennessee Press, 1976), 202–57; Fred Gearing, "The Structural Poses of 18th-Century Cherokee Villages," *American Anthropologist* 60 (1958), 1148–57.

11 Herzog essay in this volume.

12 See, for example, James D. Drake, *King Philip's War: Civil War in New England, 1675–1676* (Amherst: University of Massachusetts Press, 1999); and Jenny Hale Pulsipher, *Subjects unto the Same King: Indians, English, and the Contest for Authority in Colonial New England* (Philadelphia: University of Pennsylvania Press, 2005).

13 Pulsipher essay in this volume.

14 Dixon essay in this volume.

15 John Mack Faragher, "Commentary: Settler Colonial Studies and the North American Frontier," *Settler Colonial Studies* 4 (2014), 181–91, quotations from pp. 181–82, 186. On the enduring contest between metropolitan and what we would now call settler perspectives, see Michael Leroy Oberg, *Dominion and Civility: English Imperialism and Native America, 1585–1685* (Ithaca, NY: Cornell University Press, 1999).

16 For more on these episodes, see Daniel K. Richter, *Before the Revolution: America's Ancient Pasts* (Cambridge, MA: Harvard University Press, 2011), 265–79.

17 Charles M. Andrews, ed., *Narratives of the Insurrections, 1675–1690* (New York: Scribner's, 1915), 116–17.

18 Ibid., 25–27.

19 Ibid., 127–28.

20 Alexander Spotswood to Peter Schuyler, 25 Jan. 1720, Pennsylvania Provincial Council Records, Vol. F, pp. 13–21, Pennsylvania State Archives, Harrisburg.

21 William N. Fenton, "Structure, Continuity, and Change in the Process of Iroquois Treaty Making," in Francis Jennings et al., eds., *The History and Culture of Iroquois Diplomacy: An Interdisciplinary Guide to the Treaties of the Six Nations and Their League* (Syracuse, NY: Syracuse University Press, 1985), 27–30; Richard White, "'Although I Am Dead, I Am Not Entirely Dead, I Have Left a Second of Myself': Construcing Self and Persons on the Middle Ground of Early America," in Ronald Hoffman, Mechal Sobel, and Fredrika J. Teute, eds., *Through a Glass Darkly: Reflections on Personal Identity in Early America* (Chapel Hill: University of North Carolina Press, 1997), 410–13; Nancy Shoemaker, *A Strange Likeness: Becoming Red and White in Eighteenth-Century North America* (New York: Oxford University Press, 2004), 8–10 (quotation), 93–103; James H. Merrell, "'I Desire All That I Have Said . . . May Be Taken Down Aright': Revisiting Teedyuscung's 1756 Treaty Council Speeches," *William and Mary Quarterly*, 3d ser., 63 (2006), 777–826.

22 Jeffrey Glover, *Paper Sovereigns: Anglo-Native Treaties and the Law of Nations, 1604–1664* (Philadelphia: University of Pennsylvania Press, 2014), 1–6.

23 E. B. O'Callaghan and B. Fernow, eds., *Documents Relative to the Colonial History of the State of New-York*, 15 vols. (Albany, NY, 1853–1887), vol. 7, 301.

24 Treaty minutes, 12 July 1697, New York Colonial Manuscripts, vol. 51, fol. 93, New York State Archives, Albany.

25 Shoemaker, *A Strange Likeness*, *passim*, quotations from pp. 3, 141; Daniel K. Richter, "His Own, Their Own: Settler Colonialism, Native Peoples, and Imperial Balances of Power in Eastern North America, 1660–1715," in Ignacio Gallup-Diaz,

ed., *The World of Colonial America: An Atlantic Handbook* (New York: Routledge, 2017), 209–34.

26 Owensby and Ross essay in this volume.

27 See Lorenzo Veracini, *Settler Colonialism: A Theoretical Overview* (New York: Palgrave Macmillan, 2010), 34–49; and Patrick Wolfe, "After the Frontier: Separation and Absorption in US Indian Policy," *Settler Colonial Studies* 1 (2011), 13–51.

28 Echeverri essay in this volume.

ACKNOWLEDGMENTS

This volume emerged out of a 2014 conference on "Meanings of Justice in New World Empires: Settler and Indigenous Law as Counterpoints," organized by Brian Owensby and Richard Ross through the Symposium on Comparative Early Modern Legal History. Richard Ross oversees the symposium, which gathers at the Newberry Library in Chicago to discuss the comparative legal history of the Atlantic world in the period c. 1492 to 1815.

The editors wished to produce a volume that explored the way various groups of Europeans and indigenous people came to imperfectly understand each other's notions of law and justice. Central to this process is the challenge of "legal intelligibility": how and to what extent did settler law and its associated notions of justice became intelligible—tactically, technically, and morally—to Natives, and vice versa? We pursued this question comparatively, contrasting the English and Iberian New World empires. To that end, we drew from contributions by participants in the symposium and also invited other scholars to write for the volume. Bradley Dixon, Marcela Echeverri, Karen Graubart, Tamar Herzog, Jenny Pulsipher, and Craig Yirush presented papers at the symposium. Nancy Gallman and Alan Taylor contributed a chapter written especially for the volume. We were fortunate that two of the commentators at the symposium, Lauren Benton and Daniel Richter, agreed to write chapters presenting concluding perspectives.

The editors wish to thank the authors for their essays. All undertook revisions with skill and cooperative good humor. Several anonymous reviewers for NYU Press provided valuable suggestions for improving the volume. Clara Platter, the history and law editor at the press, encouraged the project and adeptly guided the book through the publication process. The University of Illinois College of Law provided funding for the symposium conference and contributed to covering the costs of preparing the manuscript for publication.

ABOUT THE EDITORS

Brian P. Owensby is Professor in the Corcoran Department of History, University of Virginia. He is the author of *Intimate Ironies: Making Middle-Class Lives in Modern Brazil* (1999) and *Empire of Law and Indian Justice in Colonial Mexico* (2008). His current book project is *Gain and Transformation in the Land without Evil*, about the early-modern encounter between European and indigenous ideas regarding human social order in colonial Paraguay and the Guaraní. Owensby is also director of the Center for Global Inquiry & Innovation at the University of Virginia.

Richard J. Ross is the David C. Baum Professor of Law and Professor of History at the University of Illinois (Urbana/Champaign) and Director of the Symposium on Comparative Early Modern Legal History. He has previously edited, with Lauren Benton, *Legal Pluralism and Empires, 1500–1850* (NYU Press, 2013). With Steven Wilf, he is currently working on a book entitled *The American Rule of Law: A Comparative Story*.

ABOUT THE CONTRIBUTORS

Lauren Benton is Nelson O. Tyrone, Jr. Professor of History and Professor of Law at Vanderbilt University. Her publications include the following: with Lisa Ford, *Rage for Order: The British Empire and the Origins of International Law, 1800–1850* (2016); *A Search for Sovereignty: Law and Geography in European Empires, 1400–1900* (2010); and *Law and Colonial Cultures: Legal Regimes in World History, 1400–1900* (2002), which received the World History Association Book Award and the James Willard Hurst Book Prize.

Bradley Dixon is a PhD candidate in history at the University of Texas at Austin where he is working on a dissertation entitled "Republic of Indians: Law, Politics, and Empire in the North American Southeast, 1539–1830." His work has received support from the Social Science Research Council, the Library Company of Philadelphia, the New England Regional Fellowship Consortium, the John Carter Brown Library, and the North Caroliniana Society. Dixon has presented at numerous conferences and was a co-organizer of the "Entangled Histories of the Early Modern British and Iberian Empires" workshop held at the University of Texas.

Marcela Echeverri, Assistant Professor of History at Yale University, specializes in the social, intellectual, and political history of Latin America from the colonial period to the present. Her first book, *Indian and Slave Royalists in the Age of Revolution: Reform, Revolution, and Royalism in the Northern Andes, 1780–1825* (2016) received the Latin American Studies Association's 2017 Michael Jiménez Book Prize and Honorable Mention for the Conference on Latin American History's 2017 Bolton-Johnson Prize. She is currently at work on a book-length research project about Gran Colombian slavery and antislavery between 1820 and 1860.

Nancy O. Gallman is the 2017–2019 Barra Postdoctoral Fellow at the McNeil Center for Early American Studies at the University of Pennsylvania. She is the author of "Reconstituting Power in an American Borderland: Political Change in Colonial East Florida," in *Florida Historical Quarterly* 94(2) (Fall 2015): 169–91.

Karen B. Graubart is Associate Professor of History at the University of Notre Dame. She is the author of *With Our Labor and Sweat: Indigenous Women and the Formation of Colonial Society in Peru, 1550–1700* (2007), as well as many articles. With generous assistance from the National Endowment for the Humanities, she is completing a new project, titled *Republics of Difference: Racial and Religious Self-Governance in the Iberian Atlantic, 1400–1650*.

Tamar Herzog is Monroe Gutman Professor of Latin American Affairs at Harvard. She received her PhD at the École des Hautes Études en Sciences Sociales in Paris. Among her publications are *A Short History of European Law: The Last Two and a Half Millennia* (2018), *Frontiers of Possession: Spain and Portugal in Europe and the Americas* (2015), *Upholding Justice: State, Law, and the Penal System in Quito* (2004), *Defining Nations: Immigrants and Citizens in Early Modern Spain and Spanish America* (2003); *Ritos de control, prácticas de negociación* (2000), and *Mediación, archivos y ejercicio* (1996).

Jenny Hale Pulsipher is an Associate Professor of History at Brigham Young University and the author of *Subjects unto the Same King: Indians, English, and the Contest of Authority in Colonial New England* (2005), which was selected as a Choice Magazine Outstanding Academic Title in 2006, and *Swindler Sachem: The American Indian Who Sold His Birthright, Dropped out of Harvard, and Conned the King of England* (2018).

Daniel K. Richter is the Richard S. Dunn Director of the McNeil Center for Early American Studies and Roy F. and Jeannette P. Nichols Professor of American History at the University of Pennsylvania. He is the author of *Before the Revolution: America's Ancient Pasts* (2011); *Facing East from Indian Country: A Native History of Early America* (2001); and

The Ordeal of the Longhouse: The Peoples of the Iroquois League in the Era of European Colonization (1992).

Alan Taylor is the Thomas Jefferson Foundation Chair in the Corcoran History Department of the University of Virginia. His seven books include *William Cooper's Town: Power and Persuasion on the Frontier of the Early Republic* (1995); *American Colonies* (2001); *The Divided Ground: Indians, Settlers, and the Northern Borderland of the American Revolution* (2006); *The Civil War of 1812: American Citizens, British Subjects, Irish Rebels, and Indian Allies* (2010); and *The Internal Enemy: Slavery and War in Virginia* (2013). *William Cooper's Town* won the Pulitzer Prize for American history in addition to the Bancroft and Beveridge prizes. *The Internal Enemy* won the Pulitzer Prize for American history and the Merle Curti Prize for Social History (OAH). *American Colonies* won the 2001 Gold Medal for Non-Fiction from the Commonwealth Club of California. *The Divided Ground* won the 2007 Society for Historians of the Early Republic book prize and the 2004–7 Society of the Cincinnati triennial book prize. *The Civil War of 1812* won the Empire State History Prize and was a finalist for the George Washington Prize. He will publish an eighth book, *American Revolutions: A Continental History*, in September 2016.

Craig Yirush is an Associate Professor of History at UCLA. He is the author of *Settlers, Liberty, and Empire: The Roots of Early American Political Theory, 1675–1775* (2011) and is currently working on a history of indigenous rights in the Anglo-American world.

INDEX

Aborigines, 273–74, 284

Accomacs, 188

Acosta, José de, 5

Adair, James, 20

aldeamentos (Jesuit village system). *See* Jesuits

Algonquians, 56n73, 220, 299–300; French and, 277; land tenure and, 90, 110nn4–5; murder and, 19, 26, 277

alliance making, 280, 282–83, 289n35; contraventions of, 81–82; indigenous and Portuguese understandings of, 78–82; Portuguese accounts of, 66–77; removal and, 80–81, 88n52

Alvarez, Manuel Bernardo, 251–52, 257

Amazon basin: caciques in, 72–73; Iguatemi in, 73, 75, 79; legal incommensurability and, 295; misdialogues in, 32–33; Mura in, 75–77, 79–80; religious symbols in, 70–73; Spanish-Portuguese competition in, 61

The Ambiguous Iroquois Empire (Jennings, F.), 147n76

America, invention of, 3

American Revolution, 224, 243, 302

Amherst, Jeffrey, 219–22, 224, 283

Andeans, 283, 294; *chicha* industry of, 169–70; collective ownership attributed to, 152, 159–60, 177n5; community action of, 153–54, 168–70, 173; labor of, 167–70, 173; legal languages mixed by, 34–35; slave trade of, 170–73, 180n65; *tambos* of, 169–70; transculturated justice of, 173; urbanization of, 163–67;

usufruct of, 160; *ynuvaciones malas e rreprouadas* and, 151, 293

Anderson, Virginia DeJohn, 112n17, 117n79

Andrés Moya, José, 249

Andros, Edmund, 117n86, 195

Anishanabeg, 295

anthropology, 47, 275–76

anthropophagy, 6, 21

Apalachee: caciques of, 187, 189–90, 194, 205, 208n43; demographics of, 190–91; diaspora of, 205; land law in, 197–98; present-day, 205; Republic of Indians in, 185–86, 198, 200, 205; succession in, 189; *visita* in, 194

Apalachee leaders (*holahtas*). *See* caciques

Aquinas, Thomas, 9–10

Archer, Gabriel, 300

Armitage, David, 149n108

asesor militar (investigating official), 226

Astudillo, 252

Audiencia, 23, 27–28, 55n70, 178n14

Australia, 273–74, 284

Axtell, James, 119

Aztecs, 23

Bacon, Nathaniel, 186, 198, 204, 299; manifesto of, 199–200, 296–97; Pamunkeys and, 199–200; Susquehannocks and, 199; on tributaries, 199–201

Bacon's Rebellion, 37, 148n77, 184, 186, 203, 296; aftermath of, 192, 201; Berkeley and, 297–99; ternary relation in, 297–300

bad and condemnable innovations (*ynuvaciones malas e rreprouadas*), 151, 293